HAWAI'I IS MY HAVEN

HAWAI'I IS MY HAVEN

RACE
AND
INDIGENEITY
IN THE
BLACK PACIFIC

NITASHA TAMAR SHARMA

Duke University Press
Durham and London
2021

© 2021 Duke University Press
The text of this book is licensed under a Creative Commons
AttributionNonCommercial-NoDerivatives 4.0 International
License: https://creativecommons.org/licenses/by-nc-nd/4.0/

Project editor: Lisa Lawley
Designed by Drew Sisk
Typeset in Portrait Text, IBM Plex Sans, and IBM Plex Serif by
Westchester Publishing Services

Library of Congress Cataloging-in-Publication Data
Names: Sharma, Nitasha Tamar, [date] author.
Title: Hawai'i is my haven : race and indigeneity in the Black
Pacific / Nitasha Tamar Sharma.
Description: Durham : Duke University Press, 2021. | Includes
bibliographical references and index.
Identifiers: LCCN 2020054724 (print)
LCCN 2020054725 (ebook)
ISBN 9781478013464 (hardcover)
ISBN 9781478014379 (paperback)
ISBN 9781478021667 (ebook)
Subjects: LCSH: African Americans—Hawaii. | Racism—Hawaii.
| Minorities—Hawaii. | Hawaiians—Ethnic identity. | Ethnic
groups—Hawaii. | Hawaii—Race relations. | Hawaii—Ethnic
relations. | Hawaii—Social conditions.
Classification: LCC E185.93.H3 S53 2021 (print) | LCC E185.93.H3
(ebook) | DDC 305.8009969—dc23
LC record available at https://lccn.loc.gov/2020054724
LC ebook record available at https://lccn.loc.gov/2020054725

ISBN 978-1-4780-9381-7 (ebook other)

Cover art: Kamakakēhau, a globally touring Hawaiian falsetto
singer and 'ukulele player born in Arkansas and raised in Hawai'i.
Photograph by Kenna Reed. Floral arrangement by Ren MacDonald
Balasia/Renko Floral, Los Angeles and Honolulu.

Duke University Press gratefully acknowledges the support of
Northwestern University, which provided funds toward the
publication of this book.

The open access edition of *Hawai'i Is My Haven* was made possible
by an award from the National Endowment for the Humanities
Fellowships Open Book Program.

At home in the islands
At home
In the middle of the sea.

THE BROTHERS CAZIMERO, "HOME IN THE ISLANDS"

Some of the greatest things about being of African descent can't ever exist in America.

BLACK TRANSPLANT TO HAWAIʻI

WHO IS THE BLACK WOMAN IN HAWAII?

What pulls a person
    to a family
    to a group?
What does one seek
    in a race?
If there is no family
    no group
    of one's own
How does one satisfy
    the taste?
Mechanical to seek
Inevitable to greet
Those others from
Another tribe and place.
Survival is the aim
Communication tames
And trust, not fear
Fills the space.

KATHRYN TAKARA, 1977

CONTENTS

Acknowledgments xi

Introduction:
  Hawaiʻi Is My Haven 1

1. Over Two Centuries: The History of Black People in Hawaiʻi 37

2. "Saltwater Negroes": Black Locals, Multiracialism, and Expansive Blackness 71

3. "Less Pressure": Black Transplants, Settler Colonialism, and a Racial Lens 120

4. Racism in Paradise: AntiBlack Racism and Resistance in Hawaiʻi 166

5. Embodying Kuleana: Negotiating Black and Native Positionality in Hawaiʻi 217

Conclusion:
  Identity ↔ Politics ↔ Knowledge 261

Notes 279

Bibliography 305

Index 331

ACKNOWLEDGMENTS

We usually save the best for last, but the best people in my life have waited long enough to have my attention back after taking a decade to complete this book. First and forever, to a man with unending patience who is brilliant, beautiful, and ethical: Makaya McCraven. This book is dedicated to you and our loving, adventurous, and wonderful children, Maya Naima and Jaya Jagdish. This book is also dedicated to my other "children": my Northwestern Posse I students (Sam, Macs, Jourdan, Nick, Alejandro, Sarah, Angel, Jordan, Elleana, and Huzaifa) and the fifteen students (Karen, Maggie, Henry, Makasha, Anna, Magdalena, Pooja, April, Isabella, Stacy, Danielle, Jessica, Imani, Elise, and Alicia) in "Race and Indigeneity in the Pacific," co-taught with my close friend and comrade, Hiʻilei Hobart. You are the reason we become—and remain!—professors.

This book would not have been possible without the support of my parents. My father, Dr. Jagdish Prasad Sharma, died during my first year of fieldwork but had introduced me to so many people central to this project. My mother, Dr. Miriam Sharma, has always been such a gifted editor of my work. I am deeply grateful that this project has allowed me to spend more time with this incredible woman upon each trip to Mānoa Valley, where she welcomed me home. I'm fortunate to have my brother, Arun, a powerhouse of a human being with a deeply generous spirit: thank you for always being there and for visiting us so often. I have only boundless love and gratitude for Ágnes Zsigmondi and her Hungarian family, and to Marcus and Marguerite and all the McCravens for always making me feel special and welcome—I am blessed to be in your family.

This book is the result of ten years of collaboration with the warm and generous Black residents of Oʻahu, Hawaiʻi and so many other Island residents. You have my deepest gratitude. I thank you all from the bottom of my heart for what you have shared—your life stories, your homes, and your music. My goal is to tell your stories alongside the story of Hawaiʻi. Dr. Akiemi Glenn offered years of informative discussions and lively hangs; members of the Department of Ethnic Studies at the University of Hawaiʻi at Mānoa provided nuanced perspectives, especially Ethan Caldwell, Monisha Das Gupta, Vernadette Gonzalez,

Rod Labrador, Jonathan Okamura, and last, but certainly not least, Ty Tengan. No research could be done without the guidance of friends and neighbors, like Susan and Glenn Shea, Amarjit and Mary Singh, Jim Morel Jr., and Janice Staab, and old classmates including Julie Lowe from Roosevelt High School, who (re)introduced me to Hawaiʻi's Black residents.

This book would not look the way it does without the careful eye and tireless work of manuscript editor Kimberly Banks, whose first-rate skills reshaped the book. The images in this book come from Hawaiʻi photographers who generously allowed me to reproduce their images. Dr. Chuck Langlas, as well as Dr. Hiʻilei Hobart, provided critical guidance and editing of ʻōlelo Hawaiʻi—mahalo nui loa for your expertise and care. Ideas on Fire provided helpful edits to the book's introduction, and the fantastic Josh Rutner created the index. Courtney Berger at Duke University Press is, simply, the finest editor one could have. Your dedication to sustaining deep relationships with authors allows us to benefit from your intellectual acuity and sharp editorial eye—all delivered with encouragement over delicious meals and white wine! Thank you for your belief that this book would become a reality. To the entire team at Duke University Press, including Sandra Korn and Lisa Lawley—your professionalism has no equal. I look forward to our next jazz hang, Ken Wissoker.

I am intellectually and politically indebted to the brilliant and hospitable scholars in Asian American, Black, Native, and Pacific Islands studies. I have learned so much from the work of, and conversations with, Hōkūlani Aikau, Maile Arvin, Keith Camacho, Vince Diaz, Willy Kauai, and Kathryn Takara. Angela Davis, Ruth Gilmore, Noelani Goodyear-Kaʻōpua, Gerald Horne, Miles Jackson, George Lipsitz, Gary Okihiro, and Vijay Prashad—your ideas have shaped this intellectual journey. Martha Biondi—you have been a mentor to me for over fifteen years, and your advocacy, kindness, and friendship allowed this book to happen. Colleagues supported and trusted me to accomplish this project, even as my family and work responsibilities grew: E. Patrick Johnson, Dwight McBride, Celeste Watkins-Hayes, Mary Pattillo, Jennifer Nash, Michelle Wright, Ji-Yeon Yuh, Shalini Shankar, Patricia Nguyen, Doug Ishii, Michelle Huang, Ivy Wilson, Joshua Chambers-Letson, César Braga-Pinto, and Leslie Harris. Suzette Denose, Marjorie McDonald, Seth Bernstein, Carlos Ballinas, and Cheryl Jue provided years (decades!) of logistical support: I deeply respect and appreciate you.

Northwestern University and specifically Weinberg College and its dean, Adrian Randolph, have supported me and my research. Faculty Research, Subvention, and Provost's grants funded this research, as did the Woodrow Wilson Foundation, the National Endowment for the Humanities, the Kaplan Institute, and the always supportive Center for Native American and Indigenous Research. This book is stronger due to the host of undergraduate and graduate research assistants I have had the honor of working with, first and foremost Aozora Brockman—my first assistant, now a published poet in her own right! Thanks as well to Yoonie Yang, Ying Lu Lucy Wang, Bennie Niles, Mishana Garschi, and Leah Kaplan for your assistance with research and editing.

The most difficult task was writing the book, including reading and discussion groups, attempting to do justice to the narratives of the hundreds of people I spoke to. For this, I am completely indebted to my dear friend and best writing partner, Mary Weismantel. A special mahalo and hugs to Hiʻilei Hobart, Jinah Kim, Dana Kuzwayo, and Kelly Wisecup—you have sustained me with your friendship and brilliance. Other generous readers over the years have also strengthened the book; parts that are weak are because I did not listen to your advice: Frances Aparicio, Marquis Bey, Keith Camacho, Camilla Fojas, Rudy Guevarra, Daniel Immerwahr, Lauren Jackson, Sarah Johnson, Sylvester Johnson, Doug Kiel, Simeon Man, Justin Mann, Kaneesha Parsard, Mark Rifkin, Shannon Speed, Nicole Spigner, Faʻanofo Lisaclaire Uperesa, Ana Ramos-Zayas, and so many others. Writing retreats and write-on-sites gave me structure and strengthened my friendships and knowledge. I benefited from weekly check-ins with Zulema Valdez, one of my oldest and dearest friends, with whom I have shared the best writing retreats. The Yosemite Creative Connections retreat in 2014 introduced me to new friends and smart interlocuters Tanya Golash-Boza, Vilna Bashi, Crystal Fleming, and France Winddance Twine. Thank you OiYan Poon, for modeling a butt-in-chair writing practice that held me down for over a year, along with the writing retreat you arranged. I learned so much from events like the Diaspora and Indigeneity Group at Brown University, run by Kevin Escudero and Paja Faudree, and those who collaborated with me on Pacific Islands studies at Northwestern.

I rarely wrote in my home or at my university office, until COVID-19 upended our lives. I worked for hours in cafés, wine shops, and bars across the United States and Hawaiʻi. I have a deep sense of gratitude to Colectivo and Other Brother coffee shops as well as Sandeep's Vinic Wine Shop in Evanston, where I long to return during this endless lockdown and where I hope to celebrate this book. I wish, too, that I could thank my children's caretakers in person: Jill McDuffee Wade, Imani Wilson, Saeko, and so many others without whose time and attention I would never have finished this book. It's only fitting to circle back to those people and places who made all this possible and pleasurable: thank you Makaya, to our beautiful children Maya and Jaya, to my parents, and to Mānoa Valley on the island of Oʻahu.

INTRODUCTION

HAWAI'I IS MY HAVEN

> *Field Notes, August 2009*
>
> I met E, a Black nurse from Mississippi, for our interview during her lunch break in the courtyard of Queen's Hospital in Honolulu. She said, "Hawai'i is my haven. It's beautiful: the ocean, the beach, the mountains, and mostly the people feel aloha, the spirits.... It feels like in Hawai'i you can escape your Blackness."

"Haven." "Sanctuary." "Reprieve." These are the words Black residents use to describe Hawai'i. They also experience racism, ostracism, and erasure. I illustrate this duality of Black life in Hawai'i through the life stories and experiences of hundreds of people of African descent. They include locals who were born and raised in the Hawaiian Islands as well as transplants, like the nurse Ellen, identified as "E" in my field notes, who moved here as adults. The title of this book came from my conversation with Ellen, whom I interviewed in 2009 (just my second interview of the project). While I have stayed in touch with her over the past decade (she read my work and let me identify her), it was only years later that I learned that Ellen had won one of the largest damage awards in an employment discrimination case in the Islands (figure INT.1).[1] When she mentioned her troubling encounters with fellow nurses at our initial interview, she had confided in me, saying, "It's good to speak to another minority that understands." Ellen personifies the irony of attempting to "escape" one's Blackness—or, rather, escape denigrating ideas about Blackness—while facing antiBlack racism in a place of sanctuary.

Jury awards former Queen's nurse $3.8 million in lawsuit

Ellen Harris filed a lawsuit in 2013 against Queen's Medical Center, claiming racial discrimination and retaliation after she reported multiple patient safety issues..

Former Queen's Medical Center nurse, Ellen Harris was awarded more than $3.8 million in damages by a circuit court jury, on Wednesday.

Figure INT.1 Ellen Harris, a Black nurse, in 2018 won one of the largest damages awards for employment discrimination in Hawai'i. Source: KITV Island News.

Hawai'i Is My Haven is the first ethnography of Hawai'i's Black civilian residents—a population virtually absent in the popular and scholarly imagination of the Pacific, with the exception of former President Barack Obama. "You can't really understand Barack until you understand Hawai'i," says Michelle Obama.[2] The former president concurred that the Islands shaped him when he explained, "No place else . . . could have provided me with the environment, the climate, in which I could not only grow but also get a sense of being loved. There is no doubt that the residue of Hawai'i will always stay with me, and that it is part of my core, and that what's best in me, and what's best in my message, is consistent with the tradition of Hawai'i."[3]

Yet in his memoir, Obama also describes the racism he faced growing up in Honolulu.[4] Like almost one-fourth of the population of Hawai'i, Obama is multiracial, representing the almost 50 percent of Hawai'i's Black residents who identified as more than one race on the 2010 census.[5] Black locals, or African-descended people who are born and raised in the Islands like Obama, often do not have access to Black communities in contrast to Black transplants who move to the Islands as adults from elsewhere, including members of the US armed forces. Raised within nonBlack families, it is their local Hawaiian and Asian community members who inform their feelings of belonging.

Black residents, both local and transplant, are a present absence: although more Black people live in Hawai'i than Sāmoans, who have a significant local imprint, few people recognize them. Hawai'i is at once a site of proliferating Blackness, through the popular local adoption of Black culture, and of Black absence, which includes the denial of the Black civilians who live among us. This absence is due both to the reduced *salience* of Blackness in the Islands, referred to in Ellen's discussion of "escape," and to the displacement of Black people onto the continental United States.

Contesting their erasure, Hawai'i's Black residents were impossible to ignore during the marches, rallies, and vigils held across the Islands in honor of George Floyd, an African American man who was murdered by a Minneapolis police officer, Derek Chauvin, on May 25, 2020. Among the attendees at local events were Black transplants who remarked on this unique moment of potential social transformation. In response to a youth-organized "Hawai'i for Black Lives" march on June 6, 2020, which drew nearly ten thousand people to the state capitol building, retired professor and Morehouse College graduate Robert Steele reflected, "One of the unique things not only here but nationally or internationally is how [rally organizers] hold a demonstration. The whole movement is so ethnically diverse. In fact, the majority of participants are people of color, which is so gratifying."[6] A Black man from Georgia who attended an event a week earlier at Magic Island in Honolulu that drew around two hundred people to memorialize Floyd highlighted Hawai'i's uniqueness: "This is a fantasy to me, people of different hues, different backgrounds all together," he said. "This is how it should be."[7]

The realities of racism, however, cloud sunny depictions of Hawai'i as a multicultural and harmonious society. A Black Hawaiian community organizer, Shayna Lonoaea-Alexander, told a reporter that "a lot of folks believe that because Hawai'i is a melting pot that anti-blackness doesn't exist here. . . . Anti-blackness and racism exists in Hawai'i and it's unacceptable and it's on all of us to fight for Hawai'i, to fight for a country where being black isn't a death sentence."[8] Dr. Akiemi Glenn, a Black transplant to Hawai'i, explains in a June 2020 interview at the height of protests,

Figure INT.2 *All Colors Are in This Together*. #blacklivesmatter. The Maui surfer, Roderick Nathan, holds a surfboard commemorating George Floyd during a paddle out in honor of Black men and women murdered by the police. Photo by Conan Gentil, May 31, 2020.

> In addition to watching the stuff that's happening in North America over the last week, we're ... grappling with the blatant and often unrecognized antiBlackness that's a part of Hawaiʻi culture. I'd be remiss to talk about what's happening in North America without also contextualizing threats that have been made against Black people even ... here in Hawaiʻi. ... As people here have been organizing vigils and demonstrations and socially distanced gatherings, there have also been calls for nonBlack locals to come and keep an eye on us to make sure that we don't become violent.[9]

Glenn, the cofounder and executive director of the Pōpolo Project, an organization documenting Black life in the Pacific, deciphers these responses as local adoptions of antiBlack racism: "So even though we live here and we are part of this community, there's still this suspicion of criminality that's associated with any kind of Black people and Black gatherings."[10]

Hawaiʻi's Black population faces global antiBlack racism and local erasure simultaneously. On the one hand, locals presume that the Black people they encounter in Hawaiʻi are temporarily stationed in the Islands as part of the US military, and thus as agents of state power. On the other hand, local and tourist framings of the Islands as devoid of Black civilians allow this place to imagine itself as free from the racial problems that beleaguer the United States.[11] As a result, Black locals appear an oxymoron, an impossibility. Speaking of sentiments expressed by Black community members in Hawaiʻi surrounding weeks of activism in response to George Floyd's murder, Glenn explains, "Many folks are feeling very tired. ... But what I think that tiredness is about is that exhaustion comes with constantly having to explain yourself and your humanity. And for many Black locals, having to explain that we live here, and that we are part of this community" and "part of the local people."[12] Black people are not considered to be from the Islands but rather are an ignored minority in a mostly nonWhite place. It is more the case that Blackness has been adopted by Pacific Islanders who embrace Black cultural forms, such as reggae and Rastafarianism, and Black politics, including the ideologies of the Black Panthers expressed by the Polynesian Panthers in Aotearoa/New Zealand, without concrete reference to or knowledge about the African diaspora. This reduction of Blackness to culture and ideology results in the excision of actual African-descended people from our local and scholarly understanding of Hawaiʻi.

The prioritization of frameworks of culture and ethnicity in tourism, local discourse, and research on Hawaiʻi contributes to the erasure of Hawaiʻi's Black civilians. Without an analysis of *race*, we cannot understand, or even *see*, Black life in the Pacific. In a June 2018 interview during one of her visits to

Hawaiʻi, the cofounder of the Black Lives Matter movement Patrisse Khan-Cullors stated:

> Black struggles and freedom struggles, in particular, have had such an important impact on the globe. Everywhere I go, Black Lives Matter is understood as part of a long legacy, a movement, of Black people trying to fight for our freedom. It doesn't always mean that it's going to translate into a particular place. . . . *Maybe Black Lives Matter doesn't make sense here, but maybe the conversation about Blackness makes sense here.* And how do we translate that. . . . Let's talk about Blackness and its relationship to our context [in Hawaiʻi], not Black Lives Matter in the US. (italics added)[13]

Khan-Cullors's sentiment that Black Lives Matter may not "translate" or "make sense" in Hawaiʻi is uncanny in light of the protests during the summer of 2020. Her comments illustrate the widespread erasure of Black residents described by Glenn. Discussions of Blackness in Hawaiʻi before 2020 and even during these international uprisings pivoted to Melanesians, anti-Micronesian racism in Hawaiʻi, and reflections on the widespread adoption of reggae and hip hop. Few acknowledge the presence of Black people living within these communities, except for Black community leaders like Joy Enomoto, an artist and activist who is Black, Asian, and Hawaiian, and Akiemi Glenn, a Black, Asian, and Native American linguist with genealogical ties to the areas now known as North Carolina and Virginia. They have both been called on to "translate" the importance of the recent Black protests taking place across the nation to the Hawaiʻi context.

I join these efforts to address Khan-Cullors's call for a conversation about the value of Black life in the Pacific by providing the necessary context: mapping the histories, lives, and politics of Black people in Hawaiʻi. To realize the potential of solidarity that Khan-Cullors, a queer Black woman artist, organizer, and freedom fighter, hopes for requires us to address locally specific tensions that stall Black and Hawaiian comradeship.[14] Khan-Cullors's travels across the Pacific led her to recognize the intersection of race and indigeneity. She observes, "Hawaiʻi has always been an interesting place for me when I think about indigeneity and Black Indigeneity in particular. . . . I've learned much more about colonialism in Hawaiʻi and the US military's impact here in Hawaiʻi and the kind of role Black Lives Matter has the opportunity of playing when it comes to having a broader conversation about globalization and a broader conversation about solidarity work."[15] In the Islands, the local context necessary for understanding the particular contours of Black life includes its colonial history, military occupation, and Asian settler colonialism. This

Figure INT.3 Dr. Akiemi Glenn, executive director of the Pōpolo Project. Photo by Michael McDermott.

setting informs clashing ideas about what issues matter locally and how best to go about addressing them—dynamics that shape Black and Hawaiian relations.

Some of the tensions framing relationships between Black and Hawaiian people convened around two movements that reached a crescendo in 2020, both of which I consider to be struggles for liberation: the Movement for Black Lives against police brutality and Kānaka (Native Hawaiians, or Hawaiians) self-determination represented by the kiaʻi, or Native Hawaiian protectors. The kiaʻi stationed on Maunakea, a mountain of ancestral significance that has also been claimed as a site for astronomy, have mobilized to stop the desecration of their land proposed by the construction of the Thirty Meter Telescope.[16] Earning global support, the protectors went to the mountain on the Big Island of Hawaiʻi to disrupt a planned groundbreaking ceremony on October 14, 2014. Hawaiian activists, including the kūpuna (elders), have since camped out in the cold and faced arrest while successfully blocking the ongoing march of the settler state's attempt to bulldoze Hawaiians' rights to make decisions about their land.[17]

Native Hawaiian activists have been guided by their kuleana (rights and responsibilities) and the practice of kapu aloha, or "the commitment to nonviolent direct action" that fosters "compassion and respect while engaged in politicized expressions of outrage and disobedience."[18] The same principles of kuleana and kapu aloha guide the protests against antiBlack racism in Hawaiʻi. More often, however, locals frame the struggle for Kānaka self-determination on the one hand and the desire for the recognition of Black humanity on the other hand to be discrete and contestatory aims. More concerning, when African-descended people in Hawaiʻi do voice their concerns in ways informed by a legacy of Black struggle, other locals dismiss their problems and disparage their strategies as not representative of "aloha." The Hawaiʻi reporter Anita Hofschneider reflected on this contradictory response to Black and Hawaiian activism: "Social media posts also compared violent protests [against police violence] on the continent with peaceful Native Hawaiian protests in Hawaii against the Thirty Meter Telescope on Mauna Kea."[19] She interviewed the Black Hawaiian organizer Shayna Lonoaea-Alexander, who explained, "There's a lot of online discourse right now around Kanaka (Native Hawaiians) trying to police the way black folks are grieving and protesting and I think it's so unacceptable," she says, speaking of the depiction of Black protest as "violent."[20] Lonoaea-Alexander calls out the lack of reciprocity between Hawaiian and Black activists, saying, "We asked the world to stand with us [Hawaiians] (on Mauna Kea) and I think that the world really responded but when black folks are asking it's a different story.... I'm tired of people who look like my dad or my brother or my sister being killed."[21]

Despite these divisions, the Movement for Black Lives and kiaʻi protecting the Mauna against desecration are fighting against the same sources of oppression: state-sanctioned violence, racism, and colonialism. The police enforce the White supremacist settler state even when the officers are nonWhite and are even one's family members, as they often are in Hawaiʻi. By extending themselves to learn about Black struggles, two Hawaiian collectives cultivating Hawaiian knowledge and fighting for Indigenous self-determination, Puʻuhonua o Puʻuhuluhulu and the Hawaiʻi Unity & Liberation Institute (HULI), issued a "Joint Statement of Solidarity for the Protection of Black Lives" on June 5, 2020. The statement proclaimed their solidarity with Black communities fighting against police violence:

> While we share in histories of oppression and colonialism, we recognize and understand that our lived experience is not the same as the Black experience in America and we refuse to use Kapu Aloha to judge their response to struggle for survival. We acknowledge with great pride and humility the influence that black struggle has had on the Hawaiian movement and political consciousness and call upon the lāhui (Hawaiian Nation) to learn about the relationship between black and Hawaiian struggle.[22]

The statement frames Black and Hawaiian people, experiences, and politics as distinct and calls for Kānaka to learn about their political cross-fertilization. They also recognize "our Black Hawaiian relatives," people whose voices I center in this ethnography: "Anti-blackness is a problem in our communities, and we must work to understand the many forms that it takes in Hawaiʻi. We must address this issue together and commit to stand as kiaʻi (protectors) against anti-blackness and racism," the statement urges.

This book offers a framework for understanding these discussions that acknowledge agency and oppression. *Hawaiʻi Is My Haven* maps the context and contours of Black life in Hawaiʻi that frame relationships among people in the Islands. It centers both Black locals and Black transplants to Hawaiʻi who encounter a life of integration and invisibility. My focus on Black residents includes Black Hawaiians, or the children of Black and Native Hawaiian parents, who do not abide by either the local Hawaiʻi or North American academic framing of Black and Indigenous people as disparate groups living in distinct geographies and advocating divergent politics. The kuleana of Hawaiʻi residents to urgently address antiBlack racism and Indigenous self-determination in a settler state is clear in the current predicament of Black residents. Akiemi Glenn expresses the specific needs of Hawai'i's Black residents during a period of mourning in the summer of 2020: "Of course, we are feeling the 'eha (hurt, pain) and the heaviness of what's happening in North America very much, but we also love Hawai'i and will behave accordingly as we are grieving."[23]

Black people grieve in a place they may consider their haven and sanctuary, far from the Middle Passage and the Black Atlantic.[24] Black transplants grew up in Black communities, and their perspectives are informed by the history of slavery and antiBlack racism. Their worldviews are challenged in the Black Pacific, where Indigenous epistemologies and local cultural practices take precedence. They are part of a two-centuries-long lineage of Black arrivals who have experienced historical acceptance and integration into Hawaiian society. This is what shapes a sense of optimism and possibility for African-descended people, notably personified by Obama. However, Black residents, both locals and transplants, also trouble this positive depiction through their accounts of invisibility and experiences with antiBlack racism in contemporary Hawai'i. Shifting the focus from what is exceptional about Obama, I ask, What alternative to elsewhere, and particularly the continental United States, does Hawai'i provide to members of the African diaspora? How is it that Black civilians experience antiBlack racism yet nonetheless declare Hawai'i to be their haven?

The Difference of Hawai'i

[The Kingdom of Hawai'i was] a neutral country, that sought to have friendly relations with countries throughout the world, that gave a home to people of multiple ethnicities that wanted to be here at a time when in other countries, they were enslaved.

NOELANI GOODYEAR-KA'ŌPUA, 2018

I can remember when Hawai'i became a state; I was just a little girl [in Alabama], and all the Black people were so excited. Because it was basically a nonWhite state. And we knew that. And so it was exciting that this kind of a thing could happen. [Us] not understanding all of the history, of course, and the dispossession and the overthrow—any of that. But it was just this model of equality, if you will, that was so incredible.

BLACK LONG-TERM RESIDENT

Hawai'i, a place with no clear demographic majority, has been heralded as an ideal multicultural society because of its racial and ethnic diversity.[25] In his visit to the Islands in 1959, the year of statehood, Martin Luther King Jr. commended the Hawai'i State Legislature: "I come to you with a great deal of appreciation, I should say, for what has been accomplished in this beautiful setting and in this beautiful state of our Union," particularly, he noted, "in the area of racial harmony and racial justice."[26] Today, nearly one in every two marriages is interracial or interethnic, resulting in a large number of multiracial people, at almost a quarter of the overall population. Of Hawai'i's 1.25 million residents, Asians make up 41 percent, Whites 24 percent, and Native Hawaiians approximately 20 percent.[27] Yet all this attention to Hawai'i's diversity curiously neglects a group so central to America's understanding of itself: Black people.

Residents and representations of Hawai'i remain silent on the question of its Black population, except for individuals in entertainment and politics.[28] They include Barack Obama, Janet Mock, and Dwayne "The Rock" Johnson—figures who are often read nationally as Black, but locally as multiracial. The invisibility of the Islands' Black population in today's scholarship on Hawai'i and on the African diaspora, tourism literature, and local discourse could be due to Black people's small demographics, at 3.5 percent in 2018. However, their population has increased every decade for the past eighty years.[29] The historical and current erasure of Black people is belied by their growth (a 16 percent increase in the last decade) and the prevalence of Black popular culture. Blindness to the contemporary presence of Black men and women mirrors a historical omission of what has been an almost 250-year-old story.[30]

Subject to hyperbole, Hawai'i is described by the popular press as "the most isolated population center on the face of the earth."[31] Indeed, it takes a five-hour flight to get to Hawai'i from California, and almost nine hours from Japan. The Hawaiian Islands, in the center of the largest ocean on earth, consist of eight main islands: the Big Island of Hawai'i, Kaua'i, Maui, Lāna'i, Kaho'olawe, Moloka'i, Ni'ihau, and O'ahu. O'ahu, the site of this ethnography, houses the state capital of Honolulu, the Islands' largest and most populated city, within which lies the tourist mecca of Waikīkī. These islands, together with numerous other isles and atolls, appear discrete, reachable by airplane, boat, and canoe. Yet they form an archipelago united undersea by a volcano chain, and united politically between 1795 and 1810 by King Kamehameha I.

The Hawaiian scholar Ty Tengan summarizes, "Despite the establishment of a monarchy (1810) and international recognition of the Hawaiian Kingdom's independence (1843), the nation suffered an overthrow (1893) backed by the U.S. military and annexation (1898)—both done illegally."[32] After the 1893 coup against the reigning queen, President Cleveland admonished, "It appears that Hawaii was taken possession of by the United States forces without the consent or wish of the government of the islands.... Therefore the military occupation of Honolulu by the United States ... was wholly without justification, either as an occupation by consent or as an occupation necessitated by dangers threatening American life and property."[33] Congress refused the President's orders to reinstate the Queen.

In light of this history and with respect for Hawaiian self-determination, I do not typify Hawai'i as a state or conflate it with the rest of the United States. Rather, I refer to the continental United States or the contiguous forty-eight states (rather than "the mainland," a term that decenters the Islands) in distinction to this unique site. Hawai'i is a state that is not a state. It houses the US Indo-Pacific Command. It is a place illegally occupied by the United States. It is a site of active Indigenous resistance for an independent nation.

Whereas residents are profoundly aware of Hawai'i's colonial history of usurpation, scholars and the tourist industry advance representations of Hawai'i as a site of exception, the epitome of a harmonious multicultural and multiracial society that forecasts national demographic changes. Social scientists affiliated with the Chicago school of sociology focused on its diversity, group relations, and mixed race marriages and their children to depict Hawai'i as a "racial frontier." The demographer and University of Chicago graduate Romanzo Adams came to O'ahu in 1920 when the college became the University of Hawai'i, and he founded the departments of sociology, economics, anthropology, and social work. Adams was followed by fellow Chicago graduates Andrew Lind (arriving in 1927 and retiring in 1967) and Robert Park (1931–1932), both of whom studied race and Island demographics.[34] Shelley Lee and Rick Baldoz review how these early social scientists conceived of Hawai'i as "racial laboratory," a "fascinating interracial experiment station," whose study could "yield insights about racial dynamics and social change that might be brought to bear on understanding and solving race problems in other parts of the United States."[35] Today, Hawai'i's demographics and multiculturalism continue to interest not only scholars but also mainstream Americans, whose perceptions of the isles are shaped by a tourism industry invested in obscuring its direct links to militarism, plantation histories, and the illegal overthrow of the monarchy. It is this history, however, that shapes the contours of Black life in Hawai'i.

This history—including the absence of a slave past—plays out in contemporary group demographics and dynamics. The Black and White binary is not primary; immigrants do not refer to Latinos (who constitute a full 10 percent of the population); disenfranchised groups include Hawaiians, Sāmoans, and Filipinos, as well as recent Micronesian immigrants; and local Chinese and Japanese, along with haole, or White people, have political and economic clout.[36] Rather than viewing the Black population as the primary native-born minority, locals consider them (along with Whites) to be sojourners, cultural outsiders, and part of an unwelcome military presence, or else athletes or reggae artists. The conception of Black people as arrivals from elsewhere and unfamiliar with local culture informs the subjectivities of Black transplants. They come mostly from the United States, but also from Africa, Asia, Europe, and the Caribbean, and find themselves to be just one among many nonWhite groups. In a similar reversal of their racialization in the continental United States, Asians are often presumed to be island-born residents who have created local culture through their linguistic, culinary, and other practices from the mid-nineteenth-century plantation times to the present. Much of this, along with the large mixed race population, marks Hawaiʻi as exceptional.

Black life in Hawaiʻi is exceptional as well, distinct from elsewhere. Black people made up 3.5 percent of Hawaiʻi's population in 2018, or 48,863 residents, making them the sixth-largest group, just after Chinese.[37] One-quarter of the Black population is Island born, with the rest coming mostly from the continental United States (5 percent are born abroad).[38] In a 2014 article in *Black Enterprise* crowning Hawaiʻi the state with the highest Black household wealth, Kenneth Clark extols: "Topping our list is one of the most beautiful places created by God's design. Better known as 'Paradise,' black residents who live in Hawaii make the most . . . at a whopping $66,629."[39] People of African descent also have the Islands' highest rate of high school graduation and employment while being the "race least likely to be in poverty in Honolulu."[40] What accounts for these economic opportunities and racial trends for Black residents? The answer partially rests in the institutions that bring them here.

The armed forces employ one-fifth of the entire Black population in Hawaiʻi, who, along with their dependents, make the military the second biggest employer of Black residents. More than 30 percent of Black civilians are veterans.[41] Thirty-three percent of Black residents work for the federal and state government.[42] These statistics may account for why the Black online source TheRoot.com named Hawaiʻi the "number one best state for Black people" in 2014.[43] Certainly, these figures reflect a version of Black success that some people may contrast with the rest of the nation. The conflation of "Black" with "military" is hegemonic in Hawaiʻi; it is difficult to overstate its effect on all Black residents. At the same time, this conflation is historically inaccurate and denies the realities of Black nonmilitary civilians. This ethnography expands the focus on Black soldiers in the Pacific to include Black locals, or Hawai'i-born-and-raised people of African descent, who are mostly multiracial, primarily raised in nonBlack families, and occupy a range of class statuses.

Hawai'i Is My Haven breathes life into these facts and figures, illustrating the contradictions of Hawai'i as both a sanctuary and site of antiBlack racism. After all, Black residents pay the most for rent, work more hours than all other groups, and are the tenth-highest-paid group.[44] These figures do not relate what emerges as the central theme from my interviews with sixty African-descended locals and transplants: this predominantly nonWhite society with a significant Indigenous population moderates White racism and thus expands the opportunities for Black people.

An Ethnographic Account

This inaugural ethnography of Hawai'i's Black population—also the only ethnography of African American civilians in Oceania—draws from a decade of fieldwork to address two questions: What does the Pacific offer people of African descent? And what do Black transplants bring to Hawai'i that leads to a deeper understanding of the Islands? Black locals recount how Blackness resonates differently—as both more expansive and less salient—than elsewhere, specifically the contiguous forty-eight states. Black transplants, on the other hand, bring with them a *racial lens*, or an analytical view that, in contrast to dominant representations of the Islands, both sees and dissects racism as a central component of local power dynamics. Transplants insist that a racial hierarchy prevails in this "Pacific paradise"—albeit, they find, not a Black and White one.

Hawai'i offers an alternative to life otherwise: a society that prohibited slavery in the nineteenth century and a site of "less pressure" today.[45] Participants describe their relief from relentless structural, police, and class oppression and from what they describe as the expectations of "being Black" in their daily lives. Nonetheless, Black men and women living in Hawai'i experience racism, within the intimacies of their homes and as they navigate the institutions that hire them. Whereas the general Island ethos amplifies cultural and ethnic differences to celebrate multiculturalism, Black people who move here highlight the vectors of racism that they confront. At the same time, the large Asian population, significant Indigenous presence, and notable Black absence confound them. Upon arrival, they see that in these Pacific islands, the targets of racism are not always Black, and the perpetrators are not always White.

A living contestation of White supremacy, Hawai'i offers a contrast to US racial formations. For over two centuries, Black people have experienced integration and acceptance in Hawai'i rather than segregation and systemic oppression. Black locals, who are raised in a place that lacks a large Black presence (or Black Metropolis)[46] and where nearly a quarter of people are multiracial, offer a different orientation to debates about Blackness and multiracialism within African American studies and mixed race studies. This place has been home to generations of island-born people of African descent, from the children of Cape Verdean mariners' unions with Hawaiian women in the early nineteenth century to the people I interviewed who have Black fathers and Hawaiian, Korean, and other nonWhite mothers. Rather than signaling the end of racism or upholding the sociological fantasy of Hawai'i as a "fascinating interracial experiment," Black multiracial people in Hawai'i emerge from the entangled tentacles of oppression.[47] These processes, including colonization, dispossession, exploitation, disenfranchisement, racism, and militarism, shape the lives and perspectives of Hawai'i's Black civilians.

The historical scholarship on this population is scant, based largely on nineteenth-century missionary and shipping archives. In other words, much of it comes from European and American perspectives. Other work details the military history in the Pacific with a focus on World War II, which created a diaspora of African American soldiers—and their children—across Oceania, from Hawai'i to Sāmoa, from New Hebrides to New Caledonia. Important exceptions include the narratives of women scholars and artists of African and Pacific Islander descent, including Teresia Teaiwa, Courtney-Savali Andrews, and Joy Enomoto.[48] Important recent scholarship on Hawai'i draws from Hawaiian language sources;[49] however, in centering Hawaiian-haole relations and Asian plantation histories, they have not looked for Black figures before the twentieth century. Twentieth-century sociologists, demographers, historians, and Black scholars living in Hawai'i provide the most relevant studies, but none charts the *lives* of Hawai'i's Black population.

Linking the current civilian presence to Hawai'i's history expands our understanding of the Islands beyond multiculturalism and the armed forces. Encounters between Black people from elsewhere and those from the Islands highlight locals' (including Black locals') unawareness about the history and concerns of the African diaspora. As a result, this expanded knowledge provides people of African descent with a location and sense of belonging. At the same time, Hawai'i and its residents offer African Americans and other members of the African diaspora ways of thinking about the self that decenter "Middle Passage epistemologies," which, according to Michelle Wright, follow a "linear progress narrative" that fixes the Middle Passage as definitive of Blackness.[50] I heed Wright's call to look to examples that fall outside the "Africa to America" narrative. What happens over time—and sometimes quickly—is that people begin to foreground connective relationships to land, people, and ancestries in ways not determined by the boundaries and histories of White-ordained racial formation.

My articulation of the Black Pacific does not erase Native Hawaiians but rather engages them in their home, where African-descended people find themselves read through Native Hawaiians' historical engagements with Blackness.[51] This includes Hawaiians' reverence for Pō (the generative darkness); haole missionaries' historical transference of their ideas of Black inferiority onto Kānaka Maoli (Native Hawaiians); the European construct and ensuing Pacific Islander adoption of the colonial divisions of the Pacific, including Melanesians; and the global influence of Black expressive forms.[52] (I use "Kanaka," "Kanaka Maoli" (Kānaka, plural), and "Kanaka ʻŌiwi" interchangeably with "Hawaiian" and "Native Hawaiian." "Hawaiian" does not refer to everyone from the Islands (e.g., I say that I am from Hawaiʻi, but I am not Hawaiian); it is not like calling someone a "New Yorker." These terms refer only to the Indigenous people of Hawaiʻi—to those with Hawaiian ancestry who are the descendants of the first inhabitants of the Hawaiian Islands.)[53] I add to these various layers and valences of Hawaiʻi's engagement with Blackness a missing component: the actual experiences of members of the African diaspora in the Pacific, Black people in the Hawaiian Islands.

This project speaks across the "studies": it addresses debates between Black studies and critical mixed race studies (see my analysis of multiracialism in chapter 2); it brings Pacific Islands studies into conversation with Black studies (chapter 3); and most centrally, it addresses tense debates between Black and Native studies that center historical and political disputes (discussed at length in chapter 5). My ethnographic illustration of Black and Hawaiian encounters expands theories of (Asian) settler colonialism, Black agency and abjection, and the Black/White, local/nonlocal, and native/settler binaries—all more fully discussed across the chapters. Documenting daily life fleshes out, and in some cases directly contests, totalizing abstract theories of Black life and death, Native erasure, and frameworks that prioritize some forms of oppression over others. It also animates the Islands as more than a primarily Asian locale. This is not a binary analysis. Unlike many scholars of transpacific studies, I expand beyond the "cultures of the Asian diaspora" by stopping *in the Pacific*.[54] Additionally, whereas North American studies analyze triangulated Native-Black-settler (White) relations, Hawaiʻi-based scholars analyze the relationship of Native Hawaiian-Asian-haole triangulation. How do Black people emerge within this paradigm? How do they disrupt it? I theorize the relations between Hawaiians, Asians, and Black people while decentering haole.

Less studied—and the focus of my project—is the role of race and racism in Hawai'i.⁵⁵ Members of the African diaspora illustrate how central these systems are to understanding life *for all people* in the Islands. Black transplants bring an explicitly racialized framework—a racial lens—to the Islands. Black Americans often grow up within a particular set of relations informed by the history of slavery, segregation, and antiBlack racism. This framework allows them to understand group dynamics through a continental US perspective that includes an awareness of the differential access to resources based on race. Along with a Black/White understanding of difference, they may advance the one-drop rule, or the rule of hypodescent, which states that if you have a "drop" of Black blood, you are (just) Black. At the same time, they also bring knowledge of counterhegemonic ideologies of Black resistance, cultural expressionism, and a deep sense of connectivity among members of the African diaspora. A racial lens includes an analysis of White supremacy and a deep awareness of the workings of racism that they see as crossing oceans to settle in a place where haole are not a majority. This perspective contests depictions of Hawai'i as a "multiracial paradise," challenging locals' tendency to view racism as a problem that happens "over there," as a problem only plaguing the continental United States. At the same time, Black transplants encounter a site of persistent Indigenous resistance against haole oppression—resistance they relate to and consider as a model for liberation. Local dynamics and Native politics reorient people who are used to understanding their position as oppressed within a Black and White binary.

The Black Pacific

"The Black Pacific," a term used to describe the movements of African-descended people, aesthetics, and politics across Oceania, is a growing area of study generally attended to by historians.⁵⁶ Whereas the majority of the literature on the Black Pacific centers the military and reads Blackness as embodied by either Black American soldiers or else in reference to cultural and political formations (reggae, Black Power ideologies, and aesthetics), I center the lives of civilians who identify as Black and as members of the African diaspora. I use the Black Pacific as an ethnographic, conceptual, and geographic concept. The Black Pacific is descriptive—it includes my ethnographic charting of the daily lives of African-descended people in a Pacific site. It is geographical, focusing on a place deemed "the most isolated place on earth" that is intimately tied to global imperial powers (the United States and Japan). It is contemporary, in contrast to studies fixated on World War II. And it is conceptual, offering a counterpoint to the Black Atlantic, bringing Pacific Islands studies into conversation with Black studies.

Scholars who use the term "the Black Pacific" include those who skip *over* the Pacific to speak about the Americas and Asia, including the study of African American men in East and Southeast Asia and other Afro-Asian projects.[57] In these works, as in much of transpacific studies, peoples and societies are evacuated from Oceania, which emerges as a vast, watery "flyover" expanse, a place not productive on its own. The Hawai'i-based scholars Paul Lyons and Ty Tengan explain, "'Asia-Pacific' and the 'Transpacific' often sublate Pacific Island and Islander priorities within models that originate outside of the Islands."[58] Engaging a Pacific society on its own terms involves grappling with a deeply local context.

An ethnography of the Black Pacific that centers people associated with transatlantic slavery brings the Black Atlantic theorized by Paul Gilroy into conversation with Pacific indigeneities.[59] It thus contributes to research on the appeal of Black politics and aesthetics across Oceania, which includes Robbie Shilliam's analysis of Rastafarianism in Aotearoa/New Zealand, Bernida Webb-Binder's study of Black Pacific art in the United States and Aotearoa, and Gabriel Solis's examination of music in Australia and Papua New Guinea, islands whose people have been considered Black.[60] Power is at play not only among Polynesians, Micronesians, and Melanesians but also within these categories of people as they consider notions of Whiteness and Blackness.

White colonizers parsed Pacific Islanders into a tripartite racial taxonomy of Melanesians, Polynesians, and Micronesians, informed by their encounter with Africa. Melanesians, so named owing to their melanin, emerge in discussions of Blackness in the Pacific as the result of cartographies of European colonial racial taxonomies. Pacific Islanders have generated their own conceptions of Blackness and darkness. This includes Hawaiians' reverence for Pō, or darkness, and the identification of some Indigenous Australians and Papua New Guineans with Blackness and as Black. Together, these colonial and Indigenous conceptions shape the experiences of Black people in Hawai'i—experiences that, for African Americans, are distinct from those of both Africans and Melanesians.

The racial dynamics that exist in the Pacific contextualize but do not explain the experiences of the people in my study. This project focuses primarily on African Americans and people who identify as part of the African diaspora rather than on Melanesians, whom the Fijian scholar Ponipate Rokolekutu describes "as the black people of the Pacific."[61] "In mapping Oceania," writes the political scientist Tarcisius Kabutaulaka, "Melanesia was the only subregion named after the skin color of its inhabitants: the 'black-skinned people' or 'black islands.'"[62] Linked to colonial constructs of Africans, this informs Melanesians' placement at the "bottom" of the racialized hierarchy of Pacific Islanders. Rokolekutu explains, "Oceanian epistemologies are deeply racialized." He continues: "The European discourse on race has subsequently informed racialized epistemologies and racial categorization in Oceania. Melanesia[ns] are represented as inferior while a degree of deference is accorded to Polynesians. Both Melanesians and Polynesians have internalized such perceptions which subsequently dictates race dynamics in Oceania."[63]

Blackness is a concept rather than an essence, an ideology rather than biology. As such, the people of Oceania have adopted these constructs that inform their relations. Hawaiians were conceived of by Europeans as "almost White" Polynesians and thus granted higher status than Micronesians or Melanesians—the latter considered "Oceanic Negroes" or "ignoble savages"—who lacked the former's societal development, physical beauty, and potential.[64] Yet in the nineteenth century, Hawaiians too were called "niggers" (a term that I never say aloud in any iteration), as well as "Indians," while today Micronesians are targets of antiBlack racism in Hawai'i.

Africans and African diasporic people from North America, Europe, Asia, and the Caribbean are read *through* and also *separately from* these legacies and meanings of Pacific Blackness. Melanesians and some Indigenous Australians share with African-descended people the denigration of their darkness, connecting them to colonial constructs of African inferiority, an antiBlack ideology fueled by White supremacy that belts the globe.[65] They are also bonded through their resistant and powerful identifications as Black.[66] Yet African Americans, rather than Melanesians, find that they are the ones viewed as the repositories of "the Black experience" that people in Hawai'i imagine when referring to Blackness. When African Americans move to the Pacific, therefore, they are interpolated through these existing ideological layers. At the same time, they serve as representatives of hegemonic Blackness (including Black politics, popular culture, and notions of racialized violence and sexuality) that circulate the globe, and are intercepted in specifically Black American ways.

Colonists may have tried to fix people of Oceania into Polynesia, Micronesia, and Melanesia, yet in practice, people fuck with conceptions of who is what, including who and what "Black" is in the Pacific. Hawai'i does not conform to the Black/White binary of the continental United States in part because of its large Asian demographic, strong Native Hawaiian presence, and mixed race population. Yet perhaps the most evident example of resistance to the White racial hierarchy is simply the nonsalience of Blackness in Hawai'i and Hawaiians' historical acceptance of African diasporic people. Blackness is expansive—it refers to politics, to aesthetics, and to populations that circulate the oceans. Blackness does not conform to taxonomic categories and does not stick fixedly to bodies. The Canadian Black diaspora studies scholar Rinaldo Walcott says that "the wonderful thing about blackness is that it is a sign in which we are not exactly sure what might sit underneath it or what might sit within it, but yet there is a history that shapes what we mean by it when we invoke it."[67]

(Mixed) Race and Indigeneity

I place race at the center of this study without forcing US-centric models on the Hawai'i context. Race, along with indigeneity and settler colonialism, explains the relationship between Black, Hawaiian, and Asian people; highlights the dynamics of belonging; and challenges the dominant theories of ethnicity and culture as the operative dynamic among groups in the Islands. Ethnicity is an individual's chosen identity, including cultural practices and ancestry. On the other hand, race is not always a selected identity and is often imputed on people. A racial analysis centers historical processes of racialization and racism, which highlight power and inequality among groups. People can thus have racial and ethnic identities (e.g., being identified as Black and identifying as Nigerian, or identifying as Black and Nigerian). People across the United States are also identifying in growing numbers with more than one racial category, or as multiracial—the fastest-growing population in the United States. If the scholarship on Hawai'i has focused on ethnicity—despite earlier Chicago school scholars' research on "race"—less studied and the center of my argument is how groups in Hawai'i are differentially racialized for the economic and political gain of powerful interests and institutions.

People also identify along the lines of race *and* indigeneity, such as the Black Hawaiians in this project, or people with a Black parent and a Native Hawaiian parent. I maintain the specificity of Kānaka indigeneity rather than viewing Hawaiians as just another ethnic group or racial category. At the same time, Hawaiians and other Indigenous people have been racialized through colonization and disempowerment. Although race and indigeneity are distinct processes and categories of identity, law, and materiality, they overlap in important ways for Black residents of Hawaiʻi, and particularly Black Hawaiians. The Islands' history, Kanaka Maoli practices, and local culture inform how people understand and express themselves here, expressions that arrivals from elsewhere may find puzzling.

Exchanges among groups in Hawaiʻi unsettle both hypodescent and the expectation that people identify monoracially, or with just one race. Black locals disagree with scholars who argue that the category of Black is expansive enough to acknowledge multiracialism.[68] People I interviewed forgo a "Black-only" identity and instead adopt the Hawaiian practice of hyperdescent, whereby they acknowledge all their ancestries. Rather than interpreting this as antiBlack, a flight from Blackness, or internalized racism, I read such choices through Kanaka epistemologies that reveal practices of expansive inclusion.

Critics of multiracialism argue that discussions of "mixed race" lead to the quantification of what is a socially constructed process of racialization. In Hawaiʻi, the quantification of race coexists with an elastic handling of ancestry. Federally imposed policies still require evidence of blood quantum to be eligible for certain material resources. However, people debate who is and is not Hawaiian "enough" by calling on ancestry as well as cultural capital and knowledge. Both Hawaiian and Black people, despite their multiple ancestries, often highlight their Hawaiianness or Blackness, respectively. As Brandon Ledward writes in his study of Hawaiian hapas (multiracial people), "rather than playing up our many ethnicities often times most of us choose to posture ourselves as simply Hawaiian."[69] Yet, after living in the Islands for some time, Black transplants, who formerly identified as Black only, tended to recount all their ancestries when asked, "What are you?" The Black Pacific provides opportunities for expansive identifications because of both the relative invisibility of Blackness and the prominence of Indigenous epistemologies. At the same time, Black locals are integrated into local nonBlack networks of kin and community and may not learn about the African diaspora. They come up against racial authenticators from elsewhere who apply stringent conceptions of hypodescent and monoracialism that shape Black locals' ambivalence to Blackness.

Analyzing how Black Hawaiians navigate ideas of Blackness alongside Kanaka ideas of genealogy and belonging brings Black studies into conversation with Pacific Islands studies. Brandon Ledward explores group dynamics among Hawaiians whose communities are filled with people of multiple ancestries. Ledward wants to "examine the implications of multidentity among Hawaiians who feel strong connections to diverse ethnic groups."[70] His ethnography illustrates "social factors contributing to the notion of 'Hawaiian enough' and discuss[es] the implications processes of racialization have within the contemporary lāhui Hawaiʻi (Hawaiian community)."[71] The vast majority of Hawaiians—like African Americans—are of mixed ancestry (Ledward says up to 98 percent of Kānaka Maoli).[72] His study of "hapahaole" (people with Native Hawaiian and European ancestries) attempts to bridge the divide of hapa and Hawaiian as separate categories, which emerges as one impact of US racialist thought on Hawaiian epistemologies that my research also emphasizes.[73]

If the experiences of Black people in Hawaiʻi seem primarily to highlight how race operates, the lives of Black Hawaiians reveal how race and indigeneity intersect. While Ledward looks at White and Brown Hawaiians, or Hawaiians who cross the categories of Hawaiian, local, and haole, Black Hawaiians reflect the unique ways that Blackness (rather than haoleness) functions and is de/valued within Native communities. The historical racialization of Black people and the local emphasis on being Native Hawaiian explains why participants in this project who have Hawaiian mothers and Black fathers identify as both Black and Hawaiian. Hawaiʻi's unique context reveals the problem in critiquing this mode of multiracial identification—a critique (often accompanied with suspicion) that emerges from mapping a continental Black/White, monoracial, and hypodescent framework onto both the Pacific and multiracialism.

Black Residents and Asian Settler Colonialism

The work on settler colonialism in Hawaiʻi has not yet taken Black people into account. Even in the most recent books on Hawaiʻi, one cannot find the terms "Black" or "African American" (or even "race") in their indexes. If in the continental United States, settler colonialism is viewed as a White/Native structure of Native erasure that relegates Indigenous peoples to the past, Native Hawaiians, at 20 percent of the population, are undeniably contemporary, present, and agentive. This reorients the meanings of race and indigeneity—as well as belonging in a settler state—for people of African descent.

This book bridges continental discussions of settler colonialism that theorize the role of Black people within the native/setter binary with those in Hawaiʻi that analyze Asians and other immigrants as settlers. Evelyn Nakano Glenn calls out comparative race studies for its erasure of Indigenous people and complicity with Native dispossession. Glenn, drawing on Patrick Wolfe's definition of settler colonialism as a structure and not an event, applies an intersectional approach to the conditions faced by communities of color.[74] She encourages fellow ethnic studies scholars to see how a "settler colonialism framework can encompass the specificities of racisms and sexisms affecting different racialized groups while also highlighting structural and cultural factors that undergird and link these racisms and sexisms."[75]

Bridging ethnic studies and Native studies, *Hawaiʻi Is My Haven* contributes a Pacific perspective to new work analyzing Native and Asian immigrant relations in North American settler state contexts while I decenter the hegemony of the study of Asians in Hawaiʻi.[76] I do so by foregrounding the voices of Native Hawaiians. This project engages the robust theorization of (Asian) settler colonialism in Hawaiʻi and the scholarship on Hawaiian politics, grounded in the ideas of Haunani-Kay Trask. These contributions, as seen by any number of panels at the annual Native American and Indigenous Studies Association (NAISA) conference, have primarily been about the *conceptual* contribution of Hawaiʻi and Pacific Islands studies scholarship to (North American) Black and Native relations. Zeroing in on Black and Native interaction *within* Hawaiʻi reorients debates in Black and Native studies about group connections, tensions, and liberation. It illustrates, as Tiya Miles and Sharon Holland do in their volume centering North America, how "people of African descent transported and transformed cultures, created intersectional communities, and built metaphysical as well as physical homes on Native lands and within Native cultural landscapes."[77] Like scholarship on the Caribbean, however, it expands debates between Black and Native studies that privilege the Americas.[78]

If Black people are relatively invisible, Asians form a substantial presence in the Islands, where settler colonialism and localness are primary formations. Asians, including Asian multiracial people, made up over 56 percent of the population in 2015.[79] Okinawans and Japanese are the highest per capita income earners and have the highest rates of homeownership.[80] As the Hawaiʻi expert Jonathan Okamura explains, "Since the 1970s, ethnic relations in Hawaiʻi have become increasingly structured by the economic and political power and status wielded by Chinese Americans, Whites, and Japanese Americans over other ethnic groups."[81] It is Asian—not White—settler colonialism that emerges as a living, obvious, and maintained structure.

Asians in Hawaiʻi are defined not only by their settler status but also by their various racialized positions. They contribute to the perpetuation of local culture and differentially face the effects of unequal resource distribution. The plantation economy of prestatehood Hawaiʻi brought waves of plantation workers from China, Japan, Korea, the Philippines, and elsewhere. This history of exploitation has become the dominant narrative drawn on by Asians not indigenous to the Islands to justify their belonging. However, the framework of Asian settler colonialism reveals how claims to a local identity provide cover for the ways various Asian groups advance the settler state and dispossess Hawaiians of their land and rights to self-determination.[82] After statehood, these various ethnic groups have come to occupy highly uneven positions of political and economic power. The Islands are home to a diversity of Asian communities, from those running political and economic life to the precariously housed hotel workers. As a result, Okamura has articulated why "there are no Asian Americans in Hawaiʻi," whereby "ethnic," or what I consider racialized, distinctions (Japanese, Filipino, etc.) within this lumping category are primary.[83] This explains why, for instance, someone may describe a neighbor as a "local Japanese" or may self-describe as being a "Filipino from Wahiawā," rather than identifying as "Asian American," as is more common in the continental United States.

In their study of Asian and Native relations in North America, Karen Leong and Myla Carpio explain, "Because the settler state works to eliminate Indigenous claims to the land, immigrant groups' conditional inclusion requires complicity in ignoring these Indigenous claims as well."[84] This is relevant to Hawaiʻi, where Harry Kim, mayor of Hawaiʻi County on the Big Island, explains how to "trample the souls" of Native Hawaiians in his advancement of the Thirty Meter Telescope (TMT) on the sacred land of Maunakea—a move contested by Kānaka Maoli and other residents.[85] Asian complicity in Native dispossession through their participation in settler colonialism takes place *alongside* Asian antiBlack racism: this is the same mayor who jokingly referred to a Black professional as "that colored guy." If, as J. Kēhaulani Kauanui shows, "Asian groups were racialized in contrast to Native Hawaiians vis-à-vis the haole," Black people have been both compared *and* contrasted with Kānaka to differing ends.[86]

Black locals, including Black Hawaiians and Black Asians, develop our understanding of settler colonialism, the development of racialized indigeneity, and the resonance of local identity. They include Hawaiʻi-born Black children who are raised in nonBlack communities and identify strongly as local. As a result, Hawaiʻi's Black residents do not fit neatly into the important critique waged by Hawaiian and Asian settler ally scholars who reveal how Asians in Hawaiʻi (especially the political elite) deploy "local" to deny their role in settler colonialism and advocate anti-Kanaka policies.[87] A local or nonlocal identity emerges as central categories of non/belonging in this study. Are Black people local? Black locals highlight the salience of this identity, disrupting efforts to consider "local" as only a problematic identity in debates over settler colonialism. Scholars who only analyze ethnicity cannot respond to these questions when they neglect a racial analysis, deny indigenous specificity, and downplay both racism and material inequalities.

Haunani-Kay Trask's specification of "settlers of color" frames the field of Asian settler colonialism, raising the question of other nonWhite people in settler states. Are Black people settlers? This question of the structural relation of Black people to Native dispossession has arisen in some work focusing on Black and Native studies. "Black dislocation within the settler state is always an unfinished and incomplete project," write Eve Tuck, Allison Guess, and Hannah Sultan.[88] "Policing tactics, gentrification, vigilantism, and political isolation find justification in the settler colonial truism that Black people should not be where white settlers want to be."[89] They echo critiques of Asian settler colonialism: "Yet the struggle to resolve Black dislocation can obscure the face of Indigenous erasure and resilient, radical relationships to the land. There isn't something easy to say about this."[90] Indeed, my interlocutors reflect on these politics, as I do by raising the question of Black agency in aligning with the US military occupation of Hawai'i. I also turn to the historical, political, and cultural cross-pollination that characterizes Black and Hawaiian relations. This book does not conflate Black and Hawaiian struggles for self-determination but rather looks to what emerges once we bring together Black and Hawaiian people, race and indigeneity, a racial lens and Kanaka epistemologies, in our analysis of the descendants of enslaved people living in a nonWhite settler state.

On Relations and Relationality

Hawai'i presents an alternative to elsewhere because of its nonWhite demographics and strong activist movements that critique US hegemony and imperialism. Not just a confrontation to White supremacy, it is a place where even aspirations to Whiteness are disparaged. Black people experience the pleasure of being part of a multitude of communities of color while reflecting on accountability for settler colonialism and military occupation, which are ever-present structures of life in many parts of the Pacific. Race, too, is an organizing force in the Hawaiian Islands.

Race both offers a top-down analysis and requires our attention to the adjacent everyday dynamics of a person's life. Race, combined with indigeneity that highlights connectivity, genealogy, and place-based identities, strengthens our understanding of Black life in the Pacific. At the individual level, we see how Black residents negotiate historical tropes of Blackness, antiBlack racism, and the perception that they are not local. These racialized processes intersect with the experiences of other groups, including Native Hawaiians' histories of colonization, kuleana (responsibility, privilege), and ideas of belonging, along with Asian groups' uneven rise to power and their contributions to local culture.

I detail the agency *and* oppression of Black, Hawaiian, and Asian people vis-à-vis global systems of racial power and capitalism (e.g., White supremacy, slavery, plantation economies, settler colonialism). While this context frames this ethnography, I highlight on-the-ground relations. These not only humanize global processes but trouble facile theoretical claims, including binaries, "Oppression Olympics," identity-based generalizations and cancellations, and uncritical celebrations of an alliance. I reveal, for instance, how Native Hawaiians are oppressed *and* are antiBlack, both within the context of colonization. Conversely, I show how Black people in Hawai'i face racism *and* are part of a tourist economy and occupying military force. NonWhite groups internalize and exert colonial and racist ideologies in the painful recollections of Black locals. Beyond ideology, the *practices* that inform(ed) slavery, genocide, labor exploitation, war, and diaspora also converge in contemporary life, including for those who emerge from these histories and are Black and Native, Black and Asian, and Black and Latina/o. Black Koreans and Black Okinawans recount their experiences with invisibility and the antiBlack racism they face within their Asian communities. They cannot escape racism, even on these promising shores. Black Hawaiians as well as Black Sāmoans, central to this ethnography, illustrate how people living within, among, and *beyond* these categories conceive of their relations to others in ways that privilege connections.

Native dispossession and the denigration of Blackness do not go uncontested. The combination of Indigenous epistemologies, illustrated in contemporary movements for self-determination and cultural revitalization, and the racial lens employed by Black transplants work hand in hand toward decolonization and antiracism. Black people navigate the imbrications of White supremacy and Hawai'i's occupation, but their relationships and sense of self are never fully determined by them. Because I root my analysis in the history of Hawai'i, we see how the norms in the Hawaiian Kingdom still inform contemporary life through the persistence of Kanaka epistemologies and practices. I share the desire articulated by Tuck, Guess, and Sultan, who discuss Black and Indigenous people on the "selfsame land" "to supersede the conventions of settler colonialism and antiblackness toward another kind of futurity."[91] In light of the antagonisms reflected in a range of scholarship, I join their turn toward "the need for more thought and attention given to the relationships between Indigenous peoples and Black peoples."[92]

The lives of the participants in this project emerge from the intersection of racism and colonialism; their actions reveal the link between antiracism and decolonization. While we may know this politically and intellectually, we have few examples of how this is *lived*, contributing to the literary and historical analysis of Black, Asian, and Native relations. What this ethnography shows is that no one exists outside of antiBlack racism, settler colonialism, and occupation; nor do one's given identities ("Kanaka," "settler," "African American") *determine* our relation to these systems. It is our standing vis-à-vis institutions of oppression—within and outside of them—that gauges our contribution to maintaining or decimating them.

One's positionality crafts conceptions of one's kuleana, or responsibility. The Kanaka scholar Hōkūlani Aikau describes kuleana as a central component of living responsibly with "critical positionality and reflexivity. Kuleana is not static, is not fixed; it is about understanding yourself in relationship to the place where you are."[93] It is a constellation of "responsibility, authority, and obligation" and thus shifts accordingly.[94] But it is the *actions* of people—not just their identities—that determine whether we uphold or undermine racism and colonialism. Hawai'i, and especially contemporary movements in the Islands, requires residents to reflect on their accountability and responsibility to this place and to one another. Analyzing the intersection of race and indigeneity includes how members of the African diaspora contend with living as people not indigenous to Hawai'i.

Critical self-reflection, together with action based on one's kuleana, creates a sense of we-ness among those working with expansive notions of community.[95] "What linked land taking from indigenes and black chattel slavery," explains Glenn, "was a private property regime that converted people, ideas, and things into property that could be bought, owned, and sold."[96] Yet current practices of self-determination and visions of the future in the Islands challenge imported colonial practices that were not only statist and proprietary but also based on the denigration of Native Hawaiians and Black people.[97] The lives and ideas of those living in and creating the Black Pacific expand academic debates, model both limited and expansive politics, and paint a fuller picture of daily life that moves us from a race-only, ethnicity-only, or native/settler-only lens to one that accounts for these, as they articulate.

Methods, Participants, and My Story

Born and raised in Hawaiʻi, I am the daughter of an immigrant father from rural North India and a Brooklyn-born Jewish mother who is the daughter of immigrants from Russia. I am Indian and White, neither Hawaiian nor Black. My parents, professors at the University of Hawaiʻi (history and Asian studies) for forty years, raised my brother and me in a middle-class home in Mānoa Valley in Honolulu on the island of Oʻahu. I considered myself and was considered by others to be a local girl. People knew that I was Brown but not Hawaiian, given the close-knit nature of Hawaiian communities. Other youths teased me for my Indianness and demanded clarification: as Jay-Z once rapped, "Are you red dot or feather?"[98] I attended local public schools: Noelani Elementary School in Mānoa Valley, followed by Stevenson Intermediate and Roosevelt High School in Pauoa, attended also by several participants in this project. On alternating yearlong sabbaticals, my parents relocated us to live in my father's North Indian village of Kota, the Indian city of Jaipur in Rajasthan, and Queens, New York. Otherwise, at home in the Islands, I played soccer, learned ballet, and played violin in the Hawaiʻi Youth Symphony. But it was hula that most formed me, that most informed me about my birthplace—its stories, histories, people, plants, and practices. I danced first with Auntie Maiki Aiu Lake above Puck's Alley at the mouth of Mānoa Valley. After she passed away, I joined Hula Hālau Na Hanona under Kumu (teacher) John Keola Lake at St. Louis High School for almost a decade, until I left for college in California. This book—like all my scholarship and teaching—is shaped by this marriage of factors.

I offer this ethnography as someone trained in anthropology and housed in ethnic studies (aka race studies). While too many people have heard me joke about being "divorced from anthropology," it is true that I had a vexed relationship with the discipline. Its scholarship (and scholars!) did not encourage my interests, which have always focused on the United States (not "there"), on communities and concerns (too) close to me, and on race and racism (instead of cultural difference). That said, anthropology equipped me with the ethnographic method that I remain committed to, while my political and intellectual motivations align comfortably with comparative race studies as a professor of African American studies and Asian American studies.

Hawaiʻi Is My Haven expands my previous ethnographic analysis of Black and Asian relations. The goal of my work is to detail interminority racisms shaped by White supremacy to illustrate the formation of on-the-ground solidarities. I illustrate existing models of antiracism that consider the liberation of all people. My work past and present decenters Whiteness and looks to understudied collectives through a focus on race and culture and, in this book, indigeneity—whether South Asian American hip hop artists, rappers in the Middle East, or Black people in Hawaiʻi. Working to eradicate racism that differentially affects all nonWhite people (and, yes, affects White people too—but that's not my concern), I chart the everyday lives of people who cross theoretical and commonly accepted boundaries of race, place, and politics. Their understandings of the world provide theories of difference and solidarity. Understudied, unique, and small populations, owing to their "difference" from normative expectations, *show us* (and thus disrupt) naturalized categories as they navigate divisions, including those among presumably incommensurable groups. This explains why so much of this ethnography centers Black people in the Pacific and multiracial people within Black studies.

After my father, Kumu John Lake (a voracious storyteller and cigarette smoker, just like my father) was the most influential man in my life. More than a hula teacher, this esteemed elder took our hālau (hula school) across islands to Maui, and across the Pacific to Aotearoa/New Zealand for exchanges with Maori, whom we later hosted. Our hālau comprised younger and older dancers, men and women, straight, gay, and māhū (third gender, for those who do not identify as only male or only female). Sāmoan and Tongan football players, Japanese, Indian, Hawaiian, and hapa haole Catholic and public school girls—we all together practiced complicated kaʻi (entrances), dances, and hoʻi (exits), with the better dancers in synchrony up front, me and the others in the back.

Kumu Lake drove us in his van up to the mountains on the other side of the Pali, where we climbed the deep crevasses etched by rain. He narrated the Hawaiian names of the plants and flowers we picked to make haku lei for our heads, wrists, and ankles for our performances at the Prince Lot Hula Festival. We pretended to listen but were more interested in sliding down the muddy mountains on the wet ti leaves we gathered. He had us memorize oli (chants) in ʻōlelo Hawaiʻi (I always lip-synched, never really dedicated the time to learn them); he gave us Hawaiian names, equipped us with the skills, and guided us through ʻūniki (a rigorous graduation process, which I failed to complete). He told us about Hawaiian history, the meaning of every step in each song, and gave us printed sheets with the words and movements to scores of ʻauana (modern) songs and hula kahiko (ancient) chants. I still have these materials stored in an aged yellow three-ring binder in my old woven hula bag, stuffed with my instruments—the ʻuli ʻuli, puʻili, ipu, along with the ipu mat; my green hula skirt that we printed with tapa now fits my daughter. The dark golden yellow ʻilima lei I painstakingly made, feather by feather, for weeks under his guidance is stored safely in a plastic cookie dough container.

Writing this book has been an interrupted yet long-term return home that rewarded me with memories informing my fieldwork and analysis. While my home is still there (my mother retired and still lives in my childhood house, where I edited the final version of this book during COVID-19), my father and Kumu Lake have passed on. As they and others left, my own family has grown during fieldwork, first with one child and then another. Each research trip involved at best, with no delays from a Chicago airport, a nine-hour flight (for a family of four, recent trips cost at least $3,000). My children got to play in the same backyard that I did at their age, helping my mother collect coconuts and rotting mangoes from her yard, and swimming in the same outdoor Mānoa public pool that I did. I have been able to watch the Wednesday night fireworks from the Ilikai Hotel with my mother after witnessing in awe how this almost eighty-year-old still paddles with the Anuenue canoe club, near the Hilton Hawaiian Village in Waikīkī. It allowed me to reconnect with my home after years of the growing sense that I was read as being from "the mainland," despite my Hawaiian jewelry and familiarity with Sāmoan doormen, as a result of too much time away from home.

This project reflects my love of Hawaiʻi and gratitude to the people of Oʻahu who raised me and shaped who I am. Hawaiʻi has always been home and a gift to me. My father's generous outlook, my mother's political radicalism, and Kumu John Lake's wisdom inform my kuleana. This ethnography is my attempt to tell these stories and to engage with their theoretical and political implications.

I began fieldwork in 2009 and over ten years have spoken to hundreds of island residents in addition to the sixty people I formally interviewed, many of them several times. My work centers the voices of those who self-identify as Black—people of African descent who are members of the African diaspora. After arranging childcare, I rode my father's scooter or drove my mother's car to meet generous participants at coffee shops in Mānoa and across Oʻahu, the university's Campus Center, and in people's homes. Interviewing was always a pleasant and often exhilarating experience, despite my constant low-grade anxiety that preceded each meeting ("Why am I an ethnographer? Do I have to do this interview?") as a result of feeling that I was taking and not returning something from participants when I asked them to share their stories. Part of this stemmed from the ethics of ethnography, as well as my fatigue from the heat and my persistent allergies. It was, however, always worth it, as I experienced the postinterview rush of inspiration that amplified my interest in these questions. Conducting this project in my hometown was deeply satisfying, as I was familiar with the topography, could easily suggest and find places to meet people, and understood historical dynamics and local references.

No less important, the dress code demanded a casual approach—thus my uniform of tank top, flowing and comfortable cotton culottes, and plastic slippers (slippas) worked well for me as I conducted my first stint of fieldwork throughout my first pregnancy. I began this project in the year I was on leave from my university in Evanston and lived in Hawaiʻi. During that year, I got married and became pregnant with my daughter, and my father died. He was crucial to the initial drive of my project, urging me to contact potential interviewees, including people like Ellen, the Black nurse who befriended him during his frequent hospitalizations. My mother, also a professor, doubled his effort over the past decade, introducing me to her students who were multiracial Black Asian transplants taking her courses in Asian studies. As my father's health deteriorated, he was bedridden at the Queen's Medical Center. He couldn't speak well, and then not at all. Indian family and community members brought his favorite parathas and sweets, even after he couldn't or wouldn't eat. And yet he always listened to my chatter about the progress of my pregnancy, my husband's career, and updates about my research. His hands float across this project, revealed through participants that he enlisted for me as we sat at a coffee shop in Mānoa Marketplace earlier in the year before he was sick. While my mother is the anthropologist who inspired my career, I learned how to be in the world as a social and empathetic person from my father.

Fieldwork consisted of the staples of ethnography: heavy hanging out, formal and informal interviews, and participant observation. I took notes wherever I found myself—at nightclubs, the beach, and house parties. I recorded interviews that were between one and two hours long and had them transcribed by hired students and rev.com. I coded and analyzed them both by hand and with Atlas.ti, a qualitative software analysis program I know I am supremely underusing. I wrote the book using the software program Scrivener, a writer's dream. Informing my analysis was my engagement with Black studies; the scholarship on race, ethnicity, and the history of Hawaiʻi; Native studies; critical mixed-race studies; and the work on the nineteenth-century Pacific.

The historical context for this contemporary ethnography emerged from my archival research of shipping logs, missionary journals written in English, and official correspondence and newspapers in ʻōlelo Hawaiʻi (Hawaiian language). Except for the basics I learned from Kumu Lake long ago, I do not speak ʻōlelo Hawaiʻi, and thus my research on nineteenth-century Hawaiʻi is limited. What I found suggests provocative traces of Black life in the 1800s, recorded not just in missionary journals and other English-language texts. I also searched hundreds of Hawaiian-language sources in the rich digital collection of the Hawaiian Mission Houses for particular terms to get a picture of how words for blackness and darkness developed as descriptors for things and then later for people. I scoured the correspondence of the monarchs and chiefs in the Aliʻi Letters Collection and the newspaper *Ka Lama Hawaii*; upon finding the terms, I solicited the assistance of colleagues who spoke ʻōlelo Hawaiʻi, including Drs. Hiʻilei Hobart and Charles Langlas, to help me correctly interpret their context. For other chapters, I also analyze contemporary media and social media accounts, including local and national newspapers. Census and demographic information from a range of sources, including Hawaiʻi economic and population reports, has been key to illuminating the Black presence in the Islands that has so curiously and almost completely fallen under the radar.

I spoke to hundreds of people—any Black person I could meet on Oʻahu (and I Skyped with those on outer islands) and many nonBlack residents. University of Hawaiʻi professors led me to students and Black faculty; high school friends pointed me to former classmates; new friends and family introduced me to others. I interviewed nurses, bartenders, DJs, lawyers, and security guards. However, it was only after coding, reading each interview and other source materials scores of times, and analysis that I created the primary groupings of people that structure this ethnography. These primary categories include Black locals and Black transplants; long-term residents (I also call them "old-timers") and newcomers; locals (those born or at least raised in the Islands); and nonlocals (those who moved to Hawaiʻi after high school). This book also highlights the experiences and perspectives of nonWhite dual minority biracial people, whom I call Black hapas or multiracials (more on the term "hapa" in chapter 2).

The first group consists of nineteen Hawaiʻi-born or Hawaiʻi-raised Black *locals*, who grew up mostly in their nonBlack mothers' communities in the Islands. Forty-one people make up the second group, *transplants*. Transplants are roughly divided into *long-term residents* (who had generally lived in Hawaiʻi for over ten years) and *newcomers* (more recent arrivals at the time of our interview). Overall, almost half, or twenty-eight of the sixty participants, were multiracial, including fourteen locals and fourteen transplants. There are thirty-eight men and twenty-two women; one man identifies as gay, and two women are queer identified, including one who is gender nonconforming. Black transplants and locals offer distinct life stories, with different orientations to

Black history and politics and uneven access to Black communities, families, and cultures. Together, along with the epistemological topography of their childhoods, these shape residents' identifications with Blackness, localness, and belonging in Hawai'i.

Many of these people stay in touch with me, sending me emails and Facebook messages updating me about their battles with cancer, the development of Black social life in Hawai'i, and their lawsuits against workplace discrimination. Right now our conversations are consumed by the protests against anti-Black violence emerging from the murders of Black people including George Floyd, Breonna Taylor, Tony McDade, Nina Pop, and Ahmaud Arbery. They keep me abreast of new events centered on vigils and BLM protests in Hawai'i, the growing Black community, and happenings at the university, where Black students and faculty come together to create spaces of belonging. I have stayed in touch with many of these people, as well, by sharing my writings, sending them my publications, and, of course, explaining why it has taken so long for the book to come out. Facebook has been a particularly critical technology for maintaining contact, allowing me to keep abreast of their lives, including changes in their work, the growth and contractions of our families, and evidence of our aging. It has also led to real and long-term relationships with them, as we could communicate about when we were next going to be in the same place and arrange to meet up—at least we did before COVID-19 upended our lives.

This is a ground-up ethnography. It is not determined by the most current debates and categories but rather hopes to ground some of the tendencies toward abstraction on the question of Blackness and characterizations of interminority relations, as well as some Black and Native studies scholarship. I highlight the influence of Native Hawaiians, Kanaka epistemologies, and local culture. I focus first and foremost on the islands of Hawai'i (with a bias toward its largest city, Honolulu, on the island of O'ahu) and the words, perspectives, and experiences of Black people who live in the Islands as nonmilitary-affiliated civilians. Their generosity and stories filled the hundreds of hours, thousands of pages, and years of fieldwork this book emerges from.

I do not recall growing up with any kind of Black community in Honolulu—most of the people I knew and saw around me were hapa haole (mixed race), Japanese, Chinese, Filipino, haole, Sāmoan, and Hawaiian. When I return home now, my family hangs out at Kaimana Beach with members of these groups along with Black residents of Hawai'i. We are invited to attend events hosted by Black collectives, usually by women who have come to the Islands alone or with their children. I interact with a significant number of Black scholars, from new hires at the university to emerita faculty who still live on Oʻahu. Social, arts, and political events advocate food sustainability, Black performance, and conversations with Hawaiians about coalitions. My family, including my Black and Hungarian Jewish husband (who in Hawaiʻi is sometimes read as Sāmoan), and our two children are integrated into Black communities in Chicago. Unlike the Honolulu of my childhood, in which Blackness was invisible outside the military context, my family now experiences Oʻahu as a Brown place of fellow multiracial people with a growing Black population whose cultural presence is strong, respectful, and respected, and not necessarily affiliated with the military. Things have changed over time. Given the rising demographics of Black people in Hawaiʻi over the past century, I chart this change and what it means for all of Hawaiʻi's people.

Conclusion

Hawaiʻi Is My Haven animates the liminal as a center for theorizing: the Black Pacific, the nonWhite multiracial (a mixed race person who does not have a White parent), and the porous boundaries and critical nexus between race and indigeneity. Hawaiʻi has long offered people of African descent an alternative to the places from which they came, yet US notions of race and White supremacy travel across the ocean through colonialism, militarism, and the tourist economy. Life stories of Hawaiʻi's Black civilians foreground experiences with racism that trouble images of its welcoming multiculturalism. At the same time, this society provides an alternative for members of the African diaspora, who describe Hawaiʻi as their haven. They also express feeling a respite—a space to breathe—away from the "pressures" that come with being Black in the continental United States. Racism reinforces their racial lens, while Native Hawaiian practices allow them to be "Black and ____" rather than "Black only," represented by the significant number of Black people who identify with more than one race on the census.

The Pacific expands conceptions of Blackness. In Hawaiʻi, Black people adopt Kanaka practices to develop what the activist and Black feminist scholar Angela Davis describes as the necessary expansive and inclusive community formations for revolutionary transformation, in contrast to identity-based communities, which can be exclusive and narrow.[99] The perspectives of African-descended people living in Hawaiʻi, informed by the history of both the African diaspora and the Pacific, illuminate a Black Pacific worldview that weaves together a racialized understanding of power with an indigenous understanding of place and people—and the connections among them. These illustrations contest the scholarship that, while understandably focused on Black death, also portrays Black life as only abject.[100] Hawai'i enables a sense of optimism and possibility embraced by many participants.

Between the introduction and the conclusion, this book offers five chapters that articulate Black life in one part of the Pacific. Chapter 1, "Over Two Centuries," charts the history of Black people in Hawai'i from the beginning of the nineteenth century who went on to play critical roles in Hawaiian society. Often citizens of the Kingdom, they also were central to the racialization of Hawaiians by haole. These ideas shifted considerably with the twentieth-century association of Black people with the US military. The persistence of Kanaka epistemologies and the tendency to integrate Black people within their communities and families intersected with the increasingly negative twenty-first-century reception of Black transplants.

The next two chapters focus on the experiences and perspectives of Black locals (chapter 2), which contrast with Black transplants (chapter 3). Black locals' life stories may be the most understudied of the Islands' populations. However, they answer the question of what the Pacific offers people of African descent. With an analysis of their demographics, identifications, and conceptions of Blackness, they chart the effects of racial invisibility as well as the opportunities of expansive belonging offered by local practices and Kanaka approaches to genealogy. Chapter 2, "'Saltwater Negroes'" (a term used by one local Black Sāmoan), takes on the charge that multiracialism is a form of antiBlackness while engaging questions of race and localness, making a case for the meaningfulness of local identity. Black locals, including Black Hawaiians, Black Sāmoans, and others, reveal how and why the Pacific is a place of expansive Black belonging. (Mixed) race, indigeneity, and local culture together forge the dynamics through which non/belonging and affiliation are assessed and asserted.

Chapter 3, "Less Pressure," focuses on transplants, or African-descended people who moved from North America, Asia, Europe, the Caribbean, and Africa to the Islands as adults. It charts their reasons for doing so and identifies how their preconceptions of Hawai'i aligned with their actual experiences. Illustrating a racial lens, their perspectives, formed in parts of the world with a greater Black presence, illuminate how power operates here. This chapter enters debates on (Asian) settler colonialism, addressing whether or not Black people can be settlers while also explaining why some consider Black absence to be a source of liberation. It also documents the strong imprint of the Islands on its residents, including these transplants whose views about race and Blackness are challenged in this "haven."

Chapter 4, "Racism in Paradise," the first substantive documentation of antiBlack racism in Hawai'i, brings the experiences of Black locals and transplants together. Through an analysis of antiBlack racism at home, school, and work, and in encounters with the police, we see the limits to depictions of Hawai'i's celebrated diversity. At the same time, locals and transplants diverge in their *analysis* of racism, including their perspectives on local humor as a way to contend with difference. Transplants call out and contest racism (often through the courts) because of their identification and racial analysis of local dynamics (racial lens). How does this explicit reckoning with antiBlack racism come up against local dismissals that Black people have a "chip on their shoulder" or don't understand local culture? Tensions between these interpretations have come to a head in local reactions to Black Lives Matter protests against police violence and the ongoing erasure of Black people in Hawai'i. Transplants' racial lens gives voice and structure to racism in the Islands and, along with the painful childhood memories of Black locals and accounts of their interactions with police, makes a resounding call for critical reflection of all island residents for our role in antiBlack racism—and our kuleana to challenge it.

Chapter 5, "Embodying Kuleana," centers Black and Kanaka positionalities and relations, framed by a discussion of Black and Native studies. It foregrounds the voices of Black Hawaiians but expands out to Black residents' reflections on land, sovereignty, and belonging. This final substantive chapter shows how US histories of slavery, Jim Crow segregation, and police violence, as well as class status, inform Black transplants' views on Hawaiian movements for self-determination. They revert not so much to native/setter or local/nonlocal divisions as they draw links across African American, Native American, and Hawaiian histories. Together, they map overlapping pasts and a shared present and chart routes that Black and Hawaiian people together can navigate toward liberated futures.

I end with a conclusion that reveals how people are neither just trapped by colonial categories and racist ideologies nor simply reactive to them. Rather, through everyday strategies, political exchange, and knowledge production, people in Hawai'i exceed these constructs as they consider their kuleana and act with accountability. I offer suggestions for how to bring settler colonialism and racism into account through the greater incorporation of Black people into our learning in the Islands. If knowledge is power, then in looking to the knowledge that circulates between Black and Native people, we can find existing models for antiracism and decolonization.

1

OVER TWO CENTURIES

THE HISTORY OF BLACK PEOPLE IN HAWAI'I

> *Hawai'i was different for Blacks coming here initially because they didn't have to deal with the stigma of being slaves in Hawai'i. If you step off in Hawai'i, nobody was going to hunt you down, shackle you up, and bring you back. You stepped off and stayed and dealt with Hawai'i as it was.*
>
> LOCAL BLACK SĀMOAN

> *Only by understanding colonization and its accompanying logics can one make sense of how social, political, and economic relations have been structured, restructured, and reconfigured throughout history. This historical approach does not dismiss the violence and inhumanity of slavery as an institution, but neither does it ignore the violence and inhumanity of colonization; instead, it links together forced removals and relocations, and dispossessions of land and personhood.*
>
> KAREN LEONG AND MYLA CARPIO, "CARCERAL STATES," 2016

Not so much erased as unknown, the history of Black people in Hawai'i is a story of integration and invisibility over two centuries long. Black whalers, king's advisers, and educators arrived long before the large waves of both Asian plantation workers in the nineteenth century and Black US military personnel the following century. Predominant narratives (only) link Black men and women to the Atlantic slave trade or else to their military history in the Pacific. Reading

Hawaiʻi's history through the lives of African diasporic people who arrived since the late 1700s expands these narratives. This story has been overlooked in our attention to the Middle Passage in studies of the African diaspora and by foregrounding Pacific Islanders' encounters with American and European Whites as well as Asian settlers in Pacific Islands studies. Additionally, scholarship on Hawaiʻi fixates on White-Asian-Hawaiian relations while ignoring both ideologies of Blackness in these colonial encounters and the presence of African diasporic people.

Colonial constructs of Blackness—not just Whiteness and indigeneity—shaped the Pacific as Europeans attempted to fix Oceania's heterogeneity. White people carved this vast oceanic world into categories of race, appointing Melanesians as the Black people of the Pacific because of their dark skin and curly hair, in contrast to Polynesians, whom Europeans considered closer to Whiteness.[1] African-descended people dialogically informed these ideologies in Hawaiʻi, where attitudes toward Blackness and Black people shifted over the last two centuries. In the nineteenth century, Hawaiians increasingly adopted US ideas of race, while they themselves were triangulated by Whiteness *and* Blackness.

Presenting the early Black presence in Hawaiʻi is not just a matter of demographic significance. The context to these numbers uncovers competing discourses about difference imprinting a major portion of the globe. In part, the lack of attention to Oceania by African American studies scholars reflects intellectual (and perhaps political) blind spots, including an unwillingness to approach African diasporic history outside the Black Atlantic and beyond the contiguous forty-eight states. In their attention to colonization, which prioritizes relations with White people, Pacific Islands studies scholars also have not attended to this history. Yet this is the story of Kanaka (Native Hawaiian) racialization. Haole (Whites) distinguished themselves from Hawaiians, whom they aligned with "Indians" in the Americas, but they were all also interpolated by Blackness. Centering the Black Pacific unsettles Black/White and Black/Native/White frameworks in continental and Atlantic studies of racial formations and the Native/settler framing of Pacific Islands studies.

The early history of Black people in the Hawaiian Islands marks the origins of the centuries-long presence of Black island residents whose voices inform these pages. Unlocking our gaze on the Black Atlantic, we see how Black people have not only crossed but also at times stopped to settle within and shape the Pacific.[2] Arriving a century before Hawaiʻi's annexation (1898), Black newcomers entered a society not structured by race. It was mostly men who came, owing to the institutions that brought them—whaling and later the military—creating a persistent gender imbalance that still favors them. What has changed significantly over time is the shift from the social organization of the Hawaiian Kingdom to one of a US racial and political state—a shift Black people engaged. Despite the increasing significance of race along with racist concepts and structures, Hawai'i continues to be a sanctuary for African-descended people, far from the history of slavery and the bonds of oppression. Such a sanctuary is partly created by ongoing Kanaka (Native Hawaiian) resistance to the imposition of US paradigms and thriving Hawaiian ideas of being and belonging.

The nineteenth century proved tumultuous for Hawai'i. Through the first half of the 1800s, distinctions in the Hawaiian Kingdom were between high and low chiefs, between gods, the ali'i (the ruling chiefly class), and maka'āinana (commoners), as well as between men and women.[3] One's station in life, or status as maka'āinana or ali'i, was determined by genealogical ties and recounted through oli (chants). Ali'i were primary shapers and enforcers of societal norms. However, ships brought foreigners and their diseases that eradicated over 90 percent of the Hawaiian population.[4] Within this context of "the great dying," the historian Jonathan Osorio charts the effect of arrivals, including missionaries and other haole elite, who coordinated the "dismemberment" of Kānaka Maoli from their cultural and spiritual practices that had maintained harmony and pono (balance, righteousness).[5] Growing external influence shifted the significance of genealogy and changed who could hold power, presenting the chance for members of the nonchiefly class to exercise greater clout.[6] Early Black arrivals entered this turbulent society where they, too, found new opportunities.

Race generally and Blackness specifically were less fixed in the Pacific. Accepted as free in a place not yet wed to notions of Black inferiority at the height of US slavery, Black immigrants to Hawai'i held important political and economic positions. With no slave codes, the Islands offered a place of refuge and possibility, including the freedom to be oneself.[7] Hawaiians accepted Black whalers, noticing that they were also dark skinned.[8] Categories connoting difference were not the same in Hawai'i, and the categorization of African diasporic people—sometimes as Black, sometimes as White, and other times as Hawaiian—depended on the census, whom one asked, and self-identification: a reprieve from the US obsession with quantifying "ratios" of Blackness.[9]

In 1843, as a sovereign nation-state with citizenship granted to its people regardless of race, Hawai'i became the first internationally recognized non-European territory.[10] The nineteenth century saw changes to who could hold power through laws including elections, new constitutions, and a changing land tenure system, as well as later changes to nationality. At the same time, in addition to confronting widespread death from disease, Hawaiians faced the arrival of Christian missionaries and foreign business interests. Kanaka rulers selectively adopted and merged foreign ideas with Indigenous practices; Hawaiians also outright resisted haole imposition.[11] Navigating ideas of race accompanied these drastic changes, which included the shifting political statuses of the island chain.

In a January 1893 coup backed by the US Navy, an oligarchy of primarily wealthy American businessmen, representing what became known as the "Missionary Party," forcibly sought the abdication of Queen Liliʻuokalani. Through the 1893 overthrow, a group of haole men placed themselves as the new provisional government of the republic, headed by Sanford Dole, a lawyer from a missionary family in the Islands. Later the Queen was imprisoned in ʻIolani Palace under the charge of "treason" for knowledge of a (failed) 1895 counterrevolution by her supporters and for attempting to create a new constitution as demanded by the majority of her people.

Kānaka fought foreigners' rising power against their nation and monarch that disenfranchised Hawaiian and Asian residents.[12] In her deeply moving book *Hawaii's Story by Hawaii's Queen*, Liliʻuokalani recounts her resistance, wherein she refuses to abdicate her title and her duty to her people.[13] President Cleveland had issued a directive to return the rights of the Queen, who was, according to the president of the United States, illegally overthrown. Campaigning in Washington, DC, over many months, Queen Liliʻuokalani attempted to sway Congress to follow this directive. She protested, and Hawaiian organizations and royalists fought usurpation of Hawaiian sovereignty. Nonetheless, in 1898 President McKinley annexed Hawaiʻi by signing the Newlands Resolution.[14] Two years later, Hawaiʻi became an organized incorporated US territory through the Organic Act. In 1959, with the support of US political interests and its military, Hawaiʻi became America's fiftieth state, despite Kanaka resistance. The US military's role in Hawaiian dispossession and the illegal occupation of the Islands frames shifting attitudes toward Black people in Hawaiʻi. While they were initially accepted as sailors, laborers, businessmen, and professionals in the nineteenth century, in the next century Black men arrived in greater number as soldiers participating in the militarization of the Pacific.

As Hawaiians debated political incorporation, they simultaneously wrestled with the growing hegemony of US notions of race. The 1887 "Bayonet Constitution," led by an armed group of American and British men, hastened the erosion of sovereign power and undermined the capability of the reigning King Kalākaua (the Queen's brother and predecessor). Under duress, the King created a new cabinet of powerful haole men, with a constitution that for the first time made "democratic rights ... determined by race."[15] Certainly by 1898, upon annexation, haole settlers had institutionalized US racial categories and other ideologies of race.[16] The ruling elite placed Hawaiians along a shifting spectrum from Black (calling them "niggers") to White (determining them to be "almost White" Polynesians),[17] influencing Islanders' ideas of racial difference. Those shifts also affected Black peoples' status and opportunities in Hawai'i.

Why have Black men and women consistently described Hawai'i as their sanctuary? Certainly, part of it is precisely that the Pacific, meaning a place "calm and peaceful," is not the Atlantic.[18] Early Black immigrants saw Hawai'i as W. E. B. Du Bois did: "as a land of opportunity," far from the inhumanities of slavery, and a "paradise" not structured by Black dehumanization.[19] As the prolific historian Gerald Horne writes, "Those of African descent in particular looked longingly to the Pacific as a sanctuary from their living hell in the Americas."[20] Yet positive sentiments arise also as a result of what the Islands *were*, not just what they *were not*: a place where people did not have to be defined by their Blackness.[21] Over centuries, Black arrivals have been able to take advantage of economic and other opportunities, significantly shaping a place lacking geographic concentrations of segregated Black communities that were elsewhere responding to racism. By contrast, their Hawai'i story reveals the lives of notable and educated Black individuals since the early 1800s, including formerly enslaved men and women, civil rights attorneys, barbers, unnamed sailors, and hundreds of thousands of military members. They found in Hawai'i a respite from the constraints of the places they had left; some married and settled into island life. The children of these Black and Hawaiian and Black and Asian unions are a significant portion of the people who anchor this book.

This project is partly recuperative: it places Black people into Hawai'i's history. Lauded histories of the Islands tell us a fascinating and complex unfolding of haole influence on Hawai'i's elite; newer ones reveal organized Kanaka resistance. Yet they have not looked in the records for nonWhite, nonAsian foreigners who populated the Islands. Remarkable notations of Black sailors, musicians, and others dot the pages of missionary journals and Hawaiian-language newspapers to provide a fuller account of a society thus far depicted as an indigenous place increasingly peopled with haole and a growing Asian population.

This project is also conceptual: it reveals race as an imperative analytic that becomes unwaveringly obvious when we center people of African descent in Hawai'i's history. The earliest arrivals experienced the possibilities of a non-race-based society available to African people during a time of slavery. At the same time, Black people—both as individuals and as the perceived embodiment of White imaginings of Blackness—were central to the adoption of race by the late 1800s. Their experiences illustrate both the Kingdom's uniqueness compared with the United States and its growing accommodation to US racialist (and racist) thought and structures, as it changed from a kingdom to a US territory and then to a state.

This chapter provides this historical context to correct the current notion that all Black people in Hawai'i are visitors here as a result of the US military. Hawai'i residents' association of Black people with the US military has become hegemonic since the twentieth century, developing antiBlack sentiment in the Islands. World War II brought the largest number of African Americans—again, mostly men—through all branches of the US military, which, along with media outlets, continues to inform locals' understandings of who Black people "are." However, from the nineteenth century to the present, Hawai'i is also peppered with distinguished Black civilians who made the Islands their home. I highlight several of these notables, whose accomplishments reflect the possibilities afforded by the Pacific. They are joined today by college students and professionals, newcomers and long-term residents, who have migrated from North America, along with a smaller number from Asia, Europe, the Caribbean, and Africa. While the US military has been the primary generator for the arrival of Black people in the Hawaiian Islands, it neither begins nor ends their local story. Black locals are the most invisible of Hawai'i's Black population, their narratives overshadowed by the military.[22] This neglected history reveals why Black people have considered these islands to be their haven, an alternative to life otherwise.

A Note on Terminology

The term "Black" is more accurate than "African American" in identifying African diasporic people who have migrated to the Islands. The sociologist Romanzo Adams wrote in 1945 that "the number of Negroes in Hawaii has never been large and commonly most of them are not called Negroes."[23] Yet there were enough people of African descent in the nineteenth century for Hawaiians to describe them with the term "haole 'ele'ele." Eleanor Nordyke, a demographer, translates this to "foreign black."[24] Haole referred initially to any foreigner and later specifically to White people; 'ele'ele means "Black, dark, the black color of Hawaiian eyes."[25] Hawaiian-language references translated to "black" in newspapers across the nineteenth century described color, as in "black paints" or "black hair dye," or else something dark or darkness. 'Ele'ele referred to dark or darkened things ("black bear," etc.).[26] "Pā'ele" was another term for "Negroid . . . Negro, Black" as a noun; used as a verb, it means "to be covered with dirt; to besmear; to blacken."[27]

In the nineteenth century, some Hawaiians also used the terms "negero" and less frequently "nika" to mean "negro" or "nigger."[28] Clarissa Armstrong, the haole wife of Reverend Richard Armstrong, writes in her journal: "The natives often ask if he [referring to an image on her wall] is a negro ('nika')" (parentheses in original).[29] This term is not commonly used today, although now many island residents call themselves and one another "nigga," despite not identifying as Black.[30]

"Pōpolo" is a more common term to refer to African-descended people in contemporary Hawai'i (which, like the term "haole," is used both descriptively and derogatorily), referring to the dark berry of the nightshade plant. In the Kumulipo, a Hawaiian creation chant, "Pō" refers to darkness, which is there from the beginning and gives birth to the first woman.[31] "Pō" refers here to darkness or "deep darkness" (pō-uli). The scholar Joyce Pualani Warren explains, "A pan-Polynesian concept, Pō is the darkness, a chaotic yet generative space from which life emerges."[32] Pō thus refers to "night, darkness, obscurity; the realm of the gods; pertaining to or of the gods, chaos, or hell."[33] Under the entry "pōpolo," the Hawaiian dictionary states: "Because of its color, pōpolo has long been an uncomplimentary term. . . . In modern slang, Blacks are sometimes referred to as pōpolo."[34] Yet, like the term "nigga," "pōpolo" has been reclaimed by some Black people in the Islands who use it to self-describe.

Most usually, the participants in this project and others use the common US terms "Black" and "African American" (along with their other racial identities for those who are multiracial) to refer to themselves and other African-descended people. These shifts in terminology are part of the uneven adoption of US racial distinctions in the Islands.

Possibilities in the Pacific: The Earliest Black Arrivals

Decades before plantations, Black men and women landed and often settled in the Hawaiian Kingdom. There were many important positions to occupy in the rapidly changing nineteenth century. Some acquired citizenship and land; they married Hawaiians and learned 'ōlelo Hawai'i (the Hawaiian language). While in the United States the slave system was still intact and citizenship was denied to people of African descent, former and escaped enslaved men and women could participate fully in the Hawaiian Kingdom. For one, no person was a slave in Hawai'i. Additionally, darkness was hailed as a sign of "strength and courage."[35]

On the heels of James Cook's voyages to Hawai'i (1778–1779), free Black men worked along maritime fur-trading routes between the Pacific Northwest and China. Among those aboard whaling and exploration ships leaving New England (Bedford) and Liverpool, England, were those seeking refuge from slavery. Based on shipping records and missionary accounts, we can say that "by the time Europe was ready to tackle the last unexplored ocean [the Pacific], free and unfree Blacks had been serving onboard these ships in a variety of capacities," bringing them to Hawai'i by 1800.[36] Following Hawai'i's sandalwood trade to China (the 1790s), the first whaling ship arrived in the Islands in 1819, the year before the first missionaries landed. This legacy of arrival—from Cook to the sandalwood trade, the waves of whalers and missionaries, and later the US military—points both to a genealogy of Western imperialism and to the vectors that brought African-descended people to these islands.

If by annexation people in Hawai'i had begun adopting US racial categories and ideologies of difference, this was neither an inevitable nor a complete process. Hawaiians had their own practices. Scholars describe the "assimilation" of the several thousand Cape Verdean sailors arriving on whaling ships between 1820 and 1880, who went on to learn Hawaiian and practiced local customs.[37] Former University of Hawai'i professor Edgar Knowlton Jr. compiled the names and migration stories of Cabo Verdeans of African descent, including those who married women with Hawaiian names.[38] Their children, also given Hawaiian names, tended to marry other Native Hawaiians, revealing a less rigid racial stance concerning Blackness. Hawaiians did not adopt the US one-drop rule, used the term "haole" to refer to any foreigner, and maintained an expansive definition of who was Hawaiian.[39]

The Kanaka scholar J. Kēhaulani Kauanui writes, "Kanaka Maoli genealogical practices and kinship . . . differ from the U.S. colonial imposition of blood quantum"; whereas "the blood quantum rule operates through a reductive logic," Hawaiians call on "expansive identity claims based on genealogy."[40] There is an absence of Black people in the records because individuals had difficulty categorizing African-descended people, some of whom privileged their self-identification as Hawaiian. A disjuncture emerges, too, between the ideas of difference (or lack thereof) held by the Kanaka women who married these Black men and statisticians' attempts to enforce US regimes of race as quantifiable. I am reminded of Stephanie Smallwood's account of the Atlantic slave trade, in which the historian highlights the limitations of written accounts and ledgers that commodify rather than humanize those enumerated.[41]

We have records of Black men and a few women of the nineteenth century who arrived as missionaries, educators, and entrepreneurs.[42] Four Black men made up the King's Royal Band, and soon after that, the first two band leaders of the King's Band (now called the Royal Hawaiian Band), commissioned by King Kamehameha III in the 1830s, were Black men.[43] On July 11, 1848, Amos Starr Cooke of the Castle and Cooke company enjoyed a concert in which "the Band consisted of the leader & 9 negroes - - 4 . . . with claronets (!)."[44] Others who also found a place as yet unsettled by race became advisers to the monarch and, in the early 1900s, owned small businesses like boardinghouses.[45]

Elsewhere, other scholars and I have written about important Black figures in nineteenth-century Hawai'i.[46] The story most often begins with Anthony Allen, an escaped enslaved man from New York. He arrived in Honolulu around 1810, where he became an entrepreneur and steward to King Kamehameha.[47] It was on Anthony Allen's O'ahu estate that Allen made the acquaintance of Betsey Stockton, the first documented Black woman to live in the Islands. Anthony Allen "was very kind to me," Stockton writes, "and seemed happy to see one of his own country people. I think he told me he has resided on the island twenty years, and had never before seen a coloured female."[48] Betsey Stockton (b. ca. 1798) was "gifted" as a slave to the wife of the president of Princeton University (then a college) in New Jersey and became renowned for her missionary zeal. After being granted her freedom, Stockton accompanied the friend of her former owners across the Pacific, arriving in Maui in April 1823, where she stayed for two and a half years. There, this remarkable individual learned 'ōlelo Hawai'i and founded a school for Kānaka Maoli. The Hampton Institute in Virginia was modeled on Stockton's school.[49]

Allen and Stockton are just two of the scores of Black residents in the Kingdom of Hawai'i at the time. They offer reputable stories of upward mobility to suggest why the existing narrations of "the African American experience in Hawai'i" (few as they are) usually begin with them, rather than with the nameless laboring sailors who arrived well before them. They and countless others held important positions and shaped the Islands' educational, economic, and cultural arenas. We miss these striking individuals—and those deemed "less impressive"—if we do not look for them in archives. These compelling figures existed not only outside of official documents but also outside of our contemporary and taken-for-granted categories.

Relying only on official documents like the census and English-language sources makes it appear as if annexation brought about a drastic shift in racial classification. Yet turning to the daily writings of haole, makaʻāinana, and aliʻi—not to mention the *spoken words* of Hawaiians, as Noelani Arista urges[50]—we see that Hawaiians were not yet regularly distinguishing Black people simply along racial lines in the first half of the nineteenth century. However, Europeans and Americans were steadily importing their racial science in the decades that preceded annexation as these islands became a cauldron of competing ideas of difference.

Nineteenth-Century Hawaiʻi: A Place Unsettled by Race

Nineteenth-century Hawaiʻi calls for a *racial* analysis of this island society, yet one that does not conflate its dynamics with those of the United States. Whereas "the continental triangulation of black, white, and Indian racialization provides a framework for conceptualizing the Hawaiian, Asian, and white triangle formed in the colonized islands," so too did paradigms of Blackness—and Black *people*.[51] Racialization affected this "most isolated landmass in the world" in several ways: Europeans and Americans divided Pacific peoples into a tripartite racial hierarchy of Polynesians, Micronesians, and Melanesians; they categorized Kānaka Maoli alternately as Indian, Black, and White; and African-descended people entered a society not structured along racial lines in the early 1800s but emerged at the turn of the century as "Blacks," "Negroes," and "niggers." As the archaeologist Fred McGhee insists, "The cultural geography of European exploration and colonization—and ultimately of race—in the Pacific . . . needs to be rethought, in a manner similar to the way identity and geography have been rethought in the Atlantic maritime worlds to produce a deliberately cross-cultural and trans-national Black identity and culture picture."[52] The Pacific was an(other) racial frontier. Using the term "Black Pacific" well before the current crop of scholarship, McGhee argues that "it cannot be denied that by the mid to late eighteenth century the Black Atlantic world (Gilroy 1993) was already in contact with and influencing (and being influenced by) the Pacific world."[53] New England missionaries brought some of the sharpest changes.

Christian missionaries who arrived starting in 1820 degraded Hawaiian culture and brought antiBlack racism and ideas of native savagery with their religion.[54] Part of haole attempts to control the populace included efforts at categorizing according to illegitimate racial science. Despite rampant taxonomizing, Western racial categories were in flux in the Pacific (including the relationship between Melanesians and more recent African diasporic arrivals) because people do not exist according to colonial constructs. American and

European "colonial travelers who voyaged through the Pacific sailed through a sea of islands inhabited by peoples they identified as Indians" and attempted to racialize Hawaiians as Native Americans.[55] The Spanish physician Don Francisco Marin, a confidant of King Kamehameha and "one of the most influential European residents in the Hawaiian Islands in the early 1800s," called Hawaiians "Indians" (itself transposed from Columbus's erroneous thinking that he had landed in India).[56] Haole also attempted to denigrate Hawaiian monarchs by calling them "niggers." From early encounters, White people grafted their constructed categories onto Oceania.

Hawaiians have a counterhistory of explaining their distinction from others. Queen Liliʻuokalani contests her usurpation, arguing, "The people of the Islands have no voice in determining their future, but are visually relegated to the condition of the aborigines of the American continent."[57] In the early twenty-first century, some advanced a similar argument against the unsuccessful Akaka Bill that had attempted to grant Hawaiians a status similar to that of Native American tribes.[58] In quite a different way, Hawaiians also found a likeness with Native Americans. Hawaiian-language texts show how "since the 1830s, American Indian people became a central site around which Kanaka reflected on colonialism and their own situation."[59]

As the anthropologist Virginia Dominguez reveals, the shifting terrain of the nineteenth century unsteadies the "inevitability" and hegemony of US racial terms in a place where Kānaka Maoli persistently engaged global ideas.[60] People of African descent had more play with their identifications within this society structured neither rigidly by race nor by a system of slavery. Black people were respected rather than reviled. The educator Betsey Stockton—formerly enslaved when she lived in New Jersey—describes a day in Hawaiʻi in 1823 before she learned ʻōlelo Hawaiʻi: "After service the favourite queen called me, and requested that I should take a seat with her on the sofa, which I did, although I could say but few words which she could understand."[61] Would this scene have been imaginable in the continental United States? Haole may have referred to the earliest African-descended arrivals through references to Blackness; nonetheless, Black women and men experienced integration, mobility, and prominence over generations, further revealing the stronghold of Kanaka epistemologies.

Hawaiʻi's more flexible yet increasingly solidifying racial borders are evidenced through the unstable and unexpected categorization of people of African descent. Kanaka Maoli definitions of genealogy and ancestry commingled with US racial definitions. Such unsteadiness contrasts with the fixity of Blackness and obsession over racial boundaries in the United States that instituted antimiscegenation laws regulating marriage as early as the 1660s.[62] In contrast to the one-drop rule, Black Hawaiian children were often classified as part Hawaiian, reflecting "inclusion [that] is not premised on the exclusion of one's other racial identities," or what Kauanui calls "*hyper*descent."[63] The historian Gerald Horne remarks on the fact that one could intermarry with Hawaiians and have children who were identified as Hawaiian, whereas this kind of integration into nonBlack communities was less probable in the United States.[64] This marital incorporation, along with professional and friendly relationships of makaʻāinana and aliʻi with Black men and women, signifies the receptivity to, and general lack of concern over, Black residents before World War II.

Haole, Black, and Asian people were not the only migrants; Hawaiians had long crossed the ocean. Nineteenth-century Kānaka visited the Eastern Seaboard and other parts of the United States (and many other nations), where they interacted with Native American, Black, and White people.[65] The historian David Chang shows how Kanaka racialization as Native people led Hawaiians to identify with and marry Native Americans in the western United States. Chang joins Gary Okihiro's examination of the routes Hawaiians traveled for hundreds of years, including those who fought in the Civil War, and the ties between schools for Native children in Hawaiʻi and the US East Coast.[66] These historians contribute to the work on overseas Hawaiians established in the careful research of Hōkūlani Aikau, Lisa Kahaleole Hall, and Adria Imada.[67] Their scholarship shows that not all Kanaka experiences abroad were positive.

Traveling Hawaiians were afflicted (and infected) by ideas of Blackness in the continental United States. They encountered the denigration of non-Whites abroad and aboard ships. Queen Kapiʻolani and Princess Liliʻuokalani visited San Francisco, Salt Lake City, Chicago, and Washington, DC, where they met with President Cleveland and confronted categories of race framed by both Native American genocide and the enslavement of Africans. During Prince Lot and Prince Liholiho's travels in 1849–1850, the latter prince encountered a train conductor who attempted to remove him from the train car. As the sixteen-year-old Alexander Liholiho (who later became king of the Islands) wrote, the conductor "took me for somebody's servant just because I had darker skin than he had. Confounded fool."[68] John Quincy Adams described an earlier visitor to DC, the diplomat Timoteo Haʻalilio, as being "nearly black as an Ethiopian, but with a European face and wool for hair"; Haʻalilio was similarly mistaken for a servant or slave.[69] Such Kanaka experiences with racism abroad, where they were read through the prism of Blackness, both informed aliʻi of the negativity associated with Blackness and led Hawaiians to align with other people of color, as in the case of mid-nineteenth-century Hawaiians on the East Coast who lived in Black households.[70] Upon return, the future monarchs confronted the growing racial denigration of their people.

African-descended people, too, practiced expansive Kanaka epistemologies of belonging when they foregrounded their Hawaiian identities. Reverend Andrew Iaukea Bright (b. 1881), father of the singer Sol Bright, "would say with a hearty laugh, 'Well I'm a Hawaiian, but my father was a black-assed popolo"—referring to his father, who came from the port of Bravas in the Cape Verde Islands.[71] Was the Reverend using "Hawaiian" to refer to ancestry and also to citizenship? Was he referring to his kinship and genealogical connection to place and people that would not preclude his own Blackness? Was he adopting racial categories and distancing himself from Blackness? Was his use of "black-assed popolo" a form of self-identification, an example of ethnic humor, or a term of derision? Paying attention to these fleeting references to Blackness and the kinship of Hawaiians to African-descended arrivals points us to the Pacific as a proper, if neglected, site of the African diaspora and illustrates nineteenth-century Black and Native relations.

The possibilities in this society illustrate Virginia Dominguez's bold claim that the Kingdom of Hawaiʻi (1840–1893) was a possible site for the "unthinkability of race."[72] This appealed to nineteenth-century arrivals who benefited from "Hawaii's non-exclusionary citizenship laws which gave access to civil and political rights to such African Americans . . . nearly 20 years before the US civil war."[73] Hawaiʻi's explicit antislavery stance, detailed in Willy Kauai's careful research, was an added draw: "Article 11. Involuntary servitude, except for crime, is forever prohibited in this Kingdom; whenever a slave shall enter Hawaiian Territory, he shall be free."[74] Kauai finds that until 1887, the year of the Bayonet Constitution, "acquiring Hawaiian citizenship was based on allegiance, not skin color."[75] The 1890 Census shows about 15 percent of its Hawaiian subjects were not Native Hawaiian or were "of foreign ancestry."[76] Although the Kingdom was not an equal society, Dominguez writes that "no institutional practices promoted social, reproductive, or civic exclusivity on anything resembling racial terms before the American period," despite the presence of non-Hawaiian subjects of the Kingdom.[77]

As American oligarchs debated the Islands' future with the United States, they imported racial science, transposing ideas applied to Black bodies onto Hawaiian ones. At the same time, Americans distinguished Hawaiians from both African-descended people and the Blackness of Melanesians. Polynesians were not spared the ideologies of Black inferiority; haole placed Kānaka Maoli within their hierarchy of races as well as within colonial divisions of the Pacific. They applied supremacist conceptions of Black inferiority developed in the context of slavery to Hawaiians, calling them a heathen and "shiftless" people to justify colonization while noting their hierarchical valuation as "closer to White" than Micronesians (who now face antiBlack racism in Hawai'i) and Melanesians.[78] Among these ideas was the conflation of darkness with inferiority, contrasting with Kanaka ideas of the mana of darkness, or Pō. The Maui chief Kahekili tattooed half of his body black, "just like his namesake the god of Thunder," signaling Hawaiians' "revering its [i.e., blackness/darkness] power, its sacredness, its importance to our origins and our strength."[79] Yet darkness and inferiority began to cohere in the Islands.

Colonists attempted to discredit the monarchy by crafting rumors of King Kamehameha's African ancestry—the "proof" was his dark complexion.[80] Queen Lili'uokalani faced the same "Negro-ification" when a news writer claimed that she "had no 'real hereditary royalty'" and that she and King Kalākaua "were instead the illegitimate children of a mulatto shoemaker."[81] According to Noenoe Silva, American cartoonists "borrowed stock images of Africans and African Americans" to racialize and denigrate Kānaka, depicting the queen as a "pickaninny" in the 1890s.[82] The Queen resisted these images; however, they fit too neatly within the larger narrative of White supremacy worming its way into the Islands over the course of the nineteenth century.[83] Reverend Baldwin (of the famous Baldwin family of Maui) describes a meeting in 1831 with the ali'i: "We were first introduced to Kauikeaouli, the king, a stout young black boy of 17," who was "quite French in his manners, & reminded me very much of many of our spruce College bucks," after which he made the acquaintance of "Kaahumanu, that monument of divine grace that I have long wished to set my eyes upon."[84] Native Hawaiians were and were not "Black."

Maka'āinana, or commoners, were not spared these racialization efforts, as "empire has functioned by making its victims both Indian and black."[85] Dwight Baldwin describes his reaction upon arrival, similar to that of fellow missionary Betsey Stockton: "The natives flocked around us. We needed nothing more than their appearance to tell us we were on heathen ground," mentioning their lack of clothing other than the tapa on their waists. "Here for the first [time] we found things that reminded us of home. All seemed American around the mis. establishment, except the black faces that met us every where, & *alohas* instead of, *how do you do?*"[86] Other influential haole residents, like Dr. George Albert Lathrop, who "habitually" called Kānaka "niggers," supported the haole takeover of the Islands.[87] Lathrop's racism proved fatal through his ineffectual handling of medicine. A Honolulu physician from New York, Lathrop opened his Queens Street drugstore in 1850 and was a founding member of the Hawaiian Medical Association (1856). The doctor was responsible for overseeing the compulsory smallpox vaccination program in a medical district that became plagued with "general mismanagement" and a "defective vaccine" during the great epidemic in 1853.[88] Introduced by a merchant ship that arrived that year in the Honolulu port from San Francisco, the outbreak killed an estimated ten thousand people.

Not only did haole bring diseases that physically devastated Hawai'i's people; they also imported ideologies that infected the minds of its residents for centuries to come. "To enact indigenous genocide and displacement, settler societies have drawn upon the same language of racial threat and criminality that has been invoked to justify anti-black violence," the historian Justin Leroy writes.[89] This included sentiments of disgust toward "natives" and their "heathenism" (which conversion attempted to resolve) and attempts to fit them into racial categories codified by the law and census developed through White people's encounters with Native Americans and Africans.

Hawaiians adopted ideologies of race in their ways, to distinguish Kānaka as a people. Queen Lili'uokalani asked in 1898 if it is not so that "as a race we have some special mental and physical requirements not shared by other races which have come among us?"[90] Yet because of its demographic, historical, and geographic distinctiveness, Hawai'i's racial dynamics were unlike those of the United States, in large part because of Kanaka persistence. Despite epidemics and attempts to "disappear" them, Hawaiian epistemologies and practices continue to shape island norms and propel its future orientation as Kanaka demographics and culture rebound. Hawaiian resistance to "dismemberment" through expansive ideas of belonging is largely why these islands continue to provide Black people an appealing alternative to US society.

Settling Race/Racial Settlements:
The Turn of the Twentieth Century

Hawai'i's relationship to race—and Blackness—cemented with annexation. Rather than an overnight change theorized by Dominguez, haole imported racialist ideologies (and racist practices) well before official codification and political incorporation, signified by collecting "racial" data through the US Census. But this was not a one-way imposition. As haole disembarked onto Hawaiian land, ali'i and Kanaka laborers set sail on ships abuzz with humanity, to which they contributed their own ideas and practices. They traveled to destinations where haole explained their divisions of humankind, and upon returning from Liverpool and London, and Macao and Mexico, those Kānaka brought back new notions of difference, modes of behavior, and items of desire.[91] Various ideologies clashed in the Islands, especially over the burgeoning plantation economy that came to shape contemporary Hawai'i. Twentieth-century Hawai'i also witnessed the continued arrival of prominent and influential Black individuals and their families. According to the census, by June 1, 1900, Hawai'i had 233 Black residents, and the number grew to 695 ten years later.[92] These newcomers had to navigate their status vis-à-vis the Islands' growing diversity, made all the more so by Asian plantation workers.

Haole in Hawai'i indoctrinated (and often authored) racist Black/White understandings of difference partly based on their knowledge of US southern economies. They applied this racialist discourse to emerging disputes in Hawai'i over a Black plantation labor force in the early 1900s. Some Hawai'i plantation owners hoped to resolve their labor shortage by recruiting several hundred Black southerners starting in 1901.[93] The Hawaiian Sugar Planters Association brought thirty families from Tennessee, Mississippi, and Alabama to a Maui plantation in 1907. These newcomers followed the trend of earlier Black arrivals: they "did not establish a separate homogenous community"; rather, some "merged with the residents through intermarriage and association with local groups, but others returned to the Mainland."[94] Debates over the use of Black southern labor explain these small numbers. The plantocracy may have resisted their recruitment for several reasons, including stereotypes of Black people as "unmanageable, lazy, untrustworthy and violent."[95] Abolitionists included members of the Hawaiian government and those missionaries who felt that contract labor was too similar to slavery. On their end, southern plantation owners wanted to hold on to their labor supply. The geographic and social distance of these "foreign" islands, along with reports of terrible working conditions faced by Black workers, further discouraged their large-scale emigration.[96]

A similar debate occurred in the US South over Chinese people as possible sources of labor after the abolition of slavery. Although White people viewed as unsuitable both Chinese workers in the US South and Black workers in Hawai'i, they considered Asian and Black people differently. In Hawai'i, Asians were considered desirable workers, unlike their Black counterparts; the US South preferred Black to Asian labor.[97] This represents the divergent forms of deviance that White people produced, through ideologies of difference and practices of exploitation, of Asian and Black people. This occurred both within the bounds of the United States and in their colonial considerations of Africa (to which White people attached notions of savagery and Black inferiority) and Asia (Orientalist depictions of emasculated and backward heathens). While in the US imaginary, it is laboring Black bodies we think of when discussing plantations while forgetting the Chinese presence, Hawai'i's prestatehood narratives showcase poor conditions faced by Asian laborers (whose descendants became known as "local") without recalling the island of Maui's Black plantation workforce.

By the mid-1800s, haole elite turned land taken from Kānaka Maoli into sugar plantations, followed by pineapple production and tourism, all based on exploited labor that created profits to line the pockets of an oligarchy.[98] The ruling elite melded "moral" objections to Native indolence (Kānaka objected to laboring under haole) with economic aims that racialized Asians as desirable workers. Haole missionaries, businessmen, and politicians (often one and the same), along with traveling Hawaiians, further changed the landscape to develop their capitalist interests.[99] While largely narrated as a haole, Hawaiian, and Asian story, Black people and ideas of Blackness were part of this unfolding economy.

The sugar plantation economy, which began in 1835, shapes contemporary demographics and local culture in this nonWhite settler society.[100] It led to the arrival of workers from Asia and the Pacific (as well as Puerto Rico), who together shared a working-class experience and now collectively form the majority demographic. Haole plantation owners' techniques of enforcing racial difference structured the economy.[101] Unequal living and working conditions, including the geographic separation and differing pay and status granted to groups, both distinctly racialized each group *and* led to the development of local culture. Local culture, discussed at length in chapter 2, may now be a shared expression that privileges Hawai'i-centered practices, but it exists within a society rife with racial and economic hierarchies.

As in the continental United States, indigenous people resisted their co-optation as plantation labor. The Kōloa Plantation on Kaua'i was established in the 1830s, and by 1841, Hawaiian workers resisted their conditions and objected to the destruction of land, leading plantation owners to look elsewhere for labor.[102] Beginning in 1852, about thirty thousand Chinese (mostly men) made up the first wave of contract workers, many of whom stayed on and married Hawaiian women. In the early 1880s, King Kalākaua visited Japan, China, and India in an attempt to garner laborers and assist his nation's economy.[103] Japanese came in large numbers (around 159,000) between 1868 and 1907 and contributed significantly to the development of local practices. Families of Portuguese, many from the Canary Islands, followed in two waves between 1878 and 1913 (15,000), becoming lunas (supervisors) on plantations partly because of their proximity to Whiteness. Six thousand Puerto Ricans followed, and then Spaniards and Mexicans (8,000—many of whom were also categorized as "White" on the census) at the turn of the twentieth century. Nearly eight thousand Koreans came, starting in 1903, followed by Filipinos (around 123,000 between 1906 and 1946), one of the largest groups in contemporary Hawai'i.[104]

Plantation owners, attempting to quell possible insurrection, segregated these groups through imposed distinctions (the workers overcame this with strikes in 1909 and 1920). These constructed differences, including varying levels of economic and political power, as well as particular stereotypes, continue to distinguish various Asian groups in Hawai'i today.[105] This history also marks their distinction from the racial and community formation in the continental United States, where Asians are a minor demographic and are lumped together as a racialized group of newcomers and professionals. In Hawai'i, Asians are not lumped together into a combined category. This process reflects the differential formation of racial ideas in Hawai'i referred to as "ethnicity" and reminds us of the important intermediary and shifting role of Asians between Black and White, as well as between haole and Hawaiian. Filipinos and Sāmoans, along with more recently arrived Micronesians, tend to be racialized in negative ways used to "justify" their lower status, while haole, Chinese, and Japanese dominate local politics yet are also distinctly racialized.

The hegemony of the plantation narrative erases Black people, since they mostly did not come through this system. This dominant narrative also forms the basis for Asian settler colonialism, which obfuscates the role of Asian settlers in ongoing Native dispossession.[106] Histories of Hawai'i focus significantly on the Chinese, Japanese, and Filipinos, with exciting new research on early Hawaiian history; less is known about Black workers or, perhaps more surprisingly, the other major US racial minority: Latinos. Mexicans and Puerto Ricans, who make up nearly 10 percent of the Islands' population today, have a long local history but face a similar erasure.[107] The Black presence in Hawai'i precedes these waves of Asian and Latino laborers, and we know little about their intergroup relations, on and off the plantation. In part, this is because Black men arrived earlier as whalers and sailors, yet we have been wrong to erase them from plantation history. A few hundred Black workers came from the US South to encounter a new society. But it is the notable Black men and women who came at the turn of the twentieth century whose absence from island history seems so curious, given the greatness of their contributions.

A steady stream of highly educated Black Americans at the turn of the twentieth century, including several lawyers and Black professionals with ties to Howard University, shaped residents' perceptions of their intellectual acuity and professional successes. The first practicing Black lawyer in the Islands was the South Carolina–born (1853) T. McCants Stewart. Whereas Betsey Stockton was enslaved by the president of Princeton, Stewart attended Princeton in the same class as Woodrow Wilson. The esteemed attorney, a graduate of Howard University and a friend of Frederick Douglass, was recognized for his letters comparing the situation of Black people in the South with those in the North (he was critical of the latter).[108]

The *Pacific Commercial Advertiser* celebrated Stewart's arrival from Brooklyn on November 29, 1898 (the year of annexation): "T. McCants Stewart, a distinguished Afro-American, who is a thorough-going American, if there ever was one, has arrived in Honolulu and will remain to engage in the practice of his profession—that of the law. . . . He is a lawyer of character and ability, well fitted for any business connected with the ability of Justice."[109]

Stewart "may have desired to start a new life in a land devoid of the racial limitations he faced in the United States"—his success in the Islands bears this notion out, as he was considered a possible candidate for governor.[110] According to his acquaintance Marcus Garvey, Stewart intriguingly may also have come to the territory "at the instance of British capitalists to represent them in some valuable interests."[111] Staying for about seven years, Stewart developed his practice, helped draft a city charter for Honolulu, "and represented all varieties of people in diverse Honolulu."[112] According to the Black lawyer Daphne Barbee-Wooten, Stewart "represented Chinese clients who suffered from discrimination and expulsion in immigration cases," setting the precedent for Black lawyers fighting discrimination in the Islands.[113]

The race consciousness of Hawai'i's first Black attorney represents the orientation of those following in his steps.[114] His impact was long-standing, as his daughter Carlotta (who married a Chinese businessman, Yon Lai, changing her last name from Stewart to Lai) helped develop Hawai'i's educational system.[115] She was a graduate of O'ahu College (which became Punahou School, Obama's alma mater) and was the first Black principal in Honolulu. One source suggests that "conditions were neither difficult nor racially oppressive for a black professional woman, [as] in Hawai'i, there was no substantial black community before World War II, and Carlotta saw few black people either in classrooms or outside."[116] As her father once stated, "Happy is the man, who . . . leaves such footprints on the sands of time that succeeding generations are safe in following them."[117] Generations of Black men and women have indeed followed in the footsteps of Stewart, Lai, and the much earlier nineteenth-century arrivals.

Figure 1.1 Principal Carlotta Stewart Lai (*right*) and students at the Hanamaulu School, Kauaʻi, 1933. Source: Peter Young, *Carlotta*, Images of Old Hawaii, December 9, 2015, http://imagesofoldhawaii.com/carlotta.

While massive numbers of Black soldiers arrived in the twentieth century, there was still a steady stream of Black civilians and families who became influential. Alice Ball, the daughter of Black professionals from Seattle, was the first African American and the first woman to graduate with a master's of science in chemistry at what became the University of Hawaiʻi.[118] She played a crucial role in developing an antileprosy treatment that was used for decades after her untimely death at twenty-four (1916). The Ball Method of treating Hansen's disease was erased from the record when a haole scientist who became the president of the University of Hawaiʻi created his method without citing his predecessor.

Other influential residents thrived in Hawaiʻi during the time of Jim Crow. They include Wyoming-born politician Nolle Smith (b. 1888, son of a Choctaw and Black mother and White father), whose family was featured in a 1959 issue of *Essence* magazine.[119] Fellow politician Helen Hale broke a host of barriers for which she too was recognized locally as well as by a different prominent national Black American magazine. Hale was the Minnesota-born niece of Ralph Bunche and came with her African American husband to the Big Island in 1947, just before statehood (they divorced, and she married Richard Kiyota).[120] The words of "the poet laureate of Hawaiʻi" Don Blanding pulled her to the

Figure 1.2 Carlotta Stewart, ca. 1900. Source: Moorland-Spingarn Research Center, Howard University, Washington, DC.

Islands, which she thought would provide a "racially receptive culture" that she indeed found.

During a visit to the Big Island, Blanding wrote a poem, "Tutu" (Grandma), published in 1939.[121] Dedicated to "those grand old Hawaiians you see sitting on the doorsteps of the little houses along the road in Kona watching life go by, smiling," the poem begins:

I would grow old as you are old, Tutu,
Seasoned with loving, mellow with gracious giving
I would have hair like your grayed hair, Tutu,
Each silver thread a service stripe of living.[122]

The poem is oddly predictive of Hale's future. She was featured on the cover of *Ebony* magazine in 1963 as "Hawaii's top woman politician," wearing a tapa print top and several lei. Encouraged by Blanding's descriptions, Hale moved to the Big Island of Hawai'i, where she lived for sixty years and died at the age of ninety-four. She served the county and Hawai'i Island, earning her own badges of silver hair described in Blanding's poem.

After working as an intermediate school teacher and being on the board of supervisors in the 1950s, Hale served three terms in the state legislature to become the oldest person elected in that capacity.[123] In 1962 she ran for chief executive officer (i.e., mayor) of Hawai'i County. Her feature in *Ebony* the next year states, "For a person who was not a native of Hawaii, and not related to any of the leading island families and who in addition admitted being part Negro, part Indian 'and a few other nationalities,'" it seemed that her campaign "could only lead to defeat."[124] She beat the Republican incumbent to become the first woman and first African American mayor across the Islands. Indeed, Hale was the first woman to run the island in an executive capacity since Queen Lili'uokalani in the previous century. Hale helped to develop astronomy on Maunakea (currently the site of struggle over Indigenous land rights) and fostered the creation of the unparalleled Merrie Monarch hula festival.[125] Perhaps because of her fair appearance, some sources do not mention her racial background. Others call her "multiracial," saying that her mother and father were "both of mixed African-American and Caucasian heritage," while Black long-term island residents proudly claim her as African American.[126]

The experiences and contributions of these transplants, better documented than those of early Black sailors and their children, reveal exemplary accomplishments possible in a place structured neither by slavery nor by a Black/White binary. Black people were long accepted in this Pacific site, where they tended to arrive as individuals or in smaller groups than the waves of

Asian plantation workers of the nineteenth century. In Hawai'i, in contrast to the places they left, members of the African diaspora pursued opportunities during the Jim Crow era and served critical roles in the governing, legal, educational, and social life of the Islands.

While noting these contributions, I want to caution against a dominant narrative of Black history in Hawai'i that is emerging among some representatives of "the Black community" (generally African American long-term residents, a few with ties to the military). This narrative begins with Anthony Allen and ends with Barack Obama, developing a progress story of accomplishment and respectability that erases many Black island residents—including women—who do not fit this narrative or choose not to. Marginal to this account (but central to the story of Hawai'i) are Cape Verdean whalers and other mariners who arrived before Allen, nonprofessional Black residents, and especially Black locals who do not identify with this story of Black Hawai'i.[127] One accessible timeline, "The History of African Americans in Hawai'i," presents only the most "distinguished" and respected figures, filled with nonlocal educated lawyers, doctors, and politicians.[128] It does not mention Black people's role in the domestication of Hawai'i into the United States or their role today in the Islands' occupation. Like the growing scholarship on Black Hawai'i, this narrative also excludes non-American Black people. Black residents on the margins of this curated narrative of African American accomplishment have been concerned with other questions of belonging. They contrast with Black transplants through their kinship ties to local communities that formed when race was still unsettled. If anything, however, these emerging contestations mark the recognition of a growing Black presence.

Hawai'i's history, as told either in its schooling system or in any of the recently published major texts on Hawaiian history, gives the sense that there has been no significant Black settlement. This is incorrect. This overlooked story affects the lives of contemporary Black people and deepens our understanding of the development of race in Hawai'i. Sketches of early arrivals reveal acceptance and integration in a place where Black people were not reduced to race but rather found avenues of identification that exceeded or outright challenged the one-drop rule.

Archival silences make it difficult to quantify Black people living in the Hawaiian Islands during the 1800s. But what accounts for monographs today that make no mention even of Hawai'i's contemporary Black population? Historical research conducted by African American scholars I spoke with contests Romanzo Adams's thesis that there was "probably no significant immigration" of "American Negroes . . . until after annexation in 1898."[129] Adams was locally considered the expert on Hawai'i's demographics: "No scholar has analyzed the statistics of population of Hawaii with greater skill and insight than Romanzo Adams."[130] However well regarded Adams was as a demographic pioneer, his methodology limited his findings.[131] His dependence on census statistics, which folded those people we consider today to be "Black" into the category of "Others" from 1900 to 1950, misses the lively social and demographic life of preannexation Hawai'i.[132] Neither do demographics and numbers encapsulate the opportunities Hawaiians offered to these arrivals and the respect they paid them within the flux of the nineteenth century.

The census codifies race. However, such structures are not determined; they must engage with local ideas. This may be why Hawai'i was not only a place where the child of a Black man and a Hawaiian woman could become Hawaiian, but also a place where some African-descended people became White.[133] The census categorized people of African descent variously, including as Portuguese and Puerto Rican—both of whom were later classified as White.[134] Some records listed the early "Black Portuguese" as Black, and others as Caucasian and, in at least one case, mulatto, thereby undercounting people whom today we may consider Black. The most prolific scholar on Black Hawai'i, Kathryn Takara, offers another explanation for their decreasing numbers in the last century: "Because of the stigmas and negative stereotypes associated with descendants of slaves, some Blacks in the past chose to be identified with another race that was more acceptable and familiar to the local Hawaiian community. Blacks who called themselves part-Negro in the 1910 Census found it easier to become part-Hawaiian in 1920. Even today, a few fear the possible or imagined repercussions of being discovered to be of Negro origins."[135] By the end of the nineteenth century, colonial conceptions of race had reorganized Hawai'i.

The Black encounter with Hawai'i illustrates the unfolding of racial formation and its alternatives. Enslaved and free Black men and women made their way to the Kingdom, where they became citizens and used their intelligence and compassion to learn from, care for, and cultivate Hawai'i's population through contributions in education and health, and in leisure and labor. It was specifically the lack of a slave system and the openness of Kānaka to people of African descent in this monarchal nation—one that did not systematically denigrate Black people or Blackness—that provided these opportunities. It was a world of difference from the Middle Passage. This is the foundation of what the Pacific offers people of African descent.

Black mariners encountered the Pacific as a vast site of Indigenous diversity, a heterogeneity unflattened despite Europeans' attempts to encase people within constructs of Micronesians, Polynesians, and Melanesians. The Black presence in Hawai'i questions studies that restrict island dynamics to a triangulation of haole, Hawaiian, and Asian. Members of the African diaspora also crossed the Pacific, where Indigenous people were racialized in relation to Europeans *and* Africans. Multiple vectors of Blackness overlay this ocean that covers over a quarter of the earth—vectors including transposed ideas of Blackness as well as Black women and men peopling the ocean and its island communities, including Melanesia, Aotearoa, and Aboriginal Australia.

Haole racialized Blackness and Hawaiianness in overlapping yet distinct ways. The Black presence in Hawai'i interrupted Europeans' applications of Black inferiority and "sloth" on Kānaka Maoli, just as the haole presence qualified the application of "Whiteness" to Hawaiians. The intersection of racialization and indigeneity constructed Hawaiians as nonWhite natives. With the importation of White supremacy came the conditions for forging a collectivity of people defining themselves in opposition to their shared oppressors. Black, Hawaiian, and Asian residents shared a sense of we-ness, even if ephemeral and strategic, forming local culture. Yet divisions also took root.

Shifts after annexation enforced Kānaka Maoli adoption of racial ideas. These included the census, land policy, schooling, and the denigration of Blackness and African-descended people by the turn of the twentieth century.[136] Takara writes: "That the very possibility of being Black could threaten to depose a king in late nineteenth-century Hawai'i, a land where prior to Western contact 'Black' had symbolized the greatest political and spiritual powers, should indicate just how much had changed in less than 100 years."[137] This shifting attitude comes with residents' adoption of US racial categories affecting twentieth-century Black men and women—soldiers and their families who arrived in large numbers amid US Jim Crow segregation and the push toward statehood. Leaders who favored Hawai'i's union with the United States, including some local Asian constituencies, aligned with America despite documented Kanaka Maoli opposition to these political *and* ideological commitments.

Imported ideologies and practices harmed Black and Hawaiian people in territorial Hawai'i—moreover, they transformed relations between them. If the small numbers and flexible conceptions of Black people in nineteenth-century Hawai'i shaped their acceptance and integration, this shifted to negative notions of Blackness in the next century, when the largest numbers of Black arrivals came as part of the US armed forces. The expansion of US militarism across the Pacific, including the Spanish-American War of 1898 and World War II, served to erase the Islands' Black past and Black people's histories of working with *and as* Hawaiians (referring both to citizenship and to people with African and Hawaiian ancestry). It created a new paradoxical narrative of Black people. On the one hand, they were foreign agents working *alongside* haole against the rights of Kānaka, which solidified local adoptions of anti-Black racism. On the other hand, their presence increased island residents' exposure to Black culture and struggle as nonWhite people resisting global oppression.[138]

Twentieth-Century Hawai'i, the "Black Equals Military" Conflation, and Contemporary Black Residents

Twentieth-century African American participation in the US military forms what has become the overwhelming narrative about Black people in Hawai'i. The first group of Black military men who came to Hawai'i arrived in 1913 as part of the segregated troops of the Twenty-Fifth Infantry Regiment, hailing mostly from the US South. Among these two thousand soldiers was Dr. William Waddell, an expert in veterinary medicine who joined the faculty of the Tuskegee Institute and worked with George Washington Carver.[139] Waddell retired in Hawai'i, where his daughter, the poet and scholar Kathryn Takara, has, over the past decade, invited me to her countryside home to talk story (her poem opens the pages of this book). This regiment, which had been tasked with "controlling" Plains Indians (by whom they were named "Buffalo Soldiers" during the Indian Wars of the 1870s because of their "woolly heads") and working in national parks, was now stationed in Schofield Barracks in north central O'ahu. They were later relocated to the Big Island, where, amid downpours, they arduously built a twenty-five-mile trail to the summit of Mauna Loa. Martha Hoverson's careful collection of newspapers and bulletins from the time reveals the soldiers' renown for baseball, with games drawing spectators in the thousands.[140] Like those arriving before them, these temporary transplants saw that "Hawai'i was more accepting of the African American soldiers than mainland communities had been. They did not entirely escape prejudice during their time in the islands, and they certainly remained segregated, but the soldiers did not encounter the racial hatred that had characterized their interactions with civilians in parts of the mainland."[141]

Many servicemen and servicewomen came from the southern United States and brought perspectives on difference informed by their experiences with racism and segregation—the same realities that made the military an attractive choice. In Hawai'i, young Black Americans experienced a new kind of society, finding themselves stationed in the United States (first as a territory and then as a state), but in a place that was predominantly nonWhite outside of the barracks. Soldiers earned steady paychecks, which they could spend on leisure activities "in town" (Honolulu), where they found relief from the rigid racial structures of home and their bases. Black soldiers stationed in the Pacific wrote home to their loved ones, describing the Islands as a place where "one can be respected and live as a free man should."[142] Whereas Whites warned that Black men "are going to overstep their bounds a little too far one of these days and these boys from the South are going to have a little necktie party," a Black shipyard worker was adamant that he would "never go back" "down there" to the Jim Crow South.[143]

Hawaiʻi has been viewed for centuries as a strategic military and trade location between the Americas and Asia, ideal for colonial interests and central to US imperial expansion. During our "decolonial tour" of Oʻahu, the local Japanese activist Kyle Kajihiro and Hawaiian activist Terrilee "Auntie Terri" Kekoʻolani took my undergraduate class from Northwestern University to Camp Smith overlooking Puʻuloa (Pearl Harbor).[144] This is home to the US Indo-Pacific Command, the "oldest (January 1, 1947) and largest of the unified combatant commands," responsible for operations covering half of the Earth's surface.[145] The US consolidated military occupation during World War II, when Hawaiʻi was under martial law and faced the arrival of over one million people working in and for the military. "Among these men and women were approximately 30,000 people of African descent—soldiers, sailors, war workers."[146] They did not all leave at war's end but rather solidified the US military presence in the Islands and reached into and across the Pacific to Asia.

In alliance with haole big business, the US military secured bases on the Islands totaling over 5 percent of the land today (the highest of any state), including nearly *one-quarter* of all land on Oʻahu (the island on which Honolulu is located).[147] This restricts Kānaka access to their sacred sites, and some beaches are closed to nonmilitary personnel. In 2010, about 13 percent of Hawaiʻi's population consisted of the military and their dependents, housed primarily on the island of Oʻahu.[148] In 2017, the most common job in Hawaiʻi was working in the military (followed by cooks and retail salespeople).[149] The same source finds that "Hawaii has an unusually high number of residents working as Military," at 16.3 times higher than the expected rate.[150] Black men and women make up a substantial proportion of these numbers, and of the island residents who are veterans.

The arrival of members of all four branches of the US military consolidates the hegemonic association that "Black equals military." It is difficult to overstate the dominance of the presumption that all Black people in the Islands must be in the military. This aligns Black people—no matter their actual affiliation—as participants in US imperialism across the Pacific and in Asia, and specifically in the occupation of the Hawaiian Islands. The tides of the Black experience shift here from acceptance and integration in the nineteenth century to ambivalence and hostility since World War II.

The US territory was a place of possibility and disappointment for Black soldiers. They were excited about life's adventures as they negotiated race relations in "a strange place" and site of "liminality."[151] Yet they also experienced familiar structures, including the racism of White soldiers who spread notions of Black inferiority and hypersexuality that influenced locals. In either case, they may not have considered themselves as agents of colonization. The Black studies scholar Sylvester Johnson historicizes the effect of Christianity on the formation of Black settler colonies like Sierra Leone and Liberia "spawned" by the American Revolution in the Atlantic world. At the turn of the nineteenth century, free Africans in the United States "conceived of their settlements as civilizing projects devoted to African redemption" with the goal of self-determination.[152] Yet Black people did not arrive in the Hawaiian Islands attempting to "establish their own state," as they wished to in Sierra Leone, where "they were, in essence, pursuing the same terms of racial freedom as had the White settlers of the Americas," thereby defining it as a "colonial project," according to Johnson.[153] In Hawaiʻi, they came as individuals and in small groups to a monarchal nation, and later a territory and US state, where they integrated rather than made it a place of repatriation for large numbers of Black men and women.[154] However, their participation in the occupation of Hawaiʻi across the twentieth century led to rising tensions.

The role of the US military in Kānaka dispossession through occupation and its environmental damage to the land, sky, and sea is key to the varied reception of Black people by residents. Hawaiʻi's political elite align with these US interests, further eroding Kānaka Maoli self-determination and their land base. The governor and the University of Hawaiʻi president, for instance, stand by US national and colonial interests in their advocacy for the construction of the Maunakea Thirty Meter Telescope (TMT) despite Hawaiian resistance. In response to their arrival, military personnel across racial backgrounds face ambivalence and at times outright hostility. Locals' and visitors' unfamiliarity with the long and diverse history of Black people removes potential alternatives to the "Black equals military" reference today. This conflation informs the daily lives of Black civilians.

Raised in this context, Barack Obama represents a relatively common Black local experience: he is multiracial, does not come from a military family, and was raised not by his Black father but by his mother's family (more on this later). Ironically, however, as president—and thus commander in chief of the entire US military—Obama's more recent history consolidated the association of Black people with the military. This position shaped his subsequent visits home, when the president and his family, ensconced in a protective security detail, worked out at military gyms and thanked the troops for their service. Global knowledge about Obama lacks the overall context of Hawai'i's Black history and the current racial dynamics that I provide in this project. As a result of the romanticized narrative about this Black person from "paradise" who became the most powerful man in the world, the Islands have experienced what one Black resident called "the Obama Effect"—the rising numbers of Black civilians moving to Hawai'i.

The population of people who chose just Black or African American in Hawai'i on the 2010 Census was 21,424, which jumps to 38,820 when it includes those marking two or more races.[155] Obama has influenced this trend. But since the 1950s (when Hawai'i became a state), the Black population has nearly doubled each decade. In 1930 there were 322 Black men and 241 Black women, and the numbers grew to 11,804 and 5,560 respectively by 1980.[156] These numbers reflect both a significant rise and the historic gender imbalance owing to those arriving through the military.

While dependents who move with Black military personnel also tend to be Black (based on national marital patterns), Black residents marry nonBlack spouses in Hawai'i, as they have for centuries. This should not be surprising, as Hawai'i leads the nation in intermarriage rates. As in the continental United States, Black women in Hawai'i outmarry at much lower rates than Black men, but the rates are still quite significant: nationally in 1980, 3 percent of recently married Black women and 8 percent of Black men married nonBlack spouses; in Hawai'i over 19 percent of Black women and 51 percent of Black men outmarried.[157] These may be the parents of the 34 percent of Black people in Hawai'i who checked two or more races in 2000, growing to 44 percent ten years later, a significant departure from the national rate of 7 percent.[158]

Gendered outmarriage patterns with Hawaiians are also notable. In one 1998 report, out of 433 Black grooms, 157 married Black women; 76 married Hawaiian women; and only one Hawaiian man married a Black woman, in large part due to Black women's smaller demographic, as well as the gendered racism that Black women face.[159] (This pattern is evident among the Black Hawaiian people I spoke with, all of whom had Black fathers and Hawaiian mothers.)[160] When one considers the long history of intermarriage in Hawai'i among all groups, these high rates among Black residents are only partially a result of the gender imbalance (i.e., the smaller numbers of Black women). This, combined with the acceptance of African-descended people, results in a population of multiracial Black locals who are central to my project—a population that is overshadowed by Black soldiers.

In 2010, almost 41,000 people in the armed forces were living in Hawai'i with 62,322 dependents, totaling over 100,000 people out of 1.36 million total residents. Indeed, the vast majority of Black people in Hawai'i serve in the US military.[161] By 1985, over 85 percent of Hawai'i's Black population had military-related jobs or were their dependents. In 1990, almost 2.5 percent of the state's population was Black, yet Black people made up 16.5 percent of the armed forces and 13.3 percent of military dependents.[162] Military veterans made up nearly 16 percent of the Islands' population in 2000, but nearly a third of Black people in Hawai'i are veterans—by far the highest rate among all groups. As for nonmilitary residents, the State of Hawai'i Data Book lists 7,286 Black people, 0.5 percent of the total population, in 2011; another source offers a 2010 civilian labor force for those selecting "Black" at 7,300 people.[163] Even these recent censuses likely continue to miss hundreds of African-descended people who do not identify as "Black or African American" and select other parts of their identities, including Native Hawaiian. These striking demographics structure relations *among* Black people in the islands, including military, Black, and multiracial Black locals, and newer arrivals such as college athletes, professionals, and artists.

Not all Black people in Hawai'i are tourists or work in the military. Hawai'i is now home to the largest number of Black civilians in its history. Along with college students, a growing number of Black health, education, and law professionals make the Islands their home. Some of them are former military personnel who stayed on; others arrive as young adults seeking new opportunities. They come mostly from the continental United States but include migrants from the Caribbean, Africa, Asia, and Europe. The University of Hawai'i's first international student from Africa was Barack Obama Sr., who came from Kenya in 1959 when he met seventeen-year-old White Kansan classmate Ann Dunham, whom he married. More visible in the social landscape and particularly in Honolulu are the temporary visitors who include African American tourists—groups of young Black men or older married couples—and touring bands (mostly reggae) from Jamaica and the United States.

Most invisible are Black locals who are raised in their Hawaiian, Sāmoan, Asian, and other local communities across the Islands and tend not to be affiliated with the military. Yet they are the ones who exemplify the possibilities of Black life in Hawai'i, epitomized by Obama. Local news stories, with titles like "Hawaii's Influence on Barack Obama," cite his style and ease: "Obama has oozed island cool: the black shades and khaki shorts, the breezy sandaled saunter.... He strolled near the beach, enjoyed a shave ice and a ... Spam musubi."[164] Obama appreciates the Islands' influence on him. He says, "I do think that the multicultural nature of Hawaii helped teach me how to appreciate different cultures and navigate different cultures out of necessity.... There just is a cultural bias toward courtesy and trying to work through problems in a way that makes everybody feel like they're being listened to."[165] Obama may be the most famous Black person from Hawai'i, but he is by no means the only one.

The renowned trans activist Janet Mock offers her memoir *Redefining Realness* about growing up in her mother's working-class Hawaiian home in Kalihi, where "it was the norm to have people who were not male or female" (referring to māhū) and "everybody was at least brown or tinted in some way."[166] Mock later lived with her African American father in Oakland, California, where she was forced to reckon with her racial, gender, and sexual identities. Other Black residents include entrepreneurs like Wally Amos of Famous Amos cookies, who came with the air force but stayed because of the "peace" and beauty.[167] Educators include Dr. Miles Jackson, who came with the US Navy and later became a professor and dean of the School of Library and Information Sciences at the University of Hawai'i. Kathryn Takara is another scholar, who founded Pacific Raven Press, which publishes most of the work on African Americans in the Islands. Kenneth Lawson (who codirects the Hawai'i Innocence Project) and Charles Lawrence are faculty at the University of Hawai'i Law School, whose new dean is Camille Nelson, a Black scholar from Canada.

Black and Sāmoan Dwayne "The Rock" Johnson spent his formative years in Hawai'i until he was fourteen. He describes the difficulties of growing up in the sunny islands, saying, "I'm really lucky that I didn't wind up in prison, and certain I was on that track if I had stayed there in Hawaii."[168] Like Obama, the famous actor is hailed for being a "native son" (although he is Sāmoan and not Hawaiian) and criticized for his representational choices. Johnson voiced the part of the Hawaiian god Māui in the Disney blockbuster *Moana*. He agreed to play King Kamehameha in the film *The King*, a role some felt should be played by a Hawaiian: "Some Hawaiians in the community," says one Kanaka teacher, "might take offense to a non Hawaiian, in this case a Polynesian to play this role."[169] Each of these famous Black people from Hawai'i—Obama, Mock, and Johnson—is a local multiracial Black person who faces questions about appropriation and their Blackness, whether in their activism, politics, or art.[170]

Black locals and old-timers also advance Black music. Black and Hawaiian radio personality Big Teeze works for a local reggae station; Kailua-born R&B and reggae singer-songwriter Irie Love, who is "Jamaican and Native American . . . Caucasian and Hawaiian," has toured globally;[171] Black DJs and producers Sub Zero and DJ Jrama have hosted hip hop parties for decades, and Black Canadian Chuck James and his Black and Mexican sons are respected jazz drummers. The gender discrepancy that favors Black men is evident in this recitation of famous people, yet Black women have been an important presence from the days of the educator Betsey Stockton and scientist Alice Ball to the nurses, educators, lawyers, and musicians of today. The Black Hawaiian performer Ginai is a renowned singing celebrity who performs at the Blue Note in Waikīkī, and other Black women like Daphne Barbee-Wooten and Sandra Simms work in law. The long-term resident and educator Kathryn Takara is joined by more recent arrivals, including engaged scholars and activists like Dr. Akiemi Glenn, a linguist from the southeastern United States who helped found the Pōpolo Project, an organization giving voice to Black people in the Islands.

Black locals also live across the islands, from the descendants of Black workers on the Spreckelsville plantation in Maui to Black Hawaiians living on Hawaiian Home Lands in Papakōlea and Nanakuli. They include the children of Japanese, Korean, Filipino, and Okinawan mothers and African American military and civilian fathers. Black people born in Hawai'i work in retail and as bartenders, entertainers, social workers, athletes, and entrepreneurs. Whereas Black transplants may include the women who attend Links events and NAACP meetings, Black locals perform in hālau hula (hula schools). Hawai'i's Black residents in the twenty-first century make up a diverse group, less a collective than a smattering of individuals across the islands, with Honolulu and military bases serving as important hubs. Today's civilian Black population is, like those who came over two hundred years ago, integrated and often invisible, living their lives as they face acceptance and ostracism.

Conclusion

The history of the Hawaiian Islands is not only the story of seafaring Polynesians, haole "discovery," and laboring Asians; it is also the history of the African diaspora. From the first arrivals at the end of the eighteenth century, Black people—many of whom were fleeing slave societies—encountered a kingdom not organized along racial lines. Far from the epicenter of the slave trade, the Black Pacific was nonetheless informed by the development of race that grounded that institution. Black sailors confronted these hierarchies aboard ships that then crossed the Pacific, sometimes arriving in societies that became their new homes.

This chapter has drawn on the essentially unknown story of Black people in the Hawaiian Islands—a story that calls forth a racial analysis of this shifting society. By looking beyond traditional archives and official census documents, we find a host of Black men and some Black women living in, among, with, and as Native Hawaiians, some rising to prominence and shaping the Kingdom of Hawaiʻi. From early Cape Verdean whalers to Black American sailors, from educators to activists, both with spirits of independence and adventure, people of African descent found something new—a haven, they say, that encouraged some to stay and make it their home.

Kānaka Maoli disallowed slavery and welcomed Black women and men, venerating darkness as Pō in their creation story. As a result, early Black arrivals not only witnessed but also took part in changes in Hawaiʻi's status as kingdom, republic, territory, and fiftieth US state. Black men served as advisers to kings, and some made their fortunes; and a queen invited the first documented Black woman in the Islands, a formerly enslaved and pedagogical innovator, to sit next to her in the 1820s. Sometimes they aligned with Native Hawaiians, intermarrying and forming Hawaiian families. Although these early arrivals were both respected for their diverse skills and integrated, few today know this history, overshadowed as it is by the narrative of US imperialism since the twentieth century.

While the military may offer opportunities within a racist and exclusionary nation, being part of the military also means participating *on behalf of* that nation's bombing and conquest of people across the globe. Black people in the armed forces exemplify what Ethan Caldwell calls "the colonized-colonizer paradox." This refers to the dynamic by which African Americans, oppressed in the nation that enslaved them, find opportunities in the military, through which they can leave the boundaries of the nation but participate in the colonization of other nonWhite people.[172] Black military men's nonWhite yet agentive and class status since World War II significantly affected their increasingly tense reception in Hawaiʻi. The resulting hegemonic association that "Black equals military" forged in the mid-twentieth century shapes contemporary ideas about Black people.

The history of Black Hawaiʻi—and its unknownness—reveals how race, and not just ethnicity and culture, shapes the Islands. Black people have historically found Hawaiʻi to be their haven, even as US racial ideas take root. They have, for over two hundred years, experienced both integration and invisibility in this nation initially structured neither by race nor by slavery and still not by a Black/White binary. It is from this past that the current generation of Black Hawaiians and Black Asians emerges to narrate family histories, which I detail in the next chapter, that crisscross oceans and continents, following Pacific currents ridden for centuries by members of the African diaspora. Knowing the story of Black civilians in Hawai'i expands our understanding of the Islands' diversity and provides contemporary Black residents with a sense of place and belonging. Their histories reveal an expansive and detailed portrait of the Black Pacific as a site of indigeneity and a set of racial dynamics that Black people in Hawai'i continue to negotiate.

2

"SALTWATER NEGROES"

BLACK LOCALS, MULTIRACIALISM, AND EXPANSIVE BLACKNESS

> *Less than 5 percent of Black people in the United States, and almost 50 percent of Black people in Hawaiʻi, marked "Black" or "African American" in combination with another race.*
>
> U.S. CENSUS, 2010

> Nitasha: A Black woman from the East Coast said you cannot be Black and be local. Do you feel like someone can be Black and local?
>
> Colin: I would say that she comes from a background that is Black and White, which it's just straight up and down. And so she cannot understand or comprehend, you know, the gray lines, and the mix of people or things or ideas. So, um, I actually feel sad for her.
>
> EXCHANGE BETWEEN THE AUTHOR AND A LOCAL BLACK HAWAIIAN

Black locals—African-descended people who are raised in Hawaiʻi—understand and articulate themselves in a place not structured by a Black/White binary and in the absence of a White majority. The possibilities afforded by this context reflect what Hawaiʻi offers Black people. Instead of an overbearing White supremacist presence, Black locals come of age in a site with a strong Native political and cultural presence, far from the continental United States and its history of slavery. How do Black locals come to understand the meanings of Blackness in a place without a Black Metropolis? What does being Black and multiracial mean in a society that normalizes multiracialism? Black people in the Islands are asked "What are you?" and "Where are you from?" in an experience familiar to multiracial people across the United States. Rather than the one-drop rule, which considers anyone who is part Black to be Black only, Black people from Hawai'i embrace expansive identifications. People in Hawai'i foreground connective relationships to land, people, and ancestries in ways not determined by US racial formations. Local cultural practices and Hawaiian epistemologies inform Black locals' experiences, as culture intersects with race and indigeneity to highlight how pivotal *place-based* identities are.

Visually identified as having African ancestry and generally mistaken for being part of the US military presence in the Islands, Black locals navigate Hawai'i-specific ideas of Blackness. They have to discern—often on their own and without other Black family members—what those associations mean as they uncover the meanings of Blackness. This contrasts with Black transplants or people who move to the Islands as adults and bring racialized perspectives informed by Black history and US racial binaries. By contrast, Black locals negotiate different points of reference in a place with a nonWhite majority. Their process of meaning-making in the Black Pacific contributes to debates central to, and between, Black studies and critical mixed race studies. Multiracialism, hyperdescent, freedom to self-identify, and localness make the Hawaiian Islands a unique place for African diasporic people.

We know almost nothing about Black locals, whom I define as African-descended people who are Hawai'i-born and raised or came as young children and grew up in the Islands. They are overlooked in popular representations of paradise and scholarly work, including the scant literature on Black people in Hawai'i. These sources depict people of African descent—except for Obama—as coming from elsewhere, usually through the military. Attempts to understand Obama's history, aesthetics, and politics fall short without reference to the wider context of Black locals in Hawai'i. Other than Obama, who are Black locals, and where do they live? What contours mark their lives, and what are their conceptions of Blackness in a place of Black absence? Their experiences are both exceptional and common. Theirs is a story heretofore undocumented, yet they have much to tell us about Blackness, Hawai'i, and multiracialism.

Black locals, who are usually the first generation of their families to be Black and local, do not constitute a community. However, together they navigate American ideas of race, federal policies, Kanaka kinship practices, and local cultural expectations. Colin, a sizable man in his forties who calls himself a Black Hawaiian, declares: "A Black Hawaiian is a Royal Hawaiian, a dark Hawaiian." He is the fourth generation on his Hawaiian Homestead (what I also refer to as Hawaiian Home Lands) in Honolulu. The Hawaiian Homes Commission Act of 1921 established eligibility for a Homestead Land lease: one "must be a native Hawaiian, defined as 'any descendant of not less than one-half part of the blood of the races inhabiting the Hawaiian Islands previous to 1778.' This means you must have a blood quantum of at least 50 percent Hawaiian."[1] Speaking of his access to these federal lands put aside for Hawaiians, Colin clarifies, "I don't have fifty percent Hawaiian, I'm just shy—like thirty-seven and a half [percent] or something like that. So I can't get my own property, but I have twenty-five percent, which means that it can be willed to me."

Colin came to our two-hour interview—the first of several exchanges—scheduled at the Mānoa Valley Starbucks excited to share with me his story and his interpretation of the resonance of Blackness to Hawaiian history. His Hawaiian mother went to the continental United States, where she met an African American musician. She returned to her family on O'ahu, pregnant with Colin and without the musician (Colin has never met his father). While all the Black Hawaiians I spoke with identified as "Black Hawaiian" and also had Black fathers (from Africa and the United States) and Native Hawaiian mothers, Colin uniquely explicated the term:

> To back up a little bit, a Black Hawaiian is actually a Royal Hawaiian. So now this, what I wanted to share with you, is this: the first Royal Hawaiian was King Kamehameha the Great. Now King Kamehameha the Great, he was seven foot four [inches] Hawaiian. Dark skin. He was a king that united all the islands.... But because of who he was, that's what gave people the label of what a Royal Hawaiian is. Now a Royal Hawaiian and a Black Hawaiian is actually the same thing because King Kamehameha was dark. He was a very dark, tall person. And that's kind of where it came from: people saw him, they thought of him as being a Black Hawaiian.... But it was the way he looked that made people identify with him, with the things he did. So that's why I wanted to kind of go with this, is that a Black Hawaiian in Hawai'i, or a Royal Hawaiian in Hawai'i, is considered a Hawaiian above Hawaiians. Here is an extraordinary Hawaiian, because of Kamehameha and everything he had accomplished. When people call you a Black Hawaiian or a Royal Hawaiian, that is putting you on a higher level, you know? And when you look throughout Hawaiian history, you see that a lot of Black Hawaiians have done a lot of great things.

In this chapter, I analyze Black locals' ideas and ambivalence toward Blackness through examinations of their family stories and identifications. I highlight the persistence of Kanaka epistemologies that continue to frame the acceptance and integration of Black people in Hawai'i.² Nonetheless, among local Black hapas, Blackness works as a modification or distinction from Hawaiianness, Koreanness, or their other ancestries. Race is not neutralized by indigeneity.

Spread across the geography of the Islands, with the majority in Honolulu, Black locals are tied to local communities through their friend and family networks, their jobs, and their former high schools. They challenge transplants' ideas that one cannot be both Black and local. A Black Okinawan man from Wahiawā recalls: "These two kids: they were Hawaiians and Black, but they looked just full Black, you know? They had the Afro, but they were the most local dudes. I mean, they didn't care a lick about Black anything! Just pidgin-speaking, fist fighting. So yeah, I think they feel just fine being a local Black kid." Those who grew up in these multiracial islands and were accepted as part of the communal landscape cultivate this perspective.

Most Black people raised in Hawai'i are multiracial or hapa and identify as being Black and _____. (The "and" in "Black and _____" refers to their other identifications, including nonBlack ancestries.) Yet why does the one-drop rule still resonate in the continental United States? Another local Black Okinawan describes this as the "the million-dollar question," which she confronted while attending a historically Black university on the East Coast. "You can't deny half of a person," Michiko says. It seems understandable that a local Black Okinawan raised by her Okinawan father and African American mother would identify as Okinawan, as well. Acknowledging multiple ancestries does not equalize racial categories. Rather, it *shores up* histories of colonization (of Okinawa by Japan; of Hawai'i by the United States), immigration, and slavery. In this way, a multiracial identity unsettles commonsense racial categories. "It challenges America's racial vision of itself," writes the philosopher Ronald Sundstrom, reminding us of the historical contexts in which sex across constructed racial boundaries occurred.³ Saying that one is "Black and Okinawan" or "Hawaiian, haole, and Black" does not mean that one is "moving away from Blackness," "denying Blackness," or attempting to "access the privileges of Whiteness." Rather, it can bring to mind relations among unequal racial pasts—and in the present.

US mixed race studies and the popular media's fixation on the multiracial population is frustratingly narrow, narrating people's identities as an end in itself. Since 2000, people could mark more than one racial category on the US

Census, allowing the collection of data on the nation's fastest-growing population. Every ten years, the articles describing mixed race people proliferate in the news. These stories detail their parents' unions and list their often predictable identities and angsts. In ending rather than beginning with how these individuals identify, we fetishize and apoliticize the "exceptional" multiracial person. What are the *implications* of these identities beyond their individual stories? How do they affect society, especially communities of color? How do the possibilities of these stories and identities shape and contest unequal and racist structural forms?

In addition to illustrating Black life in Hawai'i, local Black hapas show us what it means to be multiracial. They challenge our phenotypical assignations of race when they explain "looking like but not feeling like." I begin rather than end with the backgrounds and identifications of Black locals, who include African Americans and Africans, Black Hawaiians, Black Sāmoans, Black Filipinos, Black Okinawans, Black Koreans, Black Mexicans, and others.

While every person identified as Black or African American, their relationship to Blackness or to being Black was vexed, diverse, and complicated. What does it mean to be a Black child raised in a nonBlack home? Some describe profoundly individual and lonely childhoods. With few or no Black family members to guide them, they recall their singularity and uniqueness. In a tearful interview, a Black Okinawan woman on O'ahu told me: "I'm glad that you told me about the other [Black hapa] girl because I mean, I knew I couldn't be the only one who felt like that. But it's really frustrating. . . . Like why do you need validation from these people?" To be sure, with one exception, they did not describe horrific upbringings or miserable childhoods. Nonetheless, a sense of difference and aloneness accompanied their early years in their mothers' local and mostly nonBlack communities.

Cultural (non)exposure, as well as lack of access to Black family members, also informed not just their identifications but also their relationship to those ancestries. One can *look* (Black) but not *feel* (Black); one can also *feel* (Korean) but not *look* (Korean). The obverse is their initial acceptance as Black in the continental United States, owing to the one-drop rule and the embrace of other Black people. In Hawai'i, nonbelonging may occur on account of presumptions that Black people are not local; in response, they emphasize their localness. Turning to local culture and highlighting nonBlack ancestries constitute performances of belonging to the Islands.

US-centered interpretations of multiracialism can miss the politics of ancestry in Hawai'i. This oversight emerges in national readings of Obama's Blackness and general skepticism of his "enviable dexterity at navigating between black and white."[4] His election to the presidency was hailed internationally as signaling the end of racism (a common and problematic trope of multiracial representation), and yet his Blackness remains. On *60 Minutes*, Steve Kroft asks Obama when he "decided" he was Black, to which Obama responds, "Well, I'm not sure I decided it."[5] He does not deny that he is interpreted by others to be Black (although Ta-Nehisi Coates describes Obama as an "African American" whom people could accept as US President, in distinction to a "black man" they would never allow). "Obama's blackness quotient," writes Coates, the esteemed commenter on race, "is often a subject of debate." Coates deciphers Obama's flexing of Black cultural norms, "cultural cues [that] became important" during his run for the presidency: "Obama doesn't merely evince blackness; he uses his blackness to signal and court African Americans" (although Coates can't get over the sense that these performances are "mawkish").[6] Race and cultural cues bump up against one another and commingle in Obama's performances. Perhaps this is exactly something Hawai'i taught him in his youth.

Unlike half of the Black population in Hawai'i, Obama selected Black only on the 2010 census, when he lived in the continental United States. Likely this was a politically motivated move, but possibly also one that reflected his changing identity and the influence of American ideas of race and his experiences as a Black man, depending on where in the world he was. After all, as the chapter epigraph shows, Obama's decision aligns with the vast majority of Black Americans who chose "Black only." That is, Obama's shifting racial identity is an allegory for the difference between Hawai'i, where one can be Black and _____, and the continental United States, where African-descended people tend to identify as Black only. Still, he consistently mentions his Kansan White mother and the haole grandparents—Toot and Stan—who raised him (references that some people viewed as "strategic"). Although he is far from being racially progressive, Obama's refusal to be locked into the category of Blackness is not, nonetheless, *only* an antiBlack move.[7] We have to take local customs into account to understand what is common practice in the Islands—practices Obama grew up with. When US-based analyses of Obama's racial identity revert to historical tropes of Blackness, they reiterate a Black/White binary as globally relevant and seemingly inevitable. In the Islands, however, people view him through locally specific considerations.

Multiracial identification is neither only antiBlack nor always a racist project. Black locals challenge theories that presume Black only (hypodescent) as the only pro-Black identification. The demographic strength of dual-minority biracial people in Hawai'i additionally contests the application of a Black/

White binary to the Pacific. Black people in Hawai'i who identify with numerous ancestries are neither running away from Blackness nor aspiring to Whiteness. Rather, in many cases, they are avowing their indigeneity. They acknowledge rather than deny family members, including their nonWhite and nonBlack mothers, and the communities who raised them. Self-identifying as "Black Hawaiian," for instance, unearths centuries of unions between mostly Black men and Hawaiian women whose children were woven into Hawaiian networks of kin. At the same time, whereas their counterparts in the early twentieth century may have identified as Hawaiian only, "Black Hawaiians" reflect the increasing relevance of Black *and* Hawaiian identifications since the 1970s. Thus multiracialism is constitutive of Blackness for African-descended people in the Pacific, some of whom reject hypodescent.

My analysis begins with two conceptual discussions to frame its ethnographic material. The first highlights the politics of multiracialism, engaging scholars who interpret multiracialism as an antiBlack and racist project. Second, I analyze how Black locals unsettle theories of localness and settler colonialism. Whereas discussions of localness in Hawai'i do not take Black people into account, debates over settler colonialism focus on Black-White-Native North America and, in the Hawai'i context, on Asian settlers. Local Black hapas problematize these debates. My discussion of multiracialism and settler colonialism frames my portrait of the demographics and identifications of the locals I interviewed, as they describe their parents and themselves. I turn to an examination of their conceptions of Blackness, which relates to the next section, where I explain how they develop these ideas. Black locals are ambivalent toward Blackness, not as an expression of antiBlackness but rather as a response to gaps in their knowledge of Black culture and the hegemony of Black Americanness developed elsewhere. I end with a discussion of how race and sense of self disarticulate among Black hapas in Hawai'i, who "look like but don't feel like" and conversely "feel like but don't look like."

To understand the different resonance of race in Hawai'i, it is useful to see both how various modes of being intersect and how they disaggregate. We assume race is transmuted, or at least shared, between parents and children; this is not always the case (think, for instance, of transracial adoptees). Mixed race studies shows how *cultural capital* aligns or doesn't align with looks or phenotype (which is the expression of human genetic variation that often becomes the basis of racial categorization by others). Thus this rupture between looks and identifications comes about at the intersection (not the conflation) of race, indigeneity, ancestry, and culture. Multiracial people highlight this particular articulation in generative but not exceptional ways.

"Black and _____": Multiracialism and Expansive Identifications

Dual-minority biracial people, or mixed race people who do not have a White parent, are understudied in work on the African diaspora and mixed race studies. NonWhite multiracial people enhance our understanding of "the mixed race experience" and Black life. Illustrating how and why they identify contests the simple reiteration that mixed race people are privileged compared to those who do not identify as multiracial (e.g., those who identify as Black only), or that mixed race people are privileged compared to their communities of color. The argument that multiracial people are less oppressed than Black people assumes that mixed race people are (read as) White and have access to Whiteness, including White family members, lighter skin, and ambiguous racial looks. This argument crumbles when we make nonWhite multiracial people the focus of our analysis.

Nineteen of the sixty people I interviewed are local. Of them, four are the children of two Black parents, one of whom was adopted into a Hawaiian family. Thus fifteen (over three-quarters) identify as hapa or mixed race, meaning they have parents who identify with different racial categories, far exceeding even Hawai'i's significant overall mixed race population at 23 percent. (In fact, nearly half of all sixty participants are multiracial.) Hapa—which I discuss more fully in pages to come—is a Hawaiian word meaning "half" and "of mixed blood" emerging from Hawaiians' encounter with haole. It is rooted in Hawaiian history, and some people prefer to restrict its reference to part Hawaiians. I use it more expansively to refer to all people who identify with more than one race in Hawai'i. I hope to do this respectfully by centering Native Hawaiians (including Black Hawaiians) and their ideas throughout the text while remaining true to my fieldwork.

In addition to the salience of a mixed identity—to calling forth one's multiple ancestries—Black people in the Islands reveal the salience of local and nonlocal distinctions and the imprint of Hawai'i on them. Hawai'i-centered explanations of Obama's success reflect the optimism that people feel the Islands provide. A Black woman from the US South who has lived in Hawai'i for almost fifty years describes the former president: "He's a Black man.... But because he wasn't stuck in that mainland oppression, and attitude, paranoia—justifiable, but he didn't have that—so his step is lighter, his back is straighter, his smile is bigger. You know what I'm saying? I mean, he (*chuckles*), he's magic!" But a more recent Black and Mexican transplant from the continental United States was critical: "I watched as people were surprised as his presidency unfolded about how not liberal he is. That annoyed me because he's a constitutional scholar.... I think that that is a direct result of having grown up here. I think that that sort of disconnect could only happen here. You might be socially ostracized and deal with petty racism growing up here, but I could see how that evolves [into] a person who is not making those connections." Some people deploy American hegemonic notions of Blackness to discount multiracial Black people and to reflect their suspicion. However, people in Hawai'i—where Blackness is not hegemonic—consider identification differently, giving people of African descent ways of being Black otherwise. They do not deny or absolve themselves of Blackness, neither passing nor self-hating; but Blackness plays a different role in their daily lives. New epistemologies of Blackness open up in Oceania, where multiracialism, Blackness, and localness intersect. Indigenous epistemologies and local practices stretch our conceptions of Blackness and belonging, bringing culture into conversation with race.

Conflating culture and race adds to misinterpretations about the premises of mixed race studies. Scholars in this field know that race has no biological basis—or, as Terence Keel says, "there are no genes for race"—but race is a fiction with real-life consequences.[8] The "critical" in critical mixed race studies rejects and cautions against easy assumptions that "mixed race studies" advances the fallacy of "pure" and "mixed" races. "Nothing is implied about racial purity, nor does [mixed race] necessarily reinforce the poles of racial duality," writes Sundstrom. He explains: "Mixed race identity results from the positioning of individuals in social spaces where they experience, as members of multiple racial groups, various combinations of the social forces that make race and the various racial groups real."[9] Rather, "mixed race" (for lack of a better term) points to the intersection of ancestry (whereby "biological heterogeneity, or 'being mixed' is in fact the default human ontological position"),[10] culture, and phenotype in a nation that presumes the convergence of looks, behaviors, and identifications.

The experiences of nonWhite multiracial people contest the idea that a monoracial category can provide all that a multiracial person "needs." Similarly, accounting for the enormous range of ways that people express their identifications is not antiBlack so much as anti-monoracial (that is, against having to choose just one racial category). Hawai'i's robust engagement with the dynamics of (multiple) ancestries illustrates why and how people *are* (rather than how they "deploy" multiraciality). Local hapas describe lives different from those in studies of their counterparts in the continental United States and England. This is because of the cultural practices and norms particular to the Islands—practices that emerge historically, which I detail through ethnography (a lesser-used method in both mixed race studies and ethnic studies). Locals perform these practices, which in turn shake up the ways that transplants conceptualize their identifications.

A cohort of scholars in the past two decades has taken US mixed race studies to task, charging multiracialism (the premise of the field) as antiBlack. To make the argument, scholars like Minkah Makalani and Jared Sexton point to Black and White biracial people who identify as anything other than just Black as adherents to White supremacy who hope to escape Blackness. Makalani summarily describes the 1990s movement to allow people to identify as "multiracial" or select more than one race on the US Census: "It is a racist project," one at odds with the Black community.[11] But how does this play out when one's "other" ancestries are not White but include immigrant family members whose cultures and commitments are tied to nonWhite people and places around the world?

A focus on Black and White biracial people in the United States misses the complexity of multiracial people, including dual-minority biracial people. Makalani characterizes a biracial identity as being "historically unfounded" and "essentialist" and asks, "What would a biracial identity offer that a Black identity does not?"[12] One may respond the way one student attendee at the 2014 Critical Mixed Race Studies conference did, when he asked, "What kinds of silencing and oppression occur when members of the Black community request that multiracial people deny their multiple identities?" While Blackness in the United States has always been an expansive category and conception that implies African Americans' Indigenous and European ancestries, multiracial Black people do not always feel adequately seen through a sole category. Black people in Hawaiʻi, especially local Black hapas who grow up accounting for several backgrounds, show what an expansive "Black and _____" identification offers that "a Black [only] identity does not." Multiracial individuals in Hawaiʻi and across the United States are not unified in expressing "an unwanted Black identity" in hopes of becoming a "new race" distinct from Black.[13]

Black people in Hawaiʻi enact expansive notions of Blackness because of the combination of their life stories, the tempering of Black Atlantic epistemologies, and the prominence of Hawaiian practices of genealogical and place-based identifications. Whereas, speaking of the rise of Black and White biracial people, Makalani wonders "whether these people consider themselves Black or biracial," people in the Islands replace "or" with "and."[14] Jared Sexton, the author of *Amalgamation Schemes*, known for his work in Afropessimism, similarly reduces his analysis to Black and White to argue that multiracialism allies with White supremacy against Black politics, an argument summarized by his book's subtitle, "Antiblackness and the Critique of Multiracialism." Such critiques are difficult to sustain once we decenter both the contiguous forty-eight states and Whiteness.

Multiracialism is not "a racist project." Locals articulating their known ancestries are not simply celebrating multiculturalism or flattening differences. Nor are they self-hating, misguided, or naive. They bring into the familial ring the presence of their ancestors. What Sexton and others read as a disavowal of Blackness is rather a practice of recalling, unearthing, and shoring up past interactions in the places of one's ancestors. For instance, when someone local describes their mother as "English, Irish, Scottish, Hawaiian, and a little bit Chinese," this narration *calls forth* rather than *flattens* the colonial, capitalist, plantation, and military histories of Hawai'i evinced through their mother's ancestries. Black locals also often detail their father's Black *and* Native American ancestry. Some, for instance, described their fathers as "part Cherokee Indian, yellow fair-skinned Black"; "Black, American Indian, and English"; and "African American, American Indian, English, and Irish." Is this inclusive acknowledgment simply antiBlack, where identifying as anything other than just Black means that one aligns with Whiteness?

Haunani-Kay Trask is definitive: "In Pacific Island cultures, genealogy is paramount."[15] So strong is this practice of speaking to and of the spirits of their kūpuna (ancestors) that people not native to the Pacific also recount family origins and their physical locations. Hawaiians' kinship-based descent is an inclusive form of belonging "not premised on the exclusion of one's other racial identities or ancestral affiliations."[16] This explains why more often than not, people identify with their ancestry and secondarily discuss skin color and looks—factors that often take precedence in the continental United States.

Today's Hawaiians and African Americans emerge from histories of colonialism, slavery, antimiscegenation, and discriminatory laws. Members of these communities sometimes state that they are (just) "Hawaiian" or "Black." That is, both groups have a history of multiracialism but a practice of stated monoracialism. It is just as likely, however, that someone may respond in Hawai'i with "I Chinese, Portagee, Hawaiian on my maddah's side, and Irish, Scottish, German, and Hawaiian on my faddah's side." Hawaiian and Black become shorthand for complex historical relationships along with colonial blood quantum rules and contemporary racial politics attempting to maintain racial distinctions in light of the blurring color line (and thus Whiteness) through "racial mixing." Kānaka Maoli are Hawaiian in similar ways that African Americans are Black concerning the tacit understanding that they likely also have multiple ancestries; but a shared bond of being Hawaiian or of being Black, forged through historical processes of power, connects them to other Kānaka and Black people, respectively.

Black hapas do not signify the end of racism or only emerge out of master/slave relations in the afterlives of slavery.[17] These are dangerous yet common misconceptions of multiracial "identity," disproven by this research. What we find, rather, is a running *toward* something else to reveal alternative possibilities of being and belonging in a place that unsettles and expands identifications with Blackness. We can appreciate this perspective by shifting from a US race-only view toward a contextual analysis of the intersection of race, culture, and indigeneity in the Pacific.

People are multiracial because, as Sundstrom neatly summarizes, there are people who say they are multiracial.[18] They often grow up in a household with parents (or a single parent) of different racial identifications, and they may self-identify in distinction to how each parent does. Hawai'i influences how locals—including Obama—identify owing to what Haunani-Kay Trask points to as the primacy of genealogy, along with family stories and multiplicity. We know Obama's family story, which people in the continent may view as a unique story of biracialism and transnationalism. But he is practiced in telling his personal narrative because such recounting is central to belonging in Hawai'i.

What we learn about race from multiracial people nationally applies beyond the small but significant population that identifies with more than one race. Growing up in a household with a White mother and a Black father is distinct from growing up in a household with two Black parents—this includes not only the way one may (or may not) look; it also includes sharing domestic space with White relatives, having access to different racialized networks, in addition to the advantages of being fair(er) skinned (for those who are), accumulating cultural knowledge, greater access to wealth and other economic resources, and looking "ethnically ambiguous," including the possibility of not looking identifiably African-descended. Everyone negotiates who they are, what they look like, the communities to which they belong, and how they act. Yet it often appears as if only those whose looks and acts diverge, or those who disrupt single-race categories, contend with the dilemma of "what are you?" Multiracial people—often and especially those who are first-generation biracial and look "ethnically ambiguous"—present this rupture between expected actions coming from interpreted looks to a degree that *is unique*. But this experience and presentation of self are *not exceptional*.

I am not arguing that "the mixed race experience" is exceptional or the answer to the "problem of race"; nor is it the case that all multiracial people share the same experience, crosscut as identity is by family structure, gender, sexuality, class, ability, age, and so on. But there is a distinction to growing up in multiracial families, and these distinctions are clear in the narratives of Black hapas, especially for Black-appearing people who are raised without Black family members. Another example comes from African Americans in the continental United States who identify as Black only but, over their time in the Islands, change their identifications to "Black and _____."

The Black and White racial paradigm shapes the conditions shared by African-descended people across the United States, whose resilience includes expressions of racial pride and the cultivation of strong race-based communities and politics. These stakes in Blackness help explain the psychologist Sarah Gaither's findings in her study of Obama's biracial identity that "white people thought he was 'too black' and black people found him to be 'too white.'"[19] Meghan Markle, married to England's Prince Harry, faces similar ambivalence as she identifies as "a strong, confident, mixed-race woman."[20] Rather than skepticism, Black multiracialism in the Pacific offers a different interpretation of these choices, framed by a deeply local—noncontinental—context. In addition to identifying as Black and _____, members of the African diaspora raised in Hawai'i emphasize their local identities.

Localness, Settler Colonialism, and Black Hawai'i

"Local" is a panracial category referring to a place, culture, and politics stemming from the colonization of Hawai'i, plantation life, haole political dominance, and groups' uneven positions in poststatehood Hawai'i. It is rife with tensions, both as a concept and as an embodied practice. Scholars illustrate how non-Hawaiians deploy the concept to claim belonging to the Islands by denying their settler status. These debates center Hawaiian and Asian relations, Hawaiian and haole relations, or triangulate haole-Asian-Hawaiian relations.[21] People have also attempted to analyze the politics of positionality through binaries of Hawaiian/non-Hawaiian, local/nonlocal, native/settler. Yet the dynamics on the ground almost always unsettle such binaries. Each of these dualisms intuits a generally fixed power dynamic with non-Hawaiian, local/nonlocal, and settler signifying haole and Asians who have dominated island politics and economics for over a century. But none—even those highlighting the role of the military—analyzes (let alone mentions) Black people. Stated a different way, "local" may seem to be problematic when applied to economically and politically dominant Asian settlers; it is less clear that we should throw the term out when considering Black people and other communities that have little state power, like Filipinos, Sāmoans, and Southeast Asians, who are from and formed by these islands.

My use of "local" does not advocate "a hegemonic common sense position that assumes that diverse non-White groups' interests are always aligned with Native peoples."[22] (I detail these tensions.) Black residents do not use the descriptor "local" to "avoid difference through amalgamation," since they tend to view locals and their experiences as shot through with race, and thus with power and inequality.[23] Black peoples' own diverse positionalities crosscut supposedly distinct categories, thereby unsettling binaries and conceptions of (who enacts) power: Black people are Native (Black Hawaiians), and they are settlers (military personnel); they are local (Hawai'i-born and raised, pidgin-speaking surfers), and they are nonlocal (people from elsewhere who come to learn cultural norms); they fit within monoracial categories (identifying as Black with two Black parents); and they are hapa (for instance, Black Filipino or Black Sāmoan). Ethnography adds fullness—a thickness, as Clifford Geertz described—that fleshes out and disturbs slick dogma.[24]

"Local" describes a shared culture and orientation to the world based in island geographies (including the waters, the skies) that cross race. It is the imprint of a place on you, a practice, and signifies a length of time. It includes a geographic designation with attention to place, a shared culture, and a temporal signifier of those who are Hawai'i born and raised or brought to the Islands as children. They include Asian, Hawaiian, Black, Latina/o, other Pacific Islander, and haole groups. Terms like "local," "nonlocal," "newcomer," and "long-term resident" are important distinctions attentive to *time* on the Islands. "Local" refers to people who self-identify as such and are fluent in cultural practices that are recognized by others as Hawai'i-grounded ways of being and doing. Local also means having cultural and codified knowledge central to creating and expressing a sense of "we-ness" among Hawai'i's people, which distinguishes locals from transplants, whether from the east or west of the Islands.

There are Black locals in Hawai'i. Most scholarship conflates nonlocals with haole, whereby nonlocal often remains racially unmarked, assumed only to be White, much in the way continental Whiteness is presumed and unmarked. When (and if) Blackness enters debates about localness and settler colonialism, it ruptures the assumption that nonlocal equals haole, that Asian equals settler, and that both have disproportionate power. My research not only marks localness *racially* but also expands our expectations of who *is* local. Localness as a practice, feeling, and identity is a central paradigm to every participant's understanding of the landscape of Hawai'i and their location within it. I distinguish transplants from locals. I (and they, too) nonetheless maintain the distinction that they are not from the Islands and were raised elsewhere. This is not to emphasize the sense of nonbelonging that people who come to the Islands as adults experience but to reflect that the context and content of their childhoods are central to the development of a racial lens that Black locals generally do not express.

The salience of localness means that I use it descriptively and conceptually, attentive to critiques that non-Kānaka employ "local" to hide their participation in settler colonialism, and that it erases the indigeneity of Hawaiians by conflating them with other "ethnic" groups. I counter this tendency by zeroing in on Kānaka Maoli and their relationships with Black residents within my conversations and across this study, and by analyzing localness and race by thinking through indigeneity and Kanaka self-determination. While panracial, it need not erase the specificity of Kanaka genealogical ties to this land.[25] So how do Black people contribute to the question of "why . . . settler colonialism matters"?[26] Do they, like some local Asians, "see their interests as aligned with the formation of a liberal settler state" while trampling on Indigenous rights and demands?[27] According to the ethnography that unfolds here: yes and no. This largely depends on whether or not they are affiliated with the US military, a positionality that "pull[s] formations of settler colonialism and imperialism together," as Dean Saranillio does in his analysis of Asian settler colonialism.[28] We find that Black civilians conscientiously reflect on their position in these islands.

Black lives in the Hawaiian Islands neither privilege any binary (native/settler, race/indigeneity, local/nonlocal) nor exist within any single lens (race only, ethnicity only, local only, settler only). They experience the intersections of native, settler, local, foreign, and immigrant to reveal the analytical commingling of race, ethnicity, and indigeneity, especially clear in the case of Black Hawaiians. Localness emerges as a significant aspect of daily life that informs race and indigeneity. It is not so much that Hawaiians represent "indigeneity," Asians represent "local," and Black people represent "race." These are crosscutting and at times simultaneous and even contrary positionalities. Local as a cultural practice and way of belonging mediates presumptive binaries. We have much to learn from Black people in the Islands with neither the ability nor desire to further dispossess Kānaka Maoli and without the power or structures to impose their will on Hawai'i. The lives of Black locals illustrate what Colin, the Black Hawaiian quoted at the start of this chapter, called the "gray areas" between and beyond given dualisms.

Invisible and Integrated: Who Are Black Locals?

Multiracial people unveil racial negotiations, especially in a place where they make up nearly a quarter of the population. People who identify with multiple communities of color navigate interminority dynamics that include how non-White groups advance and resist racism. These dynamics and the ideas of race held within various communities shape the racial options of people who defy monoracialism, or the practice of identifying with just one race. In this section, I describe the backgrounds and parents of the Black locals I interviewed. Black Hawai'i residents' practices of identification are not celebratory, flattening, or antiBlack. Rather, they combine Kanaka epistemologies of genealogy and place with local practices of question-asking to *express* rather than hide uneven histories of enslavement, genocide, exploitation, and colonization.

I interviewed sixty people of African descent who represent enormous diversity not examined in scholarship, documentaries, or the census; this is no less true of the nineteen Black locals who animate this chapter. I culled through their terms of self-identification, looking for clear-cut patterns. Perhaps they would tell me something about the intersection of gender and racial identification? Or unite based on looks? Or geography? These are primary explanatory theories provided in mixed race theory: that multiracial people identify based on family structure, parents' racial and class backgrounds, where they grew up, their phenotype, and so on.[29] Yet the participants vary on every one of these lines, with few exceptions, and provide an enormous range of self-identifications.

In such a diverse and complex group, do their ancestries and identifications cohere? How does their Blackness modify or affix to localness? How does it relate to their other ancestries? Across a diversity of identifications, every Black local was shaped by life in the Islands. They epitomize *localness* and its salience. I describe how this unique demographic came to be (i.e., their parents' stories), their relationship to the Islands, and their self-conceptions. What emerge are disruptive *patterns* that combine uncommon *categories* ("Black townie"). How they identify (e.g., "Black Sāmoan") illustrates the role of race, indigeneity, place, culture, and peoplehood in Hawai'i.

My definition of local includes but does not require being born in Hawai'i—rather, it covers those who were island born and raised or spent their formative years (at least high school, but generally their elementary school years) in Hawai'i. The majority of all Black people in Hawai'i are not born here; this is also true of the Black locals I spent time with. Only eight of the nineteen locals (the only eight of the entire group of sixty participants) were born in Hawai'i. The majority of locals who were born off island—including some Black Hawaiians—came with their mothers as young children, usually by the age of five but in one case as old as fifteen. This group consists of eleven men and eight women, all cisgender, and one identifies as gay. At the time of our interviews, they were in their thirties and forties except for one fifty-something-year-old. They all attended schools in the Islands in the 1970s and '80s when the Hawaiian cultural renaissance was developing but was not quite as ubiquitous as it is today. Whereas I met them all on the island of O'ahu and mostly in Honolulu, they also come from the Big Island and Maui. They are local because they self-identify and are accepted by other locals as such. They adopt or are deeply familiar with local cultural practices, such as wearing slippers (but not in the house), speaking or at least understanding pidgin, preparing and preferring local foods, and understanding local references. Most important, they are local because Hawai'i shapes their conception of the world and their place within it.

They are *Black* locals, however, because their Blackness always implies their nonbelonging, their not-from-hereness. Race modifies and adheres unevenly to localness. Locals may assume that Asians, Pacific Islanders (especially those from Polynesia), and other Brown people are "local" or from Hawai'i. However, Blackness, in particular, marks one's presumed nonlocalness. This is because of their small demographic and their predominant affiliation with the US military. Black locals to some are an oxymoron, an impossibility even. To others, it is a fact of life, whereby the first modifier (*Black* local) is placed on them by others, whereas their primary self-selected identification is with the latter: Black *local*.

I chose to study dual minorities (nonWhite multiracial people) purposely (as I did nonmilitary personnel). They disrupt the expectation that Black people are monoracial or, if they are biracial, Black and White. I also *hope* to remind readers that not all hapas are hapa haole (part White). The term "hapa" is contested in part because of its decontextualized adoption by California college students in the 1990s to signify their Asian and White heritage.[30] They detached it both from its Hawaiian-language context and from Hawai'i—and Hawaiians themselves. Hapa comes from the English word "half" and initially referenced Hawaiians "of mixed blood." The *Hawaiian Dictionary* offers the following definition: "Portion, fragment, part, installment; to be partial, less. (Eng. *half*)." The second definition is "Of mixed blood, person of mixed blood, as *hapa Hawai'i*, part Hawaiian."[31] I use the term, as some people in Hawai'i do, to refer to people who identify with more than one race. It refers to Hawaiians who are hapa haole, as well as those who are of Hawaiian and African descent, or Black Hawaiians. While hapa initially referred to part Hawaiians, I apply it expansively in the context of Hawai'i, and interchangeably with "multiracial" or "biracial," to refer to any person who identifies with multiple ancestries or racial backgrounds, whether they do so on the census or in our interviews.

Fifteen of the nineteen locals are hapa, or identify with more than one race, and have nonWhite parents who consider themselves to be different races. Among them, Black Hawaiians are the largest group. Together, they include five Black Hawaiians (two women and three men), two Black Sāmoan men, two Black Koreans, two Black Okinawans, two Black Mexican men, one Black Filipina, and one Black Japanese woman. I also feature the insights of four locals (only one born in Hawai'i) whose parents are both Black and whose experiences overlap with other locals but are distinct from the Hawai'i-raised children of Black military personnel.

Black locals have varied class backgrounds, but none was wealthy and they were more likely working-class than the consistently professional class of Black transplants. Some came from Hawaiian Home Land in Papakōlea and Nanakuli, and others grew up in the mixed and heavily Asian neighborhoods of Wahiawā and Kaimukī. One was raised by her Korean single mother in a skyrise building in town, and another grew up with his two Black parents in a Kapolei single-family home. Some Black Hawaiians attended the Kamehameha Schools for Hawaiians, and others attended local public schools, such as Wai'anae High School in West O'ahu (where two Black Hawaiian women and one Black woman went) or Roosevelt High School in Makīkī, attended by several Black Hawaiians and Black Koreans (and me) in the 1980s. None attended the elite Punahou or 'Iolani schools in Honolulu.

The diversity of local Black hapas emerges from their family stories and their mothers' brave choices. Most striking is that all except one of their fathers were Black. That is, only *one* of the mothers of local mixed race participants was Black (an African American woman from the East Coast). None of the Black fathers was local; all of their fathers came from elsewhere.[32] Sixteen of the nineteen fathers were African Americans from the continental United States; one was from West Africa; one was from Canada; and one was from the Caribbean. The vast majority of fathers served in the military, and many were musicians (some were both), and these roles shaped how, when, and where they met the participants' mothers.

The second striking commonality is that the majority of their parents split and the children were raised by their nonBlack mothers. (Several Black locals did live for some years with their father's African American families in

Table 2.1 Black Local Participants' Background Descriptions

			BLACK LOCALS		
No.	Gender	Father	Mother	Self-Identification	Birthplace
			LOCAL BLACK HAWAIIANS		
1	Male	African American	Hawaiian	Black Hawaiian	Hawaiʻi
2	Male	African American	Local Hawaiian	Black Hawaiian	Hawaiʻi
3	Female	African American, Cherokee Indian	Half Hawaiian, half White	Black Hawaiian	Midwestern US
4	Female	African American	Part Hawaiian, African American, Cherokee, Caucasian	Black Hawaiian	US East Coast
5	Male	West African	English, Scottish, Hawaiian, Chinese	Black Hawaiian; not full Black	Hawaiʻi
			LOCAL BLACK SĀMOANS		
6	Male	African American	Sāmoan	Local dude with East Coast sensibilities	Hawaiʻi
7	Male	Caribbean American	Sāmoan	Identify more as Sāmoan	US West Coast
			LOCAL BLACK ASIANS		
8	Female	African American	Japanese national	Black and Japanese	Japan
9	Female	African American, Indian, English, Irish	Korean national	Part Black, Black Korean	US East Coast
10	Male	African American, Cherokee	Korean national	Half Black, half Korean	Korea
11	Female	Local Okinawan	African American, Chinese	Black Okinawan	Hawaiʻi
12	Male	African American	Local Okinawan	Black Japanese	Hawaiʻi
13	Female	Black	Filipina	Black Filipina	Western US

(continued)

Table 2.1 (continued)

No.	Gender	Father	Mother	Self-Identification	Birthplace
			LOCAL BLACK MEXICANS		
14	Male	Black	Chinese, part Hawaiian, part Filipino	NonWhite, Mexican, Blackfoot	Western US
15	Male	Black, American Indian, English	Mexican	Black, Mexican, English, American Indian; Hawaiian boy; kale	Hawaiʻi
			LOCALS WITH TWO BLACK PARENTS		
16	Male	African American	African American	Black local	Hawaiʻi
17	Female	Black	Black	Black local	Western US
18	Male	Birth parent: African American	Birth parent: African American Adoptive parent: Hawaiian	African American but Hawaiian at heart	Southern US
19	Female	Black	Black	Black local townie	Midwestern US

the continental United States.) Fourteen of the nineteen locals' parents were divorced. The four families that stayed together were all the parents of island-born Black people.[33] Eight of the eleven off-island-born locals were brought by their Japanese, Filipino, Korean, Sāmoan, Hawaiian, or African American mothers to the Islands, usually after divorcing or otherwise separating from their Black (African, African American, and Caribbean) fathers.

Hawaiian and Sāmoan mothers were from either Hawaiʻi or Sāmoa, and all had family in Hawaiʻi. As young women, they traveled through Job Corps and other work programs to the continental United States, where they met African American men. These women all returned to the Islands, pregnant or with young children they could raise in their families after their relationships ended. One Hawaiian woman met her partner in West Africa; another adopted an African American baby from the US South and raised him in her Hawaiian community.[34]

In some cases, fathers came to Hawai'i, but in each case, the relationship did not pan out, and with one exception, the father left the Islands. Hawaiian and Sāmoan mothers usually remarried or had long-term relationships with other Black (usually military) men in Hawai'i. Most of the local Black Hawaiian and Black Sāmoan participants had no relationship with their biological father. One man never met his father; one woman did not know whether or not hers was alive.[35] An exception was a man who was raised by his African American father and Native Hawaiian mother in their Hawaiian neighborhood.

Like Hawaiians, Okinawan parents were local (from Hawai'i), but they were anomalous. Whereas all the other locals had Black fathers, two Black Okinawans I spoke with had Okinawan fathers who married African American women who made Hawai'i their home. (A third Black Okinawan had a local Okinawan mother and a Black father from the continental United States.) All three Black Okinawans were Hawai'i born. The other Asian mothers were from Korea or Japan, where they had partnered and then split with African American soldiers. While I sought to write the untold story of Black civilians, the military influence persists, infusing the lives of all people living in Hawai'i, including these interlocutors. The immediate families of twelve of the nineteen locals had worked in the military. Fathers and stepfathers served in Korea and Vietnam; some mothers worked in the air force and other branches of the armed forces. Unaffiliated with the military, a single African American mother and a Mexican American mother still married to her Black husband were both from the continental United States.

The agency of single and newly divorced mothers is remarkable. They selected Hawai'i by taking their children's backgrounds into account. The Sāmoan and Hawaiian mothers wanted to be with their extended families. Asian (Korean, Japanese, and Filipina) and African American mothers of children born elsewhere had no preexisting family ties that brought them. Asian mothers were concerned about antiBlack racism in their home countries of Japan and Korea. They saw Hawai'i as an Asia-adjacent place where they could access cultural resources—speak Japanese, find familiar food—after separating from military partners. While the numerical minority, African American women who had children with African American men chose Hawai'i not because of extended family or familiarity but because they wanted distance, to get "as far away as possible" from their former partners, following a friend or chasing the adventure of settling in the Pacific.

None of the Black parents, except for one whose mother is also Black Hawaiian (her father is Black), was from Hawai'i. Almost all the Black parents, including single Black mothers, were from North America. This means that I am

Table 2.2 Local Participants' Descriptions of Their Parents

DESCRIPTIONS OF MOTHERS			
Hawaiian (7)	African American or Black (3)	Sāmoan (2)	Korean (2)
Okinawan (2)	Mexican (1)	Filipino (1)	Japanese (1)
ALL WHO DESCRIBED MOTHERS WITH MORE THAN ONE ANCESTRY WERE HAWAIIAN AND DESCRIBED THEIR HAWAIIAN MOTHERS AS FOLLOWS:			
Half Hawaiian and half White Scots-Irish	English, Irish, Scottish, Hawaiian, and a little bit Chinese	Part Hawaiian, Filipino, Chinese, "slash dog" mixture	Part Hawaiian, African American, Caucasian, Cherokee

DESCRIPTIONS OF (BIRTH) FATHERS*				
African American (10)	Black (5)	African (1)	Caribbean Islander (1)	Okinawan (1)
THOSE WHO NAMED MORE THAN ONE ANCESTRY FOR THEIR FATHERS DESCRIBED THEM AS FOLLOWS:				
Part Cherokee Indian, yellow, fair-skinned Black		Black, American Indian, and English		African American, American Indian, English, and Irish

*One person did not describe their birth father.

studying the first generation of Hawai'i-born Black people, whose presence is new and yet tied to the generations of Black Hawaiians who were born through nineteenth-century unions between Black mariners and Hawaiian women. While the Islands continue to experience small groups of Black arrivals—mostly men—who then form families with local women (usually Hawaiian and Asian), women from Hawai'i also express their agency in migrating to the continent, where they meet partners.

Fundamentally, I offer this sketch to illustrate who Black locals are—to make you aware that there *are Black locals*. They are mostly hapa—at much higher rates than the overall population, even in Hawai'i—and generally have Black fathers and Pacific Islander, Black, and Asian mothers who raise them.

They offer unexpected and exciting life and family stories, just as Black transplants do. However, they are united by growing up in Hawai'i—and growing up Black in Hawai'i—despite thinking they were "the only one." These stories and this place explain why being "local" and identifying as Black and _____ are so significant to Black locals.

Self-Identifications

Black local self-identifications, or words participants used to describe themselves, were vast and uncategorizable. I asked these contributors to "start at the beginning, tell me about your parents, your grandparents, before you were born." What an account! I was riveted by the detail and complexity of the descriptions, grateful for the generosity of those who shared their life stories.

Our conversations were not all easy. Some women, young and older, cried when recounting childhood memories. People in their thirties mentioned not having spoken about their fathers for years, sometimes not communicating with them for decades—or *ever*. Others shared memories of their time spent with fathers in the continental United States. Local men and women were confused by my poor questions that seemed to circle unclear inquiries about Blackness. They were used to the question, "What are you?" But when I followed up with "How do you identify racially?" and "What would you put down on a school form?" the children of two Black parents seemed most unsure and vexed. Several were ambivalent: "I guess"; "I don't know"; and "I think," they said. They modified their racial identification as Black: as local or a townie (someone from town, from Honolulu).

Sifting through these diverse responses, I nonetheless found patterns. For instance, every person who had a (part) Hawaiian and (part) Black parent identified as "Black Hawaiian," "the Black Hawaiian," or "the other Black Hawaiian," although their understandings and expressions of Hawaiianness and Blackness differed. Additionally, men spoke pidgin more frequently than Black Hawaiian women (more on this later). They often already knew of one another despite being raised in different Kanaka communities on O'ahu. They introduced me to one another. They were all raised in their mother's Hawaiian communities, and all but one without their biological fathers.

It is their Blackness—not their being mixed—that distinguishes part-Black Hawaiians from other Hawaiians. Hawaiians include generations of people who identify as "part Hawaiian," referring to hapa haole (Hawaiian and White), as well as people who might be, for instance, Hawaiian, Chinese, and Portuguese.

Table 2.3 Local Participants' Descriptions of Parents and Self

MOTHER	FATHER	SELF-DESCRIPTION
African American	African American	Townie local Black
Sāmoan	Black	Half Black kid; Black and Sāmoan
Sāmoan	Black	Identifies more as a Sāmoan
Korean	Black	I can't really say I'm just Black; I can't say I'm just Korean; half Black, half Korean.
Half Hawaiian and half White Scots-Irish	Part Cherokee Indian, yellow fair-skinned Black with freckles	I am more Hawaiian; I wasn't raised around my Blackness; I identify with the Hawaiians.
Mexican	Black, American Indian, and English	I'm Black, Mexican, English, and American Indian; I would say half pineapple, banana, papaya, [and] kale.
Part Hawaiian, Filipino, Chinese, "dog" mixture	Black side	I have Mexican in me, nonWhite.
English, Irish, Scottish, Hawaiian and a little bit Chinese	Togolese	I'm the dark kid, but I'm not full Black; I'm from Hawai'i.
Korean	African American, American Indian, English and Irish	Part Black; I'm just me; I'm not more African American, more Korean.
African American	African American	I'm Black; I think I identify as local.
Hawaiian	African American	I was a minority; I was just Black; I'm Black Hawaiian.
Filipino	Black	I say Black Filipino; Malaysian if I'm feeling funny.
Japanese	African American	I don't identify as local because we come from Japan; I'm both Black and Japanese.
Hawaiian	African American	Black Hawaiian

Table 2.3 (continued)

MOTHER	FATHER	SELF-DESCRIPTION
African American	African American	I don't know, I guess. Black is who I am.
Birth mother: African American. Adoptive mother: Hawaiian	African American	I would answer African American but Hawaiian at heart.
Black Chinese	Okinawan	I knew I was Black, and I knew I looked different, but I still thought of myself as a little Asian girl. I was just Okinawan.
Okinawan	African American	I'm half Black, half Asian.
Part Hawaiian, African American, Caucasian, Cherokee	African American	I'm the other Black Hawaiian.

Black Hawaiians do not specifically share a *mixed* identity. Rather, Kānaka are united through "their Hawaiian-ness, rather than their being mixed."[36] By contrast, African ancestry does not necessarily unify or lead to a shared identification among Black people in the Islands. This also contrasts with more cohesive communities of multigenerational mixed Black people like the Garifuna in Honduras or the Siddis of India and Sri Lankan Kaffirs.[37] Nonetheless, Black Hawaiians' racial difference ruptures the expectation of wholesale acceptance as Hawaiians, highlighting the sometimes tense intersection of Blackness and Hawaiianness.

People used a range of terms to describe their Hawaiianness. Often this relationship reflected their experiences with Hawaiian family—just as their relationship to Blackness reflected their non/interactions with Black people. A daughter of a Black Chicagoan and a Hawaiian mother said, "I am more Hawaiian than most of them; [they] call me haole-lover [a reversal of 'n-word-lover']. I wasn't raised around my Blackness, I still don't really relate to the Black community. . . . I identify with the Hawaiians, but they won't have me, [and] I can't go around saying I'm Scot[tish] and Irish. I don't relate to my [American] Indian self at all." The one Black Hawaiian I spoke with whose Black father and Hawaiian mother together raised him said unequivocally that he was "Black Hawaiian." A woman raised by her Black Hawaiian mother's family said of her maternal Black grandfather, "His community is Hawai'i, not a race," although she identified as a Black Hawaiian. Whether or not they were raised by Black family members, all Black Hawaiians identified similarly. A tall man working in land and water restoration found it "difficult to identify [as] either Black or Hawaiian. I do identify with being Black Hawaiian." Another Black Hawaiian changed his identifications over time: "I was really a minority," he recalls of growing up on Hawaiian Home Lands: "When I was young, I was just Black. I was different. As I got older, that's when my people, my community, started to embrace me for being Black Hawaiian." In all these cases, Black Hawaiians face ostracism from Hawaiians ("they won't have me") and highlight the dialogic link between community acceptance and identification ("my people, my community, started to embrace me").

Others referred to Hawaiianness beyond ancestry, such as Kamakakēhau (his real name), a musician who said he was "Hawaiian at heart." Some haole have deployed this phrase to claim rights in the Islands.[38] Their lawsuits allege discrimination ("reverse racism") by Hawaiian-only institutions like Kamehameha Schools or the Office of Hawaiian Affairs. Yet Kānaka accept Black locals in ways that exceed this problematic. Kamakakēhau is a globally touring Hawaiian falsetto singer and 'ukulele player who was born to Black parents in Arkansas and adopted as an infant by a Hawaiian woman who lovingly raised him in her Hawaiian community on Maui. The dark-skinned and outgoing performer says he feels "honored to share the culture I've grown to love and respect." Commenting on close-up photos of his face featuring his freshly cut fade and earrings, he explains, "Here in this picture, you see the many facets of me. By heritage, application and visually I am African American. But by soul I am Hawaiian. Either way you look, all the same always full of ALOHA!!" Hawaiians, including family members, responded with love and aloha, affirming him as a "solid Kanaka" and noting his beautiful "Hawaiian soul," as well as his "African Hawaiian features too!" Fluent in Hawaiian, this local performs expansive expressions of Hawaiianness embraced by many Kānaka 'Ōiwi who do not succumb to what Mishuana Goeman terms settler "logics of containment," including blood-based ideologies of belonging.[39]

Others were expansive in other ways, such as when a Black Mexican man stated that he was "a Hawaiian boy," or when Black Hawaiian Colin called Obama a "Black Hawaiian." Colin generously deploys nonancestral descriptions of "Hawaiian," as he does "Blackness" beyond ancestry in his discussion of King Kamehameha the Great as a Black Hawaiian in the introduction to this chapter. The community-engaged entrepreneur says, "I would say that there's one Black Hawaiian out there that holds the largest job in the state of the whole—you know, in the United States: Barack Obama. And it's kind of funny because Hawai'i is proud of him, they're excited that he's there because he represents that local mentality and then that Hawaiian lifestyle."

This Black Hawaiian was often slippery—elastic, even—in his application of "Hawaiian." He used it to refer to people who lived in Hawai'i before the arrival of Captain Cook; he described himself in percentages of Hawaiianness; he described King Kamehameha as a Black Hawaiian, as he did Barack Obama. Raised by his Hawaiian mother and a Black stepfather (who was shocked to find that this Black boy, versed in Hawaiian history, had never heard of Martin Luther King Jr.), Colin formed his understanding of race and indigeneity within locally specific conditions far from the continental United States.

Blackness outside the military context, or local and civilian Blackness, is often constituted through mixedness. Locals offer "Black" as just one component among others that make a person who they are. They also identified through fractions: "half Black kid"; "Sāmoan side"; "half Black and half Korean"; "I'm Black, but I'm not full Black"; and "part Black." They are constituted by "quantities" of ancestries, describing their parents through portions. A fourth-generation Black Hawaiian says her "mom's grandfather is a quarter Black, half Cherokee Indian, and one-quarter White from North Carolina." Mathematical fractions reflect their adoption of blood quantum rules of ancestry instituted not just through the Hawaiian Homes Commission Act; this is also how multiracial people across the United States tend to speak of their backgrounds.[40]

Mixed race studies and Native and Indigenous studies reveal the emergence of these fractional practices from the "great vanishing act" of colonial blood quantum regimes that operate in both North America and Hawai'i. They bring together what the Oneida scholar Doug Kiel describes as a "paradox" of "two paradigms for assessing Native personhood": "One paradigm regard[s] Indianness as membership in an Indigenous community defined in terms of kinship and social relations," while "European ideas fostered a second paradigm that came to regard Indianness as a quantifiable attribute that could be computed on the basis of one's lineage or bloodline."[41] This happens in Hawai'i, as the Kanaka scholar Maile Arvin explains: "Native nations are generally quite expansive in nature. Yet the imposition of blood quantum laws and tribal rolls by settler states have overlaid those more expansive notions with restricted, racialized, and gendered modes of membership."[42]

Kanaka practices of ancestral genealogical recounting tied to place coexist with European discourses of blood. An intimate connection to the Islands sometimes takes precedence over ancestry. A Black Japanese Hawaiian man who came to Hawai'i as a college student says that even after living in the Islands for over a decade (his mother is from an outer island), "I'm still not like a local. I'm just a little bit different, you know? And it comes up sometimes. People ask me, 'Yeah, what high school you went?' I didn't go to high school here." Not only is cultural adoption or background important; so is time spent in a place and how one's place of birth gives one meaning. Attending to place is critical to "local stories," which the historian John P. Rosa ties closely to families, neighborhoods, and ethnic communities.⁴³ "How do you identify?" I asked one participant. "I'm from Hawai'i," the dark-skinned Black man simply said. Participants named the tribes of their Native ancestors (most were Cherokee) and located *where* their family members came from ("North Carolina"), just as they described their particular European ancestry (English, Irish, etc.).

Whereas the nonBlack ancestry of hapas activates their acceptance as local, for those with two Black parents who do not identify as mixed, localness marks a way of belonging. Black people are constituted, as other locals are, through their relationships with other people and places: whom they know; where they live, surf, and go for happy hour. This also means they are being constituted *through the practice of responding to* "What are you?" Networks of kin and fictive kin envelop island-raised people who together enact common culture (pidgin, clothing, engagement with beach culture).

In resounding contrast to the views of some Black newcomers who state that one could not be Black and local, the vast majority of Hawai'i-born-and-raised Black residents identify as local, especially those with two Black parents.⁴⁴ "I am Black, but I definitely consider myself to be a local, a townie specifically," said a dark-skinned Black professional with dreadlocks. Another Black woman, who was fair-skinned and also "prefer[red] the natural hairstyle," said, "I think I identify as local. I know what I look like on the outside, but I don't feel anything in particular, but I feel local." A young Black college student, who was born in Hawai'i but whom many misidentified as being in the military (exacerbated by his short haircut and business casual clothing choices), had a difficult time answering me: "Well, I don't know, I guess. Black is who I am. It sometimes defines you and sometimes it doesn't define you."

Hapas also prioritized a local identity and stated their nonBlack ancestry alongside being Black. A Black Sāmoan called himself "a half Black kid," whereas another said he identified "more as Sāmoan." A woman in her late thirties said, "I can't really just say I'm just Black; I can't just say I'm just Korean. You're half Black and half Korean." A Black Hawaiian said, "I'm the dark kid; I'm Black but I'm not fully Black." A young Black Okinawan who recalled growing up in Honolulu said, "The only Black people here that I saw, unless they were like me—local, you know—then I didn't really think of them as Black. I [was] just like, 'Oh, you're local, I'm local,' you know? Black people and to some extent White people, if they are here, they're probably in the military." Another Black Okinawan, a tall man in his early thirties, said, "My elementary [school] life was pretty much I was a local boy. It was never a race thing, we were just in our local world." A Black Hawaiian reconsidered his potential move to Vegas: "I didn't [go] because I'm a local boy; you know, I would miss Hawai'i too much." Across these comments, local is about place; it is about how island influence enfolds the people who live here.

Self-identifications refer to race (via racial categories and looks, such as "Black Korean"), ancestry based on their (great-)grandparents, ethnicity ("African American, Irish, Chinese"), and culture ("local"). Kamakakēhau, the adoptee raised by a Hawaiian family, identifies as "African American but Hawaiian at heart" and disrupts the definition of Hawaiian as referring only to "Native blood" to point to an expansive orientation to genealogy and long tradition of adoption.[45] But it is his decades-long immersion in Hawaiian cultural practices ('ukulele mastery and Hawaiian language fluency) that is what he means to underscore in his cultural and heartfelt denotation of Hawaiian belonging. His is not a problematic appropriation of Hawaiianness or a desire to further dispossess Kānaka. Transracial adoptees complicate homologizing family with genealogy and ancestry. At the same time, Hawaiian hānai (adoption, broadly speaking) practices provide the language and structure for this phenomenon. The strength of cultural belonging also explains why a dark-skinned and dreadlocked Black professional insists that she is a "local townie" as well as being Black. In Hawai'i, race (in this case, prescribed Blackness), Nativeness (Hawaiian; growing up with Hawaiian family or on Hawaiian Home Lands), and culture (Hawaiian language fluency; local; townie) mesh in their lives but are clearly demarcated in their words.

Racial and local self-descriptions emerge from local practices, Kanaka epistemologies, and imported racial science. It is common in Hawai'i to ask questions about another person's background to connect to and locate people. Asking "obviously Black" (e.g., Black-appearing or African-featured) people "What are you?" or "What you?" allows the person who is asked to acknowledge their multiplicity, history, and locatedness at a remove from the one-drop rule. Locals offer detailed exegeses. Within one two-hour conversation, someone might call on numerous descriptors, revealing the difficulty in fixing and categorizing (and the fruitful outcome of asking "What are you?"). A hip hop DJ says:

> I have Mexican in me. I guess that's the best way to say it. I got so much other stuff in me, too. Pretty much everything, even when they told me you can only check one [on forms]. Even like checking American Indian. I knew Blackfoot was the tribe. Just non-White [is how I identify]. I've never played so much into it because all the Black-White-whatever race thing.

The practice of asking and answering resists haole attempts to decimate Kānaka through elimination and envelops Black people in Indigenous practices.[46]

Black and Native are not discrete and bounded groups, as ancestries, genealogies, and cultural practices crisscross colonial racial constructs. Indeed, (these) multiracial people are often the products of European and American colonization and imperialism that have displaced, dispossessed, and dispersed groups across the globe. The stakes of Black multiraciality, as we see with Obama, are no doubt different in Hawai'i than in the continental United States. But what would it mean for us to welcome people like the student at the Critical Mixed Race Studies conference to self-define in ways that grant him visibility rather than diagnosing him as an antiBlack Black person?

Expansive recounting calls on uneven pasts and ongoing forms of disenfranchisement and pride that play out within changing political contexts. Listing your ancestries and those of your children (using one's fingers for each ethnicity, a different hand for each parent) does not equalize differences. Rather, the utterance voices how these ancestries came together within that person. This is not simply an act of colonial acquiescence; this accounting is a testimony of historical imbalances and contemporary dynamics. It is not a pristine precolonial Native Hawaiian practice; it reflects nineteenth- and twentieth-century colonizing blood logics and histories of death and intermarriage. Racial science hoped, on the one hand, to dispossess Indigenous people of their land and to assist elimination and, on the other hand, to dispossess Black people of their humanity while increasing their numbers for slaveholders. Contemporary practices of multiracialism in Hawai'i reflect the ongoing contestation between Indigenous and colonial epistemologies. Through this interplay, the same person who may not be eligible for Homestead Land would nonetheless be socially accepted as Hawaiian. Expansive identification and a Hawaiian cultural renaissance have led to a growing Indigenous demographic. "After 200 years, Native Hawaiians make a comeback," states a 2015 release from the Pew Research Center.[47]

The Pacific is an understudied site of the African diaspora, yet one in which Black people pursue non–status quo relationships to Blackness that contest hypodescent. Race is geographically specific, and the topography of Blackness is vast—global, diverse, and locally specific. These findings do not make Hawai'i postracial or a multiracial paradise. Without a Black Metropolis, the small Black presence and openness to members of the African diaspora influence how Black locals relate to their Blackness. However, transplants express confusion at being asked, "What are you?" and are surprised to be questioned about something "so obvious." In this way, practices of belonging in the Islands disrupt seemingly settled categorizations, hinting at alternative possibilities. Whereas Hawai'i pushes Black people from elsewhere to expand their sense of self and reconsider the meanings of Blackness, it also creates a corresponding ambivalence, which I discuss in the remainder of the chapter, among Black locals who may not learn about the history and struggles of the African diaspora.

(Un)Conditional Acceptance and Disrecognition

I ordered a drink at a Waikīkī hotel pool bar, mustering up the courage to ask the thirty-something-year-old bartender about his impressions of Hawai'i (speaking to strangers has never has gotten easier!). My husband and I wrongly assumed the bartender was a Black newcomer; from his looks and comportment, we thought he was an African American who had recently moved to the Islands. Of course, he wore the clothing and displayed the solicitousness of the tourism service economy, but it was also the way he spoke and interacted with us.

"People assume I'm from the mainland. Especially at the bar," Damon later recounted, "people always assume I'm not from here. . . . I guess maybe because the way I speak? The way I look obviously. So people just assume I'm a transplant. From somewhere else." He clarified that he was raised by his Sāmoan mother and did not know his Black father, who was from the Caribbean. After some time in California, Damon's mother brought him to O'ahu, where he attended a public high school near several military bases. In our interview, later at a Starbucks near Ward Center, he recounted crossing the social divisions in high school to befriend Black, Polynesian, and Asian students. His friends' Asian parents, however, disallowed him from their homes: "They just didn't want some Black kid in their house." These memories illustrate the racism of locals (the topic of another chapter) who attempt to confine the cross-racial fluency of Black hapas.

While others see Damon as I had—as Black—he identifies differently: "Because I was around my Sāmoan side a lot, I probably identified more as Sāmoan. I was more proud to tell people I was Sāmoan. I think it just goes back to how I was raised. Because I was around Sāmoans so much, it kind of enclosed me to that type of activity within that ethnicity. So I never felt the need to reach out to my other side." Black multiracial individuals like Damon translate themselves through their kin relations, language, and other cultural practices so as to be *seen* both by strangers and by fellow members of their nonBlack communities. He explains, "I definitely try to let them know that I am [Sāmoan], and in certain ways, I guess I'm always trying to lead them to perceive me as someone. And if it doesn't work, then I can kind of just let it go, so I don't think about it. But I guess inside I always want them to know I'm Sāmoan. So they don't look at me different." Damon's story points both to the implications of Blackness among Sāmoans and to the significance of having the opportunity to answer the question, "What are you?" One's looks do not tell the whole story.

The racial difference of Black-appearing locals marks them as outsiders to the Islands. In response, they perform belonging. They narrate geographies of affiliation and kinship (saying who their family members are, citing their neighborhoods and high schools) and socialize with other locals. They also communicate localness by featuring their nonBlack, more "local" ancestries (e.g., Sāmoan, Korean, etc.). This is especially evident among local hapas who experience a split between their looks and their identifications.

Others echoed Damon, experiencing the phenomenon of *being* but not *looking*. Karmen was raised in Honolulu by her mother, who spoke Korean, prepared Korean food, and took her children to Korea to visit family; her father, an African American military man, passed away after the divorce when she was young. With her medium brown skin and curly long hair, Karmen expressed the emotional ramifications of her life as a Black-appearing local: "I look in the mirror and say, 'Where is the Korean? What happened?' I am half Korean, and I *am* half Black. Why can't I be accepted as that? I go to the Korean market, and some people must know, but others just think, 'She likes Korean food.' People think, 'She must be adopted.' I get head turns."

"Now," Karmen says, "I tell people what I am. I would like to identify more with both. I love Korean food, I can understand Korean. I don't speak it 'cause it would be too much of a disjuncture." Brandon Ledward, who studied "White Hawaiians," describes how "it can be truly painful not to be recognized by members of your own group."[48] Damon and Karmen face *disrecognition* from their nonBlack communities who do not see these individuals, owing to their

Blackness, as coethnics. However, part-Black multiracial people also face anti-Black racism. Damon's Sāmoan grandparents worried that the birth of a Black grandchild would harm their chiefly lineage. And Karmen says, "It hurts that cousins who are mixed Korean/Japanese are accepted [as Korean]. . . . It hurts my feelings. My mom says, 'You're darker, I can't take you there.' I tried to talk to her and tell her that it hurts, and she doesn't realize it. . . . Just the concept is hurtful. I don't see it that way."

What does it mean to face Korean antiBlack racism *as* a Korean? Whereas discussions of antiBlackness and racism assume that perpetrators and targets come from two different racial groups, in these cases, they are the same.

Disrecognition and antiBlack racism have not turned Black hapas to Black-only communities. Karmen says that "I was raised in Hawai'i by my [Korean] mom, and I couldn't identify with African Americans. But by looks I'm Black, so I can't identify as that. So I'm just *me*. I'm just *Karmen*." Black arrivals from Africa, the Caribbean, Europe, Asia, and the continental United States noted to me how their counterparts in Hawai'i neither gave nor returned the universal head nod, a seemingly simple movement nonetheless representing a complex expression of shared consciousness and community among African-descended people. Yet Black locals, who admitted to not engaging in this practice, do not always identify with this local and global fellowship.

In the continental United States, being identifiably Black—being *seen*—often signals the acceptance of presumed belonging, only to be suspended once Black locals revealed their unfamiliar speech patterns, ignorance about popular references, and a different orientation to community and self-identification. (In this way, *racial* belonging in the continental United States parallels *local* belonging in Hawai'i.) More accurately, they do not know *how* to identify with this larger Black community, discussed in the next section. These narratives challenge the assumption that ancestry (often called "biology") and identification align.[49] They also counter the overdetermined nature of Blackness presumed in studies of the United States and structured into the nation's formation. How can we imagine being in a society not forged through a Black/White binary? Karmen and Damon are examples of Black people in the Pacific still wrestling with resilient Western concepts of race based on phenotype and "blood purity."

Like fellow locals who did not grow up within Black communities, Kamakakēhau, the Black adoptee who was raised in a Hawaiian family, said that he could learn about Blackness "in other ways," such as by living with African American roommates from the continental United States. He says of his roommates, "Their goal was to get adapted to Hawaiian culture, and here

I am wanting to learn about African Americans. We had the same things in common, and we can teach each other." However, they told him, "You're not Black. . . . You're not African American. You are Hawaiian. The only difference is the color of your skin," commenting on his dark skin. Similarly, locals register their surprise when they see Kamakakēhau perform in venues across Waikīkī, remarking on his fluency in Hawaiian when "you're not even Hawaiian." Whether told he is "not really Black" or "You're not even Hawaiian," what does it mean to be defined *in the negative*? Kamakakēhau says, "I am African American but Hawaiian heart and soul." He tries to include himself as part of a larger Black brotherhood, "but I don't consider myself Black. I guess it's because I've been raised in Hawaiian culture."

These locals understand Blackness as something that can be taught and learned—as something cultural (like localness itself) and as an ethnicity with attendant foods and practices—just as they learned to be Hawaiian and Sāmoan. Ancestry does not define their identifications, nor do their looks. They affiliate along cultural lines and refute the one-drop rule, not so much because of internalized racism but because they feel they lack the cultural capital of what Black *is*. "Sometimes," one Black local says,

> I feel like I don't know enough when I'm around [other African Americans], you know? Like style. . . . And then I have to come back to my senses, and then I think about that. "Okay, well, you don't know this, you don't know about what I know." And just kind of build a little more confidence about myself to be open and to communicate with these people, and at the end of the day, that's how we learn. We're not going to learn if we keep our mouths quiet.

These boundary crossers express what it is to "look like but not feel like," highlighting how multiracialism—especially as experienced by nonWhite multiracial people—expands theories of race. Black people from Hawai'i navigate racial non/belonging wherever they are. At home in the Islands, other locals assume Black people come from elsewhere. On visits to the continental United States (described shortly), however, other Black people generally embrace them within their communities and homes. The process of growing up in predominantly nonBlack families and later learning how deeply unfamiliar they were with the experiences of African Americans together shaped their relationship to Blackness.

Ambivalent Blackness:
Black Locals' Conceptions of Blackness

Walt grew up with his Sāmoan mother and Black stepfather on Oʻahu and also lived for several years with his African American father and his father's family on the East Coast. Interactions with Black people were a daily part of his childhood, not something "over there" or elsewhere. "To me," the ebullient talker says, "Blackness wasn't something to be tucked away. Because it was something that I was living actively. My Christmas memories are always of the Motown Christmas album, in Hawaiʻi. You know what I mean? The Jackson 5 Christmas album, in Hawaiʻi." His may be a familiar narrative to some readers, but it was not representative of the Black local experience. Many Black locals did not have the opportunity to learn Black cultural practices from earlier generations.

What most distinguishes Black locals from their nonlocal counterparts is their ambivalent relationship to Blackness and insistence on a local identity. Several locals found it difficult to explain how they identify. I asked all sixty participants generally the same set of questions, including how or whether they were raised with a sense of Black history and identity, along with what Blackness meant to them. While transplants had an easier time articulating what this meant (and generally understood what I meant by my questions), Black locals often had trouble understanding my query about "Blackness" or what *Black is*. I found these interviews to be the most confounding and difficult to navigate, although they were, without exception, pleasant and congenial. It was in my conversations particularly with local Black hapas who grew up outside of Black communities where these questions seemed redundant, and the participants offered circular or unclear responses. This reflects both my poor questions and the lack of vocabulary for discussing these topics in the Islands.

Black locals from Hawaiʻi are generally oriented differently to the expressions and practices of Blackness familiar to many African Americans. With notable exceptions like Walt, they do not know the rich history of Black arrival and integration recounted in chapter 1. For them, Black history is continental US history. Most local Black hapas had complex relationships with their Black identities. They identified as Black (i.e., "I am a Black Hawaiian"), yet they were ambivalent about having properly "earned" that "title." For instance, they say, "I am Black, but I definitely consider myself to be local"; others say, "I can't really just say I'm Black."[50] A dreadlocked man raised on the Big Island says, "I'm Black, Mexican, English, and American Indian. 'Black schmack,' growing up—that ain't me." Others said, "I'm Black, but I'm not full Black," despite being "labeled as Black."

Black culture was something elsewhere and did not seem to inform Black locals' everyday lives. A woman who grew up in Honolulu with her Black mother and Okinawan father did not "flat out deny" being Black but felt she nonetheless "thought of [her]self as a little Asian girl" when she was growing up, pointing to Asian normativity in Hawaiʻi. Even a young man who grew up with his Black parents outside of Honolulu says, "I don't wake up in the morning and think, 'I'm Black, so this is how I'm going to act.'"

Black locals are not put in a position where Black is their only or primary identity. Their comments are less suggestive of a problematic relationship to Blackness than those expressed by the young Obama attending Punahou School. Upon learning that his teacher had invited his Kenyan father to speak to the elementary class, Obama recalls: "I couldn't imagine worse news."[51] Race commenters across the United States have latched onto statements like these to determine that mixed race Black people struggle with internalized racism. Do these statements signal purely distaste for being Black? Perhaps it reflects Obama's fraught relationship to his father, who left the Islands and thus left a gap in Obama's racial literacy.

In this context of not knowing, what are Black locals' ideas about Blackness? Having explained the various ways Black locals identify, I now discuss *why* they favor a "Black and _____" rather than "Black-only" identity. Why do they identify so strongly as local? After describing the factors that influence their understandings of Black life, I present what Blackness means to locals and how this understanding shapes their ambivalent identifications as Black. This ethnographic description expands news accounts and mixed race studies scholarship focused on historical and representational accounts of multiracial individuals that seem to lose sight of the everyday lives of people navigating the structures and strictures of race.

(Lack of) Black Family in Hawaiʻi

My sense that I didn't belong continued to grow.
BLACK LOCAL BARACK OBAMA, *DREAMS FROM MY FATHER*, 2004

The experience of Black people in Hawaiʻi differs from elsewhere because, as the Kanaka scholar Lisa Kahaleole Hall summarizes, "Hawaiʻi is not America. . . . Geographically, culturally, spiritually, Hawaiʻi is very far away from the United

States."[52] Black locals often do not experience residential hypersegregation or share a historically grounded feeling of communalism with other African-descended people. What do we learn from this place where Blackness is less known and less salient? What do we learn about growing up Black in a racially diverse place? And how does growing up without local models of Blackness prevail on their comprehension of Blackness and feelings of belonging and possibility in the world?

We know Barack Obama's perspective of his family's influence on him, recounted in his memoir and countless books. But what about those lesser-known Black locals and hidden hapas? How do family members shape their ideas about being Black? Mixed race studies itemize the factors affecting multiracial identification, including one's social class, the "racial composition of social networks" whereby "multiracial individuals in largely minority social contexts . . . identify more with the minority aspect of their racial parentage," family structure, and appearance.[53] Like Obama, these Black locals did not have access to Black family members at home and had limited or no contact with their biological fathers over their lifetime. This absence means they grew up sorting out what Blackness means, often on their own.

Hawai'i's distance from the continental United States informs this gap in their knowledge. A local Black Korean mother remembers having to explain the significance of Obama's election to her local multiracial son:

> I remember when he got elected the first time, and I was in tears because all I could think was, like, my [African American] father's not here to see this. My grandmother's not here to see this. You know? Like what would it . . . I know what it means to me and what it meant to my son. . . . I want to tell him about slavery. I want to tell him about [racial profiling at] the airport. I've talked to him about things and my father, and when Obama was elected and why that was such a big deal. I had to explain why it was monumental.

It was a momentous election to this local girl who was raised by her Korean mother and had to proactively seek information about Black history. Her son, whose local father is not Black, is even further removed from this knowledge. Karmen's Black family taught her that the election of Obama was "monumental" because he was "the first Black president." But it was significant *to her* for a different reason: because it reflected her experience, as a *Black hapa from Hawai'i*. "When I see Obama," Karmen says, "I see a local boy, a part of me. I think he is better for living in Hawai'i, even if he struggled."

Jonathan, who identifies as "Black Hawaiian," grew up with his Black father and Hawaiian mother in Honolulu. We had attended high school together (although we didn't know each other). This connection, along with the reference from his friend and fellow Black Hawaiian alum from our school, encouraged his afternoon invitation for me to talk story with him at his hale (home). He lived up the hill from our former high school with his parents and other family members. I was a Mānoa girl who had spent little time on Hawaiian Home Lands—I deserved their surprise at my ignorance when I asked how far the boundaries of the Homestead extended, forming a tight Hawaiian community overlooking the South Shore of Oʻahu.

Relieved by not having to drive my father's scooter—always a bumpy ride—I parked my mother's aged Toyota on the street and walked down his driveway. I found Jonathan's father along with his maternal Hawaiian relatives talking story around a fold-up table under a large tarp near their parked cars. I joined them for our conversation at the table, adding a box of malasadas to their snacks. They offered me a bottle of water from the cooler near their feet, sparing me from having to refuse a beer because I was hāpai (pregnant).

Having expected only to interview Jonathan, I felt lucky to also see his exchange with his father and his Hawaiian uncles. The keiki (children) played inside the cool house and peeked outside only when I got up to leave. It was a great session, despite my feeling a bit awkward as the only woman in a circle of male elders and feeling drawn to speaking pidgin more heavily than I do usually. Jonathan and his father, Willard, exchanged banter, playfully jockeying over whom I was there to *really* speak to and wanting to give me *their* story. And they related two very different stories.

Jonathan wore his standard uniform of baggy jeans and a T-shirt with a baseball cap, expressing a blend of Hawaiian and hip hop influences. The tall Black-appearing man displayed local style and spoke thoughtfully in heavy pidgin. Willard, Jonathan's dark-skinned father, had salt-and-pepper hair and was dressed in the Islands' casual uniform of shorts and no shirt. Willard was boisterous, confident, and full of details. The elder mostly stood while the rest of us sat, telling me his story as a veteran from the southeastern United States. After fighting in Vietnam, he came to the Islands, where he met and married his Hawaiian wife. Jonathan had not met his father's family, nor had they visited the Islands.

Willard raised the topic of African American history during our hour together. Despite growing up with Willard, Jonathan's awareness of this history and connection to it ("The past is over," he said at one point) is not supported by a significant Black presence, a school curriculum, or community events. In many ways, it is Willard who has adapted and been adopted into his wife's family, living on her family land and raising their Hawaiian children and grandchildren.

This reflects a similar process undertaken by Black men who married into Hawaiian families over the centuries. Yet he carries the African American past with him. His engagement with me (a professor in African American studies)—filling in each other's sentences about major events in Black history—reflected that he may not have had an outlet to speak at length about these topics. Local culture, and Hawaiian culture especially, prevails within their neighborhood. And while Hawai'i demographics and the family photos of locals reveal its vastly multiethnic composition, Black people *themselves* bear little and uneven influence on it. Thus Willard may find it difficult to relate African American concerns to his children, who have a multigenerational connection to Hawai'i but little out-of-island experience (Jonathan went to Las Vegas once).

Being raised by Black fathers did not always correlate to a strong Black identity or awareness about Black history and politics. Jackson, for instance, was raised by his mixed Black father and Mexican mother (both transplants), yet because "Black" and "Latino" are not categories infused with daily resonance (i.e., rarely appear in the local news, representations, or demographics), he identifies as a "local boy" and transracial, or above categories used to define humans.

Some Black fathers and stepfathers taught their sons about Black leaders, but generally youth were not equipped with this information or ways to deal with racism. A lack of Black role models shaped self-identification. "I wasn't raised around my Blackness," says a Black Hawaiian performer, whereas another Black man said that he "want[ed] to learn about African Americans." Because a Black Okinawan man "never had that father figure," the tall rapper said that he missed having "that rock to teach me how to be strong and stand up for it." His father's absence articulates a racial and gender gap—although raised by his Okinawan mother, he missed having someone "strong" who could teach him how to be proud and confront racism.

The lack of Black family members contributes to Black locals' ambivalence toward Blackness. However, they learn about "being Black"—and particularly American Blackness—as Obama did: by seeking out Black residents. Black locals often befriended the children of Black military families who attended other schools, like Moanalua and Radford, near military bases. Local youths considered these African Americans to be the embodiment of Black authenticity and affect. Karmen, who attended a school with few Black students, would travel to these military-heavy schools in her free time just to socialize with Black kids. Tommy, a Black Okinawan who attended one of these schools, crossed several peer groups; Black students found it odd that he hung out with the local Asian kids. If Black students near military bases offered one way to fill the lacuna of Black community, the media provided another powerful transmitter of racial representation.

Cultural Shifts in Mediated Blackness

Locals without military connections found it difficult to access other Black people, but they could find role models—of racial difference, if not of Blackness—on television shows in the 1970s and '80s. "Growing up," a dark-skinned Black Hawaiian said, he "used to watch *The Partridge Family*. I used to watch *Brady Bunch*. I thought I was White. (*Laughs*) Because, that's all I saw, you know. That was popular America on television." Whiteness was the prominent nonlocal identity for someone like Colin, who was othered as a result of his Blackness. (Recall that "haole" initially referred to anyone non-Hawaiian, explaining why several Black locals considered themselves or were called haole or, in this case, identified with representations of Whiteness.) Raised in his Hawaiian neighborhood, Colin "watched these other, um, colored shows or Black shows, but I never really (*pause*), I never really felt that it connected to me. At that time in my life, I didn't know anything about Black or Black history. So, for me, it didn't have a connection at that time."

Dominant cultural representations filled in the gaps, informing locals' ideas about Black people. Popular representations shaped nonBlack family and community members' responses to (part-)Black children. One Black man did not learn much about African American history from his Hawaiian family: "It wasn't until I was exposed to TV and, you know, I see the difference, how African Americans are around. You know, the wonder has always been there." Negative associations with Blackness that arrived with haole in the nineteenth century reemerged in the late twentieth-century media depictions that often related "the myth of Black inferiority."[54] Yet the media also brought the enormously influential sonic, visual, cultural, and racial expressions of hip hop culture beginning in the early 1980s (*Yo! MTV Raps*, BET, etc.). Music, more than television, has been a much stronger vector of Black masculinity for these locals.

Hip hop arrived in Hawai'i from major US cities mediated by distance. It spoke especially to local Black men. Overall, the prominence of hip hop changed the significance of Blackness, leading some locals to feel a complicated push toward, and pull away from, their claims to an African American identity. That this occurred around the same time as the Hawaiian Renaissance (including a revival of Hawaiian cultural practices) influenced the children of Black and Hawaiian parents to identify as "Black Hawaiians." Responding to media stereotypes, some Black locals described Black people as being aggressive, as having race pride, or as having a "chip on their shoulder." At the same time, a few local men like Colin and Tommy became consumed by hip hop and became practitioners (Black locals I spoke with were once rappers, breakdancers, and graffiti artists). Yet rather than identifying with hip hop as part of "his" (Black) legacy, Black and Okinawan Tommy describes his tastes and approach to emceeing as "Japanese" or "Asian" or "weird."

Black locals who were born since the 1970s came of age as part of the oft-demonized hip hop generation. Without adequate schooling dedicated to Black history, locals imbibe popular images of Black men and women without seeing its emergence from generations of Black resistance. Hip hop, a resistant and powerful cultural expression, came on the heels of Black Power advocates of racial pride, who exemplified Blackness as a beautiful and empowering identity. Without this context of Black struggle, locals adopt dominant discourses about the negativity of hip hop (as a source advocating violence and misogyny, for instance).

Being the child of a Black person does not make these young people feel unquestionably Black. This mirrors Ledward's research finding that "an alarming number of Hawaiian respondents do not feel 'Hawaiian enough' due to a perceived lack of racial phenotypes, the inability to speak their native language or their birthplace and residence," leading to their sense of marginalization.[55] Black hapas expressed a parallel ambivalence: not only by looks but also because they lacked cultural capital or knowledge of African American norms and practices. The popularity of hip hop powerfully informed conceptions of "the Black experience" as an urban, working-class, and masculine one taking place in the continental United States. Transplants further ostracized Black locals: for not being able to dance or not knowing pop culture references. Negative stereotypes and notions of Black inferiority take the place of racial pride and informed *all* island residents. Locals teased Black boys and girls for their physical attributes, calling out "cho cho lips" (thick lips) and dark skin. This denigration and a cultural gap explain why many Black locals I spoke with *also* espouse antiBlack stereotypes.

A Black woman raised on the North Shore of Oʻahu reflected, "I recognize, though, that I do have assumptions about Black [people]. My assumption is based on my experience with the military Blacks. And that's the preponderance that Blacks are undereducated or uneducated, and somewhat close-minded and ignorant." Others applied constructs of Black physicality to themselves. A Black Hawaiian MC felt that he had "natural rhythm," and a Black Sāmoan who played college football thanked his African American father for his "thick calves" and running speed, echoing the affiliation of "black male bodies" with "physicality and muscularity, or pure athleticism."[56] Nicole, a Black Hawaiian, draws parallels between Black and Hawaiian people. However, she focuses on high rates of incarceration, pregnancy, and life in what she called "ghettos." She had a difficult time explaining what being Black meant to her, "because the history to me is really horrible. How do you define being Black? I don't know what words I would use to define [it]."

Black locals' ideas about the value of Blackness was mediated by gender. Hip hop encouraged the self-expression of Black men in the Pacific in the late 1980s and early 1990s. Black Hawaiians, Black Sāmoans, and Black Okinawans went on to create rap groups, with one contributing to the first rap CD printed in Hawaiʻi, and another getting into trouble with the law for tagging graffiti. A former middle school "loner" found himself quite popular in high school in the late 1980s when his rapping and dancing career began to flourish. This highly gendered experience thus provided only a few of the locals an avenue of identification as Black. Local Black women were generally more negative about hip hop and less aware of its context and content. A Black Hawaiian woman in her fifties says, "I've been a Black person longer than hip hop has been around. I just remember being so abused by hip hop," and another Black-appearing woman, whose mother is Hawaiian, disapproved of the negative images of women in rap music.

The global media transmit new forms of racialized expressiveness across the airwaves while also spreading racism that gets picked up in the middle of the Pacific.[57] Locals experienced a gap in learning about modes of Black life because of their lack of immediate access to Black family members. Media representations, especially since the 1980s and the global phenomenon of hip hop, filled this gap in positive ways, mostly for men. If media representations frame the continental United States as *the* site of an authentic Black experience, the continental United States becomes the place to discover ways of Black being. By far the largest influence on Black locals' understanding of Blackness came from their experiences on the continent—for those who went there.

Continental Influence

The first time I went to Washington, DC, I couldn't believe it. Black people everywhere. I was like, "Oh my God. They're Black people, and they're nice." And they held the door, and they looked at you in the eye. And it was so, like, "I see you."

Well, I can walk down the street here [in Honolulu], and people's eyes slide right off me as if they don't see me, you know? Like, you almost have to get in their face to, like, smile and engage or connect.

LOCAL BLACK WOMAN

I remember going through struggles, talking to my [Black] dad about it and my [Black] stepmom [on the East Coast], when I'd be going back and forth between DC/Maryland and Hawai'i. To them, they'd just be like, "Relax. Be you. Be Black. You know, it's all right." But I'd be like, "No, you don't understand something. Sāmoa is a very small island, but its pride is bigger than the world. You know what I mean? And I have to engage it. I have to meld it into who I am. I can't leave it somewhere."

LOCAL BLACK SĀMOAN

Geography informs race; thus we get our identities not only from our ancestries and the people who raise us but also from the places we are. A website offering real estate solutions proclaims "Rock Fever Is Common for Non Islanders," diagnosing "a condition caused by homesickness, claustrophobia, or a feeling of being trapped on a 'rock' in the middle of the ocean."[58] Yet many people in Hawai'i do not experience these symptoms and never leave. The island-born, including Black locals, appreciate the vastness of Hawai'i, expanding beyond the visual landmass into the oceans and the skies. The expanse of Turtle Island (North America) is what astounds them, as do their harrowing engagements with its racial dynamics and extreme weather.

For people who grow up as the only Black person in their island communities, time on the continent can be a relief. Black locals visiting Chocolate Cities were pleased to be accepted as Black—until their lack of understanding or incorrect performances led to consequences. Ignoring, not knowing, or resisting appropriate scripts led Black cousins to comment that these exotic "Hawaiian cousins" (whether or not they were Native Hawaiian) were not "really Black" or "Black enough." (This parallels assessments of who is and is not local in Hawai'i.) Identifiably Black locals especially confronted these tests, whereby Black family and community members in the continental United States assumed they would express African Americocentric performances of Blackness.[59] On the other hand, Black locals who did not look identifiably Black were misidentified as Latino or Asian, for instance. These ethnically ambiguous people who were not connected to Black family members on their trips to the continental United States had a more tenuous relationship with African Americans.

Traveling abroad to the continent holds special significance for locals who are Black. For them, the continental United States *is* their Black experience. Many—though not all (by choice and cost)—have spent some time there for the same reasons that Black transplants move to the Islands: for vacation, college, and work. A few Black locals attended college across the United States, from small-town predominantly White liberal arts colleges in the West to historically Black universities in the East. For most of the others, their first trips usually were to vacation in Las Vegas or visit their Black fathers when they were children. Whether they returned home to the Islands, as most of them did, or stayed on for jobs and visited home occasionally, the continental United States is where they confront the factors, including racism, that inspired transplants to come to the Islands. The length of time abroad and places they stayed exposed them to the ways US Black life is differentially structured and expressed. It is this experience that influences their sense of (not) being Black.

Participants reflect on the odd mixture of being accepted and facing blatant racism across the United States. On the one hand, the experience of being around so many Black people and being accepted automatically, if conditionally, as Black was unique. But they were not "just Black." Family members called them out for their difference, especially when they found it important to tell others, as was their norm, of all their ancestries inclusive of their nonBlack mothers. On the other hand, this was the site of their harshest experiences with racism. Every contributor to this project stated the same thing: "the mainland" is where racism manifests blatantly. (As I recount later, there is also antiBlack racism in Hawai'i, but local participants downplay these experiences because of the *continental contrast*.) Visits abroad reveal mostly how different the continental United States is from Hawai'i, and Black locals, like transplants to the Islands, maintained a Hawai'i/continental US comparison.

Walt, a self-described "local boy with East Coast sensibilities," registers as African American from his accent, shaved bald head and large frame, clothing, and references to hip hop and Black popular culture. Among the local men I spoke with, Walt most recognizably and confidently identifies as Black (as well as Sāmoan). These cultural and physical clues point to his commitment to the development of Black youths' positive identities in Hawai'i. Walt's self-possession stems from his familiarity with Black family members (recall that he grew up with an African American stepfather). He says he was "listening to

Ramsey Lewis when I was a little boy, you know what I mean? And a lot of local Black kids didn't even know who that was." He also learned about Black history in graduate school in Hawai'i. However, his extracurricular lessons about race began when he was a child living in DC.

Walt learned what it meant to be a Black boy in the continental United States: "My Black experience is very broadened by my time on the East Coast. So I have a different understanding, you know?" Walt's Sāmoan mother traveled to the continent through Job Corps, where she met his African American father. She returned to Hawai'i and raised Walt with her new husband, Walt's Black stepfather. As a youngster, the Black Sāmoan went to live with his biological father on the East Coast. Beat up by other Black youths and questioned about his background ("You not just Black. You like one of them Sāmoan WWF wrestlers," a Black girl assessed), he learned the cultural norms of US Blackness. Bringing his girl cousin to the blacktop courts earned him the name "sissy," and he got into a brawl with the one other Black boy at their Montessori school in an attempt to negotiate "who was alpha male." (His dad, who he thought would console him with a hug, simply patted his head and said, "Welcome to DC.")

Life in the continental United States was not necessarily easy or fun, but it was formative. Black locals, particularly men, who visited Black family members tend to have an affirming relationship with Blackness and a confident Black identity. Like Walt, Tommy was able to access Black communities during his trip. Tommy's local Asian mother purchased him a high school graduation gift: a trip to New York, where he met some of hip hop's pioneers just as the culture was blossoming in the late 1980s. As exciting as the visit was, New York did not appeal to him, partly because he no longer felt unique; he was just one among many Black men. Tommy (Black Okinawan) and others, including Walt (Black Sāmoan) and Colin (Black Hawaiian), then brought their "newfound trade" back to the Islands—in his case rapping (he already was a graffiti tagger), but also DJing and breakdancing in the case of others. They became immediate local sources of Black knowledge and culture otherwise accessed only by television and the radio.

Local Black women also visited their fathers, and their exchanges were less confrontational than those recounted by Walt. Rather, they earned comments about their looks. Although it "felt strange," their time with Black family and in Black communities included acceptance because of the one-drop rule. Black Hawaiian Jenny visited her African American father's family on Chicago's South Side. Like the others, she found this initial welcome both comforting and awkward—comforting because she was finally around people who looked like her and embraced her along the same lines by which, at home, she was deemed different. She felt awkward, however, because she had not *lived* the experience, including experiences with White racism, that plays a role in "defining blackness" in the United States.[60] Jenny reflects what many Black locals feel: that she had not "earned" the title of being Black. This contributed to a sense of racial passing and disjuncture between how she and others felt, their ancestry, and how they looked.

Chicago was simply too cold and too Black and White for Kelly, a local woman whose Black mother brought her to Hawai'i when she was six years old: "I felt like I was on a foreign planet! There's Black and White and there's nobody in between. We're the people in between," said this child of two Black parents. Besides, she could not handle how different the city was. She theorizes, "People come over here [to Hawai'i] with that mainland attitude, you know, the haole attitude. Then there's the Black attitude, it's different." Kelly describes this as a mentality "stuck" in a slave past by Black people who are "accepted now" but can't "let go" of that past: "Even as times change, you still have those core descendant behaviors. Kind of like a phylogeny tree, right?" By contrast, she says, "If you grow up here [she includes Obama as sharing this experience], you're completely taken out of that mentality, so you never did acquire it. And for me, I never did acquire it."

It was Nicole's African American boyfriends from "the mainland" who lived on O'ahu who told her, "You're not a real Black." This upset the dark-skinned Black Hawaiian woman with straightened hair. "Why," she responded to them, "because I don't talk like you? Because I don't talk Ebonics? Because I wasn't raised in a ghetto?" She processed these memories in our conversation, asking me, "What makes me Black? I don't like rap music, and I definitely just hate rap music that puts down the race, puts down females. And they're like, 'Why, what's wrong with it?' and I'm like, 'What's right with it?'" Nicole interprets their expectations of Black people as Ebonics-speaking ghetto dwellers, while she advocates that she *is* Black despite their denied authentication. She does not—and perhaps cannot—conform to performances of hegemonic or familiar Black womanhood that her partners expect.[61] What do they mean when they discount her Blackness? And how does framing her performance as failure influence Nicole's ideas about being Black?

Time outside the Islands, media images, and the un/availability of Black role models affect Black locals' knowledge of the politics and dynamics of African American communities. These together influence their identifications with Blackness. It is difficult to cultivate a Black consciousness in a place where this positionality is not a priority and where people often lack Black family members. Unlike transplants, who may grow up in Black communities, locals must take a plane ride to "find" or experience "being Black in America." Black locals who travel note how odd it was to have their Blackness accepted—until they failed to perform the adequate gendered racial scripts. They also describe experiences with racism, hypodescent, and cultural expectations that align with other studies of Black life in the United States. But it is their commentary on the *uniqueness* of their shared experiences that reminds us that US racial formations are neither global nor universal.

Hawai'i was annexed in 1898 and became a state in 1959. However, Black people's navigation of the Islands and the continental forty-eight states emphasizes Hawai'i-US differences. Locals grow up with conceptual gaps about the African diaspora that are filled by mainstream media, Black transplants (including the military in the Islands), and trips abroad. The continental United States exposes locals to the diversity of Black life, its multiple representations, and the conditions faced by Black people. In their visits to family, for college, and as tourists, Black locals confront the racial rules that solidify Black/White binaries. There they also find themselves to be less special, only one of many other Black individuals in social settings. These experiences are the converse of those faced by Black transplants who come to the Islands.

Conclusion

Being multiracial in the United States parallels localness in Hawai'i. In fact, living in the Islands in many ways parallels the broader multiracial experience, which speaks across Pacific Islands studies, mixed race studies, and Black studies. Black people in Hawai'i who "look Black" but don't "feel Black" disarticulate race, culture, and ancestry to show how these concepts play out in—or are perhaps inadequate for describing—our daily lives. The Black Pacific represents a site of contestation of colonial categories. Belonging is not only or always race based. How do the combined factors of looks, self-fashioning, and cultural knowledge intersect to shape Black life in this place? And how do people express connections with a community whose ancestry they share but to whose members they are not immediately recognizable? Black locals, like multiracial locals, challenge presumed monoracialism and the Black/White binary.

Local Black men and women express an unresolved ambivalence toward Blackness misunderstood by US-centric racial analyses. Exporting a US lens misinterprets their mixed race identifications as expressions of antiBlack self-hatred. This is not what is happening on the ground, where a Black-only identity does not resonate. Ambivalence toward a Black-only identity emerges from Kanaka practices of expansive belonging, where Native people do not have only Indigenous ancestors, just as most African Americans have multiple ancestries. Rather, Kanaka approaches to genealogy and local practices of belonging encourage Black locals to acknowledge all their identities, thereby recognizing all their ancestors. They also identify uncompromisingly with place, as *local*.

Locals' identifications are shaped both by the experiences they have and by the ones they do not have. Their race consciousness, and thus their relationship to Blackness and other Black people, emerges from exposure and education. Black locals do not identify as Black-only because they do not feel they have the knowledge of, familiarity with, and thus claim to "the Black experience," owing to their small numbers and an absent school curriculum on African Americans. This gap in knowledge is then supplemented with media portrayals of African American Blackness, and particularly hip hop in the 1980 and '90s, when many Black locals grew up. These together shape what becomes thought of as "authentically Black." While the mainstream media advanced problematic stereotypes of Black masculinity expressed in hip hop, this resistant and powerful cultural form also provided models of Black pride, especially embraced by local Black men. Hawai'i witnessed a shift to positive evaluations of both Blackness and Hawaiianness at the time of the Hawaiian cultural renaissance. This led to the shared identification of Black Hawaiians, who in earlier times identified as Hawaiian.

Black locals are most informed about Blackness and race through their time in the continental United States. People who traveled more learned more about Black histories and socialized with Black family and friends. In the continental United States, they were accepted as Black, which proved to be unique for locals coming from a place of Black racial invisibility. At the same time, the continent was also the site of their most blatant experiences with White racism. Black locals also faced racial authenticators who commented on their difference. When Michiko was questioned about her identity by fellow students at her historically Black college, she would respond "in order of the percentage, influenced by Hawai'i customs: 'I'm Japanese (because I didn't think people would understand Okinawan), Black, Chinese, Native American.' And they'd be like, 'So you're basically Black.' And to defend it, I'd get really technical on their ass: be like, 'Actually I'm 50 percent Asian American and like 30 percent Black, and I grew up in Hawai'i where there are more Asian people, so I feel more Asian, if you want to know the truth,'" she said with exasperation. This experience led to a heightened awareness of the global and historical conditions that Black people face, leading some to identify more strongly with being

Black. Exposed to the diversity of Black life, locals' visits to the continental United States challenged their own stereotypes of Black people and taught them about the conditions of Black life in a monoracially structured society.

Those who did not—or could not—go abroad ("it's a different planet!") expressed ambivalence toward Blackness. This sentiment was compounded even at home in the Islands when Black locals were told they were "not really Black" by Black transplants, including by pockets of long-term residents who are invested in maintaining a continental sense of Blackness and for whom an African American identity is paramount. This often manifests through expected performances of African-descended people and through middle-class respectability politics—a set of politics that do not tend to inform the lives of Black locals who move in different social, economic, and cultural circles. Further distinctions between Black locals and transplants emerge when locals recount all their ancestries, a move away from a Black-only identity that puzzles transplants. Over time in Hawai'i, however, Black transplants—the focus of the next chapter—find themselves and their identifications irrevocably changed as they learn about the possibilities of Black life in the Pacific.

3

"LESS PRESSURE"

BLACK TRANSPLANTS, SETTLER COLONIALISM, AND A RACIAL LENS

> *In California, I was a Black man. In Hawai'i, I'm just a man.*
> LONG-TERM BLACK RESIDENT

> *I am the Pacific Raven, a malihini [newcomer] who found and adapted to a new environment.*
> BLACK HAWAI'I RESIDENT KATHRYN TAKARA,
> *PACIFIC RAVEN*, 1979

Black transplants, or people who move to Hawai'i as adults, forge ideas of themselves and the world in the crucible of the places that raised them. Primarily from the continental United States, but including Canada, Africa, Asia, Europe, and the Caribbean, these migrants understand themselves as Black people within the context of Black and White power dynamics. Having spent their formative years within Black communities or within race-conscious families, transplants developed an imperative racialized perspective aware of the histories of slavery and segregation with a sense of connection to the African diaspora. They bring this *racial lens* to the Islands, illuminating hierarchies in a place better known as a multiracial paradise. Such a lens proves effective in naming and combating antiBlack racism and helps navigate the politics of inequality. However, in the Islands, it comes up against locals' denials of the salience of race within a context of ethnic multiculturalism, Asian economic power, and a strong Indigenous presence. As one Black educator who moved from New York bluntly says, "Hawai'i complicates the nigger/whitey binary." How do such complications shape transplants' ideas, their considerations of Blackness, and the possibility of new, relocated lives?

The experiences of Hawai'i's Black population both contest and support the idea of the Islands as an exceptional site of racial tolerance. Kanaka ideologies shape the reception of newcomers, who unevenly navigate tensions built into the militourism complex. While Black transplants bring a racial lens, they are in turn shaped by island norms and practices that shift their conceptions of self, community, and belonging. The Pacific gifts this haven—an alternative to life otherwise. At the same time, their life stories paradoxically reflect how Black acceptance in Hawai'i is historically continuous while also complicated by the tense intersection of Black people with the US military.

I asked Black transplants questions that helped me assess how common representations lined up with both their expectations and their lived experience in a nonBlack/nonWhite place. Do they consider Hawai'i a melting pot paradise, depicted in both sociological texts and tourism brochures? A minority agreed, with one young woman declaring, "For me it is!" This college student represents one of many Black transplants who are deeply moved by the Islands. A multiracial Black man from California said, "I think it's such a beautiful place; we're able to get along. How many places do you know that are like this, really? People get along because of the aloha spirit. It's just always nice. We don't have some of the hardships." This real estate agent feels that Black people have every opportunity in the Islands, but he clarifies the limits to such possibilities: "Now, running to try to be a politician or something like that, I don't know how people would take me as." Even this skepticism has not been borne out, however, as the Islands have birthed Black politicians for centuries.

The majority of Black transplants took to task celebratory images of Hawai'i. They variously explain why "it's obviously not a multiracial paradise per se" based on what they learn of oppression—and not only that faced by Black people—since arriving. According to one Black and White professional, "In some respects, it's further advanced from the mainland. But the ingrained oppression of Native Hawaiians, the invasion and overthrow [of Hawai'i], and the cultural resurgence of Hawaiians and their language—tensions do come up." Black residents educate themselves about the conditions and resistance of Native Hawaiians. Others offered a less targeted critique, feeling that there were diverse demographics, but "that which is melting, is not melting." Rather, they feel that people learn of one another's culture but do not incorporate it or interact meaningfully. They also find that class matters. One man says,

"I guess they say Hawai'i is this melting pot concept, but once you've lived here longer, you get to unearth the goings-on and the relationships, because you don't really see it when you first get here. When you are looking in from a class structure, you see it. It's like, 'Oh, okay... as long as you're Black in terms of the class structure.' We're not there. We don't exist. There is not a very big Black population." It takes time to learn the intricacies of local dynamics because of the dominance of paradise discourse and the myopia of transplants' race-only perspectives.

A racial lens *sees* along racialized and structural lines informed by a global system of White supremacy hidden in the dominant discourses of tolerance, ethnicity, and multiculturalism. While some read this as an equal opportunity place where anyone can succeed ("home of the first Black/Asian American/Hawaiian president!" news accounts have boasted), African Americans are "skeptical of the rhetoric" of the American Dream transferred onto island topography. Black transplants are also attuned to racial absences and implications: "Where's the Hispanic people? You know, where's the Black people? So it's America, and it's diverse, but it's almost its own kind of America, and its own kind of diversity," one transplant analyzes. They bring this optic rooted in the history of the African diaspora that they learned at home or school, through the presence of Black communities, their experiences as Black people in the contemporary United States, and popular and community discourses about what it means to be Black in America, where most of the transplants come from. This lens illuminates racial hierarchy and racial invisibility. But a race-only lens has limitations.

Centering race does not automatically encourage one to learn about Native people. US-centric ideas can additionally misrepresent Hawaiians and Hawai'i's status. An educator who had just relocated from the East Coast said, "I was pleased to come here. It is like paradise—it's sunny, the water is warm, the mountains are beautiful. But relations (among people)—that's less paradisiacal. It's like a Third World country in the United States and has all the contradictions of a Third World country, or maybe Two Point Five World. It has the contradictions of the military, tourism. Hawai'i doesn't have full status." This scholar places Hawai'i near the "bottom" in his application of Western models of "development." His analysis illustrates the global comparative approach of transplants while failing to account for Indigenous accounts of this place, including the dynamics emerging from their colonization.

This blind spot also misses other complex local dynamics. For instance, Black transplants often view local Chinese and Japanese as model minorities—a US myth created in the 1960s that explained "Asian success" as a result of their cultural values rather than immigration laws and American economic priorities that privileged highly educated professionals.[1] This presentism and these racist depictions miss Asian groups' histories—on the Islands *and* the continental United States—as formerly exploited plantation laborers who faced nativism, exclusion, and lynching. Similarly, Asian American studies courses may frame Asian ethnic groups in Hawai'i (if at all) only through their painful past as exploited laborers. This narrative ignores the accountability of mostly local Japanese power brokers, for instance, who have held political and economic power since the Democratic takeover in the 1950s, including their development of anti-Kanaka legislation.[2] A racial lens illuminates conceptual limitations of a local-only perspective by zeroing in on the unequal distribution of resources and differing life chances among the Islands' racialized groups. But race alone cannot describe colonial histories that distinguish Kānaka Maoli and inform their concerns, including Asian settler accountability.

An ethnographic description of Black life in the Pacific animates debates about settler colonialism, imperialism, and Black and Native relations. Black people come to contemporary Hawai'i, an understudied site of the African diaspora, for both diverse and shared reasons. In this chapter, I explicate their experience. Black transplants' preconceptions, their reasons for leaving home and coming to the Pacific, and their encounters in this new place are unique compared with those of others, including haole (White) transplants and Black locals. Centering Black people unsettles the assumption that settlers are White while expanding the critical scholarship on Asian settler colonialism. Are Black people settlers in the Pacific? Responding to this question requires an analysis of militourism.[3] Black civilians navigate hegemonic associations with the military and tourism and thereby complicate native/settler and agency/abjection binaries. In a later section, I problematize the concept of settlers while centering Black people as agents of mobility and influence.

Of the sixty Black participants I interviewed, forty-one were transplants, or Black people who chose to come to the Islands as adults. They include newcomers as well as old-timers who have lived here for decades. Despite a diversity of backgrounds and upbringings, all were familiar with Black histories, communities, and identities (in contrast to Black locals). I detail what brought them to the Islands and what factors shaped whether or not they stayed. Included are the perspectives of those who returned "back home." How does growing up and identifying as Black or African American in the continental United States shape one's comfort in the Pacific? Is it their sense that "Black local" was an oxymoron and they never felt fully at home in the Islands? Or is it a case of, as one transplant put it, Hawai'i knowing "how to spit people out" if they do not or will not fit? Especially for race-conscious individuals, these decisions illuminate the challenges of living in a place without a Black Metropolis. Whether or not they stay, all transplants employ a US racial framework to interpret their experiences.

Following the theoretical framework on localness, race, and settler colonialism in Hawaiʻi, the bulk of the chapter is an ethnographic analysis of Black transplants, beginning with a description of where they come from, why they come, and what preconceptions they have of the Islands. This provides the context for their experiences upon arrival: Do these experiences overlap with their expectations? Are Black people drawn for the same reasons as others? Or are members of the African diaspora drawn to specific attractions? Black adults who move to Hawaiʻi apply a critical racial lens developed in their previous contexts of *Black presence* and, confronted with a different kind of place, reorient and apply this lens to a context of *Black absence*. Their ideas of non/belonging and home illustrate why Hawaiʻi offers an alternative to life elsewhere, but one that does not unequivocally bring liberation. I conclude by charting how Hawaiʻi dialogically reshapes transplants' racial understandings as they attempt to make a home in a complicated society in which a Black/White binary is not the operative structure and Blackness is often invisible.

Black Settlers of Color in Hawaiʻi?

The question of localness in Hawaiʻi is an academic, everyday, and political concern. Foundational work argued that a local identity consists of more than simply being born and raised in the Islands.[4] Early scholars defined local as a set of cultural practices and a resistant identity emerging from a shared plantation experience. Localness linked working-class Asians to Native Hawaiians in distinction to haole, who emblematized foreign business, military, and political interests. "Local has come to represent the common identity of the people of Hawaii and their appreciation" of aloha Kanaka (love for the people) and aloha ʻāina (love of the land), writes Jonathan Okamura.[5] Shared food, language (pidgin), and other syncretic cultural practices thus emerged from the colonization that shaped Hawaiian-haole relations, followed by the arrival of plantation workers from Asia and elsewhere who did not share a common language. John Rosa points to the Massie Affair of the 1930s as consolidating Hawaiʻi residents' sense of we-ness in contrast to haole: "Local culture and society emerged in Hawaiʻi as a direct response to the hegemonic control exerted by a white elite."[6] This led the Islands' diverse population to "accommodate," as Okamura accurately describes, conditions not of their own making.[7]

Centering Black people upsets both our assumptions of "local" and the native/settler binary. The term erases Kanaka specificity, which the native/settler binary addresses. Haunani-Kay Trask's foundational native/settler analysis argues that the term "local" aggregates Hawaiians as just another ethnic group alongside "local" Asian groups, thereby erasing the specificities of their struggles and grievances as people indigenous to this land. In some uses of this binary approach, everyone who is not Native is deemed a settler; therefore anyone who is not Hawaiian is a settler. Alternately, locals are Asian, Hawaiian, and other Brown people; therefore anyone who is White or Black is nonlocal. But these dualities are crosscut by other modes of power.

The native/settler binary has undergone a trajectory similar to debates about "local," with attention to power, agency, and critiques of its binarism. Moving from a native/settler binary toward the triangulation of haole, Asian, and Hawaiian, Trask offers the category of "settlers of color," recognizing that "ideologically, Asians cannot abide categorization with *haole*."[8] She explains, "For our Native people, Asian success proves to be but the latest elaboration of foreign hegemony," and calls for a "local nation" to represent a politicized Asian desire for distinction from haole and defensiveness toward Hawaiians' call for self-determination.[9] Saranillio concludes, "Seemingly in opposition to all forms of white supremacy, 'Local' serves an important liberal component in facilitating multicultural forms of settler colonialism in Hawai'i while denying the fact that many non-Native peoples in Hawai'i benefit from and many times facilitate forms of settler colonialism at the expense of Kānaka 'Ōiwi."[10] As a result, Fujikane and Okamura importantly coined the term "Asian settler colonialism" to interrogate how local Asians take part in settler colonialism.[11]

Are Black people settlers? Vice.com invited Black and Indigenous academics in Canada to respond to the question, "Who is a settler?"[12] The four scholars categorically stated that Black people were not settlers based on agency and choice. A Black scholar clarifies, "I'm not a settler. I'm actually a member of a diaspora that is here against their will. I'm unwillingly complicit in the occupation of Canada."[13] "Settler" in these definitions refers to White people and not Black people, including recent African immigrants. (Discussions about Black, White, and Indigenous people in North America fail to take Asians into account.)[14] One states, "I guess I wouldn't wanna use that term ['settler'] towards Black people because we're really indigenous to everywhere in the world." A Métis writer points not only to choice but also to power: "Settlers benefit from the privilege of having their worldview imposed upon the lands and bodies of everyone living in these lands."[15] According to all these definitions, Black residents in Hawai'i are not settlers. What happens to the presumptions held in these binaries when we center nonWhite people, and particularly the middle-class descendants of slaves as well as immigrants from Africa and elsewhere, who move to a settler society?

To maintain the distinction of Black people from Whites (or Asians in Hawai'i), we may arrive at the notion that "Black people cannot be settlers." Yet the question of Black people's relationship to Hawai'i is significant, and we must consider the Islands' history as a kingdom, republic, territory, and state. Residents today include Black professionals who chose to move and make the Islands their home. Afropessimist absolutist notions of Black abjection—that Black people do not have agency—do not work in this case, or historically. Black arrivals in previous centuries may have had less means than the professionals of today, but they did not arrive in Hawai'i as slaves.

Native and Black relations cannot be understood through a native/settler binary. Rather, we can conceptualize these relationships by recognizing settler colonialism and antiBlackness as co-constitutive processes, as structures that people with specific positionalities navigate differentially. This is the case in Hawai'i, as residents, including Hawaiians, adopt imported antiBlack ideologies. And yet Hawai'i is a settler society that has never been based on slavery and faces military occupation. My research contests the idea that Black people have no agency, that (all) Black people are slaves today, or that one group's liberation should be foregrounded above and before that of all other groups.[16]

Burgeoning North American scholarship theorizes Black and Native relationality, such as Tiffany King's concept of "Black shoals" and Mark Rifkin's study of speculative fiction.[17] These works use humanities methodologies and center a different geographic and racial context. In "New World Grammars," King praises Haunani-Kay Trask's articulation of settler colonialism *and* genocide and challenges the uncritical adoption and influence of "white settler colonial studies traveling from Oceania," referring to Patrick Wolfe and others.[18] However, King ignores Trask's central point: that there are "settlers of color" who participate in these processes. King's triangulation of White settler colonial theory vis-à-vis Black and Native studies (in an attempt to place Trask and Afropessimist scholars in conversation) sidesteps the central question of how these varying groups take part in *on the ground* systems. King wishes to submit to particular ethical critique "Wolfe's and other white [settlers'] work" to "grapple with white human(ist) and earnest intentions and attempts to enact decolonization in everyday thought and practices."[19] However, it seems problematic to categorize this group of scholars based not on their theories and research or politics but on their identities as White settlers. Such an approach misses the range of political, experiential, and intellectual thought within any group (including "white settlers' work"). Grounding our theories in the workings of everyday life reveals too many exceptions to blanket categorizations—both of theorists and of theories.

I do not categorize the participants in this project as settlers. First, this is because those who are both African descended *and* Native Hawaiian contest discrete and seemingly oppositional categories such as native/settler. Dualisms in most race studies scholarship almost always ignore multiracial people, who trouble theories that depend on coherent identity categories. Centering multiracial people, rather than footnoting them as a small, unimportant, or unique demographic, foregrounds individuals who reorient our questions of settler colonialism and Black and Native people. Second, while settler is a critical concept for understanding power and domination in settler societies like Aotearoa, Australia, the Americas, and Hawai'i, there emerges the question of nonWhite settlers and the agency of Black people. That said, Black civilians do not and cannot, even as a group, impose their will and practices on others in a systematic way in the Hawai'i context, with the notable exception of Barack Obama. If we take race and power into account, Black people are not settlers in the Hawaiian Islands. Yet Black residents' varied positions of power, from professional transplants to working-class locals, illuminate the relationship between antiBlackness and settler colonialism.

Although the Native/nonNative distinction is often critical, and Black people make alliances with Kānaka Maoli, I do not conceive of them as "settler allies," as Candace Fujikane does, or as "arrivants," a term used by Jodi Byrd and Judy Rohrer.[20] Veering from settlers, I prefer the terms "residents," "locals," and even the clumsy "transplants" to describe just part of the enormous diversity of Black people in Hawai'i. These terms tune in to peoples' time spent in, and commitment to, the Islands. The quotidian lives of people provide categories of resonance. This may be why Asians, while numerically, culturally, and economically dominant, are not at the center of this book, even though I am a local—or settler—Asian. The term "settler" not only conflates an astonishing array of various groups with differential access to power but also denotes that there is a group (Indigenous or otherwise) with a particular claim to the land from an originary point. Although Leanne Simpson and other Native scholars remind us that Indigenous relationship to land *does not* refer to the kind of proprietary relationship that takes root in the development of capitalism, nonetheless some sovereignty advocates make claims to ownership through the privatization of property.[21]

Rather than focusing on categories of identity, I prioritize analyzing individuals' relationships to systems of power and to one another. Kanaka feminist scholars have recently analyzed the potential and living relationships between Hawaiians and non-Hawaiians through "Indigenous and settler kuleana" ("rights, responsibilities, and authority")[22] toward one another and the land (aloha ʻāina). This perspective provides the conceptual and applied foundation for Hawaiʻi's people to work collaboratively toward sustainable futures rather than focusing on identity labels.[23] Noelani Goodyear-Kaʻōpua analyzes the "complexities of rebuilding Indigenous structures" in contemporary Hawaiʻi, with special attention to the gendered dynamics in cultivation practices that "both muddied and, at times, resolidified colonial logics and binaries."[24] She finds that "the emphasis on personal and collective kuleana rather than on identity allows students and teachers to productively engage in Indigenous cultural revitalization projects together without losing sight of positionality and power."[25] I adopt this perspective in my analysis of how Black individuals navigate structures of settler colonialism, militarism, and racism through their attempts to relate ethically with one another alongside—and sometimes as—Native Hawaiians.

While Afropessimism encourages group-based or positionality-based assumptions of power and politics, my research aligns with the scholar-activist Angela Davis, who finds the most "exciting potential" when we base "the identity on politics rather than the politics on identity."[26] Fieldwork reveals how politics (power) and worldviews bring people together in ways informed by, but not always aligned with, racial categories developed through and for White supremacy. By no means, as should be evident from this project, does this mean that race, identification, and the experiences of particularly racially marked bodies with the state, violence, and other systems of power and inequality do not matter—indeed, my research shows how these things *do* matter.

People who move to the Islands, including members of the African diaspora, enter a place structured by settler colonialism, among other processes of inequality. Their navigation of these structures—rather than their racial identities or nonlocalness—and their relationship to institutions, such as real estate, education, and the military, determine whether or not they advance or contest settler colonial processes. Members of the military, regardless of race, are part of an occupying force. How do we make determinations about the status of Black civilians? We do so by looking at their relations with people and places and their positions in relation to institutions. Alongside settler colonialism— rather, imbricated through colonialism—Hawaiʻi is also a place structured by racism, but race is not the sole organizing principle. Black transplants who tend to find a home in the Islands are those most open to considering themselves and their affinity to others not only through a racial lens but also through locally pertinent principles, such as reciprocity, responsibility (kuleana), and expansive connectedness.

Coming to the Islands

The Black population of Hawai'i may be small, at just under 4 percent, but it represents enormous diversity. They are island-born-and-raised locals as well as transplants to these islands. The latter include recently arrived college students as well as elders of the civil rights generation who have been here for decades. These nonlocals had different motivations for coming and differing orientations to community and identity. Hawai'i may, on the one hand, be exceptional for attracting a particularly diverse Black population; it is more likely, however, that it is a place that encourages people to disclose their complicated life paths and pasts.

Who Are Black Newcomers?

Diversity among the forty-one transplants I interviewed includes where they come from, when they came, and how they identify along gender and racial lines. Twenty (twelve men, seven women, and one nonbinary participant) are long-term residents who have been in the Islands for decades and consider it to be their home; the twenty-one (fifteen men and six women) newcomers who came within the past five years of our interview had not been in the Islands long enough to decide to stay. Thirteen of the forty-one are multiracial, and two identify as queer. They come from across the continental United States, from Southern California to upstate New York, from Arkansas to Alaska. Most are the children of African Americans. Some are the children of parents in interethnic unions from African and Caribbean nations; others are the children of African American servicemen and Asian women. Like many Hawai'i residents, they are members of overlapping diasporas: the US military, work programs, and the diaspora of families and communities strewn across the globe based on love once forged and then broken, and then reformed through divorces and new relationships.

Transplants can be divided roughly into fifths, with about nine people in each group, coming from California, particularly Southern California (San Diego, Los Angeles); the East Coast (Maryland, Virginia, DC, New York); the South (Mississippi, Alabama, Georgia, Louisiana, Arkansas, and Florida); the Midwest, especially Chicago (Illinois, Ohio, Iowa, and Missouri); and a smaller number (three) from the northwestern United States (Washington) and Alaska.

The proportionally small number of transplants from the US South (eight people) marks an important distinction between these civilians and the military population in Hawaiʻi.

The final fifth, or nine people, were born outside the United States (many more of their parents were not American). They include two people from Asia (Japan and Korea), three from Central Africa (Congo and Zambia), two from Europe (England and Germany), and two from the Caribbean (Cuba and the Dominican Republic). A substantial number of US-born participants also had significant experience living abroad with their families, spending several years in countries like Mexico, Mauritius, and Sāmoa. Most of the participants had lived in multiple places before arriving in Hawaiʻi, thereby informing their global perspectives. For some, the Islands were to be another temporary residence that they have since moved on from; for the majority, however, Hawaiʻi is home.

Hawaiʻi is not easy to get to and is one of the most expensive places to live—so what draws arrivals? Black civilians come for a set of reasons lost in the scholarly attention to military history in the Pacific. These transplants came for two main reasons: education and work, including their own or their parents' jobs. Despite this pattern, they relate a fascinating set of reasons for why they specifically selected this place, telling us what Hawaiʻi offers people of African descent. The appeal of the Black Pacific contrasts with much of the Black Atlantic: the draw of Asia and their desire for a familiar yet different nonWhite society.

Many of the recent Black arrivals I spoke with, who came after 2000, were students at the University of Hawaiʻi at Mānoa (UH), the state's flagship university. Growing up as a faculty brat, I spent much of my childhood at the university, becoming familiar with its architecture and community. I noticed the increasing Black student population over the past decade, as well as the growing numbers of Black residents and tourists in town (Honolulu). The nineteen delightful Black students I interviewed who came for undergraduate and graduate degrees (mostly at UH, but also at Hawaiʻi Pacific University) told me that they, unlike the professionals I spoke with (including four professors), intended to stay only as long as their college careers. Some stayed on to pursue their master's degrees or because they were in a relationship with someone local. Among them were those who earned athletic scholarships to play volleyball, football, or basketball and represent a much larger and recognized (and recognizable) population of Black athletes on Oʻahu. One Black Sāmoan man from the East Coast said, "I came, pretty much, just for football and education."

In lieu of a professional sports team, the UH football team—the Rainbow Warriors—is a major source of local pride. Daily newspapers update readers about college and high school athletics, especially when football teams have a good season and participate in championships and bowl games (the 2017 high school state finals drew twenty thousand fans).[27] High school teams include girl players; an exceptional number of Sāmoans coming from or through Hawai'i go on to play in the National Football League (NFL). The UH football roster consistently features a sea of Brown faces with significant numbers of Black and White players. Hawaiian, local Asian, and multiracial (Hawaiian Chinese, etc.) players team up with Sāmoans and Tongans from Hawai'i, Sāmoa, Tonga, Utah, and California to form the local and Polynesian contingent, while recruited African American and White players represent the continental United States. Annual rosters show over one hundred players; Black athletes make up to a quarter of the team, including Black Sāmoans and a few Black locals. While tensions can manifest between local and Polynesian, on the one hand, and Black and White players, on the other (a racial division similar to tensions between locals and the military), their pregame practices attempt to bring the team together. They used to perform the haka, a dance adopted from the Maori, which united the players through an Oceanic expression of masculinity.[28]

The team's success over the years has made national news, winning bowl games and producing Super Bowl winners Jesse Sapolu, Jason Elam, Ma'a Tanuvasa, and Adrian Klemm. Hawai'i is home to the Heisman Trophy winner and Saint Louis High School alum Marcus Mariota (Sāmoan), and for many decades Aloha Stadium on O'ahu hosted the NFL Pro Bowl and still holds the Hula Bowl.[29] College sports thus bring a significant number of young Black men to the Islands, where they play on a largely Polynesian team. This route of arrival reinforces the historical gender imbalance among Black residents, although universities also recruit women athletes like Eden, a basketball player I interviewed. A greater gender balance exists among those who come strictly for studies.

Black college students selected UH because of their interest in Asia. They also majored in sociology, psychology, and ethnic studies; they earned master's degrees in social work and from the School of Management; still others were housed at the East-West Center. They were drawn by the Islands' Asia adjacency, demographics, and robust offerings in Asian studies and languages. A transplant from the East Coast says, "I looked, and there was [UH] Mānoa, and then I saw the list of majors—they had Chinese and Korean and Tagalog, and all the, like, Polynesian languages. And I thought that was so cool. So I was

Figure 3.1 The University of Hawai'i Rainbow Warriors football team performs the haka. Source: Todd Bigelow.

like," she chuckles, "'I need to go to this school, right now!'" These students grew up in the 1990s intrigued by Asia and especially Japan. In Hawai'i, they could major or earn an MA in Asian studies and encounter people of various Asian ethnicities, including foreign students from Asia.

Unlike my generation born in the 1970s, these youth were less influenced by martial arts and the kung fu flicks aired on Black Belt Theater and more by Japanese pop culture and the internet. One studied Japanese in her Maryland high school: "Since I was a kid, I started to get interested in Japanese culture, like anime and cartoons. It was *Pokémon* that started it!" she laughed. These self-described nerds grew up in the 1990s in Silver Spring or Baltimore, Maryland, playing video games, reading manga, and loving anime. Avril, an exuberant undergraduate, loved Japanese language and culture (and Japanese men, she says) and went to Japan as a high school exchange student. Youngsters, like dark-skinned and quiet Ethan from Georgia, who sported an impressive Afro and told me he had a Japanese grandparent, came to study art and ethnic studies and wanted to create video games. Another Black student came intending to become an English teacher in Japan ("Hawai'i has the best Japanese program") and went on to do just that.

Graduate students were also drawn to Asia. I arranged to meet Anthony at the UH Campus Center. He was an expressive and open student from West Baltimore who wore his hair in cornrows and generously shared the details of his life for hours. He grew up in a middle-class blue-collar family during the crack epidemic, living in "bad areas" where "you didn't really talk to strangers, you made sure you watched your kids, and when you could, you got the hell out of there." Not expected to go to college ("Just don't get anyone pregnant," said his mother), he attended community college and then graduated from a four-year institution. Anthony found himself unable to compete for a good government job against those with military ties, and he couldn't afford to buy car insurance or to commute to jobs because of Baltimore's "crappy public transportation." He didn't want to live like that—his mother was held up at gunpoint (twice), and it got dark too early in the winter. Working at the public library, he decided "it's time for graduate school." Compelled to leave, Anthony enrolled in the master's program in Asian studies at UH. "I know I want to do Asian studies," he says, "I want to do something international. I want to continue Japanese language. So Hawai'i makes sense." He had played Nintendo in his youth and would watch "*Dragon Ball* or *Dragon Warrior*, and I didn't even know they were Japanese. Kung fu flicks, too. They used to come on every Saturday on the local station. And you'd be like—you had no idea—you didn't know the cultural aspects behind it. You weren't informed; it was like, 'That's cool, you know, and that comes from Asia.' It was sort of an Orientalism, in retrospect." According to Bill Mullen's conception of Afro-Orientalism, these college students reflect a cultural and at times political alignment of African Americans with Asians that describes their interest in Hawai'i as an affiliation with Asia.[30]

Getting to the Islands is expensive, and once one is here, it is nearly impossible to afford. The median price of a single-family home on Oʻahu was around $800,000 in 2019. Thus older recent arrivals, in their thirties and forties, came for work. "I was brought to Hawai'i purely on employment," says a media professional. Others include a pastor, a small-business entrepreneur, and an especially large number of lawyers and former military personnel. Because of the expense, only a few people came on a fluke or by chance, in search of adventure. They tended to be older than university students, although the older arrivals too were drawn to Asia's closeness. This was especially the case for women from Asia who hoped to raise their children in a place and culture that was near-but-not-Asia: "It was pretty random, actually," said a Black Japanese twenty-something who describes her mother's choice as less than random: "'Cause [my mom is] Japanese, so we needed a place she could speak Japanese and English, so . . . she was looking for opportunities for herself." Single

African American mothers also came to start a new life: one from the continental United States, choosing between Hawaiʻi and India, settled on one of the smaller Hawaiian Islands. The Black mother of another participant came "because her friend was coming, and it sounded like a good idea—get far away from my dad."

Single men also came for adventure and followed friends. A Black celebrity impersonator who came in the 1980s settled on the Big Island. A few Black men followed their local girlfriends to the Islands after college, while others stayed on after graduation because they met local partners. Black lawyers, surfers, and music industry folks who visited and then fell in love with the Islands decided to make Hawaiʻi their home. Given the diverse motives of these more recent transplants I spoke with, I wondered, Who are the old-timers, and what brought them to the Islands?

Who Are Black Long-Term Residents?

The twenty long-term residents, who range from their forties to their eighties and came between 1975 and 2004, represent a range of professions and share a familiarity with Black people, culture, and history. In addition to the military, schooling and work in education brought the earliest among them. Black professors, who are often hired for their expertise on race, work at UH but remain sorely underrepresented across the Islands. Former dean and professor Miles Jackson told me, "I like to remind people that I came to Hawaiʻi as part of the navy, and what united our experiences were those signs that said, 'Dogs and Sailors Keep Off.'" Jackson and the former UH ethnic studies professor Kathryn Takara are the preeminent scholars on African Americans in Hawaiʻi. In addition to her publications and publishing house (Pacific Raven Press), Takara has collected the life stories of African American residents.[31] One of the largest employers in the Islands, the university brought both these scholars: Takara left the dynamism of the Bay Area in the 1960s to pursue graduate school and married a local Okinawan man, and Jackson, who first arrived through the military, married an African American woman and relocated permanently as a professor in 1975. The Hawaiʻi-raised children of professional transplants like these work in music, the nonprofit sector, nursing, and the service industry and identify as Black locals.

In the 1980s, another set of participants arrived, looking for an alternative to the dreary Seattle landscape or because they were tired of the Los Angeles city life, for instance. They went on to become lawyers, entertainers, and state workers on and off Oʻahu. Around 1990, four young men came, two right out of high school, including a nineteen-year-old soldier from a small southern town, a Black and White Californian surfer, a Congolese professional, and a Black Hawaiian Japanese college student. The 2000s brought others who found solace here, including a nurse from Mississippi married to an African American man in the Marine Corps, and a blues musician who came from Georgia via the West Coast.

Despite living in the Islands for decades, Black long-term residents retain a Black/White understanding of race. In contrast to Black locals, all the nonlocals grew up with an *aroundness* of Blackness, even in White neighborhoods. One professional, for instance, grew up in a middle-class, mostly White suburb in New York State, where her parents participated in African American organizations and exposed her to African art. She attended a historically Black university and became an expert on race. Those from the United States, the Caribbean, Africa, and even Asia (where they had access to African Americans near military bases) grew up with and around Black people and in communities that taught them Black history and the effects of White supremacy that led to slavery, colonialism in Africa, and persistent antiBlack racism. They also experienced particular racialization and explicit and structural racism as African-descended people. In other words, Black transplants were racially literate.[32] Through this familiarity, they developed a sense of self and relationship to Blackness and a global Black community, generally framed by the one-drop rule. Thus they often identify as "Black" or "African American," or as "Black Sāmoan" and "Black Korean" for biracial individuals, in ways that were more consistent and less ambivalent than Black locals.

Hawai'i also influences the self-identifications of Black transplants. These men and women, who may generally be read as "Black" in their hometowns, often told me of an unexpected ancestor—a Chinese or Japanese grandparent, or they acknowledged their White great-grandmother—as they related their ancestries to me. While no homogeneous "Black" identity exists across the United States, nonetheless, far more people of African descent in Hawai'i identify in ways other than Black only. This practice arises from the foundational structures of the Hawaiian Kingdom as a society not based on race and one in which ancestry and genealogy, family histories, and geographic location are key. Before we get to the experiences of Black transplants, what were their preconceptions of these Pacific islands? These shape both their impetus for coming and their consequent experiences upon relocation.

Preconceptions and Appeal of the Islands

I looked outside at the dreary Pacific Northwest landscape and spotted a squirrel. My eyes returned to the picture of Hawai'i that popped up on my computer screen with its visions of palm trees, 'ukulele music. Then I looked out the window, and I looked back at the ad, and I'm thinking, "I'm outta here." I had a friend who moved to the Islands, a friend who was a pilot who got me a half-price ticket, and I sold everything I owned and I was done. So, anyway, the squirrel was responsible for getting me here.

BLACK OLD-TIMER

I would prefer to be in Hawai'i because it's very peaceful, inspiring, and spiritual. Our home is located in a small, picturesque hamlet, nestled between the mountains and the ocean, surrounded by copious tropical plants, fruit trees, and a garden with my dad's collard greens. I like that, you know, a Tuskegee girl, a country girl in a rural setting.

KATHRYN TAKARA, POET AND LONG-TERM BLACK RESIDENT, INTERVIEWED BY ISHMAEL REED, 2018

Why did one Sāmoan-identified Black man from California choose to attend college in Hawai'i over athletic scholarships from Texas and Nevada? What made a Black mother settle on O'ahu rather than in India? Black residents shared fascinating emotive reasons for the Islands' lure. Tourism shaped their preconceptions, along with "what you see on television," including the show *Magnum, P.I.* They figured it would be a "tropical paradise" or would "be like an Elvis movie." Given the power of the tourism industry, they knew it was a vacation destination, with images of women dancing the hula, volcanoes, and Waikīkī filling their imagination. "That was it—beach, beach, beach," a man from Southern California thought, "but I knew there was gonna be a lot more once I got here." Of course, climate and topography were at the front of their minds; a musician articulated the appeal: "If you just draw a line across the latitude from Hawai'i, you would end up in Georgia [where he is from], so the climate suits me." They opted to leave the rainy and too gray parts of the Pacific Northwest for the O'ahu surf. These reasons only touch the surface of their motivations to relocate.

Black people are drawn to Hawai'i for reasons different from those that draw haole and Japanese tourists wishing for an exotic yet welcoming paradise. Transplants are propelled from their homes by experiences specific to African-descended people, including persistent racism. When some "mostly White adult males" cautioned a Black Mexican student about the reverse racism she would experience as a non-Asian person in Hawai'i, Angel conspiratorially recounted to me her response, enjoyed with a laugh: "Yeah, but I'm not White, so I don't think that's going to be an issue." The social appeal includes the fact that this is (not) the United States—it was like a different country ("Do I need to call you long distance?" asked a student's mother), yet familiar, using the same currency and language. Others highlighted its difference from their past that they wanted to leave behind: a mother brought her Black Mexican child so that he wouldn't end up in a California gang; others wanted to get away from their small hometowns in the South or escape a bad relationship.

The move to the Islands is a response to daily life with racism, surveillance, and the "pressure" that Black men especially and some women say they faced across the United States. An old-timer wanted a change from her East Coast suburban White community, ostensibly because she "didn't have anything to do." Yet she went on to recall that "I would go to the stores where they've seen me for ten years, but they'd still follow me around." An older man witnessed the corporate development of a massive new jail on the West Coast: it "looked like a college campus—it was way big. Big, big, big—expansive." He reasoned, "They didn't seem to have enough criminals to fill up a jail that size," and he took that—along with divination from a squirrel—as a sign that it was "time to get out of this place." "I can't spend too much time in racist environments," said another Black man, who lives on the Big Island. They invoke their relief from being monitored and the threat of police violence they faced in cities like Chicago and Phoenix. "Of course, being an African American in [Los Angeles], I would get harassed by the police, stopped or thrown in jail for traffic light violations." A man in the music business grew up amid rival gangs on the South Side of Chicago and came "just to get away. Away from everything." Another multiracial entertainer explains, "I just came initially just to get away, and now to discover." These reflections point to another emotional draw: the opportunity for chance and adventure.

Transplants are drawn to island demographics. If a couple of people purposefully did not read up on the Islands beforehand ("I didn't have any preconceptions," recalls a southerner who arrived two decades ago), prospective university students tended to conduct preliminary research, checking the internet for information. A student from the East Coast whose parents are from West Africa "did a lot of research" and thus knew that the population was mostly Asian, "which is a factor in why I wanted to come here." Despite their awareness of demographics, one young man had not realized "the Japanese influence would be so strong." But they were particularly interested in the position of Black people in their new home.

"I just saw stats . . . and then I saw [the numbers of] Black [people], and I was like, whoa! It was like 2 percent or something! . . . I was like, wow: Blacks are 1.7 percent!" citing nonmilitary figures. A dark-skinned and athletic man from California saw photos of "the original Hawaiian people. I was like, 'They look Black, man.' 'Cause I see Africa is like the root, and then we expanded. So I was like, 'Man, African people are from Hawai'i too?' So I said, 'I'm gonna go there.'" Echoing this graduate student, a professor says, "I always found the location interesting for some of the same reasons that you're looking at in your research . . . as a place not framed by the Black and White binary." People were generally drawn to this diversity, including an athlete who felt "closer here, because I was close to Polynesians" back in Los Angeles.

Island demographics were both different from these people's previous communities and familiar to them. It reminded one of her family's home in the Caribbean, and another concurred, "People live outside, and there is shared space [and] extended family." Others, such as a Black and White man I met while he was working at the Apple Store in Ala Moana (a large outdoor mall), compared Hawai'i with different Pacific islands. He said it was like the Marshall Islands, where he had gone for work: "Dude, it's like a bigger version of it."

Their reasons diverge significantly from those of tourists looking for an exotic escape or soldiers placed on rotation. Not just its "diversity" but Hawai'i's nonWhiteness hints at the unique set of possibilities for Black arrivals. They experience a "majority-minority" society, but one in which Black people are not the primary minority group, in contrast to their former homes. Like their predecessors over the centuries, recent arrivals feel encouraged to cultivate communities based not on ancestry but on affinity. A Black Mexican long-term resident described finding

> sort of a camaraderie that was available to me that was never available to me in [my home state], because it was easier to find cultural commonalities and outlooks in life with other Brown people, like Filipinos, et cetera, et cetera, local people, Hawaiians. It was easier to find commonalities in our ancestors' histories, even though they're unrelated, but similar experiences that we can relate to, that made it more conceptual, that I could

have a bond with them that I could never have with my White friends [back home]. They were my friends, but they were also White, and you always knew that.

This transplant found commonalities with other people of color and forged camaraderie that did not need to take White people into account. Simple multiculturalism or the social desire to temporarily be around a multitude of difference was thus not the total draw. They had racial—that is, political—motivations.

Hawaiʻi does not conform to the US racial paradigm. While Black transplants make comments similar to those made by other newcomers ("it is diverse and beautiful"), Hawaiʻi is also a new place to fit in as a nonWhite person attuned to racial dynamics. Angel, the multiracial Black woman from Alaska, says, "I wanted to live in a place and finish my degree that I didn't feel so isolated in." She had "heard about the whole quote-unquote 'reverse racism.' To be honest, that kind of appealed to me. 'Okay, that sounds kind of interesting, kind of a reprieve.'" Doing his homework before arriving for graduate school, Mark appreciated what he learned about the Hawaiian sovereignty movement: "I noticed that they had an indigenous Native movement, and being in Southern California, I recognized that amongst Native Americans. So I was like, they are trying to get sovereignty too, like the Native Americans. That's what's up." He identified with this as part of a broader struggle: "I figured, there's people struggling there. People with dark-skinned complexions. I think I could make it, you know what I'm sayin'?" He was not unique: a Black musician from Miami had not learned much about Hawaiʻi, but he was aware "that it was occupied territory." This shaped Deonte's understanding of its status: "When you have those kinds of roots, essentially, whatever the ruling class is doesn't really coincide with the soul of the people. So that was my very initial understanding coming here: I was coming to a place that may have been appropriated by America but was not America." In other words, these Black transplants did not superficially appreciate island demographics or simply think of Hawaiʻi as an exotic getaway; rather, they commented on the political implications of this site of Indigenous resistance against haole oppression—resistance that they related to as Black people.

Black transplants had race- and gender-specific reasons to move thousands of miles away from their homes, in addition to having the finances to do so. Leaving the pressures of the continental United States, and especially antiBlack racism, is key, along with practical reasons to attend a school or start a job in the middle of the Pacific. These pressures emanated from the police, from structural and everyday racism, and from the desire to leave the tight spaces of small towns or hectic city life; women, in addition to looking for a reprieve and something new, also fled relationships or came to an Asia-adjacent society for a fresh start where they could raise their mixed children.

Although they did some research into their potential home before arrival, these transplants were struck by the alternative racial structure of these Islands, with their robust Native presence. Here they reflected on being in a majority nonWhite space, and one in which Black people did not constitute a significant population. These contours made Black transplants hip to the possibilities of Black life in the Pacific, a place of "less pressure." But how did the Islands measure up to their expectations? And did these transplants continue to integrate into Hawai'i's society, as Black people throughout the nineteenth century had done? Or did the twentieth century bring a conflation of Black people with the military forceful enough to call forth dominant misconceptions about Black men and women in the twenty-first century? Additionally, would they find it too jarring and unfamiliar, or would this become their new home, luring them with new possibilities of belonging?

Black Life in the Islands

One thing that is different is that Hawai'i is not frightening. There isn't the terror like there is south of the Canadian border. It's a little bit easier, not having to fear someone gunning down Mānoa Center or a tea bagger. There's not that sense of terror, and social violence is ratcheted down.

BLACK NEWCOMER AND EDUCATOR

Hawai'i is a unique place; I guess all the states are. Part of the reason it's nice to me is that there's no White majority. It's different that way. Some Caucasian folks can't handle that. They don't get some of the so-called White privilege that they're used to getting. At the same time, I don't think there's the same paranoia about Black folks, which is not to say that everything is hunky-dory.

BLACK PROFESSIONAL AND RECENT ARRIVAL

As anyone who has moved to a new place knows, one's hopes and expectations of one's new home (especially one so deeply mediated as Hawai'i) do not always pan out. Turning to Black transplants' experiences in the Islands, we see that what begins as an expected commentary on the beauty and distinctiveness of the Islands soon turns to more complicated discussions of belonging, race, localness, and racism. Black transplants' perspectives, which are distinct from those of nonBlack transplants, inform their interpretation of these experiences. This distinction is especially articulated in Black transplants' interactions with—and desires to differentiate themselves from—haole.

Unsurprisingly, arrivals commented on Hawai'i's beauty and warmth. Several "fell in love" with the Islands right away. This is a special place, to be experienced somatically: "It was amazing. The environment, it's just beautiful here. I see the mountains, and it's just lush and green," say even those who prefer colder climates. Indeed, their experience is rapturous, much as Honolulu-born Barack Obama reminisces: "I can retrace the first steps I took as a child and be stunned by the beauty of the islands. The trembling blue plane of the Pacific. The moss-covered cliffs and cool rush of Manoa Falls, with its ginger blossoms and high canopies filled with the sounds of invisible birds. The North Shore's thunderous waves, crumbling as if in slow-motion reel. The shadows off Pali's peak; the sultry, scented air. Hawaii!"[33] Hawai'i nurtured their spirits, as well: "I felt the spirit of the land, of the people, and it really connected with me," said more than one person. Alice, a dreadlocked woman raised in a military family, felt that access to nature made her new home "healing. I love the weather. I love the look. I love the vibe," she reflects. Commentary on warmth extended to people, who were "friendly"—especially to Black people.[34] "It seems that people tend to talk to us [Black people] more and have a dialogue with us more" than in Texas, said this recent transplant. If a Black southerner was intrigued by this "kindness," a man from Los Angeles was skeptical: "I took certain things as 'what do they want from me?' because people were just so nice."

Once they reached Hawai'i, transplants experienced the demographic diversity that they had heard so much about. "It just felt like a bigger Carson [in Los Angeles County]. You got Asians, you got Blacks, not many Blacks, but you got everybody here." It's a place where "you can get people [from] all over the world in one place and interact with them." The large footprint of Hawaiians and their political and cultural presence strikes many Black Americans used to being the main minority within the context of Native "disappearance" across the United States. The Asian predominance, while expected, was surprising: "I had culture shock. Seeing all these Japanese, menus in Japanese, even street signs. [It's] like Los Angeles with its Spanish/English mix."

Living among such a heterogeneous population also called on them to explain and perform Blackness. "In some ways, it's liberating if you have close friends that are not Black and they really understand you," one basketball player found. The lanky and striking dark-skinned student describes happily dispelling myths about Black people to her roommates. In a context that is both majority nonWhite and has few Black people, "Now we can see how people interact with each other here, even though their skin is like mine."

If before they arrived, transplants were aware of Hawai'i's difference from "the mainland," how did they experience this difference after they resettled, and what do island demographics do to the Black/White binary? Hawai'i challenged transplants' ideas of belonging as they attempted to find home—and possibly liberation—in a place where Blackness has a different significance. Do Black immigrants experience the Islands as a multicultural paradise, or would their transplanted racial lens stall their adoption of a local perspective that advocates an expansive, rather than racial, sense of belonging?

Understanding the Islands: Nonlocal but Not Haole

Hawai'i is known for its "diversity," but its various groups experience island life distinctly. For instance, everyday and scholarly accounts document White people's discomfiting sense of being outnumbered, with some additionally charging reverse racism. We know less about how Black people experience the Islands. To their surprise, Black people often find that locals conflate Black and haole people, conceiving both as foreigners and as part of the military and thus deflating the Black/White binary. Living in Hawai'i challenges the dominant framework of race relations in the United States; it also uncovers robust social lives outside the binary.

Every transplant mentioned the local/nonlocal divide that grouped Black and White people as nonlocal, outsiders, and in the military. In response, Black transplants wish to clarify their relationship to White people. They engage dialogically with this process by refusing to align with haole who attempt to bond based on their shared "discrimination." For example, two Black women (with equal bemusement) discussed the "reverse racism" that haole experience. Eden the college athlete said, "I hear so many stories of White people who are like, 'Man, we're so discriminated against [here].'" Shaking her head, the southerner exclaimed her mocking response: "You don't even know the half!" referring to the racism Black people face regularly. Alice, the more recent transplant from Texas, described a coworker pursuing connection over their presumed sameness: "I was talking to a coworker of mine—she's a White lady—and she said, 'They see us as foreigners.' I was just like, 'I felt this way my whole life.' I don't feel like [an] other because I've been that way. She couldn't understand that. She's like, 'No, no, we're all together.'" Alice clarified in no uncertain terms, "No. This is just what *you're* experiencing. I know what it's like to feel that."

These patterns pull together the scholarship on local culture in Hawai'i and race in the United States. (Non)localness and race together shape the experiences of Black residents. Questions about being local or not, or aspersions and jokes about one's nonbelonging, point to the political debate over rights to call Hawai'i "home" moderated by race (Black and White presumed nonlocalness) and one's relation to the military and tourism economy.[35] Local and nonlocal are racialized and performed through acts of cultural adoption or refusal. Identifiably Black men with shorn hair, local or not, *all* described being mistaken for members of the military, and they learn and understand why this is so. A professor explained, "You're either military, a tourist, or if you happen to be a young guy of a certain size, you're playing for a sports team at UH." Eden said the same: "If a Black man [is] walking in, he has to be in the military. He cannot be anything else." However, drawing from her women's studies and ethnic studies courses, she specifies locals' particular tropes of expected Black womanhood: "As far as the intersectional approach with race and gender and class, when I'm walking down the street and somebody looks at me, they either think, 'Oh, she has to be in the military, or she has to be a prostitute or a stripper.' Like, they objectify me in three groups." Eden *is* here as an athlete; however, she is not, unlike her male counterparts, presumed to be so because of her gender. Black transplants' experiences are based on what locals presume Black people *to be* and what they presume they *must not be*, ideas that are informed by twentieth-century encounters with Black people instead of knowledge about earlier Black histories in the Islands.

One distinction from the rest of the United States is the local practice of marking Whiteness. This includes using "haole" as a common descriptor, contributing to the awareness haole have of their Whiteness. Additionally, there is a local denigration of White social norms ("No ack so haolefied!" ["Don't act so White!"]). As such, African-descended people see these practices as examples of Indigenous and multiracial resistance to White supremacy. Black people find a society that is part of the United States, but where its mostly nonWhite population does not broadly aspire to Whiteness. One can often find oneself in nonWhite spaces—these do not have to be planned. Transplants remark how explicitly many locals of various backgrounds speak about White people and theorize Whiteness through critique: "We are surprised because in Hawai'i we are made aware of our whiteness," writes the Hawai'i scholar Judy Rohrer.[36] In her analysis of haole, Rohrer explains that in Hawai'i, "We are suddenly in the racial minority, which is uncomfortable or at least unusual for most of us, and all around us people are using racial terms and talking about race. Additionally, there people are not Black, the racialized 'other' we are most familiar with, or rather think we are."[37] Without exception, every participant felt that haole people faced "the worst" social denigration of all groups.

One participant explained how "Whites in Hawai'i have a different experience. It's a bittersweet experience being White in Hawai'i." This includes dismissals or the irrelevance of haole to central conversations, some jobs not available to haole (or, more accurately, jobs [as well as land and schools] reserved for Native Hawaiians), and denigrating White social norms ("Braddah, da meteorologist stay so haolified" [Brother, the meteorologist is so haolified]). Some claim this to be "reverse racism" and pursue litigation—a strategic misinterpretation that highlights the limits of a race-only view that purposefully rejects the legal specificity of indigeneity.[38] By contrast, a local (including Hawaiian) approach names White people ("dat haole cashier") and sometimes denigrates Whiteness ("dat fuckin' haole cashier") as anticolonial critique: of haole economic domination, the political incorporation of Hawai'i into the United States, and the military occupation. Rohrer, a former Hawai'i resident, reflects, "The problem of being or becoming haole has never gone away," because residents often raise "the problem of being ... haole."[39] In attempts by onetime Honolulu mayor Mufi Hannemann, a German Sāmoan, to garner support from the Hawai'i Carpenters' Union, he told them, "I look like you, you look like me," marking the racial distinction of his opponent, New York–born haole long-term resident Neil Abercrombie.[40] Does this lifelong (racial) distinction bear out for Black people?

When I asked whether or not Black transplants considered themselves to be local, even long-term residents were at times unsure. Whereas every Black local except for one (born in Japan) identifies as local, newcomers understandably express greater ambivalence. As a Black long-term resident describes, "Hawai'i has managed to complicate things a bit. If you are an outsider, you are, period. You can be here for a long time, but it doesn't necessarily have to do with your race." This ambivalence parallels Black locals' hesitation in claiming Blackness. In both cases, the doubt comes less from negative ideas about that identity, and more from the sense that one was *not familiar enough* with the experience and lacked cultural knowledge to claim it. This includes reminders of their nonbelonging such as when locals ask transplants, "You military?" and when Black locals were told, "You're not really Black." Transplants felt that fellow Black people who left the Islands did so because they did not adapt to local culture and needed to have access to a larger Black community. By contrast, those who have made the Islands their home found that adopting local customs was key to their acceptance.

There is no one prescribed way to "be local," and Black people expand our understanding of who is local. A Black and White California surfer at one point had ʻehu (sun-dyed) curls and skin darkened by hours in the sun. A Congolese transplant, by contrast, worked for a corporation and tended to dress "business casual," which can include short-sleeved button-down shirts (I haven't seen him in an aloha shirt), dress pants, shoes, and hair shorn with more style than allowed in the military. Maira, a Black and Japanese woman who wore jeans and a sweatshirt and worked in a mall where she was often called on to interpret for Japanese clients (they were surprised by her bilingualism), spoke to me in proper English rather than pidgin. On the other hand, a long-term resident from Alabama living in the countryside enjoys wearing large flowers in her curly reddish hair, and her gold Hawaiian heirloom bracelets and sundresses reflect the Islands' bright and relaxed style. Black transplants adapt to local culture in a variety of ways to reveal localness as a cultural and often panracial embodied category.

Whereas "local haole" is an acknowledged and significant part of Hawaiʻi's population, according to some Black transplants, you cannot be a Black local—that is, locals will not accept you as being from Hawaiʻi. "There's *no* sense that you could be local or belong here in any other context," a Black professor says. Black locals sharply disagree—as do those transplants who chose to settle here and have families. Black newcomers who decide not to adapt to local customs will likely encounter the presumption that they are not from the Islands; on the other hand, those who adapt to local cultural practices can be and are seen as local. Among those who became old-timers, some felt at home in Hawaiʻi. Yet as one Hawaiian Black Japanese transplant clarified, "I mean that home is Hawaiʻi but I'm not local," despite speaking pidgin to his friends in Waiʻanae and later becoming fluent in Hawaiian. Localness, feelings of home, race, and belonging, thus interrelate in these stories.

Black arrivals highlight their *racial* distinction from haole to drive home a point: antihaole sentiment is specific to White people for the unique power they have wielded across the Pacific (and the globe, for that matter).[41] Haole continue to enjoy a high economic and political status that stems from the takeover of the Islands, a history that students generally learn about in local schools and witness every day. These dynamics make it particularly unpleasant for haole in Hawaiʻi. White people—whether locals or newcomers—face the manifestation of antihaole sentiment, including verbal insults and sometimes physical assault. This comes as a relief to Black people, who note the irony of seeing White people as the target of discrimination. But racism and antiforeign (anti-nonlocal) sentiment are not the same. Whereas Black people face racism in Hawai'i, they *also* confront antimilitary sentiment (shared with haole), which is *distinct from,* and not completely encapsulated by, antiBlack racism. At the same time, their overall positive acceptance by locals means that Black transplants can have a very real sense of "belonging" that proves more challenging for haole, whether island born or not. These disparate responses to Black and White people contest the idea of a blanket "antiforeign sentiment" (e.g., nonlocal prejudice). A local/nonlocal binary, like native/settler, which also conflates Black and White people, is crosscut with crucial racial distinctions.

Haole attempt to create a sense of shared oppression with Black people as nonlocals, perhaps to remain unaccountable for their Whiteness. Black people may extract themselves from this uneasy alliance to maintain White accountability. Discrimination against nonlocals, understood by aggrieved haole as "reverse racism," becomes a way not to discuss the specific reasons for antihaole sentiment. How does the assumption of nonlocalness influence Black transplants? Is this what causes some to leave, or does it paradoxically become a source of freedom, inspiring them to stay in the Islands?

Responding to the Islands: Expansive Identifications

It feels like in Hawai'i you can escape your Blackness. People don't assume you are Black. People don't assume what is your ethnicity.

BLACK LONG-TERM RESIDENT FROM THE US SOUTH

> AMY (fair-skinned Black student with a large brown Afro): One of the things people would ask me [when I first came to Hawai'i was] "What are you?" or "Where [are] you from?" I'm like, "What do you mean, what am I?" I didn't understand it, and I got offended and thought it was none of their business. Because I'm like, "I am human?" But then a lot of people actually confuse me to be Hawaiian. I'm like, "I'm not Hawaiian." Like one woman thought I was Asian. I'm like, "I have no Asian blood in me whatsoever." I thought it was weird at first, like, "Why do you want to know?" I would just say "Black." But then my friend Nico actually was like, "Why do you say that?" (*in an offended tone*). I'm like, "Because I am" (*short laugh*).

NITASHA: What is he saying?

AMY: He's saying I should recognize everything that's in me. I'm like, "That's a little difficult to do." But [now] I'm usually just like, "I'm mixed, multicultural—I have lots of things going on in my family." So I think it's because of the mainland mentality, or if you're mixed with Black, you're Black. I never really thought about it before.

EXCHANGE BETWEEN THE AUTHOR AND A BLACK NEWCOMER

If locals find the one-drop rule puzzling, transplants find this mirror exchange confusing. At first, Amy from Maryland was taken aback when locals repeatedly asked her what she was. She grew up practicing hypodescent and also considered the question rude, something that was "none of their business." However, her local friend explained that "you aren't just Black—you should name all the things you are." As a result, she and other recent arrivals told me that they were Black, and also, without my prompting, told me of their Native and White ancestries (multiracial transplants, except one, were already accustomed to recounting their backgrounds). In this way, Black transplants adapt to local practices as the Islands affect their identifications.

In Hawai'i, Blackness becomes less salient, shown in the prevalent practice of identifying as "Black and _____." Hawaiian epistemologies of self-location through genealogy and place rub against the one-drop rule. A Black-only identity is not the default among African-descended people in Hawai'i, despite centuries of exposure to US racial ideologies. As revealed in chapter 2, Black locals often identify as local and with their African and nonBlack ancestries. This is not naïveté about how Black people elsewhere identify or about hypodescent; rather, it is an expression of Hawaiian approaches to self and others. Hawai'i also influences people from elsewhere, leading transplants to change their identifications and feel more at home.

One exception is Janet, the daughter of a White British mother and an African American father. This older long-term resident identified as "African American. No hapa, no mixed. I don't identify as hapa. I'm Black. Because of the one-drop rule. [I'm] African American and proudly so." As an advocate against racism, Janet discussed the discrimination that Black people faced, including when others did not consider her "Black enough" because of her fair skin. When we spoke, she assumed I was Black, likely because why else would I conduct a decade-long project on Black people? She confided, "Well, you're so light-skinned also, so you probably heard those same stupid remarks," growing up in Hawai'i. When I told her I was not Black but that my mother is Russian Jewish and my father is Indian, Janet doubled down, "Well, you look Black."

Having been mistaken for many things in my life, but not for being Black, I responded that "I look Indian." Not having it, Janet finalized our amiable discussion, saying, "We all come from Africa," and insisted that I was still Black.

Local practices informed by Hawaiian epistemologies lead Black transplants to *change* how they identify; that is, they respond to "What are you?" *differently* than they did "back home." They did not identify in any one way. While the majority describe their parents as Black, including African, in many cases they also mentioned their other backgrounds through stories rich with the history of the African diaspora: Black, African not African American, half Black and half White. Some transplants recount their African-Native-haole-Chinese ancestry to bring forth the history of the US South, including the former Chinese coolies and railroad workers who settled in the Mississippi Delta. Indigenous and slave pasts—crossovers between Native Americans and Africans—come into relief through the incantations of ancestry.

Transplants from the more racially stringent US South do not provide a set pattern of identification and ancestry, either. A southerner who is resolute about being Black grew up in a small town structured along a Black/White binary. Forty-something-year-old Kurtis acknowledged that he probably had other ancestries, especially given that his grandmother "looks straight-up Native American." Nino, a man in his sixties, also from the South, offered quite a contrast to Kurtis. Without explicitly mentioning his parents, Nino describes older generations. His great-grandmother was a Scots Irish woman who came to the United States from Ireland. "She was White." His grandfather was "Cherokee, born Cherokee." He recalls, "I look at a photograph of my great-grandfather, and he looked like Jack Johnson, the boxer, the bare-knuckle boxer, that's what he looked like. And then my great-grandmother looked like Rosie O'Donnell or somebody. You know, she's a potato-eating Irish woman. She was about four foot tall, and he was about seven foot tall. So they were an interracial couple in the 1800s." Nino cannot forget this past—a past he does not want to return to because of the violence faced by his immediate family and by his Black and Native ancestors. His grandmother told him "stories about seeing people get burnt to death." These experiences inform his identification. He explains, "I'm a hybrid. But on the mainland, based on visuals, I'm considered a Black man. What I actually am is I'm a Cherokee, African, Scots Irish, hodgepodge." His family history and the openness of Hawai'i to what he "actually" is led to his feeling that Hawai'i is his sanctuary.

Skin color and gender also shade old-timer self-identification. Growing up in small-town Mississippi, where she attended a predominantly Black high school, Mary describes her mother as "very very very fair-skinned." If in the South people like her and Kurtis find a constricting Black/White structure despite a range of phenotypes and histories, in Hawai'i they may take the opportunity to embrace open and varied relationships to race. When I asked how she identified, Mary first responded as many old-timers had: "Black, White, Native American." However, she concluded firmly, "I don't." She does not identify racially.

By contrast, Bobby, a business professional from Central Africa, identifies as Black, as Kurtis does, but distinguishes himself from African Americans. "I do not relate to the Black perception and how they view themselves," Bobby said. As we ate burgers for lunch at the Gordon Biersch restaurant at Aloha Tower near the business district in downtown Honolulu, he explained, "I don't like to call them African American; they're Black American. They have a chip on their shoulder." This is a dynamic between African Americans and Africans found in the anthropologist Jemima Pierre's scholarship on the work ethnicity does to distinguish Black immigrants from African Americans.[42] Bobby was lively and kind. He drew my brilliant eighteen-year-old research assistant, Aozora Brockman, and me into the conversation as we asked him follow-up questions about his experiences at work. His colleagues, including White men and women, would remind him, "You are the only brother here." "Oh!" he responded, as if it were a revelation, unconcerned, and quite comfortable with that phenomenon. "I'm a dude. I'm not a Black guy from Africa with an accent," he clarified to us, much like Mary, who prefers not to identify racially, or the Black Mexican local who identifies more with "pineapples, or kale!" Another man, whose father was from Africa, grew up with his White mother in California and "thought I was White. I don't think I identified as 'the Black guy' in school." He states that he's proud of both heritages, but he "feel[s] there is a missing [piece of the] pie in my life. I'm half Black and half White, and that's about it." (This missing piece may refer to his having no relation with his father.) Long-term residents who may have had a vexed relationship with Blackness elsewhere feel more resolved in the Islands, where they find it to be less determining of who they are, or who they opt to be.

Some transplants named other ancestries along with African and Native American. For instance, an older long-term resident from New York explained that in addition to having "family on the Chinook reservation" and "never talking about our White ancestors," she is part Chinese because her father's mother is Chinese. Kimo, a Black Japanese Hawaiian man raised internationally, came in the 1990s to attend college in Hawai'i, where his mother's

Hawaiian Japanese family is from. We were speaking in his living room in a Honolulu high-rise with a beautiful view of the ocean; Kimo's Japanese wife and children were in another room, patiently leaving us uninterrupted. His mother met and married his "mixed Black, French, Native American" father from North Carolina. In fact, during our two-hour discussion, his father phoned from the continental United States. Kimo put him on speakerphone and explained my project, and we spoke about some of the ideas I was discussing. Kimo, who did not identify as local, is now (a decade after we first met) a malo loincloth-wearing, Hawaiian-speaking man who reads entirely as local and whose daughters dance the hula. He identifies, as all the other Black Hawaiians did, as Black Hawaiian. "I say Black Hawaiian, mixed with a lot of different things. Actually, a quarter Japanese.... I also have Norwegian and something else."

The family stories of Black residents are remarkable for their breadth, the product of globe-crossing meetings, marriages, and migrations. Their ancestral identifications are without cohesion or pattern. Some say they are African American, Native, and White; others who have Black and White parents identify with both or only as Black. There are transplants from the African continent who distinguish themselves from African Americans, and there are the Hawai'i-born children of Africans who identify as local. There is no pattern of Black identification in Hawai'i, except for the prevalence of multiracial identification and the clear influence of these islands on people's ideas of what is possible.

Finding Liberation in Hawai'i

In Hawai'i, I don't have to be that thing of what I thought was Black. Here I can be Brown, or have my melanin, or I could just be human. I don't really have to play along. That's the one kind of freedom that comes with the sacrifice of being in the gridlock [of California]. Where you might feel like, I know at least twenty blocks deep [in Compton] there's all Brown and Black people and we could wage war, but you don't have what it takes to be who you are outside of that Blackness. Unfortunately, they are assisting you to kill yourselves because we don't have this opportunity that I got here, because of the ignorance about Black people: which is a chance to be in dark skin and not have to be Black. When you have a choice ever in your life where you don't have to be what you perceive to be

Black, I think you become a different kind of Black person in general.

BLACK LONG-TERM RESIDENT

If Hawai'i is a haven, a sanctuary from continental forms of racism and White norms, is it therefore a site of liberation for members of the African diaspora? Transplants responded to this question in various ways. Only a minority of those who came were so critical of Hawai'i as to leave—and they offer insights. Others describe the importance of adopting local culture to homemaking. Some participants interpreted "liberation" to mean the ability to be outside of Blackness—including being free from expectations held within Black communities. For others, it meant the opportunity to create hegemonic and middle-class Black social groups without the "interference" of working-class Black folks. Representatives of these two perspectives did not tend to create strong social bonds with one another.

"Less pressure" combined with the "kindness" of people provides for a new way of living. "I think in Hawai'i I really have the opportunity to be me. I don't have to be what my neighborhood says I should be," says a Congolese long-term resident. The forty-something-year-old professional figured he could "belong" here, whereas he may not (as an African) were he to live in the continental United States. Island demographics that initially drew these arrivals also affect a sense of belonging. "For the first time I didn't feel as a minority," says a scholar of the Caribbean; "it's easy for you to be a minority." But whereas on the East Coast, "it's very easy for me to be aware of my Blackness, here I never felt that, which is great. You know, in terms of that, it's paradise."

Transplants compare their lives in Hawai'i with other places and highlight its relative positivity. For instance, one Black student from Baltimore said, "This is an alternative to the hell, out of a bad area." "I look at Hawai'i," says another transplant, "as one of those places where it's still kind of open." This openness comes partly from the invisibility of Black people, of *not registering* among locals. Transplants experience this in sharp contrast to Black hypervisibility in the continental United States; therefore invisibility can come as a relief.[43] A young man explained that in Hawai'i, "people don't know Black men, so they don't pay me any mind."

Less pressure includes freedom, too, of *not belonging*, and specifically of not belonging *to prescribed groups*. Black transplants were surprised when locals asked them, "What are you?"—especially those who thought they were obviously "just Black!" This question is one of the most common in the Islands, alongside the ubiquitous "What high school you wen?" (What high school did you attend?), which helps people geographically and socially locate others. Kurtis, the tall man who came to the Islands as a teenage soldier, was puzzled when people asked him what he was. He chuckles, remembering the time we first met, twenty-five years ago: "I think *you* asked me that question!" Locals do not take for granted or assume others' racial identities, since there are so many combinations that one could be, so many histories one could be descended from.

I had previously resisted interpreting these comments about freedom from Blackness as internalized racism. However, a Black scholar in the audience at one of my presentations in Chicago clarified, "They *are* running away from Blackness. From the negative ideas associated with it." This is true: they are fleeing racist conceptions of Black people (i.e., racism), not the meaningfulness of Blackness, per se. For example, a student felt that "if you go to the store in [Los Angeles], you need to look like you got [properly dressed and] ready so the store owners don't think [you] are going to steal something. . . . Here people don't mind so much that I don't fit. It's more laid-back. I haven't had any negative experiences here." The relative absence of this kind of pressure adds to the potentials of life otherwise. "One of my goals is to live a good life in Hawaiʻi," says a Black and White Californian. He felt he could achieve this here, in contrast to the "closet racism" of his home state.

Scholarship on African Americans in Hawaiʻi describes it as a place to leave behind the racism of the United States. "One good reason for wishing to live here," the Hawaiʻi scholar Shirley Abe wrote over seventy-five years ago, "is that they don't experience as much discrimination as in some parts of the Mainland."[44] Albert Broussard includes early nineteenth-century residents Anthony Allen and Betsey Stockton among those "attempting to escape racial discrimination in the United States" who found a "relatively tolerant and tranquil racial atmosphere."[45] Over a century later (and two centuries since Allen and Stockton), this is what the people I spoke with also find. This is not to say that racism does not exist in the Islands (it is the topic of the next chapter), but here life is less intense.

Hawaiʻi is a place where Blackness is neither presumed nor determines one's quality of life. Instead, Black transplants can self-define and expand their social lives. They adapt to local customs to varying levels—levels that generally align with their sense of ease, belonging, and homemaking in the Islands. The nonsalience of Blackness, on the one hand, means that one does not always and only have to be what White people have constructed Blackness to mean. On the other hand, it allows people to be Black *and* elsewhere, including other ancestries and non-race-based affinities, including one's job or preferred surf break. Nonbelonging is also an option: one does not have to belong to a Black community or have to perform along expected racial scripts patrolled by White people or Black community members.[46] Race shapes gender and sexual relations, yet demographics orient these dynamics. Does all of this mean that Hawaiʻi offers Black people a place of liberation? From Blackness?

Black arrivals experience some freedom from overriding assumptions of who one is and what one's capabilities are compared with the continental United States. Yet Lili felt burdened and irritated for having to prove that Black people can "walk and talk and chew gum." This educator not only experienced how Hawaiʻi residents' unfamiliarity with (or what another participant called "ignorance" of) Black people led to misconceptions, but also noted problems among Black folks locally:

> No, I don't think this is necessarily a liberating environment in that sense. I think, if anything, it becomes constraining, because even within the African and larger African American community [in Hawaiʻi], there's a presumption that if you are doing anything with the [African] diaspora, it's kind of boiling down to meet the needs of those in the African American community that might not have any sense of the field or what's going on, but just may want some kind of history, occasionally—kind of a Black History Month celebration, or to make those connections.

Lili felt that even Black residents did not want to pursue a depth of knowledge about the African diaspora, which was of deep interest to her. So if for some, Hawaiʻi offers relief from Blackness and Black people, others seeking Black community may find local iterations too confining. Lili has since left the Islands.

Forming Black community is a way to maintain a meaningful identity, including cultural and aesthetic alternatives to local culture. A small but strong "Black community" primarily comprises old-timers who came as professionals or students or formerly served in the military. These older Black professionals work hard to establish organizations and insist on Black people's long presence and contributions to the Islands. They have created an important safety net that can advocate for newcomers. As one community member says, "If something negative happens, we have friends who will create circles of defense. . . . They circle the wagons." On the other hand, others interpret these elders as Black authenticators.

Being Black in Hawaiʻi "doesn't necessarily mean that everybody is (*slight pause*) you know, in line with each other, has a connection. It's hard to connect just because you're Black alone," one transplant describes. Black newcomers do not always find comfort in the existing Black community, with its middle-class, civil rights, and pro-military orientation. The Facebook page of Hawai'i's NAACP chapter celebrates Black military accomplishments, including Black graduates of military academies and Tiger Woods's Presidential Medal of Freedom from President Trump, while bemoaning the death of George Bush Sr. with no accompanying sense of Black people's participation in the militarized occupation of Hawai'i.[47] In this way, these particular Black veterans in Hawai'i parallel moves by Asian politicians who "align ... with the settler state."[48] Black residents may not have the overarching "power to represent or enact settler colonialism" in the way local Japanese do, for instance, because of their small demographics and political lack of representation; yet as lawyers and other professionals, these representatives of "the Black community" have the power to endorse US state domination through their celebration of military service in the name of national security and full citizenship.[49]

Blending in and invisibility both make the Islands a site of im/possible liberation. Feeling easy almost requires one to relinquish stakes in hegemonic Blackness. This is particularly trying for Black parents who wish to raise their children (including multiracial keiki) with Black pride. Although the Islands are particularly receptive to interracial couples, Black mothers recall having to make compromises with little racial reinforcement. Invisibility, the sense of not being part of the multicultural fabric, is an odd experience for those raised in places of heightened racial awareness. Black children do not learn their histories at schools. In response to my inquiry about the possibilities of Black liberation in Hawai'i, a Black professional was partly affirmative because she liked being "in a majority space of color" and liked that the parents of her children's friends were also in interracial marriages. For mixed children, Hawai'i "is a different environment, to grow up in a space where being multiethnic is normalized. And that's really very positive." However, she continued:

> The other side of it is that local identity isn't fully inclusive of the part of them that is of African descent, so I still have to constantly articulate what that means. I think the bottom line if you come here, if you're not trying to adapt [or] change yourself, you're not going to survive. What I mean by changing is following the culture and embracing all of the culture—you need to be able to do that. Being able to live outside of your race. That's what Hawai'i is intended for. If you can do that, you can [survive].

While some might view Hawai'i as a haven particularly from US racism, others (who tended to leave) found it a challenging place and mention the effects of living in Hawai'i on a Black person's psyche. A parent who recently arrived felt that "it's important that anybody who's African American, or kids who are African American, have some sense of universal experience and connection with other community [members]." She felt that it is not "healthy to be isolated in any form," and expanded this to include transracial adoptees, as well: "Looking at that experience, you think about what that means to be of color in an environment that is majority White but can't communicate what it is to be [of] color effectively, and that's a concern." The combination of small demographics, a local lack of knowledge, and the particular contours of Hawaiʻi's "Black community" prove challenging for those wanting to inspire racial pride in their Black children.

This difference emerges because Hawaiʻi is at once part of and apart from the United States; it is a place not wholly determined by the nation. Interpreting the contemporary context through a *longue durée* approach to local dynamics, rather than refracted only by modern US history, means that Black people can be more than what White people have constructed of Blackness. They can be what Hawaiians have historically witnessed them to be. For African Americans who feel deeply attached to Black communities and movements of resistance and uplift, the Pacific can be discomfiting; it has not developed the infrastructure to support substantial communities and networks central to Black survival in White places. But these may not have *needed* to develop, because these islands are *not a White space*, despite colonial settlement. For the majority of people I spoke with, aspects of the Islands, including multiculturalism and Black invisibility, offer respite specifically to Black people: a break from violence, surveillance, and other traumas of racism. One can also break from hegemonic Blackness and imposed expectations. This explains a Black professional's comment that became this book's title: "Hawaiʻi is my haven," said Ellen, the Black nurse; a Black man, also from the South, said as much, "It was like a sanctuary to me when I got to this rock."

The racial lens that Black transplants bring to the Pacific illuminates its potentials as well as problems. Hawaiʻi offers a place of healing for many Black transplants, inspiring them to adapt to local culture and make it their home. They become old-timers and possibly local. Hawaiʻi "spits out" others, for whom it is too expensive, too relaxed, and not Black enough. The latter tend not to adapt to island culture and hold strong to their Black consciousness, part of which is a race-only perspective that misses some of the complexities of local dynamics. This makes it difficult to understand island customs and to connect with people who seem to be so differently oriented—invested as many residents are in their localness, getting along, and not seeing Blackness. In all cases, transplants think about their location in the Islands through a racialized perspective attuned to structural racism and unequal power dynamics. This perspective informs the established and emergent Black social formations on Oʻahu.

Responding to the Islands: Black Community Formations

Invisibility resulting from locals' lack of knowledge about the African diaspora can make for a challenging initial arrival. Black residents have responded differently, in some cases by integrating into island communities, in other cases by re-creating the social groups that gave them meaning in their previous homes. Older long-term residents who proudly identify as African American, including patriotic former military personnel, have developed community and organizations rooted in civil rights conceptions of belonging. However, Black locals do not identify with this community or express a desire to be around other Black people, integrated as they are into their nonBlack local families and communities. Dr. Miles Jackson, for instance, told me of the difficulty he had finding Black locals to participate in telling their stories for his documentary on African Americans in Hawaiʻi.[50] Black social life that is centered on upward mobility and veterans also does not always appeal to a politically active and younger group of newcomers, including those both critical of the US military and inspired by the Movement for Black Lives. They have, in turn, developed new kinds of social gatherings—ones that we have not seen in the Islands before, as they center a Black feminist consciousness along with explicit attention to Hawaiʻi's Indigenous communities and the environment. These various community formations point not only to the diversity within burgeoning Black groups in Hawaiʻi but also to the tensions implicit in the variety of responses to living in these islands.

Long-term resident professionals—those working in the law, education, medicine, business, and the military—have formed the most established Black communities on Oʻahu. These are the racial representatives that Black newcomers meet upon their arrival—at church, the Martin Luther King Jr. Day Parade, and upon being invited to events sponsored by the NAACP or the Links. These organizations are sustained by Black residents who are older than most of the Black locals I interviewed, and who are part of the civil rights generation that grew up during the Jim Crow era. This history is important for their distinct—celebratory—stance toward the military. With some exceptions, they arrived between the 1960s and 1980s and continue the legacy of Black contributors to Hawaiian society since the turn of the nineteenth century.

Older Black professionals have done much to establish, recognize, and fight for equality for Black and other nonhaole residents in the Islands. They have formed and are members of organizations they found missing in Hawai'i, including the African American Lawyers Association (AALA), the Links (an international professional women's organization), fraternities and sororities, and a local chapter of the NAACP. Additionally, they felt that unaddressed racism against Black people in the Islands created a *need* for these educational and advocacy groups. The AALA, whose members include Daphne Barbee-Wooten and her husband Andre Wooten, was formed in response to the treatment of a fellow Black lawyer, Sandra Simms, who was denied a second term as Oʻahu Circuit Court judge (some say she was too soft on criminals). The organization also successfully lobbied the state to officially recognize Martin Luther King Jr. Day and to host an annual parade in King's honor.[51] The government first resisted, stating that not enough African Americans lived in the Islands to warrant such a commemoration. These lawyers, who have historically served multiple communities in Hawai'i, including Chinese as well as disabled state workers, argued that recognizing the great leader was important for *all* state residents, not just Black residents.

Old-timers also conducted the foundational research on Black people in the Islands. Daphne Barbee-Wooten wrote an important history of Black lawyers in Hawai'i, published by the press of fellow Black author Kathryn Takara.[52] The cover of Barbee-Wooten's *African American Attorneys in Hawaii* boasts a blurry photo of her husband (the lawyer Andre Wooten) with a young Barack Obama. A combination of historical research and personal reflection, the book celebrates professional accomplishments and contributes to the visibility of middle-class African Americans locally. Barbee-Wooten tells a story hundreds of years old about the ongoing work of justice-oriented men and women of the law who advocated and educated on behalf of African American rights and equality.

These Black residents call on their racial consciousness and professional training to create organizations and knowledge bases that are undertapped and yet thriving. They educate Hawai'i's people about Black issues in college courses, helping to found the law school, appearing on public television, and mentoring youths. This decades-long work of education and representation is severely underappreciated by more widely acknowledged groups. Yet it has offered relief to those Black newcomers, including university students and young professionals, who are homesick and seek a sense of community. Members of these organizations and their narratives of Black accomplishment reflect their orientation toward Black respectability and education. They continue to fight for uplift through existing systems rather than questioning those very systems, as younger generations may.

The new generation of recent arrivals may find these Black elders familiar, but they are drawn to what is *different* for Black people in the Pacific. What characterizes these emergent young communities is their balance of attention to curating Black-affirming spaces while being inclusive of the Islands' diverse communities, including their relationship to Native Hawaiians. They are culture centered, tuned in to recent Black studies scholarship, and filled with the skills of people engaged in music, dance, and art. Some express an Afrocentric or "hippie" orientation to the land and water, and they encourage the full range of gender and sexual expression. Black women are the backbone of these developments.

Centered on Oʻahu and especially in Honolulu, new organizations and individuals are hosting Black social gatherings that celebrate Black life with attention to their imprint on the Islands. These gatherings include dance parties, film screenings, and women's retreats. Picking up steam, the organizational framework of the Pōpolo Project serves as a nexus for Black-related social events. Developed less than a decade ago, this nonprofit organization "works to make the lives of Black folks visible among what we commonly think of as local, highlighting the vivid, complex diversity of Blackness."[53] Under Akiemi Glenn's leadership, the project has produced some of the most important documentation and discussions of Black life in Hawaiʻi. There has never been such an organization in the Islands.

Young Black residents also create a host of other social groups, gatherings (often in February [Black History Month] and August [Black August]), and regular events that center the arts, land, and wellness. The Cocoa Collective is an online and communal meeting of Black queer and straight women, both local and immigrant. These, along with undergraduate university students and more "solo" arrivals who connect with locals through beach culture, may not identify or interact with older Black professionals.

Young people hosting events celebrating Black life and informing Island residents about Black people's concerns are notable developments. They are creating spaces of comfort for the growing and diverse Black population that bring locals and transplants together. They are fulfilling law professor Charles Lawrence's hopes:

Figure 3.2 Dr. Kathryn Waddell Takara, Luanna Peterson, and Tadia Rice at the Pōpolo Project 2020 "Black Futures Ball" held at the Hawaiʻi State Art Museum. Photo by Michael McDermott.

When I think about what I would like to have in a Black community [in Hawaiʻi, it] is just more places that [one] could just be surrounded by Black folks. And that there would be these things: you know, you wouldn't have to explain, you wouldn't have to think about, you would just all have the same response. That to me is what I envision, there [would] be kind of enough of us who understand that it's fine to be intentional about that. It's fine to seek each other out.[54]

In the wake of the growing Movement for Black Lives, Lawrence initiated a gathering that gave Black people the space to process the violence of police brutality and systemic racism that was happening thousands of miles to their east. Some of those who attended are now fulfilling his vision, bringing locals and transplants together while "be[ing] intentional" about centering Black concerns.

At Lawrence's gathering was the Black long-term resident and North Carolina transplant Dr. Akiemi Glenn—a brilliant and generous collaborator in my study—who serves as the executive director of the Pōpolo Project. The organization's board chair was the local Black attorney Jamila Jarmon, who was recognized as a young leader by the *Pacific Business News*. The Pōpolo Project hosts events and is a hub for other Black-oriented networks. In 2019 the project promoted "Saltwater People," a "monthly rooftop party that celebrates the global flow of Black cultures with music you won't hear anywhere else in Honolulu. . . . Saltwater People brings the flavors of African and Pacific diasporas together where our lineages and histories converge here in Hawai'i."[55] Significantly, the advertisement cites an African American Pacific Islander scholar: "The Black Pacific poet and scholar Teresia Teaiwa writes, 'We sweat and cry salt water, so we know that the ocean is really in our blood.' . . . Here in Hawai'i . . . we are all saltwater people. The ocean links us and is a source of our nourishment, sustenance, healing, and joy."[56] The Islands are small, and often the same individuals socialize across groups and events, running into one another as they nourish their intellectual as well as social, political, gender, and racial commitments.

The "Hawaii Free Women of Color Library Pop-Up & Retreat" draws inspiration from the Free Black Women's Library based in New York. This event, hosted by Javonna Hines and Luanna Peterson in affiliation with the Cocoa Collective, is "an all-community book exchange and mini retreat highlighting Black and women of color authors and entrepreneurs."[57] People can enjoy CBD massages by Karma Love Bodyworkx or get henna tattoos by Immortal Sol, and Marisa Brown demonstrates Black hair techniques. The flyer exclaims: "ALL ARE WELCOME! Additionally, this event WILL be highlighting Black female authors and entrepreneurs—special space is given to support Black women. This event is a safe space for women & femmes, gender nonconforming and trans folks, as well as all other LGBTQIA+ identified individuals." People affiliated with these groups also attend events hosted by the Honolulu-based Shangri La Museum of Islamic Art, Culture & Design, headed by Konrad Ng. In that capacity, Ng, Obama's brother-in-law, has hosted Black artists from across the diaspora to perform and work with Hawai'i-based practitioners in collaboration with local farmers like Daniel Anthony, who are working to revitalize Hawaiian land-based practices.[58]

Black transplants respond to life in the Pacific Islands in a variety of ways. Rather than, as the younger generation is wont to do, seek alternatives to or more expansive identities than "Black only," the older generation offers a formidable group of elders seeking occupational and lifestyle opportunities. Others who come alone may integrate into island communities and do not feel the pull of being around other Black people. Newcomers also include Generation Y college students who may call on the services of Black lawyers, and members of Gen X who are also educated professionals and include artists and

Figure 3.3 Artists hosted by the Shangri La Museum of Islamic Art, Culture & Design perform at Mana Ai farms in Kāneʻohe, Oʻahu, 2019. Photo by author.

others seeking new opportunities, creating the Pōpolo Project, and performing as musicians at dance parties that draw multiracial crowds. Organizations like the Pōpolo Project reflect emerging Black politics in the Islands that are both expansive *and* Black affirming. They support wide-ranging gender and sexual expressions and host conversations about their kuleana concerning Native Hawaiian self-determination. These collaborations reflect Lawrence's vision of fostering Black community in the Islands.

Conclusion

It can be a relief, and it's insidious—being Black in Hawai'i.
BLACK TRANSPLANT

Despite their various takes on Hawai'i as a multicultural paradise, home, or place where one can become local, Black transplants to Hawai'i find themselves in a nonWhite yet somewhat familiar society where they are afforded relative invisibility. Here they experience "less pressure" in their daily lives: less pressure from repressive state violence, and less pressure to perform restricted notions of "being Black." The need to navigate a White social structure and affiliate primarily along racial lines is less prominent here. In this way, Hawai'i offers sanctuary and a reprieve.

While this identifies what is *alleviated* in this society, Hawai'i also holds certain promises for African-descended people. They pursue avenues for professional, personal, and spiritual development and create communities of affinity. An older transplant from Georgia felt that "Hawai'i offers an opportunity for you to change your perception of yourself." Indeed, a young student said that he had "changed [his] identity," losing ninety pounds and becoming a new and healthier person. In Los Angeles, he explained, "Image is really important. It was protection. I got out of it, I got out of my shell. Here, I've grown a lot as a person." Black people do not just take what the Islands offer; they mindfully help cultivate a racially aware society.

Black people come from across the globe but tend to represent the span of the continental United States. From Chicago to Compton, they include multiracial people from Black neighborhoods in Los Angeles and those with Asian ancestors who grew up in White suburban New York. They include light- and dark-skinned Black men and women from the US South, along with mixed race Black Sāmoans, Caribbean Islanders, Africans, and people from Asia and Europe. Across this diversity, growing up in North America and in parts of the Caribbean and Africa means that they were familiar and identified with a dominant Black experience and knew some rendition of African diasporic history.

Including the recently arrived in their teens through old-timers in their eighties, Black transplants come for school and work; some mothers come for the adventure and to get away from their situations at home. These were, notably, middle-class and educated individuals who could afford to come to the Islands, where they did not find segregation or experience ghettoization. They were pushed from the "pressures" of their home, particularly the surveillance and tragedies of racism, and drawn to the opportunities and Asia adjacency of these islands. Tourism and the media crafted their expectations. Beyond that, however, they researched demographics, searching for a Black population, and became interested in a majority-minority society. Hawaiʻi's racial demographics, lack of a Black/White binary, and closeness to Asia mean something different for these transplants than for haole and other tourists. Inspired by such conceptions, transplants found "much more" than a racial paradise once they arrived.

Because Black transplants learned about race, slavery, and the history of the African diaspora within their communities, they are not particularly ambivalent about their Black identities. This frames the critical *racial lens* that informs their understanding of island dynamics. This is a lens that, if adopted more widely by all island residents, could bring into sharper focus the inequalities structuring life in Hawaiʻi that I document in the next chapter. It too would challenge local tendencies to brush away allegations of racism to explain away differences. A race-aware focus instead reveals that all of Hawaiʻi's people experience forms of inequality, but that this is particularly evident in the lives of Black residents. The racially attuned perspectives of Black people who move to the Islands as adults expand studies of Hawaiʻi that have centered on questions of ethnicity, multiculturalism, and settler colonialism.

Transplants do not unquestioningly consider Hawaiʻi to be a "multiracial paradise," noting the tensions of negative experiences and the patterns of political and economic power. They find Black men and women framed through tropes different from where they came: military, tourists, reggae artists, or college athletes for the men; military dependents, tourists, or sex workers for young women. While they are presumed not to be local, they understand why they are mistaken for being in the military.

The presumption of being nonlocal and being in the military links Black to haole people in the Islands, a connection that does not sit well with all Black arrivals. In part, this signals discomfort with being lumped together with a group responsible for many of the conditions of Black life—of being linked to one's oppressor. This desire for distinction is also a critique of White supremacy and a refusal to be seen as an undifferentiated "settler." This is a proper refusal of being granted the same accountability for domination in the Pacific that haole must answer to. Additionally, *their experiences* are distinct.

We would only be able to parse out some locals' antiforeign sentiment as specifically antihaole if we study the experiences of Black residents—arrivals who have found a more welcoming reception. This demands that we see anti-Black racism as distinct from antihaole sentiment, that settlers have distinct experiences crosscut by race, and how antiforeign sentiment or resentment against nonlocals is not transracial but rather refracted through racial specificity. In sum, "local" incorporates but is not predetermined by race (Black people can be local), and anti-nonlocal sentiment is distinct from antiBlack racism. This clarifies how (local) *culture* is distinct from *race* in Hawaiʻi. Both are mediated through Hawaiʻi's relationship to the US military and Native Hawaiians.

In the Islands, Black people express themselves beyond racial identifications and expectations; they find the space to reinvent themselves without this signaling internalized racism. They find comradeship with people of multiple backgrounds while learning of Hawaiians' struggles for sovereignty and the history of colonization. But they are also asked, in some cases, to place their Blackness on the back burner through both silences and questions.

If not structured along a Black/White racial binary, economic and social advantages nonetheless fall along racial lines, with some Asian groups as well as haole in positions of power. As a result, Black transplants resist describing Hawaiʻi as a "multiracial paradise." Because of their invisibility, the lack of a Black community or access to cultural resources (restaurants, hair products, etc.), and their concern over Kānaka struggles, some newcomers do not consider Hawaiʻi to be their "forever home." Others feel comfortable in the Islands, marrying locals, raising their (second generation) mixed race children, and adapting to local culture. Yet unlike Hawaiʻi-born-and-raised Black people, they do not all identify as "local." This distinction between "home" and "local" recognizes local as a performance of adopted cultural norms that include language, clothing, food, and ways of being—a performance that has to be accepted by other locals.

I hold on to "local" as a concept and description for those who are Hawaiʻi born and raised and those who enthusiastically adapt to a shared sense of we-ness along with Hawaiʻi-based knowledge and practice. In light of critiques that Asians use the concept to obfuscate their accountability for settler colonialism and erase Kānaka Maoli, "local" maintains integrity as a practice when we center Kanaka concerns and their relationships with Black people. Local includes a panracial, if complicated, fellowship among Hawai'i's people. Participants' experiences were shaped through encounters that made them feel local or nonlocal, which then affected their sense of non/belonging. These experiences combine to shape whether or not Black transplants stay or leave. Not feeling or identifying as local does not, however, preclude the sense that Hawai'i could be home.

Being local almost requires that one relinquish a racially strident view. Those preferring to hold on to ways familiar to their upbringing can find community among the civil rights generation of Black old-timers in the military, law, medicine, and education. They, along with newer generations of arrivals, are creating events for Black people that increase others' awareness of their presence. Young and politically attuned newcomers, especially Black women, want to enhance their love of Hawai'i while maintaining their racial and feminist consciousness. As a result, they are cultivating Black and also women-centered spaces in which to socialize and discuss life and politics.

Black immigrants to the Islands express worldviews and ways of speaking about life in Hawai'i that contrast with the perspectives of Black locals. For one, transplants speak about race—and identify racism—more explicitly. By contrast, race does not take center stage for Black locals, and they express a lack of clarity about racism. Transplants understand local society as a hierarchy of racialized groups with differential access to material and other forms of power, including political representation. A *racial lens* analyzes race relations in ways that help us significantly address existing inequalities and acknowledge practices of racism. The next chapter describes racism in paradise, as it affects every person of African descent, whether they choose to see it or not.

4

RACISM IN PARADISE

ANTIBLACK RACISM AND RESISTANCE
IN HAWAIʻI

"Pick your Paradise!" urges Hawaii.com, informing potential visitors that "each Island of Aloha offers distinct travel adventures, and discovering which slice of Paradise is ideal for you is all part of the fun!"[1] The Hawaii Tourism Authority is no less shameless in urging outsiders to "discover the Islands of Hawaii."[2] The multibillion-dollar tourism industry has perfected images of Hawaiʻi as a multicultural paradise, a diverse and harmonious place that awaits consumption. The ethnic studies scholar Noel Kent describes how Hawaiʻi was transformed from a plantation economy to a tourist one when corporations like the one headed by Henry J. Kaiser turned stolen land into resorts populated with American hotel chains in cahoots with major airlines to promote travel.[3] This further drained resources away from Hawaiians and other local workers in a burgeoning service economy, shaping current inequalities. Hidden behind the rainbow of aloha luring tourists is the darkness of discrimination and prejudice (people do not tend to call it racism), houselessness, and incarceration. Hawaiʻi's Black residents, both locals and transplants, expose in painful detail the existence of racism. Families, schools, and workplaces are the sites of everyday and systemic racism, borne privately for life or battled publicly through legal campaigns. The defacement of Cedric Gates's campaign banners for his House of Representatives run (figure 4.1) is just one example of anti-Black racism brushed aside in the *New York Times* article applauded by Obama (figure 4.2).

Figure 4.1 Defaced campaign banner of Cedric Gates, running for Oʻahu's District 44 House of Representatives, 2016. Source: Facebook screen capture.

During the summer of the 2016 Democratic and Republican National Conventions, I spoke with Black people in Hawaiʻi about national politics, local campaigns, and the Movement for Black Lives. Democrat Cedric Gates was running for Oʻahu's District 44 seat, a heavily Polynesian area that includes Mākaha and Waiʻanae (he won). Someone spray-painted the words "NO NIGGER" across Gates's campaign banner, and this image circulated online. (In this chapter, I spell out this racist term when others speak it; otherwise I write "the n-word.") Cedric Solosolo Asuega Gates responded on Facebook that he

Figure 4.2 Obama's retweet of Moises Velasquez-Manoff's Opinion column. Source: "Want to Be Less Racist? Move to Hawaii," *New York Times*, June 28, 2019.

was "not only a PROUD African-American, I am a PROUD Afakasi as well. (Half Polynesian/Half African-American Ethnicity)" who was "BORN & RAISED IN #WAIANAE."

Scores of people on his Facebook thread expressed support for Gates and their disappointment in others' ignorance. Almost no one discussed the actual racial epithet or the Blackness of the young Black Sāmoan. This is typical in Hawai'i, where "ethnicity," not race, is both celebrated and joked about, while protests, including Black Lives Matter rallies and charges of racism, are dis-

Figure 4.3 A United Airlines advertisement for its flights to Hawai'i in a magazine targeting Black American readers two decades after statehood. The multipage ad declares, "Newest state in the middle of the Pacific Ocean gives one a chance at an exotic vacation without leaving the U.S." Source: *Ebony*, January 1981.

missed as rude, ignorant, and not representative of aloha. In other words, demonstrations against racial wrongs are seen as not aloha; locals, including Black locals, often brush aside the wrongs themselves. As one woman who grew up as the only Black girl at her public school in Mākaha said, "Now, I think there's a difference between racial and racist, and I think Hawai'i is extremely racial. . . . Now, that doesn't mean that there isn't racism here. I think it's a different brand than it is on the mainland."

Popular depictions of "paradise" and the colonial history of Hawai'i lead to Black transplants' confusion and disappointment upon confronting antiBlack racism in the Islands. In 1981, *Ebony*, a long-standing magazine for African Americans, featured a multipage article attempting to lure Black tourists, inviting them to take part in the colonial settlement of the Islands. The article states that Black people make up close to 1 percent of the population and "today, the treatment of Blacks is just about the same as in any of the other states of the Union."[4] This is not and has never been the case. Racism looks different and operates differently in Hawai'i, complicating binaries of perpetrator and victim, unfixed and distinct from White and Black.

AntiBlack racism has heretofore gone unexamined in the literature on Black people in Hawai'i or on racism in the Islands more generally.[5] Among the few contemporary scholars to analyze disparity through a racial framework is Judy Rohrer, whose work focuses on haole in Hawai'i. Exceptions to the startling silence on Hawai'i's Black population come from Black educators who move to the Islands and conduct research on African Americans in the Islands. Despite their focus on transplants and the US military, these accounts add to the earlier scholarship on "Negro soldiers" in the wartime Pacific theater.[6] Black academic transplants are motivated to do this work because they were raised in Black communities in the continental United States that highlighted the significance of the African diaspora. They analyze African American lives through a focus on Black and White relations. The thrust of such studies is that racism exists in Hawai'i and that Black soldiers faced integration *and* discrimination over time. This repeated finding contradicts popular celebrations of Hawai'i's diverse and multiracial population meant to discount discrimination.[7] But what about Black civilian life in contemporary Hawai'i?

Black locals and Black transplants confront different forms and patterns of racism and thus recount distinct narratives and analyses. Locals zero in on experiences from childhood, while transplants discuss workplace racism faced as adults. These two groups tend also to locate the sites of racism distinctly—in the Islands or elsewhere. After my framing discussion of settler colonialism, antiBlackness, and ethnicity, I separately describe locals' and transplants' experiences with racism. I then turn to their complex understandings of power and hierarchy to analyze their comprehension of racism. If any case is to be made for centering a racial, rather than ethnicity-only, lens in the Islands, it is because of the persistence of racism. Black people who move to the Islands in adulthood describe Hawai'i as their "haven," a "reprieve," and a place of "less pressure" from the structural racism they faced "back home." But paradoxically, they note (as Black soldiers stationed in the Islands during World War II reported), people's openness toward difference is accompanied by a "shrewd under-handed prejudice in Hawaii which hurts more than open discrimination."[8] This is not just in the past; residents today provide numerous accounts of antiBlack racism in Hawai'i.

Unlike transplants, Black locals do not use the term "racism" and have difficulty putting into words the kinds of processes and experiences I define as racist. Locals' ideas about racism often are limited to histories of enslavement and US segregation; more subtle forms tend to be characterized as "prejudice." Yet as I pull together the corpus of the stories of Black locals, what emerges is a clear pattern of antiBlack racism by nonBlack family members, by people in power in schools and the workplace, and through unique dynamics in encounters with local police. This echoes the rich body of research on structural racism experienced by Black people across class statuses nationally; however, those tend to frame it as White-on-Black racism.[9] What do we learn when we see other nonBlack people of color advancing structural racism through hiring, firing, and housing discrimination?

Transplants to the Islands also face an exceptional form of racism: racial invisibility. The same racial invisibility that offers some relief from racial expectations also becomes a form of pernicious erasure. "It's like a crack in the door," describes a Black Sāmoan social worker, bemoaning local Black youths' limited access to knowledge about their people. This gap opens the Islands to problematic notions about Black people. This means that racial ideas of Blackness are not so sedimented as they are in mainstream US discourses as to be consistently and repeatedly negative; but it also means that Black people tend to be *invisible*, the inverse of racialized hypervisibility that Black people experience in the continental United States. In her analysis of the surveillance of Blackness, the Black studies scholar Simone Brown samples Judith Butler's discussion of the "racially saturated field of visibility" to describe "the ways of seeing and conceptualizing blackness through stereotypes, abnormalization, and other means that impose limitations, particularly so in spaces that are shaped for whiteness."[10] How does this work outside the context of dominant Whiteness?

Black people in Hawai'i confront racial invisibility—the experience of not being *seen*—in daily interactions and mainstream discourses. Is this an alternative to what Lyndsey Beutin defines as "racialization as a way of seeing," referring to "a historical formation that brings together the history of policing, the development of visual epistemologies, and the history of the naturalization of the criminality of blackness"?[11] Simone Brown analyzes how laws in colonial New York "sought to keep the black body in a state of permanent illumination."[12] Using "the term 'black luminosity' to refer to a form of boundary maintenance occurring at the site of the racial body," Brown reveals it to be an "exercise of panoptic power."[13] What happens in the *absence* or *lessening* of the "scrutinizing surveillance that individuals were at once subjected to, and that produced them as black subject"?[14] I chart in this chapter how a dimmed subjection to surveillance, or racial invisibility, leads also to racism unacknowledged by other locals, along with the relative freedom from the trappings of racist constructs of Blackness discussed previously.

It is both true and untrue that Hawai'i is "less racist" than the continental United States, as the *New York Times* columnist asserts in figure 4.2. It is more the case that racism exists in Hawai'i and people in Hawai'i do not call it racism. That is, power and inequality operate in the Islands through the nonrecognition of racism, amid other processes of oppression. Racism becomes particularly *evident* when we center Black people, but it signifies dynamics affecting *all groups*, as simultaneous targets *and* perpetrators. The accounts that I gathered exhort us to also see this unacknowledged form of inequality in Hawai'i and to hold ourselves accountable as participants in systems of oppression. The poignant narratives of Black residents butt up against hegemonic depictions of the Islands crafted by economic and military interests and embraced for different reasons by locals living in shared—and often tight—spaces. These forces cannot wish into existence their fiction of an exceptional society free of racism, especially when these are the forces that enact racism.

In this chapter, I offer the most detailed scholarly explication of antiBlack racism in Hawai'i. I begin with a framing discussion that locates antiBlackness within a settler colonial context that the predominant ethnicity paradigm cannot account for. The first half of the chapter then analyzes the main vectors of racism. For locals, these coalesce in childhood memories, sometimes narrated for the first time, since they rarely spoke about—or were ever asked about—these incidents. These take place in the intimacy of home and bleed out into experiences at school and with peers. In her analysis of the mythologization of multiracial people, the critical mixed race studies scholar Minelle Mahtani writes of her and her Indian Iranian siblings, "It is hard to describe the feeling of alienation we felt from our extended family."[15] Mahtani's experiences with ostracism and alienation in Canada echo in the narratives of local Black hapas, and I take up her call for better historical contextualization of these dynamics. On the other hand, transplants who migrated as adults face racism in their professional workplaces, not unlike that experienced across the United States; yet some critical differences lead transplants to consider Hawaiʻi's version "racism lite." Locals tend to diminish their experiences with racism and foreground both ethnic humor and a deeply local and anticolonial understanding of power relations in the Islands. Black long-term residents and newcomers, however, name and resist racism. Some pursue legal recourse. At the same time that they illuminate racism, transplants are compelled to adjust their Black and White perspective as they confront new perpetrators of racism. I draw on these painful stories in hopes that we can reflect on our kuleana to address antiBlack racism.

Settler Colonialism, AntiBlackness, and Native and Black Studies

The frameworks that have been used to interrogate the antiBlackness of Indigenous groups must be adjusted in Hawaiʻi. The Hawaiian Kingdom prohibited slavery, and thus critiques of slaveholding Native peoples do not apply. As discussed in chapter 1, Hawaiians accepted and integrated Black arrivals in the nineteenth century, who earned citizenship and rose to prominence. Hawaiian royalty and commoners were simultaneously adopting race in strategic ways. Blood quantum, as used in the distribution of Hawaiian Home Lands, was a practice imposed by the US government. While Hawaiians do not usually deny Black ancestors per se, the erasure of Black people in Hawaiian history and the aporia in contemporary knowledge about the African diaspora inform locals' conflation of Black people with the military, especially since World War II (discussed in chapter 2). I turned in chapter 3 to how Kanaka epistemologies survive, shifting the way Black transplants identify themselves, embracing expansive forms of belonging as they recalibrate the salience and meanings of Blackness. Here I trace the racism Black civilians experience and resist in their homes, schools, places of work, and encounters with police. These contemporary dynamics relate to the colonization of Hawaiians, including centuries-long haole attempts to Americanize Kānaka Maoli.

In the United States and Canada, academic interest in Black and Native relations, and particularly the relationship between slavery and settler colonialism, has been rising. (This similar discussion has not informed studies of

Hawai'i.) Some scholars have articulated overlapping histories of oppression among nonWhite people to cultivate shared visions for self-determination.[16] Others have centered on the distinctions between indigeneity and race and the tense ties between Black and Native people.[17] For instance, what is the relationship of formerly enslaved people to settler colonialism?[18] Some Native scholars and activists have also taken Black people to task for contributing to Native erasure and undermining the history of genocide by focusing primarily on slavery and Black suffering (note the converse—Black erasure—in Hawai'i). On the other hand, Indigenous antiBlackness points to Native people's participation in slavery, the adoption of racist ideas, and their denial of ancestral Blackness and ostracism of those who are part Black (such as the expulsion of Black Indians from southern tribes).[19]

In a 2016 special issue of *Theory and Event*, scholars debated how antiBlackness and Indigenous dispossession, or slavery and settler colonialism, were both constitutive of "US colonial projects."[20] Indeed, they are co-constitutive processes. Yet current scholarship often pits Black and Native people against one another in attempts to claim greater oppression. "Recent work in black and indigenous studies," writes the historian Justin Leroy, "has made claims to exceptionalism that leave the two fields at an impasse."[21] Indeed, the debate is not merely theoretical. The historian Tiya Miles understands Black and Native unity to be "aspirational": "The reality of black and Native relationships, especially within nations that had once owned black slaves, was rough, tumultuous, and in many ways characterized by conflict."[22] While these historians are attentive to these relations, race studies scholars are not always attentive to settler colonialism.

Native erasure takes place in the significant work on Black incarceration and policing that does not extend the genealogy of the "New Jim Crow" to take into account Native containment and displacement.[23] Analyzing Asian and Indigenous experiences, Leong and Carpio explain how "the erasures of colonization as a process and genocide as a colonial technology from discussions of slavery and the carceral state manifest the settler state at work even in critiques of the carceral state."[24] In Hawai'i, we see how the two processes reinforce each other when we integrate processes of colonization into the structural understanding of the carceral state.[25]

The bulk of the scholarship on Black and Native people distinguishes the racial status of Black people in contrast to Native indigeneity. My fieldwork shows how individuals embody both ontologies; they are constituted through and shape Indigenous epistemologies and our understanding of race. Hawai'i, which unlike the United States and Caribbean nations was never a slaveholding society, offers different ways to conceptualize Black and Native relations.

Indigeneity brings to the fore the ongoing colonized status of Native Hawaiians. Concerning the material living conditions of Kānaka Maoli and the experiences of Hawai'i's Black population, it is evident that race (which in my definition highlights relations of dominance and oppression and access to material resources) and indigeneity (which highlights colonialism and dispossession) structure island life well after the initial haole oligarchy was replaced by local (Asian and haole) leaders. Black and Native Hawaiian communities are both grossly overrepresented at nearly double their proportion in Hawai'i's incarcerated population. According to a 2010 Prison Policy report, at 2 percent of the state population, Black people made up 4 percent of the incarcerated population.[26] Hawaiians, whom the report counted at only 10 percent of the state population (the report did not count people who selected more than one race, who make up over a fifth of the Islands' population), constituted just under 40 percent of the state's imprisoned population and in some prisons made up over half of the inmates.[27] How does colonialism inform antiBlack racism?

This project exceeds binaries that posit Black and Native as always separate groups, as well as claims that prioritize a particular group's oppression or the chronology of their liberation. It also challenges the depictions that both groups have been (only) subjugated. Sexton writes, for instance, that "slavery . . . precedes and prepares the way for colonialism. . . . Colonialism, as it were, [is] the issue or heir of slavery, its outgrowth."[28] This scholar speaks to Miles's diagnosis that "at our present moment, in the second decade of the twenty-first century, the mood writ large of black and Native relations is sobering."[29] Whereas Sexton imagines the "unsovereign slave" as distinct from the "colonized native," Leroy, among others, shows how in historical fact (rather than scholarship "at the highest levels of abstraction")[30] settler colonialism and antiBlackness, "settlement and slavery," are "entangled" or "mutually reinforcing" rather than discrete.[31]

Leroy states that "there has not yet been sufficient theorization of how to integrate non-indigenous, non-settlers—primarily the enslaved—into a theory of colonialism without subordinating the dispossession they experience to that of indigenous people."[32] Much of the scholarship attempting to do just this turns to nineteenth-century US history, examining Native slaveholding, Black settlement, intermarriage, and alliances.[33] My work turns to contemporary Black people negotiating and living in and among—and *as*—Native people. Rather than subordinating one to the other, I analyze Black and Native relations dialogically as inhabited within particular bodies.

If scholars today who study Black and Native relations prioritize the concepts of race and indigeneity, the scholarship on Hawai'i tends to privilege ethnicity and culture.[34] However, the ethnicity paradigm privileges culture without sufficient attention to racism. Ethnicity is a selected identity that, according to Jonathan Okamura, refers to a group's "shared identity, culture, and social relationships," which can form the basis for shared social interests.[35] However, self-identification (as opposed to imposed, or racial, identification) does not fully explain Black life or the political economy of resource distribution in the Islands. An ethnicity-only analysis highlights a group's ancestry and cultural practices, and attendant concepts like "multiculturalism" flatten out differences (for instance, by defining Hawaiians, haole, Filipinos, Japanese—and Black people—as generally equivalent ethnic groups). How does this speak, then, to the material inequalities whereby "people of Japanese and Chinese descent and white people make the most money on average, while Native Hawaiians and people of Filipino and Samoan descent make the least on average"?[36] Ethnicity is insufficient because it conceals the unequal methods and material impacts of power.[37]

Applying an ethnic paradigm to Native Hawaiians is specifically problematic because "talking about Hawaiians as simply another ethnic group tends to negate their indigenous claims to land and government in Hawai'i."[38] This ethnicization of Kānaka Maoli parallels the Guyana scholar Shona Jackson's argument that "the continued identification of Indigenous Peoples in terms other than those in which they see themselves, and consequently relate to the land, represents their real and figurative displacement. It also reflects attempts to not necessarily disappear Indigenous Peoples but to subvert the radical difference they represent."[39] The Native studies scholar Jodi Byrd levels a similar critique in her interpretation of the Black feminist scholar bell hooks's listing of groups that include "Native," "Asian," and "Hispanic Americans" as those who express antiBlack sentiments so as "not [to] be seen as residing at the bottom of this society's totem pole, in the category reserved for the most despised group."[40] "Ironically," writes Byrd, "hooks's framing of white-black paradigms [or local framings of haole-Japanese paradigms] refracts a . . . foreclosure with regard to indigenous dispossession."[41] In a twofold move, ethnicity flattens out power differentials among groups and hides the racial and state power of nonWhite groups, including local Japanese.

Understanding the dynamics of Hawai'i requires us to center race and to account for settler colonialism and antiBlackness simultaneously. Examining ethnicity alone not only conceals the workings of power but, more insidiously, is also part of the process of how in the Caribbean, North America, and

Hawai'i, "those brought in as forced labor (racialized capital) now contribute to the disenfranchisement of Indigenous People."[42] In Hawai'i, these laborers include not only Asians, Portuguese, and Latinos; members of the African diaspora, too, continue to labor in the Islands.[43] They cannot simply be viewed as oppressive settlers or as only representing a state of abjection; they are also not "just another ethnic group."

The Places of AntiBlack Racism

Black locals and transplants alike shared experiences that map the spaces of antiBlack racism: at home, school, and work. Black locals tended to focus on home and school during their childhoods. Transplants who usually arrive as adults focused their descriptions on workplace discrimination, which was familiar yet disappointing to them. After all, fleeing racism was a central reason they moved to the Pacific. I conclude this section by illustrating Black people's encounters with local police—a topic that came up significantly during the rise of the Movement for Black Lives. In contrast to Black civilians' interactions with White and Black police officers in the continental United States, what does it mean when police officers are neither White nor Black and are often respected family and community members? Do we find an absence of police brutality in this site of "less pressure," or does it take on different racial and gender contours?

Taken together, these powerful testimonies affirm the existence not only of racism but also specifically of antiBlack racism in Hawai'i. Our analysis must account for both settler colonialism *and* racism in the Islands. Adding to the growing scholarship on settler colonialism, the experiences of Black people make the presence of racism evident. These findings call for further study of the institutional and everyday racism encountered across island communities, including those of Micronesians. By collecting evidence of Black civilians' racist encounters and their resistance to them, I analyze the foundations of racial inequality in hopes of, in the book's conclusion, formulating methods to address antiBlack racism in Hawai'i.

Family Words, Fighting Words

Pōpolo
Pōpolo Hawaiian
Hawaiian Nigger
Saltwater Niggers

Indians in Hawaiʻi
Black Nigger Cousin
Nigger
Toads

Almost without exception, every Black local I spoke with has been called "nigger" (a term that, as a nonBlack person, I never utter). Missionaries in the 1830s used the term "nika" in their journals. The word "nigga" is now a common term bandied about by nonBlack locals, especially men, as a result of the popularity of hip hop. I delve into the repercussions of hurling this epithet or otherwise using it to distinguish and denigrate Hawaiʻi's Black children. While Sharon Chang's study of multiracial children illustrates how people outside their families called some the n-word, Black children in Hawaiʻi faced this within their families.[44]

Locals recounted the times they were called the n-word by a schoolmate, a friend, or a cousin. Only one Black man stated that he had not experienced anything that vulgar in his Hawaiian community. Perpetrators used the word to tease these children for their dark skin and African ancestry, but not always along those lines. In some cases, locals used the term to describe dark people whom they knew were not African descended. Several people told me of Hawaiian family members for whom this was their nickname. A Black old-timer recalls when the family members of her former Hawaiian partner would casually call their sister the epithet. The Black southerner said to me in disbelief, "That was just her name! She was browner, but it was not seen as a derogatory thing. And I just went nuts: 'How could you call her that?!' 'She's always been called that,' the family responded, 'she doesn't mind.'"

Ignorance about Black people is neither an excuse nor the full explanation for this practice. Local Black childhoods are peppered with denigration and ostracism, revealing residents' complicity with centuries of White supremacy. Colonizers divided Pacific people into differentially valued "races," drawing from their devaluation of the people they constructed as "Black" in order to justify the colonization of Africa and enslavement of West Africans.[45] These processes shape the lives of African-descended people even in the "most isolated landmass in the world." American imperialism compounded these associations, particularly since World War II, when large numbers of Black and White soldiers—and their ideologies—invaded the Islands. From the 1970s through the 1990s, when many of the locals were young, they further had to contend with historical stereotypes of Black deviance advocated in the media frenzy around early rap music.

Hawai'i has much to teach us about interminority racisms, beginning with the fact that race is more than simply about "the color of one's skin." Several local Black hapas were fairer skinned than their family members, yet they were taunted. Island residents used the n-word to distinguish and disparage—and sometimes simply to describe—people of African descent in their families and communities. It was also used as a fighting word. A police chief's son hurled it at one young local girl, whose mother was Black and father was Okinawan. Another Black Asian woman was assaulted with the label when she was twelve; she did not know the meaning of the word. As elsewhere, people insist that the context, intent, and familiarity framing the exchange are key (e.g., it depends on who says it and how they say it), similar to debates over the familial and in-community use of "nigga" versus the epithet ending with -er. But a Black Hawaiian remembers, "We were teased for being dark skinned. The word-slang was 'nigger' by Hawaiians and non-Hawaiians. It had a negative vibe. It's ignorant."

Most locals did not feel these to be lasting wounds from childhood. A Black Hawaiian said that, regardless of their other ancestries, "they saw us as Hawaiians growing up here!" Others suggest that the pain remains. A Black Hawaiian recalls how her cousin—"just as dark as me"—would introduce her. Apologizing to me before she went ahead with the story ("pardon, this is her exact words"), Nicole said her cousin introduced her to people by saying, "This is my Black nigger cousin." Like others in the 1970s and '80s, Nicole wasn't aware of "how bad [this term] was." She didn't know how to react until she went home and told her grandmother. What she learned from her tutu, however, was how exactly she and the hurtful cousin were related—that her cousin was also part Black, just like their Hawaiian tutu. The next time her cousin tried to introduce her in the same way, Nicole responded: "You're a Black nigger, too," she says, laughing at the memory.

This story arouses complicated reactions. The cousin's antiBlack racism is disturbing, as, perhaps, is the fact that she did not know of her own ancestry. Tutu also linked Blackness to skin color. Nicole followed her tutu's advice when she next encountered her cousin: "'Hold out your arm,' I told my cousin. 'Your arm is darker than my arm.' And she just went speechless. I said, 'My grandma told me that you are a Black nigger, too.'" What does it mean to clap back with the same terminology used to cause hurt and surprise, denigrating what could bond them? There are no hard-and-fast rules for these exchanges, as people attempt to figure out their meanings outside the context of a Black community. These children patch together information, often asking non-Black elders—or even (part) Black kūpuna in this case—who themselves may not have all the answers.

Black locals did not respond aggressively, perhaps because they did not initially know what these words meant. A local boy, Ryan, was called the n-word in elementary school and decided to "tell on him." The offending boy was sent to the office, but Ryan did not "hold a grudge or want to beat somebody up." Ryan was one of the few Black locals with two Black parents and says that he and his friends commonly used the term "nigga." However, he distinguished this usage from its more problematic employment: "You'd have local [nonBlack] boys trying to emulate or White guys trying to emulate Black people."

"Black," "pōpolo," and the n-word are all terms used to refer to Black people, but they resonate differently, from being descriptive to hurtful, and sometimes as terms of self-identification.[46] A Black Okinawan vividly remembers almost getting into a fight as an adult. Tommy told me about an instance when he overheard locals at a house party telling a joke: "'What do you call a Black baby?' and somebody else yells, 'Oh, you mean what do you call a nigger baby?' I didn't really want to start anything, so I muttered under my breath, 'You know, it's not like a Black guy is standing right here.'" Someone from the party heard his comment and instigated his friends: "Oh, there's this pōpolo guy here talking to you guys." Losing his temper, Tommy responded, "'WHAT?' And I started going moke [almost starting a fight]. 'I don't want to hear that. Don't give me that pōpolo [shit]!' And they were just quiet."[47] After he left, Tommy heard them say, "Did you know there was a Black Sāmoan guy who lives across the street?" further racializing and misreading this tall Black Okinawan through tropes of Sāmoan *and* Black physicality and excess.[48]

People in these islands have gleefully cultivated ethnic and racial nicknames of all kinds, smartly and often lovingly exchanged in banter. Scholars theorize local humor as a way to share tight spaces across difference and include "haole" to refer to White people as uptight outsiders, "pake" referring to Chinese people and stinginess, and "Portagee" referencing the long-established Portuguese legacy, many of whom intermixed with Hawaiians and Chinese.[49] Portagee jokes are often coded as "stupid" jokes, performed routinely by the beloved local Portagee-Hawaiian–chop suey comedian Frank De Lima.[50] Walt, a Black Sāmoan, analyzes local humor in this way: "It's almost like a bad parody of stereotypical parodies from the mainland, where you see the frugality of what's stereotypically applied to the Jews applied to the Chinese. You know, the Polish jokes applied to the Portuguese. You see these mirrors. We're just mimicking bad mimicry, you know. But that exists here, and I would get the brunt of some of that because there were very few kids in my neighborhood, you know, ethnically African American or Black."

Figure 4.4 A fake advertisement for "Popolo Suntan Lotion." The advertisement, from a 1981 book featuring local ethnic humor, states that the formula is based on the discovery of a "new hormone, AFRO-102" and ends with the comment, "You may also discover a new talent for sports like basketball and track." The bottom of the ad offers: "CAUTION: Overuse of POPOLO Suntan Lotion may mislead other local people to assume you live at Schofield," referring to the military barracks on Oʻahu. Source: Simonson, Sasaki, and Sakata, *Peppo's Pidgin to da Max*. Photo by author.

Walt's description of "*ethnically* African American or Black" echoes state representative Cedric Gates's description of his "Half African-American *Ethnicity*." This aligns Black people as (just) another ethnic group in the Islands while shying away from racial matters. People in Hawai'i are much more comfortable coding race as ethnicity and find it difficult to name racism as such; recourse to ethnic humor allows this obfuscation. As a result, many Black children do not know what to do in these encounters.

Rather than a jestful enveloping into the collective "we," Black people's experiences illuminate the racist deployment of words used to denigrate and hurt people. Every local is familiar with the terms "pōpolo" and "nigger."[51] They remembered family members, neighbors, and classmates using these names to distinguish them from other cousins or peers and to denote ugliness. The friend of a Black girl said, "You can't trust Black people," and her best friend told her, "I know what can make you mad: if I call you a nigger," revealing her awareness of the word's power. With regard to "pōpolo," Black locals who grew up with the term mostly object to or at least pontificate about it; transplants don't mind as much. A Black and White long-term resident didn't consider himself to be hapa, which he thought meant "half Japanese," but he didn't mind "pōpolo." The recently created organization Pōpolo Project is a clear reclamation of the term.

A few Black locals preferred the term "pōpolo," including Kamakakēhau, who shared his preference for the term online:

> ["Pōpolo" is] a choice of word I use because every other person who is from Hawai'i knows and relates to when speaking of someone that looks like me ... it's never offensive unless you make it offensive. The term actually again referred to the pōpolo [nightshade] berry. And it would be a good thing to look up, cause it's uses are quite profound and in a humans case, relatable through the actions some people choose to put out into the world. Does it offend me? Nope! Even the N word. None effect me because, I never grew up in that era nor did I have to deal with the struggle of a black American. It's my race but not my story. At the end of the day we all the same ...

Rather than advancing a color-blind ideology that refuses to acknowledge (racial) difference, people in the Islands obsess over difference—*ethnic* difference. We see this in Kamakakēhau's profession of an ethnic reading of labels that is not so much colorblind as race blind. Like several other Black Hawaiians, he asserts a global universality among people as all being the same (human) and focuses on the intent of the person using the term.

A Black Mexican Hawaiian man also reframed pōpolo on his terms, recounting, for instance, "You do run in with a few knucklehead locals that could call you an olopop and shit like that," Daryl laughs. The music producer follows locals who have linguistically flipped the script, saying "pōpolo" backward to invert its negativity, a playful engagement with terms of difference. "I mean locals here all make fun of each other, whether you're flip, bukbuk buddha head, Japanee, chink. It's all in good humor. [But] it's still fighting words the way you say it." A Black Hawaiian Japanese man says, "I've heard Black guys say, 'Hey, don't call me fucking pōpolo.' . . . They equate it as meaning the same thing as 'nigger.' Or White people, they think haole is the same as calling them a 'cracker.'" Other locals were opposed to the term.

A Black Korean woman raised by her Korean mother stated, "Pōpolo is offensive to me." A Black Sāmoan man made a Polynesian linguistic link: "For the record, I hate the word 'pōpolo.' I think it's a derogatory word. Sāmoans say 'meuli,'" which I was told means "dirty," and his understanding was that "it means Black. But it [depends] on the way people say it" to determine the intent, similar to the difference between saying "haole" descriptively and "fuckin' haole" aggressively. He would prefer that people not feel the need to categorize others: "When they say 'meuli' instead of just saying 'that guy,' they always have to point out that he's Black, you know?" He represents a small number of Black locals and transplants who preferred not to be racially defined at all. Another local grew up with the term in his Hawaiian community, "But for me, I never embraced it. I never thought of myself as being a pōpolo. I thought of myself as a Black Hawaiian." Colin suggests that "some people, they embrace the [word] 'pōpolo' because it's a Hawaiian word meaning Black. But for me, I just had my own ideas of what I wanted." He felt his chosen term more accurately reflected him: "If I say I'm Black Hawaiian, you already know what the ingredients are, the package, you know?"

While much has been made of Hawai'i's multiculturalism and the plentitude of terms referring to its demographic diversity, the popular media and scholarship on ethnicity and local humor have paid little attention to Black labels. Numerous stories of Black childhoods in Hawai'i test the feel-good and often valid celebrations of ethnic humor as a form of bonding. In some cases, Hawaiian-language terms like "pōpolo" envelop people of African descent in local communities. The term's adoption by Black people may reflect integration, or perhaps Black transplants find it positive relative to more familiar derogatory terms.

"Pōpolo" may signify a connotation more grounded in the Islands than terms like "Black" or even "African American." At a 2019 social event in

Waikīkī that celebrates the African diaspora, Black men wore T-shirts emblazoned with "PŌPOLO IN HAWAII." (Another Black man wore a T-shirt that read "More than an Athlete," also to contest expectations.)[52] Conversely, locals sometimes adopt terms like the n-word.

The law professor Randall Kennedy opens his exegesis of the term in his best seller, *Nigger: The Strange Career of a Troublesome Word*, with a reflection from childhood. (Note how the book's title provokes readers to contend with their use of the term.) When did he, a young Black boy raised in the US South and East Coast, first hear the word from a White person? It happened in DC in the early 1960s, and yes, a White boy did it. He was able to walk home "and at dinner calmly related the events of the day. I asked my parents for advice on how best to react to a white person who called me a 'nigger.'"[53] While he received a bundle of advice from his mother and father, Black locals often return to homes without Black parents. And in all cases that locals recounted, White people were not the first to volley this term. Indeed, several recalled that it was a term first used by a family member.

Racism at Home

I've had to disavow myself from the whole victim status. But it still hurts me when I talk about what it was like growing up experiencing the racism that existed here. But it was there, in my own family, and it sucks. I'm sorry to say, but it comes from the Hawaiian community. . . . My mother's mother is pure Hawaiian descent, and she was the most evil, rotten person I think I've ever experienced in my life. I was mortified. . . . I was her little nigger. It was awful what I went through as a child. She was rotten. I couldn't say anything about her because all my other cousins, they revered Grandma because they were White. And I was the nigger grandchild, you know what I mean?

TINA, A LOCAL BLACK HAWAIIAN WOMAN

Black people may be integrated into local communities through their nonBlack families, but in our embrace, we may not recognize the ways that we disparage them on account of their racial difference. Black locals faced stereotypes of Black people along with racial epithets from their families, friends, teachers, and community members. These denigrating experiences distinguished African-descended members of Hawaiian, Sāmoan, and Asian families who often had nowhere—and no one—to turn to for solace. Locals also experience more intimate forms of racism within the domestic sphere—an experience shared by many multiracial people across the United States. The sociologist Joe Feagin writes: "Parents do not teach their multiracial children substantial anti-racist lessons about our racist system, its principal discriminators, and the omnipresent white framing."[54] Yet what of the racism by nonBlack parents of Black children that happens within the intimacy of the home? Zeroing in on the dynamics within nonWhite and nonBlack families raising Black children expands studies that analyze the racism encountered by both multiracial and Black people. Studies of multiracial youths are usually based on surveys and analyses of visual and other representations.[55] Those based on interviews tend to record a moment in time rather than a long-term engagement with people. Ethnographic documentation can inform our everyday interactions and suggests strategies for societal change.

Transplants and locals may *describe* the same kinds of incidents (being called the n-word, facing workplace discrimination), but they do not *define* these experiences in the same way (as "racism" or not). Black locals did not easily address my questions about whether they had ever experienced racism. Far more often, they used versions of the term "prejudice," employing it in ways that seemed foreign to the tongue, describing "prejudism" and "being prejudist upon." In part, this is due to local understandings of difference. As Roderick Labrador explains, "The local foregrounding of ethnicity elides the importance of race, racism, and racialization processes."[56] Labrador, Rudy Guevarra Jr., and I show that Filipinos, Mexicans, and Black people in Hawai'i each experience "marginalization, racism, and discrimination" through "ethnic" humor, politicians' anti-Mexican nativism, and everyday antiBlack racism within the context of Kanaka dispossession in a settler state.[57] Explicitly using the vocabulary and lens of race allows us to confront, rather than deny, these problems.

Tina's powerful story of racial abuse recounted at the start of this section was unique among the locals I spent time with. Nonetheless, others were also unfavorably compared to hapa haole or part-White relatives. Brandon Ledward writes about the general receptivity of Kānaka toward "White Hawaiians," who emerge from centuries of Hawaiian unions with haole and their population decimation similar to Native Americans.[58] Yet the same cannot be said for Hawaiians with African ancestry. Black Hawaiian men and women recounted instances of nonbelonging and rejection, from Papakōlea to Nanakuli. They felt like outliers as the darkest and tallest in their families or outsiders because of their absent fathers and because most of their cousins, who were also mixed, were part haole. Whereas being hapa haole is a way of being Hawaiian, Black

Hawaiians contended with racially specific labels as well as racist actions and comments about their physical difference. These comments shape Black locals' understandings about the value of Blackness—and thus themselves—leading to their ambivalence toward identifying as Black, discussed earlier.

Within the context of US colonization of the Islands, race intersects with gender, class, and Kanaka epistemologies to shape the experiences of Black Hawaiians who faced racial denigration from multiple communities. Lisa was adopted by her tutu—her mother's mother—and is the darkest person in her Hawaiian family. It was only later in childhood that she learned that not just she, but three generations on her mother's side, had African ancestry. Lisa's tutu warned the youngster not to speak pidgin, as she already had four strikes against her: she was from the Hawaiian community of Wai'anae, she was Black, she was Hawaiian, and she was a woman. Parents and other elders, who came of age around the time of statehood and explicit Americanization efforts to assimilate Hawai'i's population into patriotic Americans, often taught Black Hawaiian girls to not speak pidgin. With two exceptions (two Black Hawaiian men from a Hawaiian Homestead community), none of the participants spoke pidgin with me during our interviews. As Ty Tengan and others have shown, pidgin connotes a marker of ethnic masculinity and can be employed situationally as a form of code-switching.[59] The literature scholar Kara Hisatake defines pidgin: "the language developed by the multiethnic plantation laborers of Hawai'i in the early 20th century, the major common vernacular language of the Hawaiian islands today, inflected with the languages of the people of the islands, including Hawaiian, English, Japanese, Chinese, Portuguese, and so on. It is not a substandard language, but it does not come with the prestige of English or Hawaiian languages."[60] Yet many of the participants feel that not speaking pidgin is a way to distinguish who they are from how they look—or their abilities from people's expectations of them.

Despite—or perhaps because of—her experiences with racism and people's constricting expectations based on her identifiably African features, dark-skinned and gregarious Lisa implores us to consider culture over race: "Rather than race, I would like to talk more about culture. And the uniqueness in everybody's culture. It would be wonderful if we could embrace culture versus race. Especially when you're gonna decide something, you make a decision when you judge someone by their race. You do it subconsciously, we do it, but it would be great if we didn't." Her perspective calls to mind the singer Kamakakēhau's ethnicity-conscious but race-averse approach to difference discussed earlier. This optimistic turn to culture, however, does not address the codification of racial differences into cultural ones. Étienne Balibar terms this cultural racism "neoracism": "racism without race," wherein cultural (rather than racial) differences are called on as being "insurmountable."[61] Having lived through Americanization efforts, elders attempted to protect their children by molding them into proper national subjects. In the process, however, they understood and at times advanced economic (being from Waiʻanae), colonial (being Hawaiian), racist ("you're Black"), and patriarchal ("you're a woman") stereotypes. This also played out in the unequal treatment of Black hapas in comparison to their fairer-skinned hapa haole family members. The cross-generational transfer of knowledge from women charged with raising Black children communicated that Black girls faced particular forms of regulation, signifying how their race, gender, class, and nativeness intersected.[62]

AntiBlack racism and sexism communicated through these lessons are symptoms of colonial oppression—that mechanism by which Black and Hawaiian people are linked and continue to be so through enduring "interrelated logics" of racism, colonialism, and heteropatriarchy.[63] This emerges in local beauty standards. Hair is a particular issue for women like Nicole, a Black Hawaiian, given the centrality of beach culture to social life. This combines with the hapa haole ideal of feminized beauty that favors long hair that flows down the length of one's back (although very long hair with volume is especially important for hula dancers). Black Asian and Black Hawaiian girls found it challenging to get ready as quickly as their Asian peers whose hair needed little management.

Other forms of gender-specific rules about race existed within their homes. Hawaiʻi is not just infected with racism from its east (the continental United States and Europe); it also arrives from its west, from Asia. Asians in Hawaiʻi include Asian nationals or immigrants from Asia, including businesspeople and students, as well as the mothers of Black Asian locals who participated in this project. In Vietnam and Korea, for instance, Black soldiers and their mixed race children—the reminders of war with the United States—face antiBlack racism, motivating their mothers to move to the Islands.[64] However, Hawaiʻi did not pan out to be problem free. Arrivals from Asia encountered people, often immigrants, from the same Asian countries living in the Islands. Black and Asian girls confronted colorism—a global phenomenon within both Black and Asian communities.[65] Mothers could not always protect their children, even within the home, such as when they advanced antiBlack racism themselves. Family members did not want their daughters to get too dark in the strong island sun (much as my father warned me), and Asian mothers advised their children against dating Black people.

Colorism and antiBlack directives hold particular and painful resonance for Black children. Their experiences align more closely with the at-home racist experiences faced by transracial adoptees that Heidi Bub illustrated in the documentary *Daughter from Danang*. White and Vietnamese, Bub's relationship to Vietnam—and being Vietnamese—is irrevocably complicated by the anti-Asian racism of her strict southern White adoptive mother and White siblings.[66] However, this film and writings from transracial adoptees tend to highlight the stories of nonWhite children within White homes.[67] Hawai'i is home to a greater percentage of multiracial Black children raised in nonBlack—but also nonWhite—families. Local Black hapas thus recall navigating the complicated and problematic terrain of their mothers' antiBlack ideas without access to sources of Black pride.

Family and community knowledge of a child's Hawaiian, Okinawan, or other genealogy does not buffer them from facing less than total community acceptance. Although family members may not have access to information about Black history, they *do* know not to confuse their children with nonlocals or soldiers. As a result, the general assumption that "Black equals military" does not apply in this context. It thus requires us to confront the very real antiBlack racism that cannot be mistaken for being an antimilitary critique or local humor.

The antiBlack racism that flows across oceans combines with the local specificity of Hawai'i's colonial history and plantation narratives that erase Black people. Yet the experiences of Black children in Hawai'i are not simply the outcome of residents' naive espousals of colonial and racist epistemologies; antiBlack racism is entangled in current political moves that aim to *contest* colonization. As the Kanaka Maoli scholar Stephanie Teves explains, "Defiant indigeneity is an amorphous performance of Indigenous refusal and defiance, a purposeful performance that sometimes articulates heteropatriarchy, colonialism, and even antiblackness, but it also affirms Indigenous strength and pride in your ancestors."[68] Part of the current Hawaiian resurgence could take on the task of probing the antiBlack racism of Hawai'i's people through the accountability insisted on by the principle of kuleana.

The flourishing of Hawaiian practices and pride since the 1970s renaissance is gaining momentum, with the protectors of Maunakea defending the 'āina against the construction of the Thirty Meter Telescope (TMT). This activism is now also happening, as of the final editing of this manuscript, during a massive global protest against racist state violence. Sparked by the police murder of George Floyd, the intersection of protests for Black life and the COVID-19 crisis is leading Hawai'i residents to reflect on the conditions faced by Black people "over there," across the ocean. Part of Hawaiian activism and the kuleana of all locals should include our acknowledgment of antiBlack racism *in Hawai'i*—the pain of which is often carried by family members. The historical and transnational complexities of White supremacy, colonialism, and antiBlack violence shape but extend beyond the dynamics of Black childhoods in local families. They reverberate at school, not only in the taunts of peers who may not know better, but also in the actions of teachers, who occupy positions of influence. Home is not always a space safe from racism or a place that protects Black children. Neither are local schools.

Racism at School

Locals' negative grade school experiences sometimes were an extension of what they found at home; other times, these incidents confounded them. Schools in Hawai'i do not sufficiently teach African American history, nor do they provide the context for the presence of Black students in their classrooms. K-12 teachers often advance antiBlack racism through neglect and by their unequal treatment of Black students, which affects peer relations. Overall, Black locals enjoyed diverse friend groups based on being local; none primarily affiliated with haole. They attended public schools spread across O'ahu, including Roosevelt and Kalani in town and schools in Wai'anae, Wahiawā, and Mākaha. None of them attended the elite private schools ('Iolani or Punahou) populated by larger numbers of haole and Hawai'i's elite, although several graduated from the Kamehameha Schools for Native Hawaiians.

Intersecting dynamics explain antiBlack racism in schools. A Black Hawaiian woman who went to school in the 1960s and '70s clarified that "it's not just the Hawaiians that are being racist—the Filipinos, always. They didn't want anything to do with me, you know. The Japanese . . . the only reason I was allowed in their little clique was because I was smart and they had to be with me, because I had good grades like they did, you know. We formed alliances because they had to let me in." Strategic and temporary bonds aside, Black students also had to contend with their peers' parents. "No, you can't come to my house because my mother doesn't like you," said one friend. I asked if this adult's reaction was because she was a Hawaiian child. She clarified, "Because I'm Black. That was the experience I had with my Japanese friends at school. I couldn't come to their house, I wasn't welcome." A Black Sāmoan man had the same experience, as did several other locals, painting a damning, albeit unsurprising, picture of Asian antiBlack racism.[69] Elsewhere, I show how (South) Asian immigrant parents cultivate hegemonic norms and expectations for their children within the United States by, among other things, praising their unique cultures, aligning with the model minority myth, and enacting antiBlack racism.[70] This allows them to distinguish themselves in a racist society as non-Black people of color.

Yet instead of forming insular communities, locals have multiracial peer groups, including that of a Black Hawaiian whose best friends included a Filipina and a girl who was "part Caucasian, part Hawaiian, and some other stuff." While they all had different kinds of hair (theirs was "wash and go," as Nicole called it, whereas she had to take the time to flat iron hers), she says, "[I] definitely didn't feel isolated. I felt different, as a female . . . in middle school, and there's a difference," but she felt that growing up amid the diversity of Hawaiʻi "was the best part. We didn't really talk about race all that much." A Black Hawaiian man who attended Lincoln Elementary in Honolulu agrees: "Everybody's kind of young and accepted of everybody's difference." It was in intermediate school when things changed, and he found himself with few friends.

In high school, racial differences solidified, especially for those who attended schools with Black children from the continental United States. This did not make Black locals' friend groups any less mixed. A Black Okinawan man was "just going from elementary school where everything was safe and all my friends were together" to "these other schools [with kids] from military bases being on the same campus. . . . People start to gravitate toward what, who they look like. I wanted to hang out with a lot of my local friends. But then I noticed, you know, the Black kids." These children of Black military transplants found Tommy odd: "Why are you cruising with the locals? What's your deal?" they asked him, "'cause nobody could ever tell I'm half Asian," he explained to me. A local Black woman who went to Kaimuki High School in Honolulu explained, "This is going to sound horrible, but growing up I didn't have any contact with other Black [people]," except for a friend who was Black and Asian. But when she "did have contact, the girls from the mainland who were Black were really mean to me." To this day, she doesn't understand their reaction but points to the influence of place: "I think a lot of it had to do with culture—those people from Boston are just rude." Nonetheless, she, like the others, maintained her "eclectic" group of friends, including punks, haole, and gay boys.

AntiBlack racism within schools developed out of a colonial context of the forced assimilation of Hawaiian, Japanese, Puerto Rican, and other island residents. In 1906, the Department of Public Instruction in the Territory of Hawaiʻi adopted the "Programme for Patriotic Exercises in the Public Schools." The fourteen-page document hosts a title page bearing an image of the American flag; the back page is simply adorned with a picture of George

Washington. The pamphlet includes requirements to "salute to [the] flag," speak the Lord's Prayer ("in unison"), and sing any of the suggested "Patriotic Song[s]" followed by "formal talks" by teachers on any given "Patriotic Topic of the Day."[71] Black children face school-place racism from nonWhite sources within the context of this century-long implementation of Americanization, including English-only learning.[72] Thus contemporary antiBlack racism takes place within the colonial public school system (elite schools were formed as missionary schools). While many studies have looked at schooling for Indigenous and Black students separately (e.g., the Carlisle Indian Industrial School, the development of segregated schooling for Black children), what do we know about Black children in schools populated by Native and Asian students? Or about those who are Black and Native? Some Black Hawaiians attended Kamehameha, a school for Native Hawaiians influenced by the Hampton School. (The Hampton School, founded by a haole missionary from Hawai'i, was modeled on a school founded on Maui by a formerly enslaved missionary, Betsey Stockton.)[73]

Black adults from the continental United States are often shocked by these accounts of school-place racism, and they advocate on behalf of their children and other local Black youths. They issue firm statements about the unacceptability of racism and demand accountability, all of which may be denied. However, locals who offer their interpretation of these events frame it as a discrepancy between "mainland" African Americans' racial baggage and local ways of "doing things" that include ethnic humor doled out to all. As Labrador shows, however, "local humor" tries to level out inequalities and functions on behalf of Hawai'i's multiculturalism, which is "largely ethnicity- and culture-conscious, but not race and racism-aversive."[74] Taking offense at these jokes (the most popular ones are not about Black people, signifying their invisibility) becomes a sign of one's nonlocalness, whereas "the emphasis on ethnicity is a strategy that helps shift the focus away from race and constructs a racism mute ideology."[75] In response to this denial, Black parents who are transplants, rather than the nonBlack parents of Black hapas, may turn to the courts.

A 1998 article, "Racism at Wailuku School 'Really Wrong,'" reports the physical and verbal harassment faced by a Black boy at an intermediate school on Maui and the weak response of school administrators. The boy and his mother came from Chicago and Minneapolis, where they had "never encountered such a great degree of racism" as the boy did while attending school in this Hawaiian community.[76] His mother filed a complaint with the Office for Civil Rights in the US Department of Education.

Long-term Hawai'i resident and Black attorney Andre Wooten, who has argued several antidiscrimination lawsuits, told me about a 1997 case he fought against an O'ahu public school. Under the photographs of three African American students in that year's Kalaheo High School yearbook, the caption read: "I like pigs feet! I like hog mollz! Where da collard greens? Who got the chintlinz." In an op-ed in the *Honolulu Star-Bulletin*, "Slavery Still Haunts Us at Kalaheo," Wooten explains that "this particular joke has negative racial connotations" and the statement refers to "slave food. That is food African Americans were forced to eat because the master ate 'high on the hog,'" and thus "the slave was left to eat the pig's intestines and feet." He raises the legal ramifications of the incident as "racial harassment," which is "illegal under U.S. Constitutional Law under the 13th and 14th Amendments." Wooten not only asserts that the "yearbook slurs emphasize a deficiency in the competence of Kalaheo teachers and administrators," but also provides potential remedies: "We suggest that schools make it a point to include in their curriculum the history of Africa before the introduction of the slave trade."[77]

Illustrating the tension between Hawai'i and continental US perspectives, Reuben A. Ingram, who self-identifies as "black American" in his penned response, insists that "Blacks must stop using slavery as a 'crutch.'... The [African American students] in the [yearbook] photo need to rise above this and get on with their lives."[78] Taking on the lawyer directly, Ingram writes, "I disagree with Andre Wooten's July 19 View Point column that the students were made fun of, libeled and emotionally damaged. Mr. Wooten, how can this be? We continue to eat these great foods today. If they were so bad, bringing back memories of slavery, we wouldn't continue eating them."[79] Wooten's $28 million lawsuit was deemed "crazy." Another letter writer, Ms. Robertson (the school's head librarian), expressed her anger over the lawsuit, feeling that asking for and getting apologies should have been sufficient. In her op-ed in the same paper, the librarian advises the students to "rise above the dubious insult. Get over it. Your ancestors were not you, and you are not slaves"; she admonishes the Black boys for "playing the victim."[80] Rather than supporting the Black students (the victims of this racism), Ms. Robertson clarifies that "of greatest concern to me are statements about Kalaheo High School."[81]

Ms. Robertson sums up: "Racism comes in all colors." She denounces Wooten's suggested curricular changes, stating that "we do not need education to 'stop attacks on blacks.' We need education to stop attacks on people, period. If there is racism at Kalaheo, it exists because the school is on the third rock from the sun and inhabited by Homo sapiens. Sometimes even African Americans insult non–African Americans. If the AALA [African American Lawyers Association] demands 100 percent success, it might try another planet."⁸² Robertson advances a universalist perspective (we are all "Homo sapiens") similar to that expressed by Kamakakēhau and Lisa. But this race-blind view rests uneasily with the fact of unequal difference in the Islands. For instance, schools, many of which were founded to Americanize Hawai'i residents, teach the plantation history of the Islands, but they do not teach anything about Black migration to the Pacific.⁸³ In the end, whereas Wooten advocates a curriculum focusing on African Americans ("Who will decide whose history should be deleted so there is time to teach more African-American history?" Robertson asks), she ends with this proposal: "I propose we stop calling ourselves African Americans or Hawaiian Chinese Scottish Irish English Americans [she identifies as the latter combination]. Let's just be Americans, people or human beings." Robertson suggests that racial identification and tribalism are the problems, as is Black-on-Black violence ("We should also teach how Africans were enslaving other Africans long before the white man came along"). In this view, the whopping $28 million lawsuit seems excessive in a place where "ethnic humor" is exchanged daily.

This distinction—locals' denials and Black transplants' adamancy that these are racist incidents backed by institutional power—is based on perspective. However, could it be that, in Hawai'i, this is *not* racism? That perhaps African Americans from the continental United States have a "chip on their shoulder" and "don't understand the islands," as locals have told them? It may be true that it takes a long time to understand island dynamics—the particular brand of humor, the significance of where one went to school, or the meanings ascribed to different terms and backgrounds. However, this is what Black transplants, including Black attorneys, argue: antiBlack racism exists in Hawai'i; it is used to benefit the existing power structure on behalf of the Asian and haole elite; and this benefit in part works when locals, including Black locals, cannot identify racism.

In our conversation two decades after the lawsuit, Wooten says that he first sent the school a letter asking them to "take this out of the yearbook, and they wouldn't respond." It was after this exchange that Wooten and the students filed their lawsuit. Winning the case, each of the three students earned a payout from the state—albeit *far* from the requested compensation. Wooten says that "three of them went to college with the portion of money, which was really gratifying. Of course, they didn't go here. They all left; they would not go to college here."

Distinct priorities and interpretations of harm and injury personify the split between the perspectives of Black transplants and locals (Black or otherwise).

This particular case, however, was far from unique: it is just one of several lawsuits alleging racism against African American students, but it is one of the hundreds of other examples that go unreported, especially by locals, but emerged in my conversations.

Racism against Black students brings Black transplants and Black locals together when old-timers draw on their knowledge of both racism and the law to advocate on behalf of targeted Black students. Transplants did not go to grade school in Hawaiʻi, but their children do, as do the Black children of local Asian, Sāmoan, and Hawaiian women. Black parents recount experiences they more immediately (than locals) identify as "racist." A Black long-term resident who raised her multiracial daughters on the islands, years ago intervened upon witnessing a Black girl on the Windward Coast of Oʻahu being harassed near her house. Classmates taunted the large girl with frizzy hair, inspiring Karen to go to the school grounds. "This is not healthy," she schooled the principal, "this is not good for this child."

Another Black arrival to Oʻahu related several depressing anecdotes about her ten- and twelve-year-old local son and daughter, whom she raised with her African American husband. Teachers—primarily local Japanese—told her son that he was dumb and cast him in the role of a monkey. These ideas rubbed off on his classmates. If trouble happened at school or if a kid misbehaved, a classmate said, "We'll just say he [her son] did it." Not all locals expressed especially negative childhoods, but one girl came home from school and told her mother, "I hate being Black, Mommy." This pair of Black parents were upset enough over these kinds of incidents that they homeschooled their children, in line with the pattern of Black transplants advocating on behalf of (their) local Black children.

Racism causes some Black people—women more than men—to leave the Islands.[84] Kathryn Takara, who has collected an impressive number of oral histories of young Black women in Hawaiʻi, is attuned to the gendered dynamics of being Black in the Islands. She commented on the findings advocated by a Black principal at a local intermediate school:

> Some of the observations she made was that the Black boys here had an easier time than the Black girls because it was an "in" thing. But they're supposed to be the bad boys—you know, the rappers, whatever. So there was that popularity of the Black boys. But the Black girls with their often different body types and hair type and all of that, they had a much harder time. . . . Black girls have the hardest time here, in terms of high school.

Takara discusses how Black girls "don't fit the model. They don't feel pretty because of this Western standard of beauty. There's the Greek standard and then there's the local standard [privileging hapa Asian femininity], and they don't meet any of them." While Black girls and boys faced racism at school, the taunts are gender based, with Black boys "benefiting" from images of Black masculinity advanced in hip hop culture. Gendered assumptions about Black men and women extend beyond assumptions that they are only in the military (men) or sex workers (women) to the gendered forms of racism they encounter. Many men and women I spoke with concurred, explaining that their sisters or other family members moved (back) to the continental United States, since life was more challenging in Hawaiʻi for Black women. This includes challenges related to me by some Black women who found it difficult to meet partners, especially if they preferred to be with a Black man or make Black friends. As Takara wrote in 1977, "Many Black women would agree that there is alienation; distance separates Black women as most tend to live in separate communities and neighborhoods."[85]

Black college students also faced everyday forms of racism and presumptions based on their race. Lili, a Black professor, was troubled by other faculty members' expectations of their Black students: "I think sometimes they are real and biased. In a classroom at the university, opinions of Black students are either not called upon, or sometimes they are mocked or put down in a subtle way. Or the assumption is, 'Oh, well, you're an athlete so you must not be smart.'" Early in our interview, Lili lobbed examples of racism confronted by her Black students. One was pulled over by the police in the wealthy neighborhood of Hawaiʻi Kai. In another case, a campus employee put the customer's change on the counter instead of in the Black woman's hand. (She watched and saw the same employee deliver another—nonBlack—customer's change directly into their hand.)

Institutional racism affects not only students but Black faculty, as well. Whereas Black locals and the children of transplants faced racism from coaches, teachers, and classmates in their public schools, the K–12 system was also a site of racism against Black administrators and teachers. In these cases, plaintiffs pursued—and sometimes won—lawsuits. Black professors, primarily all transplants, faced their share of discrimination, which affects their work and everyday experiences on campus. While Black locals' most poignant recollections are of the intimate forms of racism at home and school, Black transplants point to their places of work as the site of institutional and everyday racism.

Racism at Work

In a public meeting about the Kilauea volcano eruptions on the Big Island, Hawaiʻi County Mayor Harry Kim referred to the Deputy Federal Coordinating Officer, Willie Nunn, as "that colored guy in the back there." Nunn laughed off Kim's comments and later said he took no offense. Mayor Kim did not regret his statement and explained that in the multicultural context of Hawaiʻi, this is how people joke. "Somehow, the comment I made in that context," Kim says, got "twisted into racism. I guess that's the sadness of where we are today." News columnists related their disappointment, stating that Kim sounded like a "racist grandpa" (Lee Cataluna), and that "calling a Black man a 'colored guy' in 2018 is not so funny. It's unfortunate."

EMAIL TO *HONOLULU CIVIL BEAT*, 2018

Middle-class status does not protect Black people from racism, which plays out uniquely within white-collar occupations.[86] Black transplants, who tend to be middle-class professionals, articulate a distinct set of encounters with workplace racism compared to their local counterparts. African American chancellors, professors, and teachers have been removed from their posts; Black medical professionals face harassment by coworkers. Do Black professionals from elsewhere face workplace racism in Hawaiʻi because they are middle-class (and thus work with more Asians and haole) or because they are Black or nonlocal?

One way racism operates is through who is deemed eligible and appointed to positions of authority. Many top positions in Hawaiʻi go to haole transplants. In 2008, Alabama-raised Rex Johnson, the haole CEO of the Hawaiʻi Tourism Authority, was embroiled in a scandal. An auditor had discovered "emails whose contents are racist, sexist and bigoted on the official business computer."[87] The Black environmental activist and Hawaiʻi resident Carroll Cox, who hosts a local radio news show, wrote a searing indictment: "Though African-Americans here in Hawaiʻi don't have to be out of the City limits by sundown [referring to "sundown towns"], and we don't get dragged from our homes and beaten, many of us have to cope with subtle acts of discrimination and disparate treatment in the form of systemic and institutional racism projected on us in a variety of ways."[88] Black transplants recognize how racism creates institutional inequalities resulting from people in power making decisions about hiring, firing, and other policies that affect the lives of those under them. They comprehend the devaluation of Blackness as a global phenomenon—one adopted in the Islands by nonWhites. State auditor Marion Higa found the emails, but Cox argues that she "elected to ignore and conceal [their contents] from the public."[89] This led Republican governor Linda Lingle to "ask for [Johnson's] resignation," primarily based on the sexually problematic content; Johnson's resignation earned him a $290,000 payout.[90] He was nonetheless hired soon thereafter as project director of the National Disaster Preparedness Training Center, which worked in partnership with the University of Hawaiʻi, revealing the lack of seriousness with which both the state and the university viewed Johnson's racism and sexism.

While it is difficult to find the content of these emails, a Black lawyer I spoke with said they included remarks like "make sure you don't vote for Hillary [or] Barack Obama because you don't want a beaver and a coon in the White House." The lawyer, who had testified against Johnson, was still incensed ten years later in our interview when she exclaimed, "Number one, how did he get to be the head of the Tourism Association?! Number two, felt so comfortable exchanging these jokes with people from Alabama?"

Black residents debate the definitions of racism. What these African American lawyers clearly classify as racist is dismissed by other Black people. Bankole Idowu, identified as an African American pastor by *Hawaiʻi News Now*, stated his support for Johnson: "I don't know the man but I can tell you one thing. He's not a racist. I can smell a racist a mile away. He's not a racist. I know what a racist is and a racist does not send emails that are jokes. A racist sends emails that are designed at wiping people out, and I'm disturbed that so many people would jump on the bandwagon with no more facts than they have."[91] This definition designates racism as a genocidal logic of "wiping people out" (which is one way it operates). More accurate is Ruth Wilson Gilmore's powerful definition of racism as a "state-sanctioned and/or extralegal production and exploitation of group-differentiated vulnerability to premature death."[92] Black transplants like the reporter Cox often interpret workplace racism in the Islands as an extension of White-on-Black racism, especially when the perpetrators are haole.[93] Rex Johnson imported racist ideas from the context of Alabama, just as many of the soldiers and officers stationed in World War II brought with them their southern racial paradigms.

While a continental Black/White dynamic seems to be operating in this case, transplants also face confounding encounters that disrupt their binary racial interpretation. Workplace racism in Hawaiʻi is shaped not only through its unique demographics; antiBlack racism and settler colonialism also work together to shape group relations in Hawaiʻi. Thus antiBlack racism in the Islands is and is not like racism across the United States, especially when taking

Asian demographics into account at over 40 percent of the Islands but under 6 percent of the US population.

Attention to Black and Asian relations in Hawai'i not only expands the focus beyond Black and White but also contributes a Pacific perspective to Afro-Asian studies.[94] The ethnographic evidence in these islands underscores national patterns of Asian antiBlack racism, but Asia also informs these processes. Each of the examples that follow highlights Asians, both local and from Asia, as agents in positions of power with the ability to affect workers' lives.

Black transplants who face discrimination at work are both surprised and disappointed by its perpetrators. A Black and White real estate agent said he was puzzled why, after a decade of working in the Islands, he still had no Japanese clients. Another real estate professional was questioned by clients and coworkers who did not believe that this young Black and Mexican woman occupied the position that she had earned: "It's apparent in the way they interact with me and speak with me that they don't believe I've been here as long as I've been because I'm not Asian. It's like (*laughs*), 'What are you doing here? What is your place here?'"

Sometimes racism is intangible and intuitive—something that others can thus refute or not see, and legal courts will not accept as evidence in their demand for documentation of discrimination. In our first meeting, a Black professional apologized to me for her mood. She was solemn and pensive: "I don't know. I may have faced some discrimination today with my . . . manager. I'm sorry to be a downer." Locals often interpret these as "claims" by people who have a "chip on their shoulder" and erroneously read everything as "racial."

Other incidents, however, are accompanied by irrefutable, precise, and targeted actions. In March 2018, *Hawai'i News Now* reported, "Nurse who found photo of noose on locker gets $3.8M payout"—the largest damages awarded in state history.[95] Based on her account, Ellen, the Black nurse whose story opens this book, had reported her concerns with patient safety at Queen's Medical Center, where she worked closely with Filipino nurses, and then faced racial threats. She found a photo of a hangman's noose taped to her locker at work and a note in her mailbox with the n-word directed toward her. Similar to the Kalaheo yearbook incident, although both won their legal cases, neither the hospital nor school administrations took clear responsibility for the harassment, and neither was forthcoming with an apology.

Mayor Kim, who had joked about "that colored guy in the back," also did not apologize for his infraction. The Hawai'i County mayor more recently made the news when advocating for the development of the Thirty Meter Telescope (TMT) on Maunakea, magnifying the Kanaka fight over sacred lands. Activists took the local Korean politician to task for his statement: "If you're going to trample on their [Hawaiians'] soul, please do it with care [and] with caution and compassion."[96] Kim made these insensitive remarks just one month before his notorious introduction of Willie Nunn (quoted at the beginning of this section). Viewed as an interpersonal interaction or gaffe, Mayor Kim's unapologetic stance after the incident reveals his lack of both judgment and accountability. More systemically, however, it underscores his participation in Asian settler colonialism *as well as* antiBlack racism. The *Hawai'i Tribune* reports Kim's explanation that "being open about race is the multicultural local style he grew up with. As schoolchildren, it was typical to cast aspersions on the contents of other kids' lunchboxes, while sharing each culture's offerings around the table."[97] While this description of multiethnic Hawai'i may be the case, note the slippage from teasing banter to the one-sided and specific antiBlack racism repeated by locals—primarily Asians—in Hawai'i. What passes for "just jokes" can serve as a cover for racist ideas that denigrate groups in patterned ways—ideas that are foundational to systems of oppression that create unequal rates of incarceration, access to resources, and homelessness.

Locals may have agreed with the mayor's explanation that this is the way people joke in Hawai'i. After all, even as other state workers are found guilty of discrimination, sexism, and bigotry, locals debate the application of "racism."[98] Transplants, on the other hand, are both firmer and more public about exposing harassment, especially when it is clearly no joking matter.

The attorney Andre Wooten, who won the Kalaheo High School yearbook case, told me he also won a $1,055,000 jury verdict in a discrimination case involving Umar Rahsaan, a Black high school teacher in Honolulu who was overlooked for promotions.[99] Wooten related to me what he thought was important in the case, which he fought and won twice in the early 2000s: "This was the same Japanese principal. . . . He picked a Japanese woman who had two years' experience in the system [versus Rahsaan's two decades' of experience]; both of them have their master's degrees." Wooten also calls Rahsaan's entrance into that school a form of "integration": "He was the first tenured Black teacher to ever teach at Kaimuki High School." Rahsaan received hate mail, including an anonymous "no Niggers" sign sent to his mailbox—just like the kind received in the mailbox of Ellen, the Black nurse who won the multi-million-dollar lawsuit.

To be clear: winning lawsuits does not prove that racism exists, just as losing lawsuits does not mean racism was not enacted. The Hawai'i law professor Charles Lawrence argues that "the law's claim that we are 'color blind,' its post racial tale of 'no intent, no fault, no injury,' covers up and hides the wounds that racist, sexist, homophobic images still inflict."[100] The law is neither colorblind nor evenly applied, as it was created to benefit White people at the expense of Black people and other disenfranchised groups. Michelle Alexander starkly illuminates how "the current system of control permanently locks a huge percentage of the African American community out of the mainstream society and economy. The system operates through our criminal justice institutions" to create an "undercaste" of "individuals who are permanently barred by law and custom from mainstream society."[101] Linked by a federal system, these dynamics extend across the Pacific to the "justice" system in "the fiftieth state," generally run by local Asian and haole lawyers, prosecutors, and judges. The details emerging from lawsuits—against nooses and other forms of racial terror—reveal the underside to the "it's just jokes" brush-off that locals often give in response to charges of racism by people from elsewhere. Lawrence understands that, especially in these small islands, "it may seem unbearable to see and feel the open wounds of our racism, sexism, and homophobia, but if we can listen to each other's stories we can begin to heal."[102] This suggestion shores up the principles of restorative justice rooted in communication and repair and kapu aloha, which Maile Arvin defines as "a prohibition against acting without kindness and love towards all."[103]

Although I interviewed a number of professionals in law and medicine, the largest number of transplants I spoke with worked in higher education. The UH system—one of the biggest employers in the state—has placed Black faculty in a precarious position. Some are not hired for tenure-track jobs, others are not granted tenure (effectively, they get fired), and those who do earn permanent positions are often persuaded to leave the Islands for jobs elsewhere. The faculty I spoke with provided copious examples of workplace racism, accompanied by a sharp analysis of the institutional and racial dynamics they navigated.

Black scholars who are invited to teach in Hawai'i recall being overlooked, excluded, and disregarded. A faculty member was mistaken for being a student for years by a restaurant worker, which the professor interpreted as the worker's sense of the impossibility of a Black professor. In classes on race, the Black diaspora, and African American studies, Black faculty (few as they are) teach a range of Asian students, including locals and those from across the United States and Asia. A Black professor from the East Coast noted his Asian (from Asia) students' suspicion toward him and felt they questioned his intelligence. Black students and faculty contend with various iterations of Asian antiBlack racism, both from the United States and from Asia.

Black newcomers who discuss implicit and explicit antiBlack racism link racial hierarchies with material inequities to challenge discourses of equality. According to an educator:

> A lot of that is about talking about the local culture, the experience of everybody getting along, everything's fine. But everybody isn't equal. So what does that mean when certain groups are of a particular ethnic background and they live in [the wealthy Asian and haole area of] Hawai'i Kai, and others are living in [the working-class Polynesian neighborhood of] Kahuku? What does that mean? And so that's what we work with a lot, and how those experiences are racialized.

This professor reflects, "I think there are some [experiences] that are more subtle and that I will continue to encounter. I've seen it with other African American colleagues here—you know, dealing with levels of racism and presumptions within the administration." Her words highlight the aching repercussions of intangible forms of racism that are so often glossed over:

> It's not always that they're explicitly called the n-word, though sometimes that does happen. But sometimes there's always this subtleness that's either through the administration or through teachers and other students that it's okay to devalue Blackness, or that it's not relevant, or that the pain or offenses that the [Black] students have experienced are supposed to be swept under the table, because "we're all multiethnic, and we just joke here!" And so, when you have people who should know better at the administrative or at the faculty level, not necessarily giving any positive input or helping out the situation just reinforces that—for the student—that Blackness doesn't matter and that this is who I am: I don't matter.

It is perhaps not surprising that Black studies, or the study of the African diaspora and race, is not a priority of either K-12 or higher education in Hawai'i. The flagship university's "Black or African American" student population is a mere 1.5 percent (less than half their overall representation in the population), but they make up a large proportion of the football and basketball teams.[104] The numbers are even more embarrassing at the faculty level: 1.2 percent in 2015 ("Caucasians" or White people were 53 percent; the combination of Asian ethnic groups was 35 percent; Native Hawaiians were underrepresented at 5.5 percent; American Indian or Alaska Native were a paltry 0.4 percent).[105] (The official university website still uses the archaic term "Caucasian" to refer to White students.)[106]

The almost eighteen thousand UH students at the flagship Mānoa campus have almost no opportunity to learn about local, national, or global Black history, although the strong Department of Ethnic Studies offers courses on race. This department has had one position dedicated to an African Americanist, yet even this minor institutional commitment has been tenuous. One professor did not get tenure; another left for a faculty position on the continental United States, only to be replaced by an adjunct who was then displaced by a new tenure-track hire. A few other departments (history, sociology, American studies) offer courses on race in the United States, but few scholars focus on the Black diaspora. None is an expert on Black people in Hawai'i, except for emeritus professors like Drs. Jackson and Takara. However, this may be changing with the latest professor to fill the position for an African Americanist. When in 2017 the ethnic studies department hired Ethan Caldwell (my former PhD student, a Black and Asian scholar from California who examines Black and Okinawan relations in Okinawa), the new hire was required to teach courses on the Black experience in Hawai'i and to reach out to campus and local Black communities. One hire at the state's flagship campus, however, is insufficient to adequately cover such an important part of Hawai'i's population while working with community members. (This is perhaps even truer for Hawai'i's Latina and Latino populations.)

These accounts hold repetition and tension. In numerous documented instances, Black people face erasure, racism, and the threat of violence, all of which create a hostile workplace environment. In response, some residents, like AALA cofounders Andre Wooten and Daphne Barbee-Wooten, express outrage. Their response is typical of older Black transplants who voice their resistance against racist treatment. What facilitates such resistance? Is it working in professional sites, which in the Islands tend to hire haole from abroad who together create an environment more like the rest of the United States, including Black and White hierarchies? How do Black transplants' experiences contest (Black) locals' insistence that this is not racism but rather a form of communication and relationality in the Islands? Locals use racial terms to describe and tease, rather than just to denigrate ("the haole guy over there" and "eh, you get pōpolo?"). Is this because locals do not see, or even deny, racism because they are more fully integrated into island life, or because they have a distinct understanding of difference? That both locals and transplants related experiences with police and offered various perspectives on policing—an issue central to Black life in the continental United States, highlighted by the Movement for Black Lives—illustrates the parameters and stakes of this question.

Policing in Paradise and the Movement for Black Lives

And I know you brothers wanna know, what's the cop situation out here, and I will say this: the cops don't mess with brothers. A lot of police out here are Polynesian, Hawaiian, Samoan. . . . And lot of them . . . say, "Howzit, brother," and "Welcome to the island," and they'll talk with you, man. So you don't have a lot of cops out here sweatin' you man, and shaking you down and pulling you over. You know what I'm sayin', so. You can just live in Hawai'i, you really can.

A BLACK MAN IN HAWAI'I

There is institutionalized racism here [in Hawai'i], and for a long time, I think Black men were demonized by the judges here. . . . A Black man could go before a judge for theft and go to jail, whereas a Japanese man would not. You know what I mean? Nobody wants to touch it. You don't get any response. . . . Another avenue to look at is the disparity in our Hawai'i justice system: a majority of people in prison are Hawaiians, and that tells you something is wrong. There are a disproportionate amount of Black men also in the prison, which tells me something is wrong there, too.

BLACK LAWYER AND LONG-TERM RESIDENT

Police relations with Black community members in Hawai'i contrast markedly with those in the continental United States, highlighted by the Movement for Black Lives. For instance, a Black Sāmoan athlete from the East Coast felt that the police disproportionately pulled over haole in Hawai'i. Another Black arrival felt that "it's not as intense. Just when I have encountered, or my husband has encountered, any police, the exchange has been more pleasant." Black locals, too, comment on this "difference," driven by the international protests against police brutality sparked by a Minneapolis police officer's murder of George Floyd. Several Black locals took to social media to publicly declare their mahalo to Hawai'i and its people for raising them in conditions that protected them from possible murder. As one Black local participant tearfully recounted in a live Facebook post during the national 2020 uprising, "What would have happened if I wasn't raised here? My life would be so different." What accounts for this difference? Many locals agree with the sentiments of the Black man in the first quote above, despite their interactions with law enforcement. Black men call on this as one of the reasons they experience "less pressure" in the Islands. However, Black women, both local and transplant, recalled experiences with the police quite distinct from those of Black men who had moved from across the United States.

Although police surveillance and the tension of city life are what pushed some people to immigrate to the Islands in the first place, some recounted incidents with the police. In general, however, they were surprised by police demographics and their interactions with the public. A Florida-raised dark-skinned Black man with short dreadlocks engages with police for his work. This has allowed him to see their "human side," whereby comprehending them "as locals first" has led to positive interactions. He had been told "by so many Black people ... that the police are great" in Hawai'i. He contrasts this with the time he lived in New York as a "tall bearded Black guy" when 9/11 happened. His mother was concerned that he would be profiled and asked him to tie his hair back, whereas, he said, "I don't have that fear here."

This greater sense of ease resonates with a Black old-timer who reflects on her upbringing in the Jim Crow South and as an activist in the 1960s: "My interactions with police have been essentially okay. My neighbor up here used to be a policeman, and actually being here was the first time I felt free of that police intimidation and violence and fear." She "definitely also think[s] that there is less overt tension, discrimination, fear of the police. But I think that's also a class thing," because Hawai'i does not have a large or concentrated population of working-class Black people. Or, as a Black man quoted earlier went on to describe, "You don't have a lot of hood, thuggish black folks here."[107]

When one Black transplant was homeless and sleeping on the street at the edge of Waikīkī, he recalls a police officer using his foot to wake him up. But the situation did not escalate. The elder from the South says, "When I see a police car now, I don't get a tight feeling in my shoulders that I'm about to have a problem—that it could potentially be a nightmare. And so, regarding that, I relaxed a lot, and I mellowed out a lot. But I have to remember, though, to keep my skill sets sharp in case I do go back to the mainland." Some, however, had negative experiences with police, who generally are not Black or White and are members of so many local families. If nonlocal Black men found relief in Hawai'i, Black women, especially Black Hawaiians, recounted their run-ins.

The most memorable story was told to me by a Black Hawaiian woman whose father was a Black police officer in the continental United States. She grew up on O'ahu, where her "experiences with HPD [Honolulu Police Department] has been nothing but crap!" Pulled over several times, she argues that "they give me a hard time because I'm Black. I had a (local) Japanese officer throw me up against the car" as she was trying to tell him where she was headed.

She has been pulled over by a haole officer who called for backup and "yanked me out of the car, threw me up against" it. Another darker-skinned Black Hawaiian woman was shaken by her more recent encounter with an HPD officer who "abused his authority" and was a "prick." She publicly recounted the officer's intimidation of her. Yet in the scores of responses on social media, only one asked about race ("Was he haole?"), and another person hoped that she hadn't been profiled (they didn't say "racially profiled") once the officer saw her. Both of these experiences suggest that Oʻahu police may be antiBlack *and* anti-Hawaiian *and* wage their violent abuse of power against women, as well as, I recount shortly, gender-nonconforming people.

Black men had their share of encounters, but they focused on the outcomes: they turned out better than they may have elsewhere. A forty-something long-term resident from the US South "got into it with a sheriff" outside his place of work. The officer was upset about a parking situation, "but he really tried to impose his power on me, and maybe unjustly so," the identifiably Black man said. Having been shaken after viewing videos on social media of police murdering Black people across the United States, Kurtis told the sheriff, "I don't feel safe with you." The encounter took place at the height of the Movement for Black Lives, and Kurtis considered how the situation could quickly have taken a turn for the worse: "They both had guns and dogs; I put my hands on the car."

I discussed the #BLM movement with participants, especially since the summer of 2016. Transplants understandably had more to say about this and expressed having a greater handle on the dynamics of what was being protested than did locals, who do not necessarily connect to, or feel that it is critical to keep in touch with, what is happening "over there." This is still the case during the nationwide unrest protesting the police murders of George Floyd and of Breonna Taylor, whom Louisville, Kentucky, police killed in her own apartment. Transplants felt that the Black Lives Matter protests were powerful, and politically engaged Black women said they felt "guilty" that they weren't part of them. At the same time, these women were relieved to be able to raise their (sometimes multiracial) Black children far from it all. A Black Mexican long-term resident feels "that tension and conflict" of living in Hawaiʻi but being connected to the continental United States: "Like, I want my [future] babies to grow up and not be shot to death by the police. I also want them to have some connection to what I had a connection to." The activism of Black women in Hawaiʻi pays homage to the work of Black mothers protecting their children from gun violence, including Chicago's "Mothers/Men Against Senseless Killings," two of whom—Chantell Grant and Andrea Stoudemire—were themselves tragically shot to death in 2019.[108]

The perspectives of Black transplants and Hawai'i locals can clash in the contestation over protests against racism. Hawai'i residents organized sizable rallies in support of #BLM in May 2020 in response to the murder of George Floyd. A Honolulu protest on June 5, 2020, organized by teenage public high school graduates drew over ten thousand supporters. Black Lives Matter events in previous years brought much smaller crowds. Ainy, a Black transplant from California and long-term Hawai'i resident, helped to organize a 2014 rally at the State Capitol. Inspired by the Black Lives Matter movement founded by Alicia Garza, Patrisse (Khan-)Cullors, and Opal Tometi, this rally was motivated by the murders of Black boys and men, including Trayvon Martin (Florida), Michael Brown (Ferguson, Missouri), and Eric Garner (New York), followed by the #SayHerName movement commemorating the murders of Black women, including Sandra Bland and the Black trans woman Nina Pop.

With a growing but peaceful crowd yelling, "Hands up, don't shoot," the 2014 Hawai'i rally happened to take place alongside a local children's performance of Christmas songs (it took place in December). With a crowd of about thirty supporters—mostly Brown and including UH students—yelling "Black Lives Matter!," local parents there to support their singing children told the protesters, "Shut up already! Nobody cares." Ainy interpreted this sentiment as meaning. "We don't have time to hear that shit"; one woman even threw her water bottle at a Black woman chanting for Black lives. Ainy recounts, "She was screaming, 'You guys are disrespectful! This is rude! This is our ceremony,'" pointing to her crying daughter, who had stopped singing. Another Black long-term resident chimed in to the recollection, theorizing that "they really don't like protesting about fucked-up shit. It doesn't matter how fucked up it is, [locals think] it's really offensive and rude to be loud about shit that's messed up." As the Black and Mexican long-term resident put it, "Screaming 'Black Lives Matter' in the street [in Hawai'i] is like a complete disconnect." This is the case despite the high-profile murders of young Hawaiians, like twenty-three-year-old Kollin Elderts, whose name graced the posters of several attendees at the 2014 rally. The sentiment to "keep that shit [protests against police violence] over there" in the continental United States remains in the May 2020 social media discourse coming out of Hawai'i, as the National Guard clamps down on those fighting antiBlack racism, and scores of cities burn.

Despite "less pressure" in Hawai'i, a state with one of the lowest murder rates (fifteen murders on O'ahu in 2017), concerns over police brutality and racial profiling remain central to Black people's interactions with the police.[109] Kurtis told the officer with whom he had the run-in at work, "I've seen Black

Figure 4.5 National protests spurred local conversations about policing in Hawai'i. This program titled "Hawai'i Matters: Black Lives Matter," featuring participants in this book, was hosted by local radio station KUMU. Source: Radio 94.7 KUMU.

people get shot on TV, and I'm not going to be one of those guys." The officer calmed down; they each called their supervisors. As it often happens on the Islands, Kurtis's supervisor knew a police officer, and "everything got diffused. And we walked away with nothing, with no tickets. Everybody was Kumbaya at that point." The incident worked out well because his coworker knew the officer, who "was local. I don't know, could've been Hawaiian." Who you know in the Islands—which is a function of how long you have been here and how well integrated you are—goes a long way in shaping whether an interaction turns tense or diffuses. Personal ties to locals help individuals, including the police, to connect and can overwrite indiscretions and positionalities that frame the initial encounter. Yet this was just one of Kurtis's encounters with officers.

Kurtis is a tall, lanky man who sometimes grows an Afro and has been pulled over numerous times during his three decades on Oʻahu. He believes the police attempt to charge him for things without any apparent reason. They ask him, "What do you do for a living?" perhaps suggesting that "me being Black in a particular kind of [nice] car [is suspicious]. In Waikīkī, you get pulled over because it's a perception that you are of a certain kind of stripe." The police may have thought he was a pimp. This happens less often now that he drives "a more sensible car," he says with a laugh, mentally recalling the outlandish vehicle he drove in his younger years.

Another long-term resident, too, has been pulled over "too many times," including at "every damn sobriety [check]point." Many of this gender-nonconforming person's interactions have been with women police officers. They theorize that their "masculine spirit" in combination with their Afro (since shorn) likely inspired these stops, some of which turned into getting "arrested a couple of times." In contrast to the views of other transplants, Ainy finds the police in Hawaiʻi to be a "little bit more aggressive" (in contrast to Los Angeles, where their father was killed as a young man), possibly due both to Ainy's Black and nonbinary gender expression. Ainy also is younger and not wealthy compared with Black professional transplants.

Even Black transplants who are spared these interactions scrutinize exchanges with the police. A long-term resident employs a racial lens when he determines that "it's just as institutionalized with these [Hawaiʻi] police forces [as] any police force. They're here to protect the people who pay their tab, which doesn't usually include someone of your color." A Black Mexican who has lived on Oʻahu for over a decade stated with anger, "Well, we fucking pay taxes, too!" to which they clarified: "I guess my concepts of the police are, they're protecting what is classified as the rich here. In Hawai'i, if you are rich, you are not Black. . . . You have been trained like a soldier to basically take out a group of people for the sanctity of the rich. That's it." On the other hand, a Black Hawaiian local who encountered an aggressive police officer tempered her anger at the incident with respect for "the men and women of the HPD just doing their job."

The reason policing is different in the Islands is that police are primarily nonWhite, although chief of police Susan Ballard is a haole long-term resident and the first woman to occupy the position. Many locals are proud to have family members or former classmates who are in the police force, leading to large networks of residents who know the officers in their daily lives. That familiarity also gives residents the discretion in encounters to be able to call on an officer's last name or to remind them of shared relations. There is not the practice of White police officers targeting Black and Brown men and women.

In 2013, Honolulu County Police Department ranked among the police forces with the highest minority representation: 86.7 percent of its officers were minorities (in contrast to only 8.5 percent of the Edison Township Police Department in New Jersey, for instance).[110] The Police Diversity Report listed "Hispanic" and Black full-time officers as less than 2 percent each of that total in 2013 (or 28 and 33 full-time police, respectively); Whites were 13.3 percent, or 277 officers, whereas Asian officers were over 30 percent, or 660 full-time officers.[111] Owing to the report's federal-based application of "relevant" racial categories, it does not offer percentages of multiracial, Native Hawaiian, or Pacific Islander officers. However, it lists 45 Hawaiian full-time officers (about 2 percent) and 23 American Indian/Alaska Native officers. A whopping 1,010 officers (out of a total of 2,076, or 50 percent) identified as "2+ Races," or non-Whites who likely included a large number of hapa Hawaiians, Asian multiracial people, and other Polynesians.[112]

Black scholars in the Islands have tried to explain these dynamics through a locally specific racial lens. The law professor Charles Lawrence has been an advocate for racial justice throughout his impressive career, from a defense of affirmative action to holding space for Black community members to mourn Black deaths resulting from police violence. In a beautiful video made by the Pōpolo Project in honor of his retirement, Lawrence says that Hawai'i became his home because he married an extraordinary woman from the Islands (fellow renowned UH law professor and Roosevelt High School graduate Mari Matsuda). In the video, Lawrence expresses a racial lens:

> One of the things that was apparent to me immediately when I came here was that I was in this place where there was this mythology about "we don't have race out here." A lot of my work had been about saying that racism still exists and exploring the ways that it works and that White supremacy is the framework that justifies and shapes discrimination against many different people of color.... So [in] Hawai'i [it] just seemed obvious to me that that was going on. Not just that it was going on that all these people of color were being discriminated against, but that they were all *positioned* differently by White supremacy. When you look at the history of Hawai'i, there's a group of people who are gonna be the n-people—they're gonna be treated like the Black people for purposes of getting everybody else to not see the way they're positioned by White supremacy.[113]

Lawrence's article "Local Kine Implicit Bias," offers an academic illustration of the components of the racial lens he describes and is advocated by those familiar with the US racial framework.[114] However, like his statements in the video, Lawrence does not center the experiences of Black people *in* the Islands in this article. He analyzes the court's harsh sentencing of a Micronesian man for the murder of his cousin.

Similar to the views of the Black transplants I interviewed, Lawrence's racial lens includes analyzing anti-Micronesian racism as a community-embraced form of implicit bias that is also *structured* within the court system (Lawrence questions the Micronesian defendant's long sentence), attention to racist terminology used by (Asian) lawyers and judges (prosecutor Darrell Wong "urged the judge [Randal Lee] to impose a hard penalty 'to send a message to the Micronesian community'"),[115] a racial reading of the defendant's photograph as antiBlack, and his interpretation that locals read Micronesians through the same stereotypes interpolating African Americans (criminality, racial lumping, and excess). These connections critique the idea of prejudice as simply an exchange between individuals and instead foreground structural and ideological analyses rooted in the history of segregation and the lynching and criminalization of Black people in the continental United States. With this historical, ideological, and contemporary lens, Lawrence links the structural reasons for the legal system's harsh treatment of the Micronesian defendant to the police murder of (other) Black boys and men across the United States. He points to the police murder of Trayvon Martin, just as other local reporters linked the young Black boy's death to that of Filipino Hawaiian

Kollin Elderts by a White US agent in Waikīkī (see the next chapter). Both these cases result from the racist criminalization of nonWhite boys and men by agents of the state.

Lawrence's conception of Blackness is expansive; it includes Micronesian and Hawaiian men whose lives are burdened (and cut short) by racist people in positions of power—who in Hawai'i include Asians. It privileges a structural analysis of racism informed by the historical racialization of Black people. The fast-growing population of Micronesians in Hawai'i experiences high levels of homelessness, lack of access to care, and other forms of structural oppression resulting from their forced migration due to US nuclear testing (e.g., bombing) on their islands.[116] They also face in-person racism and online hatred in Hawai'i, including comments that they should be deported, "killed, hunted, purged, and cleansed." Anti-Micronesians attack their phenotype (darkness), calling them "monkeys" and mocking cultural practices (clothing and language) while blaming "FUCKIN MICRONESIANS" for being an economic burden to the state.[117] Micronesians, who are neither African American nor Melanesian, face antiBlack racism, nativism, and adopted colonial hierarchies of Pacific Islanders. Anti-Micronesian racism is so extensive, including at the structural level, that the Palauan activist and Hawai'i resident Sha Ongelungel created an "anti-Micronesian thread of shame" to document it.[118] Such a dire situation benefits from a perspective that charts the transnational development, ideologies, and current practices of racism to contest local dismissals. Dismissal includes the charge that arrivals "just don't understand" local culture and are "too sensitive." Perhaps the most common response to Black articulations of racism is that "they have a chip on their shoulder" and should "get over" the past. By contrast, Lawrence's analysis places Micronesians as stand-ins for African Americans, as they share overlapping yet distinct racialization. Some Micronesians themselves do this, such as when a Micronesian tweeted that they were "the Black people of Hawai'i," in reference to the May–June 2020 protests against antiBlack violence. While critical, this approach further evacuates Black people—who also face racism—from view in Hawai'i.

AntiBlack racism in Hawai'i cannot be explained away as local humor or an interpersonal misunderstanding. Black transplants uncover structural race-based inequalities in "paradise."[119] Black people face harassment from Asian coworkers in hospitals and schools; Black children are discriminated against and disparaged by classmates and teachers. Addressing a subject especially pertinent as a result of the spotlight on police brutality on the continent, Black locals and transplants related to me their negative and traumatic interactions with local police—who tend not to be White. While these encounters may seem familiar to transplants raised in Black communities, US conceptions of White police encounters with Black and Brown men and women are not borne out in the Islands, where haole are a minority within police forces across the Islands.

At the same time, Hawaiian and Black people have many stories of getting pulled over and confronting the police. The racialization of Black and Hawaiian communities overlaps and expresses itself through contemporary inequalities, such as disproportionate rates of incarceration, shaped by antiBlack racism and colonialism—forces that are faced simultaneously by Black Hawaiians. The Movement for Black Lives, along with advocates of prison abolition, inspires Black transplants to remain connected to social movements "over there" across the Pacific. This has led some Black residents to host conversations on Black Lives and educate the public about Black history, accomplishments, and concerns here *in Hawai'i*, such as through the increasingly popular African American film festival. The Pōpolo Project has worked against the local erasure of Hawai'i's Black residents, demanding that the voices of African-descended people be at the center of local #BLM protests.[120]

For locals, however, their engagements with police are confusing, as they do not know if they are pulled over because they are Black, Hawaiian, women, not wealthy, do not conform to gender expectations, or are driving the wrong vehicle in the wrong neighborhood. (Black Asians did not share experiences with the police, possibly because of their higher-class status and affiliation with groups in political power.) This uncertainty influences their overall ideas about how racism operates in the Islands.

Conclusion: Confronting Racism in Hawai'i

I let my Afro grow, knowing it was a sign. I walked around with it and did shows with it. I was a part of pushing a Black Lives Matter kind of movement and protest out here with some other people. I was really feeling extremely provoked all the way up until then about not being identified as local, not being identified or smothered out just because there's only four Black people on the whole island. I felt really pushed about it. I definitely took it to the max when it came to Black History Month.

BLACK LONG-TERM RESIDENT

The thing that jumps out to me is that [Hawaiʻi County mayor] Mr. Kim [who called the FEMA *official "that colored guy"] said that this is how we talk about things in Hawaiʻi. While that may have been true in the past, it's not how we have to talk about things today.*

AKIEMI GLENN, EXECUTIVE DIRECTOR OF THE PŌPOLO PROJECT, 2018

I wanted to write an ethnography of Hawaiʻi's Black residents in part because of their erasure from local and scholarly narratives.[121] From my first interview, they described these Pacific Islands as an alternative and a "haven." I wanted to find out what *is* this haven where I grew up (as a South Asian and White local). How does it offer a counterpoint to the difficult subject matter that I cover teaching African American studies and Asian American studies just outside Chicago, the home to a Black Metropolis, hypersegregation, and rampant antiBlack police violence? What is it that the Pacific offers people of African descent? And how does the racial lens articulated across the work in Black studies apply to the Islands, where inequality rages and yet is submerged beneath state justifications for tourism and military occupation? I became more compelled to tell the stories of the Black people who allowed me to spend time with them as I also continued to hear their concerning confrontations with racism.

By now I hope to have illustrated the variety of forms of racism that exist in Hawaiʻi—that despite its hailed diversity and the opinion of a writer in the *New York Times* that one can become "less racist" by moving to the Islands, it is not immune to hierarchy and the differential valuation of people based on race. Even Obama's recollection of growing up as a Black boy in Hawaiʻi contests his uncritical applause of the *New York Times* piece. Important recent scholarship analyzes Kānaka Maoli conditions and political demands; this work by Hawaiian scholars and activists now influences the burgeoning fields of Native American and Indigenous studies. Hawaiʻi's inequality is also undeniable when we center African-descended people who face global and local denigration. This means that when patterns of racism familiar to scholars of African American studies who focus on the United States and the Black Atlantic emerge in the Pacific, we cannot dismiss it as a misunderstanding about local culture. I hope this ethnography, which coarticulates race and indigeneity, antiBlackness and settler colonialism, compels people in Hawaiʻi to address these forms of inequality, as they also distinctly affect Hawaiians, Filipinos, and Micronesians in differentiated ways, as they do other groups.

Black locals and transplants recount different experiences with and reactions to racism, invisibility, and ostracism. Black locals may not emerge unscathed by these dynamics, but they privilege local belonging over racial difference. They generally relegated "subtle" experiences with racism to their childhoods, when they were called the n-word, distinguished by their looks, or not allowed into their friends' homes. Locals are less likely to use words like "racism," preferring iterations of "prejudice," perhaps to be less damning of their family and community members. Transplants are less ambiguous. They were up-front in providing a host of examples of their unequal treatment. Locals and transplants also pursued the *meaning* of these experiences distinctly, thus shaping their reactions. Locals understood these exchanges within the context of local culture and especially the panethnic sharing of *ethnic* stereotypes that make the n-word similar to terms like "haole" and "pake." Transplants did not generally accept this as a joking matter.

Their stories together point to Asian perpetrators of antiBlack racism in Hawai'i. The Movement for Black Lives has inspired a generation of Asian American youths across the United States to analyze their relationships with antiBlackness and Black people and politics.[122] This is an uphill battle, as many of the older and immigrant generations were indoctrinated and preach anti-Black racism that is pernicious across Asia (or, rather, the world over). Asian parents in the United States monitor their children's peer groups, despising Black people, not letting them into their homes and thinking of them as negative influences. The same happens in Hawai'i. Black professionals disproportionately work with Asians and haole (and fewer Hawaiians and other Pacific Islanders) because of their white-collar occupations.

Transplants note the specific injuries of antiBlack racism that they were unwilling to let slide. As a result, they advanced lawsuits against their places of work and the state, often hiring Black lawyers who have lived in the Islands for decades and understand verbal, structural, and everyday harm as clear patterns of racist abuse and exploitation. This is especially the case because so many who come are middle-class and educated professionals of the civil rights generation who grew up during Jim Crow. They believe in using existing institutions of the law, medicine, and education for economic advancement and racial justice, advocating for *Black people*.

Centering Black diasporic experiences gives rise to spaces that air these grievances and for teaching the vocabulary to comprehend the global development of race and racism. Yet we find more generally that difference is leveled and dealt with playfully in the close quarters of island life. Locals, who respond to charges of racism by not discussing negative experiences and resorting to comedy, charge oversensitivity and unfamiliarity with Island culture, just as Mayor Kim did. This perspective is supported by the lack of knowledge about the histories, conditions, and concerns of Black people. The wounds and significance of these repeated reports of racism and erasure demand attention and repair. Some people in the Islands are working to alter these tendencies. In reference to Mayor Kim's description of "that colored guy," AF3IRM Hawai'i's Mykie Ozoa and Nadine Ortega explain that "the term recalls the Jim Crow era" of segregation. "Using this term today as if it is devoid of its original use and reference is unacceptable," say these members of the group that advocates for a transnational feminist transformation of society.[123]

Dissecting how the same words can be used both to create a joyous community and to harass and terrorize allows us to discern how and whether we employ these terms. I am not suggesting that we discard local humor—it is a critical component of local culture that cultivates community and humility and joy. Humor also has the power to express and alleviate pain in trying circumstances. But our unwavering defense of using epithets *in every instance* is clearly neither sustainable nor ethical. When one's concerns are repeatedly discounted in this way, Black transplants face a poignant repercussion: "When you're told over and over again what hurts or what is offensive isn't supposed to have much meaning, it does change your engagement with what hurts and what doesn't. It doesn't make it less of a pain, but somehow you realize, my pain is not valued here." This became apparent to Black professionals, including educators whose job it is to teach young Black people in Hawai'i.

Racism exists in Hawai'i. Black people's experiences help us *see* this more clearly; they also suggest how to address this (I discuss how to address anti-Black racism in Hawai'i in the book's conclusion). We are complicit in—if not actively accountable for—everyday forms of antiBlack racism against community and family members, sometimes mimicking the worst of what has developed on the continental United States. Not *needing* to open our eyes to the plight of African-descended people, as some who brush off the national protests throughout 2020 may claim, does not absolve us of our kuleana to educate ourselves.

If ignorance is not an excuse for racism, then education offers one remedy. The stories of contemporary Black residents provide us with a wealth of information for self-reflection. According to a Black professor, "Ignorance doesn't fly as well in other contexts, but here we see that kind of odd moment of either ignorance masking what should (*pause*)—what could potentially be a problem—but the idea that it's just ignorance and not being aware becomes the default over all colors, so 'get over it.'" What does it mean if Hawai'i's Black residents feel that "somehow there needs to be some kind of translation made in terms of local culture, the local experience, or my presence . . . always has to be filtered through this presumption of what it is to be Black and so forth," when, in fact, we don't know what "Black," in all its complexity and humanity, *means*? Rather than berating ourselves, this seems to present the opportunity to revisit what motivated the positive responses to Black arrivals by members of the Hawaiian Kingdom. It also presents the opportunity to return the openness of Black residents who took part in this project—a chance to learn from them and engage in dialogue and self-reflection—and insist that it lead to structural change, including divestment from the police.

5

EMBODYING KULEANA

NEGOTIATING BLACK AND NATIVE POSITIONALITY IN HAWAI'I

> *For me, it's not specifically a Black thing. It offends me that all of our disparate minorities—like whether it's Hawaiian or Asian or Black—it offends me that this colonization of the mind has been so successfully adopted. Our struggles are the same. The individual stories are different, the geography is different, but it is the same kind of aggression over and over and over again. That's why I'm so invested and want to learn more about my [Black and Mexican] heritage, because unless you're White, people are really sensitive to you taking on struggles that you don't have a genetic connection to.*
>
> BLACK MEXICAN LONG-TERM RESIDENT

The process of decolonization must also advocate antiracism, just as antiracist activism must also account for settler colonialism. However, the positions people take on matters of importance often emerge from their positionalities. Said otherwise, identities inform priorities and politics. What would it mean were the obverse to be the case? Angel, the Black Mexican long-term resident quoted in the chapter epigraph, seeks out knowledge of her histories to better understand how they link to others. As shown in figure 5.1, Patrisse Khan-Cullors, a cofounder of #BLM, reveals her support for Maunakea protectors and connects the struggles of Native Hawaiians to the Movement for Black

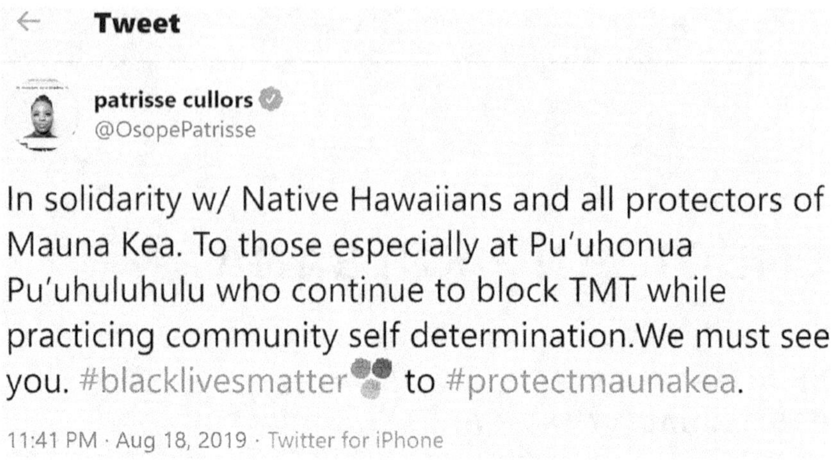

← **Tweet**

patrisse cullors ✓
@OsopePatrisse

In solidarity w/ Native Hawaiians and all protectors of Mauna Kea. To those especially at Puʻuhonua Puʻuhuluhulu who continue to block TMT while practicing community self determination.We must see you. #blacklivesmatter✊🏿 to #protectmaunakea.

11:41 PM · Aug 18, 2019 · Twitter for iPhone

Figure 5.1 Patrisse Khan-Cullors's tweet in support of the kiaʻi on Maunakea, August 18, 2019. Source: Twitter screen capture.

Lives. What would it mean to exceed our standpoints and to consider "our people" expansively rather than through ancestry and exceptionalism? After all, communities have been forged not only as divided and distinct but also as related and intertwined—as will be our futures.

What do Black residents tell us about Hawaiian pathways for self-determination—and what is their role? Their imaginings of the future do not align with native/settler binaries, do not prioritize Black liberation over others, and do not depend on claims to greater oppression. However, they do take race and responsibility into account, especially through their consideration of the Islands. By offering an ethnographically informed analysis that decenters both Whiteness and Asians in Hawaiʻi, this project shows how people who cross multiple boundaries, including those of race and indigeneity, Nativeness and Blackness, inform new ways of being and ethical belonging.

A significant and internationally recognized example of Kanaka political and cultural strength is the movement around the kiaʻi (protectors) of Maunakea who are resisting the development of the Thirty Meter Telescope (TMT) on sacred land. Hawaiians on Maunakea have developed Puʻuhonua o Puʻuhuluhulu (place of refuge), mentioned in the tweet by Khan-Cullors (figure 5.1), which includes a university with a Kanaka-based curriculum teaching Hawaiʻi's history, hula, and ʻōlelo Hawaiʻi. This resurgence of Hawaiian practices and practitioners presents an opportunity to reconsider theories of power and dispossession and to reflect on who "our people" are. What if the

Hawaiian practices of kuleana, kapu aloha, and knowledge of the past motivated an ideological shift back to precolonial notions of Blackness, to the esteem of Pō, the original darkness?

Kānaka resistance to the proposed TMT is already motivating some reflection. For instance, Larry Kimura, the Hawaiian language professor, and Doug Simons, the director of an observatory on Maunakea, took part in a discussion on the "Physics of Pō." They explored "the intersection of astronomy and Hawaiian culture" through an examination of the Kumulipo, the Hawaiian creation chant.[1] Can a similar approach inspire people of Hawai'i today to take the same stance toward African-descended people that Hawaiians took during the Hawaiian Kingdom? Hawaiians in the nineteenth century accepted people of African descent, including those who were enslaved in the continental United States, and cultivated a society that recognized their full humanity. Integration—rather than the exclusionary practices of the US nation-state—was a principle foundational to belonging and citizenship in the Hawaiian Kingdom.

While contemporary scholarship focuses on the distinctions and parallels between Black and Native peoples, the historical record shows centuries of engagement and intersection between them. This refers both to the historical systems of oppression (colonization, enslavement) and to social formations and relations on the ground. Dispossession is not a thing of the past, nor is African-descended people's particular vulnerability to premature death; equally, Indigenous people face dispossession, displacement, *and* racism, as—in differential yet overlapping ways—have Africans, who are also Indigenous people.[2] As one Black Hawaiian reflects on his coming-of-age in the 1970s, "Back then, it wasn't a good thing to be Black, and it wasn't a good thing to be Hawaiian."

The denigration of both Hawaiianness and Blackness ties to their distinct racialization and role in the US expansionist market. While White people constructed Native peoples as being outside the domain of "useful" (or cooperative) labor and as needing to be eradicated or removed for their resource (land), people of African ancestry have been more closely bound in the New World to their labor in a growing capitalist market.[3] The Hawaiian Homes Commission Act of the 1920s, which mandates that one be at least 50 percent Hawaiian to be eligible for certain benefits, works to eliminate Native peoples, thereby "freeing" Hawaiian land and resources for colonial settlers.[4] On the other hand, the much older one-drop rule, stating that any person with a "drop" of African "blood" is Black, is part of a legal regime that categorized the children of Black and White unions as Black and thus enslaveable.

The continental United States privileges a Black and White conception of race, leading some Americans to learn, for instance, how White settlers forged Whiteness in contrast to Blackness. This binary perspective depends on Native erasure and is central to justifying the continuing settler state, as "settler colonialism obscures the conditions of its own production."[5] Foregrounding settler colonialism reveals how, hand in hand with Native erasure, the "native" is pivotal to constructs of race and nation from its initial colonization. We cannot, therefore, conceive of this nation's founding as beginning in 1619, marked by the entry of the first enslaved Africans, because such a Black and White framing does not account for the Indigenous inhabitants of this place.[6] Evelyn Nakano Glenn summarizes, "While acknowledging the centrality of enslaved blacks to the formation of white racial identity . . . the Founders' first Indian policy 'was the inaugural step in defining a White racial identity for the United States as a nation.'"[7] As the Australian Goenpul scholar Aileen Moreton-Robinson observes, "Native American dispossession indelibly marks configurations of White national identity."[8]

Black enslavement and Native genocide and dispossession, along with nativism, exploitation, and exclusion of Asians and Latinos, co-constituted the formation of the US nation-state. These processes were justified through White settlers' distinct racialization of Black and Native people, both subjected to inferiority under White supremacy. Yet "given the transformation of Native Americans as ghosts [through elimination/erasure], it is not surprising that everyday conceptions of race came to be organized around a black-white binary rather than a red-white binary."[9] What happens when Black people, raised in a society in which this binary is dominant, come to the Hawaiian Islands, where neither "black-white" nor "red-white" is a hegemonic structure? And how does centering Black people within Hawai'i similarly disrupt accounts of Hawaiian history as an encounter between Hawaiians with haole?

Studies on Black and Native relations in North America focus on the relationship between settler colonialism and antiBlackness and between genocide and slavery.[10] Some scholars articulate overlapping histories of oppression to cultivate shared visions for self-determination or discuss the "proximities" of Native and Black colonization. Others remind us of the tense ties between Black and Native people.[11] Such debates presume these groups to be distinct, thereby ignoring the indigeneity of African-descended people. This includes the Native American ancestry of many African Americans and Africans' indigeneity to Africa.[12] On the other hand, scholars of Hawai'i have focused less on race in their analysis of indigeneity and ethnicity.[13] Kauanui argues that considering "Hawaiian" as a race denies their indigeneity and limits their political and legal rights as Natives.[14] Does applying a racial framework to Hawaiians contribute to the "logic of elimination" that, according to Patrick Wolfe (who was familiar with Hawai'i), feeds further on Indigenous assimilation through intermarriage, cultural absorption, and US citizenship?[15] No. Rather, analyzing race and indigeneity together reveals how colonizers deployed the logic of elimination to decrease the numbers of Indigenous people and "clear" the land for colonial settlement—including the establishment of racist ideologies. "Racialized knowledge and white possession," writes Moreton-Robinson, "work in tandem. These are white possessory acts, heavily invested in maintaining control and domination, that in our daily lives we experience as a form of racism, in which parts of our humanity are stolen and denied."[16] Moreton-Robinson pulls together Indigenous dispossession with racism: "Racism is inseparably tied to the theft of Indigenous lands."[17]

Viewing Black and Native as discrete groups may lead to abstract theorizing that does not play out on the ground. For instance, Afropessimist scholars argue for the irreducibility of Blackness and the priority of Black liberation above all.[18] In response, Native studies scholars and activists have taken Afropessimists to task for contributing to the erasure of Native peoples and undermining the history of genocide by focusing primarily on slavery and Black suffering. This tension, rooted in the view of incommensurability and identity-based politics, erupted in one of the Twitter debates surrounding the *New York Times'* "1619 Project," which commemorated the year the first enslaved Africans arrived in the British colony of Virginia.

The 1619 Project, led by the MacArthur Fellowship–winning journalist Nikole Hannah-Jones, cited that year as "the beginning of American slavery" and argued for "understanding 1619 as our true founding."[19] In response to this framing of "foundings," the Mojave poet Natalie Diaz asked: "But who are we willing to forget in order to be remembered? 'The Iroquois Confederacy/Haudenosaunee, founded in 1142, is the oldest living participatory democracy on earth[.]' Erasing one doesn't make the other more visible."[20] Project curator Hannah-Jones responded to such charges: "It is deeply painful to me that anyone has a problem with black writers wanting to mark and commemorate the most atrocious thing that has ever happened to our people, which is the start of our enslavement here and what it has meant. How does this possibly equal erasure of others?"[21] A tweetstorm emerged in support of Hannah-Jones, contesting the charge of Native erasure. The fast and furious response by scores of people characterized Diaz as "antiBlack," requested that she "stay in her lane" (only speak to and on behalf of Native issues), and admonished her to tell "her" story instead of belittling the project's narrative of slavery and celebration of Black American history. Hannah-Jones raised the ire of people across backgrounds more recently in her support of Black men in the US armed forces.[22] People called out the myopia of her US-centric focus on Black American integration that did not account for the impacts of US imperialism.

As should be clear from my work, I do not think people have "lanes" that they need to stay in mandated by our given identities (although acknowledging one's positionality is key), nor that one cannot contribute to the development of knowledge about the world's people, including those "outside" our "own" particular groups. As just one example, multiracial people illustrate the limitations of this expectation. What is the "lane" of people who identify as Black and Indigenous? What is the "lane" of Black people in the Pacific?[23] They have cultivated insightful if silenced perspectives about Black and Native relations based on their unacknowledged stories—perspectives that offer insight on these debates between Black and Native studies.

In previous chapters, I addressed the role of Black people in settler societies.[24] On the other hand, Indigenous antiBlackness points to Native people's participation in slavery, adoption of racist ideas, and denial of ancestral Blackness, which includes ostracizing part-Black Native peoples.[25] The historian Ingrid Dineen-Wimberly relates her disappointment with Black scholars who berate Black Americans who want to assert their Indigenous ancestry. The Black Native (Makah) Filipino family members she studied "stay Black while being Native" but grapple with "tribal relations and racism from within."[26] Dineen-Wimberly acknowledges how "studying multiracial identity within the context of the African American experience is frequently met with resistance, even suspicion."[27] In his study of tribes in the southern United States, Brian Klopotek argues that "this collective erasure of indigeneity in people with African ancestry should take its place among the massive acts of genocide in United States history."[28] How do such dynamics affect Black and Indigenous relations in the Pacific?

Black people's perspectives on their relationships to other nonWhite communities provide a model for informed solidarities that compare but do not conflate group histories. Black people in the Pacific make evident how a racial analytic must be part of debates at the theoretical, political, and ethnographic level. These debates include how antiBlackness relates to Native dispossession enacted by White colonizers, how this past relationality of racialized peoples and practices of oppression influences the conditions of these groups today, and how these ideologies and practices shape everyday relations among them.

We must consider these factors holistically to imagine and work toward liberated futures rooted in the self-determination of all people.

How can members of the African diaspora, nonindigenous to Hawai'i, continue to find sanctuary in the Islands without this being an exploitative process? We see people in the Islands articulating collaborative political visions of the future. The work of Hawaiian activists and their supporters, such as the local Japanese antimilitarism activist Kyle Kajihiro, has illustrated kuleana as a guiding principle for living together responsibly. This is a principle that can model future Black and Native relations through self-reflection, trust, and ethical care for people and land. Goodyear-Ka'ōpua explains how kuleana can shape our way through (rather than remaining stuck in) categories of being. The scholar-activist calls on kuleana to argue that "individuals who may be differentially positioned vis-à-vis land and ancestors [should] be accountable based on those specific relationships. Such a recognition does not relieve anyone from kuleana but rather acknowledges our different social, genealogical and spatial locations."[29] More an orientation and epistemology than a prescribed act, kuleana "can be an ethical praxis that asks one to consider what responsibilities a person has given their positionality in a particular locale and time."[30] Black residents consider their status and relationship to Hawai'i, reflecting on Hawaiian concerns and their relationship to the land.

I share Black residents' ideas of their kuleana to Hawai'i and Hawaiians, offering a Pacific counterpoint to debates in Black and Native studies that center North America. This includes analyzing the accountability of Black people in the military occupation of Hawai'i. Taking a deeply local approach to examining the negative experiences faced by Black transplants complicates their presumptions of antiBlack racism. I offer a framing discussion of how the conflation of Black people with the armed forces informs a local anticolonial critique of the US military. I then discuss Black residents' theories of sovereignty, liberation, and land—all articulated through a lens informed by their knowledge of African diasporic history, people, and politics. This understanding frames their global historical approach to considering Black and Native relationality.

AntiBlack Racism and an Anticolonial Critique of the Military

The negative accounts of Black people living in Hawai'i detailed in the previous chapter are not simply the result of antiBlack racism. This is because African-descended people are not only racialized; they are also imbricated in other systems of domination, including the military complex (note, for example, news outlets' uncritical celebrations of Lloyd Austin, the "barrier-breaking" first Black secretary of defense selected by the Biden administration).[31] The military emerges on the heels of a legacy of Kānaka-contested American domination of Hawai'i, including Christian missionaries from the 1820s, followed by the plantation and big business owners, and the illegal takeover and incorporation into the United States.[32] These interests represent a through line of haole commandeering of land and resources with blatant disregard for local needs and Hawaiian rights.

Black people across the United States who join the military are implicated in its flexing of influence and power in the Islands. They enter the armed forces for a variety of personal and structural reasons directly related to conditions shaping Black life. Yet enlisting is an exercise of agency—one that requires accountability, particularly (but not only) in wartime. By extension, Black servicepeople stationed in the Islands bear responsibility for the consequences of their presence, both locally and globally. Likewise, Black tourists are agentive visitors responsible for exacerbating the precarious social relations and worker exploitation that underlie the housing crisis. The state of Hawai'i, literally invested in the military and tourism, celebrates military contributions to the Islands by appropriating Hawaiian concepts of aloha and 'ohana (family) in the name of national security and "paradise."

Militourism and State Power

The dynamic between US continental racialist ideas and antiBlack racism is shot through by the current context of Hawai'i's illegal occupation. What is the role of Black people within what Teresia Teaiwa and Vernadette Gonzalez call "militourism," or the nexus of militarism and tourism? A scholar of Oceania, Teaiwa developed the concept to illustrate the "intersection of tours of duty with tours of leisure."[33] Gonzalez, an ethnic studies scholar, expands on this idea in *Securing Paradise* to reveal tourism and militarism in Hawai'i and the Philippines as sharing a "strategic and symbiotic convergence" that works to maintain US imperialism in the Pacific.[34] According to local scholar-activist Kajihiro, "Hawai'i remains one of the most highly militarized places on the planet, a 'linchpin' of U.S. Empire in the Asia-Pacific region."[35] Islanders are made to do the work of hiding the military "in plain sight," as Kajihiro told our class during our "Decolonial Tour" of Oʻahu.[36] What work does it take to make sure that tourists remain uninterrupted by soldiers in camouflage holding assault rifles (watch out if you take the wrong exit to the airport!), miles of inaccessible beachfront, the sound of military jets, and training grounds in the lush mountainside used to simulate the warscape of Asia and the Middle East?[37] How does the state make its people labor to keep tourists innocent of their role in Native houselessness, poverty, and dispossession?

The twentieth-century US military presence—with its hierarchical and segregated structure—shaped locals' view of Black and White people as outsiders. Two lethal cases—the Massie cases of the 1930s and the Deedy cases in the 2000s—highlight explosive and framing tensions in which race Nativeness, and US militarism figure significantly.[38] Rather than being exceptional cases that particularly require a racial analysis in contrast to the daily goings-on of life shaped by ethnic difference, these incidents reveal how racial politics undergird island dynamics across the twentieth century.

Race, militarism, and violence in a settler state come together in each case. The infamous Massie cases illustrate Navy transplants' interpretation of local difference through a Black/White framework, whereas Islanders responded through a local lens. This case in the 1930s, based on the White navy wife Thalia Massie's account of being kidnapped and assaulted by "some Hawaiian boys," rocked the Hawaiian Islands and garnered national attention. It was a watershed moment that the historian John Rosa shows helped to consolidate a "local" identity.[39] A second trial resulted from the kidnapping and lynching of one of the defendants, a Hawaiian named Joseph Kahahawai, by Thalia's mother, her husband, and two navy men (all White). The murder fractured relations between haole and Hawaiian elite and led to a collective resistance against haole oppression. "American dominance included powerful ideologies from the continent," Rosa shows, ideologies that were rooted in the Black/White binary and "then transplanted onto the terrain of Hawai'i."[40] Rosa links this case to the Scottsboro Boys and the oral history of the Black sharecropper Nate Shaw (b. Nate Cobb) to illuminate the specter of overlapping racism in the continental United States and in the Territory of Hawai'i enabled through the United States military.

The deadly combination of militourism marries national racial dynamics to local ones into the twenty-first century, framing the 2011 murder of local Hawaiian Kollin Elderts by the State Department special agent Christopher Deedy. A White man from Arlington, Virginia, Deedy was in town to provide security at the Asia-Pacific Economic Cooperation (APEC) summit (further evidence of Hawai'i's economic and military significance at the crossroads of the Pacific). He was inebriated, jet-lagged, and armed after a night of what he describes as barhopping "craziness." At 2:37 a.m. on November 5, 2011, within two minutes of their first interaction in a Waikīkī McDonald's, Deedy murdered

Elderts with a bullet to the chest.[41] Altercations rarely crescendo to this point in Hawai'i—the state with some of the toughest gun laws despite high levels of gun ownership—and prosecutors argued that Deedy "was fueled by alcohol, power and a warning from a fellow agent about the hostility of Hawaii locals toward government employees and outsiders."[42] The first trial in 2013 ended in a hung jury, and the next year, a second jury acquitted Deedy of murder. Prosecutors are pushing for a third trial.[43]

Racism and ideas of race were central to this fatal interaction, as US/national ideas clashed with Hawai'i/local dynamics during the Obama presidency. People linked the murder of the young Hawaiian to the state-sanctioned murder of Black boys like Trayvon Martin in Florida. The Hawai'i writer David Harada Stone describes Elderts as a "brown-skinned part-Hawaiian local" and writes that "the victims in both [Elderts and Martin] cases were young, unarmed men of color."[44] In a podcast also linking this case to the police brutality that inspired the Movement for Black Lives, a Hawaiian woman says that these dynamics are historic, pointing to the "mistreating of the Hawaiians—that will never go away, I don't care how many generations you have. Again, you mistreating us."[45] The confrontation between Hawaiian and imported US racialist discourses is not new.

The Deedy case points to a clear connection to the dynamics surrounding the infamous Massie case of the 1930s. The allegations of rape followed by the murder of Kahahawai were fueled by the age-old ideologies that posit non-White men as dangerous threats to the purity of White womanhood and the integrity of White masculinity. (Deedy had been forewarned about the ire of the "natives.") These constructions are used to justify White domination and the dispossession—including murder—of people who block such "progress." Intersecting racial projects founded on White superiority inform these processes: the genocide and dispossession of Indigenous people, slavery, and the exploitation and exclusion (and, in some cases, lynching) of Asians and Latinos. Thus, if for centuries Hawai'i has proved to be a "haven," Black people in the Hawaiian Islands have nonetheless had to contend with both continental ideologies of race and racist practices of White settlers as well as their *own agency* as agents of militourism.

While much of my work here has explicated the usefulness of a racial lens, imported continental ideologies, without locally specific attention to Indigenous history, misdiagnose Black and Hawaiian relations. The US Black/White binary and continental theories of antiBlack racism do not fully explain the experiences of Black people in the Islands. A locally informed anticolonial understanding of occupation explains its place-specific iterations. They are better—if only partially—captured through an understanding of local and nonlocal, and a comprehension of Hawaiʻi's colonial status and the current conditions of Native Hawaiian life. Whereas Black agency in the US military may be celebrated as a mode of national incorporation, the military's occupation and bombing in the Pacific and the Middle East call on participants to account for their complicity with imperialism.

The twin economic pillars of militarism and tourism are celebrated through national and fiftieth-state narratives of progress and local gratitude. The website of the Chamber of Commerce Hawaiʻi declares May as "Hawaiʻi Military Appreciation Month." According to the site, this designation is to "honor our troops and their families. Please join us as we celebrate the military's presence in the islands and extend our deepest appreciation for its vital contributions to the social, cultural, and economic well-being of our *Ohana*, along with a heartfelt *Mahalo* for protecting our nation, Islands and families."[46] What an offensive statement, especially with its co-optation of Hawaiian concepts ("'ohana" means family, and "mahalo" expresses thanks), to those who consider Hawaiʻi to be colonized or illegally occupied—both achieved through US militarism! This remains the case despite the reality that Native Hawaiians, other Pacific Islanders, and other locals also enlist in the military (just as they work in the police force).[47] State-level discourses about this "island paradise" contradict the reality that tourism booms despite (because of?) the economic precarity plaguing Micronesians, Filipinos, Sāmoans, and Hawaiians—people whose homelands have all been affected by the US military. Micronesians, who "suffer from discrimination [and] a lack of understanding of their culture" in Hawaiʻi, include people from the Marshall Islands, home to the Bikini Atoll, where the United States tested its nuclear bombs—a testing site recently celebrated on a can of beer.[48]

Given these patriotic discourses about the military and its warm welcome to tourists, visitors may feel affronted by a less-than-sunny welcome, and soldiers are surprised by any antimilitary sentiment. This may also explain Hannah-Jones's support of Black military personnel. Black soldiers and civilians may interpret their negative experiences as antiBlack racism. However, we cannot understand antimilitary sentiment in Hawaiʻi only through a US-nation paradigm; that is, antimilitary sentiment is attached to antiBlack racism, but the two are not the same. Rather, the local lens of Hawaiʻi's colonial history contextualizes this tension. Michelle Alexander historicizes contemporary incarceration as part of a legacy of slavery, while the scholar-activist Angela Davis calls for prison abolition.⁴⁹ Similarly, militarism in Hawaiʻi is a continuation of the haole takeover of the Islands, leading some residents to call for deoccupation and an end to tourism.

What Responsibility? Black Tourists and Military Personnel

African American families who visit for an island reprieve are among the 10.5 million tourists each year to Hawaiʻi (engulfing the 1.5 million residents) who enjoy watching natives dance and serve them cold drinks. At sixteen billion dollars, tourism is the largest contributor to the state's gross income, responsible for over 20 percent of the economy. A close second is the US military at fifteen billion dollars and fifty thousand people. These institutions shape the tropes of Blackness in Hawaiʻi discussed earlier. The disproportionate number of Black enlistees in the military is a response to the obstacles preventing other avenues of advancement. In some American narratives, the military is lauded as a force for desegregation and incorporation. A 1986 article in *The Atlantic*, "Success Story: Blacks in the Military," praised the institution for the opportunities it provided African Americans for upward mobility and recognition with the subheading "Blacks *occupy* more management positions in the military than in any other sector of American society" (italics mine).⁵⁰ These material factors led *The Root*, a Black publication, to name Hawaiʻi *the* best state for Black people.⁵¹ Federal celebrations of the military join official state praise. The infrastructure of the Islands makes it so that the military and tourists are similarly cordoned off—whether within barracks with their commissaries, social life, and even private beaches, or in the confines of the less than four square miles of Waikīkī—to maintain a distance from non-service-providing locals while participating in the occupation of the Islands through militourism. Given this context, it may be challenging for Black visitors, including soldiers, to be self-reflective about their role in Hawaiʻi.

The military is a racist institution that often relegates Black people to the lowest ranks and places them in the most vulnerable positions. Nonetheless, it draws Black enlistees, especially when other avenues are shuttered. (Almost as many Black women as White women serve in the US Army.)⁵² With recruitment centers targeting vulnerable communities, the military complex promises a host of benefits: a paycheck, the opportunity for travel and adventure, and the possibility of paying for college or securing a housing loan. Kurtis, a former recruit and long-term resident who was motivated by "really trying to get away from" his small town, recalls, "The crazy thing about the military is that they tell you when you first join up, 'Yeah. You can do whatever you want. You can go wherever you want in the world.'" He joined a legacy of Black soldiers coming to Hawaiʻi going back to the Buffalo Soldiers in 1913, who seized the opportunity to leave the racist South.

Studies of the military in Hawaiʻi that focus comparatively on Black and White soldiers miss the colonial context that leads some in Hawaiʻi to criticize the presence of *both* as part of an occupying force in World War II. It is, however, specifically the analysis of antiBlack racism in a settler society that reveals how the negative experiences of Black soldiers increased over the twentieth century as a result of the adoption of US racist notions of Black inferiority *and* locals' opposition to the military presence.

A local anticolonial perspective *and* a US Black and White understanding of racism are necessary for explaining antiBlack sentiment in Hawaiʻi. The racism of White servicemen from the US South stationed in Hawaiʻi during World War II greatly influenced locals' ideas about Black men. Black soldiers faced growing discrimination. Compounding their forced segregation in military housing and social events, Black soldiers were also refused service by local barbers and at other public establishments. Advancing stereotypes of Black men, local Asian women refused to attend segregated dances for Black soldiers. Scholars writing sixty years apart explain this "violation of the racial code" of relative equality Black men experienced in 1945 as a "carry-over from the continental United States."[53] Locals adopted the American racism brought by haole and supported by media representations of Black criminality in national and local newspapers.

Tensions between locals and the military exist today. At times they manifest as a gendered contestation between men over local women, exacerbated by economic differentials. The former enlistee Kurtis explains the heightened antimilitary sentiment:

> Partially, you know, it's economic, meaning a lot of [local] people are doing bad now. But it never changes for military people. During [tough] economic times, the government just ups their pay. So they don't feel that stress. You know, you're out here nineteen to twenty [years old] with disposable income, and you're not really savvy in your mannerisms and how you operate. So you're doing wild, dumb stuff. And a lot of people take offense to that. And it's just worse now, you know.

Echoing Kurtis's observations in a different context, COOLDADDY offers his perspective in an online forum about "Hawaiians hating blacks": "I've heard them Somoans be hating when brothers pull their women though."[54] These gendered and sexual contestations are framed by the fact of Black men's participation in the military. Many of these soldiers are young men just out of high school who are excited to earn a regular paycheck and spend it socializing in town. Desires for social life take them from cordoned-off bases to downtown Honolulu and Waikīkī, where there is an active nightlife. However, alcohol leads to tense and sometimes physical altercations with local men and (over) women.

Negative experiences Black people face in Hawai'i stem from US racism *and* an anticolonial critique that some locals wage against the military. Black people who confront this hostility may understand it as antiBlack racism. However, Black and White people, and particularly servicemen, face resistance to occupation that is not simply racist or antihaole. Anticolonial sentiment and resistance run deep, if unevenly, in the Islands. It is thus no wonder that it was a Black Hawaiian who stated, "To us, Black and White is like, the same. They come here, impregnate our women, and leave." Other studies that compare the experiences of Black and White soldiers in 1940s Hawai'i argue that Black men faced segregation in the military and discrimination from locals.[55] However, Hawaiians may look at Black and White servicemen together, viewing them as part of the occupying force that has access to a quarter of O'ahu's land, whereas houselessness among Hawaiians (as well as Micronesian immigrants) is not only a cruel paradox but at crisis proportions.

Black Civilians' Views on Militarism in Hawai'i

What does it mean to grow up or live in a place where people presume not only that you are not local, but that you may even be part of an occupying force? Walt is a Black Sāmoan local dedicated to broadcasting local Black history. He ties the "lostness" of some local Black youths to both racial invisibility and the legacy of militarism in the Islands. Walt says:

> There's cultural PTSD [related] to the military's [1898] annexation of the [Hawaiian] Kingdom that resounds up 'til now. So what happens is you transplant people [through the US military]. You're invested in your [military] part of the community, which is a federal part of the community that's not organic; [it] didn't spring up here. You're here as a matter of defense, global positioning. And the hard part for people coming here is, if you have a set way of being, you don't understand: Hawai'i is a very unique state, because it's a country. You know what I mean? It was a country that got colonized. You don't have too many states that can say, "Yeah, we had a monarchy." You know what I mean? We had a whole system of doing things, and now that's turned upside down.

Walt animates a history that accounts for slavery as well as the effects of colonialism and imperialism. Considering the disorientation experienced by Black servicepeople stationed in the Islands, he conceives of Hawaiian and Black people's engagement with the US military through post-traumatic stress disorder.

While many Black residents named White people and racism as the common denominator for historical oppressions, Nino, a Black transplant I interviewed when Obama was in office, specifies the role of "the [US] government":

> We have a government that gives money to people, and sometimes you wonder why. Because there are people here [in Hawai'i] that they should be doing more for, if you look at their past history. I understand how they [Hawaiians] feel about the fact that the military ended up annexing—because I lived in Washington, DC, and Capitol Hill is an annex.... Well, I can see how the military came in here and they took up [a] huge part of this island ... and I think there should be a fund that the federal government and the state pay into that help people here get back on their feet when they have a problem.

Pointing out the seat of US militarism (DC) and the homes of the president (DC and Hawai'i), Nino analyzes US imperialism's effect on numerous groups, both in the past and today, in the continental United States and across the Pacific. A military-critical perspective theorized through PTSD (Walt) and annexation (Nino) is shared by some of the Black Hawaiians I spent time with, although many have Kanaka family members who are veterans.[56] They contextualize their experiences in their Hawaiian communities within broader histories of race and nation, rather than interpreting difficult childhood experiences as unpleasant interpersonal exchanges or "microaggressions." Instead, they understand the contemporary denigration of Blackness as part of an inheritance from the US nation-state that includes the takeover of the Hawaiian Kingdom and the resulting antiKānaka sentiment they also had to navigate.

That civilian Black Hawaiians reflect on the nexus of antiBlack racism and the oppression of Native Hawaiians may not come as a surprise. However, what would inspire the acknowledgment of these systems by Black soldiers who may inhabit what Ethan Caldwell calls "the colonized-colonizer paradox"—or the role of African Americans in imperialism across the Pacific?[57] To consider this is part of the kuleana of Black military personnel. Requiring accountability of members of the military-industrial complex refutes the characterization of Black abjection by Afropessimist scholars. These scholars reduce Black people to "Black bodies" whose only experiences in the afterlives of slavery are ones of agentless abjection.[58] Black men and women in all branches of the military are part of an institution that dispossesses Native Hawaiians, displaces other Pacific Islanders, and ravages nations in the Middle East. Weapons testing across the Pacific creates tensions among Pacific Islanders, as larger numbers of displaced refugees arrive in Hawai'i specifically because it is part of the United States. An *entire island* sacred to Hawaiians was "transformed into a bombing range," says a 2018 Hawai'i news article ominously titled "The Bombing of Kaho'olawe Went On for Decades. The Clean-Up Will Last Generations."[59] Island residents do not have a say in the use of this land as a training ground for soldiers waging war across Asia.

These are not just the effects of things *past*; military occupation chokes Hawai'i today. In fact, in 2018 residents were subjected to a terrifying false missile alert sent out across the Islands. Speaking of the technical error, Goodyear-Ka'ōpua explained, "In many ways what happened today reinforces for many of us why it's so important to keep educating others about the truth of our history, the truth of Hawai'i's history and not only to think about why Hawaiian sovereignty is important because of the *historical* wrongs that were committed but because of the *ongoing present conditions* of *occupation* that make us a target of missiles" (italics mine).[60]

This context fuels locals' presumptions that all Black people in Hawai'i are military personnel. Imagine how this affects those Black locals who are critical of Hawai'i's militarization! When Colin says that "Blacks and Caucasians is, you know, one and the same: just military" who come here and "sleep with our women, get them pregnant, and leave," he is offering a critique of the military presence that extends to a combined critique of Black and White people. A local Black Asian rapper, Tommy, also discusses his relationship to Blackness and the military.

> Yeah, that was kind of the struggle I went through. To this day, when I say, "I'm from Wahiawā," the first words out of that person's mouth is, "Oh, you're from Schofield [Barracks]?" Or "Your dad's in the military?" Or [assuming that] I'm in the military. And I'm like, "No." I have this kind of pride thing in me where I want people to know that my experience is unique, you know. My mom and dad met in college.

Not only men wished to distinguish themselves from the military. Angela is the local daughter of two Black parents who were radicals critical of the US government during the civil rights movement. Her father dreadlocked his hair, as do Angela and her mixed race sons. I asked if she preferred to lock her hair to prevent being misidentified as someone in the military. "Absolutely," she responded, "do not confuse us." She recalls "being forbidden from dating military.... For me, the worst thing that I could have been confused with was to be a military wife. I actually don't dress very conservatively possibly because of that."

Militourism is a major structuring force in the Hawaiian Islands, affecting not only their economics but also the daily lives of its people. Black residents include transplants who arrive to work in the military as well as locals who may be critical of the presence of tourists and the military. As such, the militarization of the Islands, also dependent on a tourist economy, demands people's accountability for the occupation of Hawai'i that desecrates the land, exploits service workers, and creates a housing crisis.

On-the-ground realities reveal how the native/settler binary consolidates Black and haole, enhanced through their shared participation in the military. However, a racial analysis shows how Black and haole are not the same. If a racial lens provides the language and vision to see the operations of race-based inequalities, we misinterpret an anticolonial and antimilitary critique as (only) antiBlack racism. Global ideas about Black inferiority in an Asian settler colonial context inform residents' views of Black people. In return, Black residents' particular racial positioning leads them to articulate Black and Hawaiian comparative and historical lateral ties not evinced by haole, whose relation to colonialism and people of color is distinct and hierarchical.

"I Am of the Land": Sovereignty, Land, and Ethical Belonging

I am of the land. I always share with people that it's the land that really gives people their energy. You know? I say that because I understand the creation, the beginnings . . . we are of the land. Because of today's modern society, you're going to have a place where we claim that land. I mean, that's how it was back when. I guess families have portions of the land. I mean, no matter where you are, if you come from these soils, you've been raised in these soils, with Hawaiian understanding and value, you're the 'āina. You are from Hawai'i Kanaka.

KAMAKAKĒHAU, BLACK LOCAL RAISED IN A HAWAIIAN FAMILY

Black people in the Islands often practice aloha ʻāina and kuleana. Goodyear-Kaʻōpua tells us that "both settler and Indigenous people must take part in dismantling the structures that prohibit sustainable Indigenous self-determination and caring for lands upon which all depend for life."[61] She articulates "three key aspects of kuleana," a word that translates roughly to "privilege and responsibility," which

> may be useful to others considering the dynamics of Indigenous-settler collaboration in projects of Indigenous resurgence and education: (1) genealogical connection to place, (2) active commitment and contribution to the community, and (3) self-reflexivity and the desire to learn. . . . A settler aloha ʻāina can take responsibility for and develop attachment to lands upon which they reside when actively supporting Kānaka Maoli who have been alienated from ancestral lands to reestablish those connections and also helping to rebuild Indigenous structures that allow for the transformation of settler-colonial relations.[62]

Questions about land, sovereignty, and the concerns of Hawaiian activists elicit a range of responses from Black residents, who think about these questions at varying levels. We spoke about what sovereignty means and its implications, especially as my fieldwork drew to a close and these questions became more central both to activist movements in Hawaiʻi and to Native studies scholarship (and studies of Hawaiʻi). Black civilians (like Native Hawaiians) do not necessarily agree about land, political power, and Hawaiian independence. Their differing views highlight tensions between Kānaka and non-Kānaka viewpoints; in other cases, they align in solidarity.

How do Black people learn about Hawaiʻi and familiarize themselves with Kānaka Maoli concerns? Black residents have varying levels of knowledge about Hawaiʻi and familiarity with Native Hawaiians. Some are Black Hawaiians and thus learned as they grew up in Hawaiian communities. Old-timers include those who have chosen to study deeply the history of this place and befriend Hawaiians, as well as those who have not. Newcomers, on the other hand, and especially college students, seem most unfamiliar with Hawaiians, explaining how their social worlds revolve around the university and its demographics; their friend groups include Asians (local and from Asia), but they do not know many Polynesians. Older professionals learn about local issues from their coworkers. Black scholars of Africa, the Black diaspora, and African American history teach local students theories of race while in return learning about sovereignty from their Kanaka and local students.[63]

Black Resident Views on Hawaiian Sovereignty

Black people in Hawai'i engage the question of sovereignty with an understanding that it may include independence for the Hawaiian Nation, in which Native Hawaiians would have political power. They understand this, as many people do, within a nation-state or statist conceptualization. Kauanui criticizes Hawai'i activists whose statist desires for independence replicate conservative sexual, gender, and religious politics. Some activists do assert the continuity or reinstatement of the Kingdom of Hawai'i. Maile Arvin explains, "Many Kanaka Maoli have spoken ... of their support for an independent Hawai'i that is guided by Kanaka Maoli forms of governance but is (like Hawai'i was before the 1893 overthrow) a multi-ethnic, multi-racial nation."[64] Yet Manu Karuka adds, regarding the North American context, "Black and Indigenous self-determination exceed[s] resolution within a U.S. framework."[65] Pushing beyond these seemingly natural "logics of containment" denies nation-state formations as inevitable or desirable. Karuka continues, "These are future-oriented visions, not the dust of nostalgia."[66] Such visions critique nationalist paradigms, demonstrated by movements of Indigenous people across the Pacific and the Americas, including Latin America, that are both internationalist and locally specific. Native feminists in particular are imagining and enacting practices that not only counter nation-based conceptions of autonomy but also extend beyond them in service of visions of self-determination. These imagined futures depend on models for living responsibly today.

The field of Native studies also provides alternatives to the regime of private property. According to the Native studies scholar Mishuana Goeman, "Maintaining relationships to the land is at the heart of Indigenous peoples' struggles, and it is a struggle that benefits all who rely on water and land to live."[67] This reprioritization contests the presumption of Indigenous land reclamation as a desire to "own" property—a misinterpretation that emerges from current capitalist practices through which land is scarred by the power of the settler state: "A consequence of colonialism is the flattening of land with property," explains Goeman.[68] Some Black residents also held the misperception that Indigenous claims to land are about the desire for private property rather than a reclamation of the role of land as a relation, sustenance, and relative; as Kamakakēhau expresses in our interview quoted earlier in the chapter, the land gives people their energy. Goeman continues, "Land is a meaning-making process rather than a claimed object," highlighting relationality and contesting native-state, nationalist, and settler ideologies.[69] She reminds us that we should center "Indigenous conceptions of land as connected, rather than land as disaggregate parcels at various European-conceived scales, which is a project of accumulation."[70]

These academic conversations parallel changing Island politics, as activists and Hawaiian community members flesh out and adapt their stances over time. For instance, in the early 2000s, some Hawaiians vigorously debated the unsuccessful Akaka Bill, which would have granted Native Hawaiians recognition by the US government, a status similar to Native American tribes. No one sovereignty movement prevails in the Islands, and sentiments vary from wanting to have an independent nation to those seeking food sovereignty, or the viability of the Islands' population surviving on locally sourced rather than imported food. Perhaps the most prominent form of sovereignty activism today involves reclaiming Hawaiian cultural practices, from an explosion of traditional body tattooing to land reclamation with the restoration of waterways that facilitate the cultivation of kalo, the plant whose corm is made into poi. With these conversations in the air, Black residents over the past decade have expressed a range of views on Hawaiian sovereignty—almost always framed by race and a power-inflected analysis of future outcomes.

Transplants understand sovereignty as the desire of Hawaiians to reclaim control over their land, for Hawai'i to become an independent nation once again, and, in some instances, for Hawai'i to be a Hawaiian-only place. Thus there are those who actively support Hawaiian self-determination, those who dismiss any discussion of secession from the United States, and those (including new college students) who are fully unaware of these issues. Black residents thought about the viability of independence. For transplants, this was based on their understanding of the governmental and racial dominance of the United States; among locals, it was based on their sense of discord among Hawaiians. Some felt that desires for sovereignty were unrealistic. Deonte, a Miami transplant, stated "as a realist" that Hawai'i "was a strategic outpost for American business as much as American military, so they are never going to let it go. That's not to say that the fight for sovereignty is a waste; I think that that voice always has to be there." A slightly different take on the inability to "go back" was the view of a Black athlete. Twi, a university football player recruited from Southern California, felt that

> the history of the businessmen [who] came over and took over and made rules, I feel that wasn't right. But then, since the US see that they done something wrong they apologized but, it's kind of tough for me to say like, "give them their stuff back," to give them land because it's been all beat up and used. There's so many thing[s] on it, like the malls, schools

are on the property.... What I'll say [is] give the Hawaiian people access to those things.

While Twi noted the abuse of the land, Deonte represented a perspective based on the "reality" of what was and thus what was likely to always be. Indigenous feminist scholarship and the communal activism on Maunakea, however, not only remind us of ways to imagine new futures and to question the inevitability of existing systems, but also are already enacting different ways of being.

On Maui, more than five thousand people in support of the Maunakea kiaʻi (protectors) came together for what was called a "Kapu Aloha March." It was so named for the "kapu aloha code of conduct, historically part of Native Hawaiian practices" rooted in principles of "restraint, love and respect" that are regaining momentum.[71] The march and support across the Islands (and the globe), showcasing the "power of a unified people," according to Kahoʻokahi Kanuha, is imagining life otherwise.[72] People contest the occupation of Hawaiʻi through self-determination and resist the inaccurate framing of Hawaiians as "antiscience"; rather, the movement against the TMT—like movements for demilitarization—represents anticolonial resistance.[73]

In their press statement listing five central points, HULI—one of the groups advocating access to sacred land—concludes with the following: *"We will forever fight the TMT, until the last aloha ʻāina.* Truth and history are on our side, and our commitment and mana is only rising. We are prepared for intense and lengthy struggles but stand firm in *Kapu Aloha*—peace and nonviolence. We ask everyone to honor this kuleana and to conduct ourselves in *PONO*."[74] One may interpret these activists as calling on "traditional" practices that are "backward" (looking) instead of advancing new possibilities. However, in their calls to fulfill past promises (returning Hawaiʻi to independence; access to stolen land) through practices of their kūpuna (ancestors), Hawaiians on Maunakea and elsewhere are in fact "backing into the future." Vicente Diaz, a scholar bridging Pacific Islands and Native American studies, uses this phrase to denote moving with our backs to the future while looking at—and learning from—the past.[75] This is to say that while Deonte and other transplants may feel that Hawaiʻi is irrevocably part of the United States now, Kanaka and other Pacific Islander activists and scholars imagine otherwise, as "protectors of the future, not protesters of the past."[76]

Other Black transplants approached the topic of Hawaiian sovereignty by being protective of their economic holdings, perhaps fearing, as others have, that independence means the ejection of all nonNatives.[77] A Black lawyer commented, "I own property here. I look at it as an American. I just try to coexist with everybody." This view advances an integrationist vision of an individual's "rights" to the (US) nation. This is perhaps less reflective than the set of questions posed in Stephanie Smallwood's analysis of settler colonialism and slavery: "For the enslaved settler arrivant, whose own ancestral indigeneity was sundered by forced removal from Africa, what avenues were available to unseat the colonial relations of power that conditioned Black life in the colonized Americas? . . . Does birthright citizenship implicate Black freedpeople in settler colonial disavowal of Native sovereignty? Or does the fusion of enslaved Black labor with American soil give Black arrivants a claim to American belonging that is not colonial?"[78] Hawai'i-based scholars who focus on another nonWhite group—Asian settlers—may help respond to these questions that conclude Smallwood's article.

Noelani Goodyear-Kaʻōpua, Candace Fujikane, and Dean Saranillio articulate aloha ʻāina and support what they call "Asian settler allies" working in collaboration with Kānaka Maoli, rather than advocating what some fear is the call for all nonNatives to leave the Islands. This fear is rooted in a proprietary notion of land, rather than reflecting on how best to care for the land and the lives that it sustains. We are stretched to consider some conceptions of sovereignty that, as Saranillio writes, "are beyond the political imagination of Western and settler sovereignty."[79] Close domestic ties across groups (i.e., multiracial family composition) complicate the presumption that most Hawaiians are calling for the removal of all non-Kanaka, including local Asians.

In contrast to the lawyer who feared for her property was Laura, a Black Filipina who accepted accountability in the ways articulated by these scholars: "I feel like I am a guest here and a settler. I don't feel conflicted about that because I know the history of this place. But at the same time, it is a little frustrating because I don't feel like I have a home anywhere." This sense of rootlessness resonates among (children of) immigrants, settlers, and multiracial people—all identities that Laura claims. Black locals and transplants alike debated not only the viability of Hawaiian activist demands but also the very need for a sovereignty movement.

Few transplants were outright dismissive of movements for greater Kanaka self-determination; more often they understood what motivated this activism but had differing ideas about their roles within such movements. A Miami man felt "the call and the memory and the education of what needs to happen always needs to be there, or what is justice—that we can't forget. We can't forget that justice was not served." Transplants also saw the desire for greater autonomy through a class lens, explaining that because things have gotten economically challenging in the Islands, this has spurred people to feel that "we need to be our own [advocate of our] people because the government is not doing" what is necessary. Yet he and fellow transplants did not feel it was their place to determine the direction of Hawai'i's future. "As much as I support the will of the people," said a Black long-term resident, "I put myself in positions to learn a lot from people."

Nino, a Black musician from the US South, agreed with this view. Among the older participants, he is a long-term resident who found that Black people's issues were not prominent in Hawai'i. Despite his awareness about local history and engagement with sovereignty struggles, he feels he would be "the last person on this island" that people will ask to "solve this problem. . . . I might have a solution, but they're not gonna ask me." He shared the feelings of local Asian activists like Mary Choy, who experienced a "growing realization that Kanaka Maoli and non-Kanaka Maoli must come together in support of independence for the Hawaiian nation."[80] This dynamic was quickly evident to Black people, no matter how recently arrived, because they were already attuned to group-based exploitation.

On the one hand, Nino's sense that Natives "must lead" heeds Haunani-Kay Trask's admonition to Asians to "support a form of Hawaiian sovereignty created by Hawaiians. . . . Truly supportive Asians must publicly ally themselves with our position of Native control over the sovereignty process."[81] On the other hand, it allows for easy sidestepping of one's kuleana for what may be characterized as "other people's issues." For instance, if incarceration is deemed as being only "a Black person's issue" or immigration only a "Latino issue," this perspective limits the development of a broad-scale movement for the abolition of the criminal and immigration systems. As one local Black hapa stated in the case of activism in the Islands, "If you are bringing in other people that help your case instead of segregating them," this expansiveness makes for a stronger movement, "because they need as much people on their side as they can." The directive to "follow rather than lead" is also in some sense a reminder for people to "stay in their lanes"—a perspective I commented on previously for its limitations. Recall Goodyear-Ka'ōpua's discussion of kuleana as an orientation that both takes positionality into account *and* calls on each person to contribute together in creating sustainable pathways. Participants reminded me, however, that there is no consensus on the "proper" pathway to sovereignty.

As individuals closer to the epicenters of Hawaiian activism, several Black Hawaiians critiqued aspects of these movements because of their own experiences with exclusion, their sense of infighting, and views on the economic conditions faced by Hawaiians. A woman in her fifties said:

> I think that the Hawaiians are trying to form their own little group, and they can't come together well enough to re-create the Kingdom. And it's not going to happen because there's too many cultures in the kitchen, too much infighting. 'Cause it's all watered down. The quantum is so watered down that I'm like, "What are you thinking? And then here, I have quantum, but y'all don't talk to me" [because I'm also Black], so, sorry, I gotta say, "No." I didn't agree with the anger, I didn't agree with the hate, I didn't agree with the going back a couple of generations.

Tina reads these political demands as regressive through her lifelong experiences with exclusion and antiBlack racism from community members. Another Black Hawaiian, who grew up on Hawaiian Home Lands, was also concerned that people "could not come together as one group." Naomi said, "Yes, I agree with you that the way things happened was wrong. However, you need to look at how many Hawaiians receive benefits from the government, the state government, who are relying on it." She felt that breaking from the United States would lead to the withdrawal of these services.

These Black locals relate a common sentiment in Hawai'i about wrongs being a thing of the past, expressing a "get over it" sensibility that they also applied to Black people's claims of contemporary racism. "Just like Black culture—you can't keep blaming society or the White man. It's like, 'get over it,'" Naomi insisted. Perhaps locals hold these views because they live too far away from convincing evidence of the enduring effects of slavery and White supremacy.[82] Yet even some Black transplants from the continental United States agree.

A Black Korean graduate student from the Midwest who came to UH for advanced Asian language training to become an officer in the air force echoed this sentiment. He says that "there's a very, very, very heavy victim role being played. And it's not necessarily warranted. This sovereignty thing? I don't see it happen[ing]. It goes back to my whole global view. Let's move forward, let's move forward." This dismissive view—perhaps a result of his unfamiliarity with Hawaiians' history and his alignment with the military—nonetheless resonates with others. A local Black Hawaiian concurred, making the argument that Black people, too, used prejudice as a "crutch" that stalled forward-looking thinking. However, these views do not acknowledge that Hawaiians are facing economic precarity, health problems, and landlessness as a *result* of US government actions that prevent their access to resources and opportunities. That is, this perspective, while common, lacks a historical and structural analysis of the *ongoing* conditions of oppression and dispossession that affect the health and well-being of Hawaiians.

Expanding the range of perspectives is the commentary of a long-term resident. This former soldier offers a structural and class analysis of the potential political changes as he looks to current landholdings on Oʻahu: "I think it's disingenuous for the Hawaiians to be pissed off at White people for one, for taking their land and they want it back. Because what are they going to do when they get it back? They're just going to sell it to the highest bidder. So the transfer of wealth is just going to go from who has it now to the Hawaiians." We find evidence for his prediction in the history of new governments in postcolonial nations (like postindependence India, formerly colonized by the British) that have re-created (other) forms of inequality; yet his views rely on current formations as an unchanging given rather than seeing how people are reconceptualizing society. He called on "the Bishop Estate" (established by Princess Bernice Pauahi, it is now called Kamehameha Schools Bishop Estate, or KSBE)—the largest private landowner in the Islands—as an example of how new leaders would "lease out . . . prime land in the Hawaiian sovereign nation to the highest bidders": "The Bishop Estate got some of the most expensive property."[83] "They own everything," a Black local chimed in as I interviewed them together. "They're killing it. So at the end of the day, that's what it boils down to: that old boys' network of the racism, it's more of an economic discrimination."

Many Black transplants view Hawaiʻi not just through a racial lens but also through a class analysis—whether it accounts for their side-eye at corporate interests or leads them to prioritize their material benefits. These two men I spoke with reflected on their relative protection from racism in the Islands, where they, as Black men in the music industry, were shielded both from continental-style racism and also from the widespread poverty experienced locally by Micronesians, Hawaiians, and members of other communities living in makeshift camps across the island of Oʻahu. Their overall attitude reflected a healthy skepticism of governing bodies—whether that of the United States, the current state government, or possible leaders in an independent Hawaiian nation.

Transplants are not cohesive in their views on sovereignty; some actively support Hawaiians, others do not, and still others are unconcerned or want to learn more about these issues. What cropped up across these discussions of the viability and potential playing out of a sovereign nation were questions about people's belonging.

We Belong to the Land

Kamakakēhau was born to African American parents in Arkansas and adopted as an infant by a Native Hawaiian woman from Maui, where she raised him in her small Hawaiian community. His mother and her extended family loved the little dark-skinned baby with tight curls. Kamakakēhau went on to become a singer and ʻukulele phenom, fluent in Hawaiian and integrated into his Hawaiian community. We met in the upstairs lobby of the Sheraton Hotel near Ala Moana Shopping Center for the interview, a wonderful conversation that covered topics that span and spill beyond this book. Many times, it felt as if we were exploring aloud new ideas, rather than rehashing common perspectives. His story and ideas unsettle the many categories I have used in this book and have used to describe him (is he Black, Hawaiian, or Black Hawaiian?). His ideas about land, energy, and belonging take us to the spiritual realm—a place and condition never far for many Hawaiians, like my former kumu hula (hula teacher), John Keola Lake, who always insisted on our relationship and loving obligation to plants, people, and practices of aloha. Kamakakēhau's views unraveled several presumptions about the ties between ancestry and identity, "blood" and family, identity and politics, land and ownership. At the same time, he unsettles binaries of Black/Hawaiian, race/indigeneity, and native/settler. His perspectives provide a model for developing ideas of identity, belonging, land, and liberation.

As a Black man raised in a Hawaiian family, Kamakakēhau feels that Blackness, like Hawaiianness, can be learned, that it is a cultural formation. He adds another element to debates central to this project by taking race away from the body more completely, distancing genealogy from blood, and separating land from private property. Clearly African descended, he says, "I am of the land. I always share with people that it's the land that really gives people their energy, you know?" Given how central land claims are to Native sovereignty, Kamakakēhau offers a fascinating twist to this discussion—particularly the assumption of Black people as settlers in the Pacific and of land as proprietary. He is not arguing for the right to be granted land *as* a Hawaiian, does not view himself as a Black settler, and does not state that only people with Hawaiian ancestry have connections to the land. Rather, his evocation exceeds material "rights," ancestry-based indigeneity, and phenotype-based race, moving into the realm of spirituality and the connectedness between people and the ʻāina that resonates with Kanaka epistemologies. His thinking reflects aloha ʻāina, which translates both to love and care for the land and underscores how the land symbiotically gives (us) life and sustains.

Figure 5.2 Ryan Kamakakēhau Fernandez performing at the Pōpolo Project "Black Futures Ball." Photo by Michael McDermott.

Questions of land and belonging can be vexing for the descendants of enslaved Africans and Native people. Transplants and locals respond differently to the depiction that Hawaiians lived on land that was stolen from them, whereas African Americans were stolen from their lands. Black residents know about Hawaiians and their struggles in large part because they, too, are members of an oppressed group. While Black people recognize that Hawaiians, in contrast to many African Americans, can recount their genealogy and point to particular places as their home for generations, Black people identify with but distinguish themselves from Native Hawaiians' struggles out of respect for their distinctions. According to a recent transplant, Alice, "In my mind I feel like, from what I've learned, Hawaiians can trace their history. They can go back and say, 'This is where I grew up. This is where my grandparents grew up.' They can still see it versus those African Americans, we don't have any recollection of that because that's gone. You know the fact that all of this happened, you have all of the military here, which has affected the way that Hawaiians live, see themselves, it's affected their whole culture."

However, in his earlier quote, Kamakakēhau reframes the same question: "I mean, regardless, we are of the land. Because of today's modern society, you're going to have a place where we claim that land. I guess families have land," he says, referring to land as private property. But he moved on to say, "But I mean, no matter where you are, if you come from these soils, you've been raised in these soils, with Hawaiian understanding and value, you're the 'āina. You are from Hawai'i Kanaka," he concludes. From the perspective that people come from and are birthed by the 'āina, it is the land—not blood or ancestry, deeds or mortgages—that gives people their identity. This means that land does not restrict whom it gives meaning to; it gives meaning to all people, who have differential relationships to the 'āina. This forms the basis for Kānaka and non-Kanaka, local and nonlocal partnership as people living in a place, working together to nurture the place that nurtures them, living as a collective while being aware of, rather than limited by, distinct positionalities. Thus being in Hawai'i makes it one's kuleana to live here ethically. (This, of course, poses a significant question to military personnel, tourists, and major corporate interests.)

Kamakakēhau contributes to scholars' theories of decolonization that reframe belonging and land. If some presume that Black people are "stolen people on stolen land," then, as Andrea Smith has asked, "Why is some land for some people? How did the notion of land belonging to someone emerge? How can one not have a relationship with the land that one is on?"[84] Kamakakēhau addresses these provocations by pointing to the connectedness between people and the land, a Hawaiian conception of relationality: land does not belong to us; we belong to the land. His move away from framing Africans as being "stolen" people now living on "stolen land" illuminates the fact that Africans are also indigenous to Africa, as articulated in Robin D. G. Kelley's analysis of South Africa as a settler colony.[85]

Settler colonialism and antiBlackness, in and *outside* North America, are not two distinct processes happening to two distinct groupings of bodies. Smith's questions about land may come closer to Kamakakēhau's articulation: "But the very idea[s] of land as something to be had; as labor as the way through which the body is defined, are both constructed. How can you not be home? How can you not have a relation to the land where you are? How was that concept of land constructed—that *that* was his or her home and now he/she is not home. What is this concept of land?"[86] Yet, of course, distinctions are crucial. Hawaiians are forced to operate within the US blood quantum mandates to access material rights.

Kamakakēhau was not the only participant rooted in the land. Keli'i, a tall Black Hawaiian, worked to re-create Hawaiian fishponds at the He'eia Fishponds. He attended college on the West Coast and returned home to be with his Hawaiian family, earned an advanced degree, and began working. He says:

> I feel absolutely blessed and lucky to be able to practice culture. It's my job, and I'm part of restoring something and reviving something hundreds of years old, as opposed to, which I did try, just working downtown, working in an office, resting every day. I did that. And this makes me much more happy, and this is my dream job and the reason why I got my minor in environmental studies. I've always had this [sense that] "I need to work outside" in the back of my mind. I got involved in a lot of outdoor activities in college on the mainland. I knew I always wanted to get back to outdoor activities in Hawai'i.

At the time of our interview, I hadn't realized what an important revitalization project he was undertaking, and I wished that I had asked him more about it. However, years later, I was able to bring students from Northwestern University near Chicago to O'ahu to help reconstruct this very fishpond. The seventeen of us—fifteen undergraduate students, a seven-months hāpai (pregnant) fellow professor Hi'ilei Hobart, and I—hauled rocks for three hours and swam above rust-colored he'e (octopuses) nestled on the ocean floor.

It may be that leaving and then missing the Islands is what motivated Keli'i to embark on this restoration project:

> When I came back home [from college], I started really getting involved. I was volunteering, really feeling my way around the Hawaiian community and getting into the Hawaiian community, 'cause I had been away for four years. I was [like], "Oh, I miss UH, I miss going to UH football games. I missed that UH college experience." But I was meeting up with all my friends, who then were all getting into their communities back at home. And so I started getting in with them, and volunteering, and going hunting and fishing on different islands. And that was super important to me.

Scholars who work within academic communities and with the land, or what Goodyear-Ka'ōpua calls "EAducators" (ea means breath, sovereignty), have taught us about the revitalization and political work taking place in Hawai'i over the past several decades. Keli'i is one among many Kānaka, along with non-Kanaka helpers, who are reanimating water, agricultural, and fishing practices.[87] The local farmer Daniel Anthony and his community have cleared nonnative plant species on a Kāne'ohe farm, called Mana Ai, to plant kalo; they have dug an imu (an underground oven with hot rocks for roasting pua'a [pigs]), raised pigs, and built a stone oven to make pizzas for the numerous collaborations hosted on the farm—including with the Pōpolo Project.[88] Culture workers, such as kumu hula across the Islands and Hawaiian music practitioners, including the falsetto singer Kamakakēhau, accompany this land-based work. Kamakakēhau states, "What I do is beyond me. I'm just a vessel, and I choose to represent this gift that God has given me. I think being Black in Hawai'i is awesome.... You can still hold your head high and not be so tight about certain situations. And I encourage other friends of mine to visit and feel, feel the land. Because . . . this world is crazy. And Hawai'i can bring you to a place of serenity, in a sense." Whether other participants shared Kamakakēhau's conceptions or struggled with the tensions between Black and Hawaiian communities, many articulated comparative links informed by a global and historical perspective.

Comparative Links: A Global-Historical Perspective

A global-historical and comparative analysis of deeply local issues links the systems of oppression and the color line that "belts the world," as Du Bois once articulated.[89] This perspective also charts foundational principles for articulating a global mass resistance attuned to the specificities of particular communities and places. To present their perspectives on Hawai'i's political status and visions for the future, participants made comparisons with other groups at other historical moments, looking to examples in Black American history or at Native American struggles for recognition, for example. This orientation mirrors the work within African diasporic studies and on global indigeneities while expanding *across* them. Black locals and transplants discussed Hawaiian struggles of the past and self-determination through a cross-racial (Black/Native) and transIndigenous framework.[90] While some articulated similarities to make common cause and express support for Kanaka activism, others pointed out distinctions. Their structural and historical analysis almost always took root in their individual experiences and interactions with different communities.

Black people viewed questions of belonging and nationhood in terms of "segregation" and "integration"—terms central to the civil rights narrative of Black non/belonging to the United States. Tina, a Black Hawaiian, felt positive about the integration she experienced. She said, "I would like to see the Hawaiian culture perpetuated as much as possible. But not, I think, more than anyone else. It's an integrated society now. My life has pretty much led to prove that integration works. I don't believe in the ethnocentricity of it. I don't believe in exclusionary identification." Another Black and Hawaiian woman also appreciates the Islands' multiculturalism, which she views as "local" rather than "Hawaiian": "We all contributed to the local culture, so it's a great mixed bag. Little bit of Portuguese, a little bit of Japanese, Filipino, some White, some Black." Black transplants also advocated integration. Deonte from Miami felt that "it's important to embrace new souls, to uphold the same traditional values and expectations, and basically reroute your energies into making sure that those who are coming here are taught and given the opportunity to understand and respect the values of this place." He sensed that failing to integrate people, a challenge the Micronesians he worked with faced, was a lost opportunity. "To segment ourselves off from what we are, or what they are, and to not really look at the value of other people or [the value] that other groups bring in . . . you miss out on something," he claimed.

Along with critiques of multiculturalism as a cover for settler colonialism, Indigenous studies scholars remind us of the inadequacy of a civil rights and integrationist framework for addressing Native questions, as this framework deracializes indigeneity.[91] Troubling court cases brought by haole who charge "reverse racism" against Hawaiian-only policies and institutions are one result of viewing Hawaiians only through a racial framework and misusing antidiscrimination laws.[92] Advocating integration within the context of a dialogue on sovereignty also implies that pro-independence Kānaka are "segregationists" (much as Black Power advocates were viewed). This does not bear out in practice, given the multiracial makeup of most Hawaiian families and the small number of those in favor of a Hawaiian-only society. In response to a scathing review of the foundational text *Asian Settler Colonialism*, Patrick Wolfe calls out the reviewers' "unfounded fantasy that the critique of settler colonialism represents a desire to expel Asians from Hawaiʻi."[93] This fantasy, Wolfe shows, illustrates a discursive settler move of (to paraphrase) settler victim/Native victimizer.

Deonte, a Black transplant from Miami who does community advocacy work, also draws on the popular integrationist framework but shifts to the troubling phenomenon of racism among Pacific Islanders. Like local Black Hawaiian Tina, Deonte's personal experiences with antiBlack racism inform his perspective of Hawaiians' kuleana toward other communities. Speaking with Micronesian elders, Deonte concluded: "For every wave of Micronesians that have come here, there should have been ceremonies held to invite these people in . . . and you can say that you have a hand in these people learning and passing on the spirit of aloha. But when you are too segmented, and too protecting the purity of your group and your traditions, you miss out on being able to really bring people in who are going to help continue that tradition." Shifting from Hawaiian sovereignty to spotlight anti-Micronesian racism, Deonte adopts a racial lens to reflect on questions central to Indigenous self-determination. He recalls a Micronesian woman's sense that "she wanted to be invited here. They [the Micronesians he works with] wanted to feel like they were part of this community [in Hawai'i] and that they can bring in something [that has now been] marginalized and pushed off to the side. Two wrongs don't make a right sort of thing. That was done to the Hawaiian people." Failure to be greeted with the proper protocol—the set of practices of welcoming them as fellow Pacific Islanders, part of Hawaiians' kuleana—initiated these Micronesians' sense of nonbelonging in the Islands, which only increased when they experienced racism. Reviving Hawaiian protocol (for instance, requesting entrance to a place in Hawaiian, receiving a welcoming oli [chant] in response) has been a central practice among the kia'i on Maunakea, in Hawaiian-language schools, and should be extended to Micronesians.

Rising activism in Hawai'i has led many residents to reflect on political precedent. In their coauthored statement of support for Hawaiians protecting Maunakea, Charles Lawrence (a Black transplant to the Islands) and Mari Matsuda (who is local Japanese)—renowned critical race and constitutional law professors at UH—tied activism on the Big Island to a global legacy of Black resistance. "The Mauna Kea protectors stand in an honorable line of those called to civil disobedience," they state to contest claims that the protectors are "crazy Hawaiians breaching the rule of law.... Historically, settled law can give way when a committed minority heeds the justice call."[94] They contextualize this claim by drawing on the examples of contesting slave codes, challenging race-based housing discrimination, and the US Civil Rights Act of 1964, which "are products of citizen rejection of prior law."[95] Hawaiian resistance reflects the principles motivating Nelson Mandela and Martin Luther King Jr., as well as those underlying today's movements for justice: "In 2019 people everywhere are choosing resistance. The Mauna Kea protectors are one with the Japanese-American elders ... to stop incarceration of immigrant children, one with churches and synagogues giving sanctuary to families hunted down by ICE, one with students walking out for climate change."[96] This letter of support exemplifies the global and historical connectivity of movements for social justice that Native Hawaiians are part of and that Black and Asian residents support.

Black transplants I spoke with similarly analyzed the basis of these connections: a shared enemy. Nino, an old-timer from the US South, felt that "minorities, in general, tend to relate with one another. So when the oppressor has white skin around the world, it's very easy to use that white skin as a common enemy, right? So I totally understand what Native Hawaiians feel like, what their fears are for the future.... It's the struggle. Is it better to become like one people, or is it better to have all these differences?" Nino thought about this question by considering his identity. His Black and Cherokee background and our discussion of Black people's views of Native Hawaiian struggles highlight White domination as a "common enemy."

Locals of African descent unsurprisingly considered these relations more deeply, finding them relevant to their being. Having African ancestry and living in Hawai'i frames their understanding of Black and Hawaiian relations in the past, present, and future. They joined Black transplants in finding parallels between Black and Hawaiian people as part of communities that have histories of oppression and shared experiences with White racism. A Black newcomer to Honolulu says she hasn't interacted with too many Hawaiians during her stint as a college student. However, "I feel that we have a connection because, one, we're oppressed by White people. And second is that we try to get our own thing and try to make something of it, but at the same time, we discriminate against others." Through this racialized understanding of colonialism, Black residents align themselves with Hawaiians in distinction to oppressive White people while addressing their accountability for cross-group antagonisms.

A Chicago-born pro-union labor journalist who arrived in the late 1940s made it his job to link the struggles in his adopted home with those in the broader world. Frank Marshall Davis, a decades-long Hawai'i resident, was an important Black male figure to the young "Barry" Obama. Davis offered an expansive and insightful perspective on the Black diaspora, reflecting on the changing ideologies of Black people since World War II. Obama, who like other locals grew up with few Black role models, describes "a poet named Frank who lived in a dilapidated house in a run-down section of Waikiki. He had enjoyed some modest notoriety once, was a contemporary of Richard Wright and Langston Hughes during his years in Chicago.... But by the time I met Frank he must have been pushing eighty, with a big, dewlapped face and an ill-kempt gray Afro that made him look like an old, shaggy-maned lion."[97] Readers may recall from Obama's memoir that he sought guidance from Davis after his grandparents voiced racist fears about a Black man his grandmother had encountered at a bus stop. Davis explained to the young Black local the difference between Barack's White Kansan grandfather and Davis: "He *can't* know me, not the way I know him. Maybe some of these Hawaiians can, or the Indians on the reservation. They've seen their fathers humiliated. Their mothers desecrated. But your grandfather will never know what that feels like."[98] Davis reads the racism of Obama's grandfather within a nonWhite/White binary rather than as Black/White or native/settler, quite possibly due to living in Hawai'i. This experience with racism is one that leads Black men and women to form what Du Bois famously termed a double consciousness that stems from the necessity of knowing White people as a matter of survival in ways White people are free from. This double consciousness and awareness of White domination are ties that bind racialized groups.

Davis made these Du Boisian connections among Third World people in his news columns, highlighting Du Bois's global understanding that the "color line belts the world" rather than being a dynamic restricted to Black and White in the United States.[99] The journalist describes how power operated in Hawai'i, drawing links between Black and Hawaiian people and remarking on instances of racism in the Islands to highlight the relevance of race in mid-twentieth-century Hawai'i.[100] He "openly discussed imperialism and colonialism" and "compared Hawai'i with other colonies and attacked the press for its racist propaganda," says Kathryn Takara.[101] Davis articulated these connections in his "Frank-ly Speaking" column in 1950:

> To the people of Hawai'i, Africa is a far-away place, almost another world. And yet in many ways it is as close as your next door neighbor. The Dark Continent suffers from a severe case of the disease known as colonialism which Hawai'i has in much milder form. The sole hope of the dying empires of Western Europe is intensified exploitation and continued slavery of African workers through US money and munitions. There are strikes in Africa against the same kinds of conditions that cause strikes in Hawai'i.[102]

The historical and global links Davis draws across colonialisms with a focus on labor epitomize a key aspect of the racial lens of African-descended transplants.

Kathryn Takara, a Black long-term resident who wrote a biography of Davis, describes her childhood in the 1950s Jim Crow South: "I was born and raised in a place and time when black was *not* considered a beautiful color and was associated with many negative things." She was surprised and bothered by the stereotyping and denigration of Hawaiians when she taught at the University of Hawai'i: "I saw a lot of parallels. But one parallel that was different was, of course, the migration experience—forced migration of the Blacks versus the native homeland of the Hawaiians." Whereas Black locals often find parallels between Hawai'i's colonization and the enslavement of Africans, Takara distinguishes their impacts and raises the question of Black people's relationship to Native land outside Africa.

If older Black transplants looked to the legacy of slavery, Black locals are more likely to mention the history of Black Hawai'i. A Black man raised in a Hawaiian family said, "You know, I read something that, it was back in history when African Americans from these early lands [were] working with royalty as well." He could be mentioning Anthony Allen, one of the first Black men in the Islands who worked as an adviser to the King and rose to prominence (see chapter 1). In attempting to locate himself in the Islands, Kamakakēhau says, "So I often think about that [past]. And that's what kind of gives me the encouragement." He then also refers to the marriages between Black and Hawaiian people that are also noted in the historical archives: "I was having a conversation with somebody, and they brought up the fact that why are Hawaiians so dark? You know? Where does that come from? And then, you know, African American got mixed into the conversation, because we [we]re here way back when." A Black Hawaiian of the same age spoke about growing up on Hawaiian Home Land with his Hawaiian family as a child in the 1970s: "Back then, being Black wasn't a good thing. It was considered being a bad thing. But I think what it did for me is it also identified America as being racist, and that if you weren't White, then you were considered [a] minority. So then, at that point, you know, me being part Black and part Hawaiian, you know—here I have these two histories that both were affected by America in negative ways." Like the news columnist Frank Marshall Davis, the younger generation of Black people living in the Islands (including those who are also Hawaiian) connects Hawai'i's colonization to the enslavement of West Africans and acknowledges the global experience of antiBlack racism, albeit with local inflections.

A Black old-timer who grew up not far from Frank Marshall Davis felt that Hawaiians had a greater kinship with Native Americans than with African Americans concerning political struggles, while Colin, a Black Hawaiian, felt otherwise. Colin stated that with his increasing involvement with Hawaiian politics, "The first thing I started to look toward was Black history. To see how they dealt with Americans. The second thing is that we started looking towards the Indians because that's more what we've replicated." At the first sovereignty movement rally he attended over a decade ago (he now attends them regularly, wearing a malo and holding a Hawaiian flag), "They had these three Indian chiefs that came to speak to this Hawaiian body. And I remember that this guy stood up and he said, 'I don't know why you Indians are here because we're nothing like you guys,'" an insistence on difference by some Hawaiians documented in the work of Jodi Byrd and J. Kēhaulani Kauanui ("We will never be Indians," states Mililani Trask).[103] Colin saw this reaction to tribal leaders as a reflection of Hawaiians being "too proud for their own good," and he wanted to distinguish himself from this thinking. Hawaiians, to him, were "not even recognized from the United States as being indigenous people to our land.... And until we can accept that we are the Indians of Hawai'i, we're never going to be" granted rights. This debate marks the careful charting of connection and distinction among Indigenous communities—communities that appear unified in their demands for autonomy and self-determination.

Nino, an older transplant, contextualizes the issues plaguing the Islands today with history, linking Native Hawaiian land concerns with those faced by Native Americans; he saw connections between Hawaiian and Black people and charted the influence of the US military from DC to Hawai'i, all working together to influence his sense of self in settler colonial Hawai'i. His take on Hawai'i is informed by his past as a farmer in the US South and his Native American peers. Like Native Americans, Hawaiians, he posited, "feel the same way: they feel that their land was stolen and taken away from them and they didn't get just reward and they were mistreated. And they feel that there is a stain on the flag, that there be people in power that still be trying to wash it out. They still be trying to correct that." Nino's expansive and interlinked theories of land dispossession—his global Indigenous perspective—contrast with deeply local iterations of the conditions of Native people.

The experiences of Hawaiians and Native Americans are distinct, and yet the US government has been a central actor on these communities, exploiting their resources in ways that bind.[104] Disputes about Hawaiian land remind Nino of ongoing Native struggles in the continental United States and their negotiations with political actors for correctives.[105] He then ties these fights to those of African Americans, whose issues are not ostensibly about land but center on persistent trauma (like Walt's conception of PTSD). Nino emphasizes, "You know, the slaves were brought here against their will, and they were forced to work for four hundred years. You know, even though slavery's over now, the repercussions that it's had on their families and generations of people.... If any other group of people suffer a similar type of situation, they're not just gonna forget about it! You know? (*hits table*) They're not gonna just forget about it!"

The trauma, history, and memory of seemingly discrete groups converge in these narratives—from journalist Frank Marshall Davis to local and transplanted educators Walt and Kathryn, as well as Nino the Black Cherokee former farmer. Yet this complexity of alliances and relations emerges from the narrative of Frank Marshall Davis's mentee who went on to become the commander in chief of the US armed forces. Described as a "Black Hawaiian" in both Michelle Obama's memoir and by a local with African and Hawaiian ancestry, Barack Obama was a wartime president who maintained the militarization of the Pacific in the name of national security, thereby further dispossessing Hawaiians and displacing Pacific Islanders across nations. Guam and Okinawa continue to be sites occupied by the US military.

Participants also discuss how Black and Hawaiian movements coarticulate. In a slightly different and critically useful frame, a politically active Black Filipino and local mother attempts to bring together Black women transplants with local concerns. In our discussion of the Movement for Black Lives as something that seemed to be happening "over there," on the continent, Laura points out "how important it is that we draw connections to what's happening here and what's happening there. If we can do that, I think we can find a lot of Brown allies in the Black Lives Matter movement together with this sovereignty, because it's really the same story. I think it's a story of power and control, materialism, and capitalism. It's all connected." However, there is not enough knowledge about Black history in Hawai'i for people to make consistent connections.

The epigraph to this chapter illustrates the result of such awareness, represented by Patrisse Khan-Cullors's tweet supporting the activists on Maunakea. This Black activist supports *and sees the link with* Pacific Indigenous futures, in large part because she came to the Islands and broke bread with Black and Hawaiian residents. This is a significant rebuttal to those who do not engage in discussions outside either Black or Native concerns, as well as to scholars and others who see Native and Black issues and responses as unconnected, irrelevant, or competing. Laura's stance as a Black Filipina troubled by the persistent and state-sanctioned murders of Black people across the United States informs her sense as a settler in Hawai'i, together shaping her understanding of her kuleana to support Hawaiian struggles for self-determination and against antiBlack racism.

As scholars debate the distinction between Black and Native peoples' conditions—or more likely do not take them both into account—Hawai'i's Black residents reveal the limits of race-only or Indigenous-only, or local-only or global-only, frameworks for understanding island dynamics. They contest Afropessimist presumptions of Black abjection and refute the presumption that Black and Native concerns are incommensurable. Rather, they highlight these groups' linked experiences with White domination, their overlapping yet distinct racialization. They point to a shared interest in overcoming oppression that takes into account the global devaluation of Black people without proffering antiBlackness as a global structure that dismisses the foundational experiences of Native people across the Americas and the Pacific. At the same time, this orientation to Black and Native relations disrupts the native/settler divide and decenters Whiteness without claiming or erasing indigeneity as a way to further possess people and places.[106]

If, when growing up in the 1950s Jim Crow United States, being Black was not good, and growing up Hawaiian in the 1970s, being Black *or* Hawaiian was not a positive thing, today things have changed. Now, says a Black Hawaiian, "being White is not a good thing" as a result of movements for self-determination and the increasing politicization of island residents, including some local Asians' recognition of their status as settlers.[107] The past informs people's notions of existing—and future—loyalties. A Black local prophesied that "if there was a war, Blacks would probably side with Hawaiians." This idea of a united front against the unspoken White enemy is linked to their shared pasts of oppression based on colonialism and slavery that has shaped and continues to inform their subjectivities as nonWhite people.

Conclusion

The Department of Ethnic Studies at the University of Hawai'i at Mānoa has been a long-standing advocate for progressive and antiracist politics. Faculty in the 1970s protested the war in Vietnam and the repressive Marcos regime in the Philippines. In more recent years, the department has focused on Black issues, becoming a central site of knowledge production on the Black experience in Hawai'i and across the Pacific. The department's advocacy for Black students and community members is notable. In a June 2020 statement against the police murder of Black people, the department "condemn[s] and call[s] for an immediate end to anti-Black racism."[108] It previously cosponsored a discussion called "Linking Oppression" that focused on "the importance of solidarity in fighting different forms of oppression."

The department was a community partner of the 2017 African American Film Festival that hosted Patrisse Khan-Cullors, the aforementioned cofounder of #BLM. Khan-Cullors also was part of a panel titled "Black Lives Matter in Hawai'i," held at the state capitol. The event was sponsored by AF3IRM Hawai'i and hosted by Black Sāmoan afakasi (mixed) House of Representatives Democrat Cedric Gates along with Kaniela Ing, a self-described feminist Kanaka Maoli politician from Maui who is the youngest chairperson in Hawai'i's legislative history.[109] *Flux* magazine interviewed Khan-Cullors:

> FLUX HAWAI'I: What made you agree to fly out to Hawai'i to speak?
> PATRISSE KHAN-CULLORS: Well there's been a lot of movement inside of Hawai'i, and specifically in Honolulu, about why black lives matter in the Hawaiian Kingdom. When I was out there last November, I met with a few black folks who live on the island, and specifically mixed-race

Figure 5.3 A Black Lives Matter in Hawai'i event featured Patrisse (Khan-) Cullors. Source: Poster for event at the Hawai'i State Capitol hosted by AF3IRM Hawai'i during Black History Month, February 10, 2017.

black islanders, to have an informal dinner to discuss blackness in Hawaiʻi.

FLUX HAWAIʻI: What were a couple things that came up during that dinner that you expect might come up again in this conversation [at the Hawaiʻi state capitol]?

PATRISSE KHAN-CULLORS: The erasure of blackness on the islands, the anti-black racism that exists in different communities. Also, that there is a really complicated history with a lot of black people being in the military and being on the island, and the history of colonization by the American government on the island. Black people sometimes roll in that.[110]

Khan-Cullors has now come several times to the Islands at the behest of some of the same people excited to hear the author Ta-Nehisi Coates speak the following September. Among them was Akiemi Glenn, cofounder of the Pōpolo Project.[111]

As the moderator for Coates's talk, Glenn—a woman with African, Native American, European, and Asian ancestry from the North Carolina and Virginia area—asked him about Black and Indigenous intersections and futures. Like Khan-Cullors, he was just learning about the context of Kānaka Maoli and about Blackness in Pacific sites, like Australia, where he had just been. Coates was surprised to see Indigenous Australians identify with Blackness.[112] (Khan-Cullors, separately, also commented on her surprise at Indigenous Australians' Black identification, including by "White appearing Black people.") That the esteemed commentator on Black life in the United States was unfamiliar with the long history of Black politics and people in these island nations reveals the need for scholarship on the Black Pacific.

Khan-Cullors expresses her sense of the dynamics and history of Hawaiʻi (acknowledging its status as a kingdom, for instance) and recognizes "mixed-race black islanders"—the center of this study, but a most overlooked population. This surprised the audience at her talk. The Black activist also spoke more recently at an event at Northwestern University. After her talk, I asked Khan-Cullors how she knew about multiracial Black locals in Hawaiʻi. She explained that she liked to do her homework before going somewhere, upon being invited to visit someone's home.[113] This kind of respect is well received and practiced in Hawaiʻi, where no one shows up without a gift in hand—a bag of homegrown mangoes or avocados, a haupia pie from Ted's Bakery. She was interested in movements for sovereignty and said she met with activists during her two visits to Hawaiʻi. Her time in the Pacific informed her tweet in support of the Maunakea kiaʻi that opened this chapter.

Black Americans visiting the Pacific, from Hawai'i to Fiji to Australia, come across expansive and global renditions of Blackness that question the hegemony of US racial formations. These are individuals who may become part of growing collectives of people who hope to learn and participate in what Scott Morgensen calls models of "how comparative, border-crossing, antiracist, and anticolonial feminist work on Indigenous lands might proceed."[114] Joy Enomoto enacts this cross-sectional work to address Black and Hawaiian relations. The scholar-activist explains why Kānaka Maoli should, in a return embrace, support the Movement for Black Lives. In her powerful challenge written in 2017, "Where Will You Be? Why Black Lives Matter in the Hawaiian Kingdom," Enomoto details the centuries of denigration Hawaiians faced, which included being indoctrinated with and about antiBlackness. She tells readers that "the first people of the Pacific were Black."[115] Similarly, the Hawaiian educator and independence activist Kaleikoa Ka'eo speaks of the African ancestry of two ancient migrations of people who crossed the Pacific, reminding us that the first humans to arrive in the Pacific came from Africa.[116] Yet Kānaka Maoli, in reaction to the racism they have faced in the continental United States and at home, have distanced themselves from their histories and have adopted antiBlack racism. In response, Enomoto asserts that "by supporting Black Lives Matter, we do not lose Hawaiian ways of resistance and knowing, we do not stop perpetuating our culture or lose our language. By supporting Black Lives, our ea [breath, sovereignty] is enhanced."[117] And just as fellow Black Hawaiian Colin described the shift from the denigration of Blackness and Hawaiianness of the 1970s to positive evaluations of these identities in the 1990s, Enomoto writes that "when we embrace Blackness in all its forms, we no longer let the mark of Blackness hurt us."[118] She states, unequivocally, "Let us stand up for Blackness and protect Black lives. BLACK LIVES MATTER IN THE HAWAIIAN KINGDOM."[119]

Conversations about Black life in Hawai'i and Black Lives Matter in the Pacific were amplified among locals in 2020. Academic responses to the topic fit into what some scholars have described as the "Indigenous turn" in American studies, with particular attention to the relationship between Black and Native peoples and Black and Native studies.[120] Rather than approaching these as bounded groups with autonomous political futures and from a historical account that centers people of African descent, we see the intersection of processes, politics, and conversations that have been taking place within and across the Pacific for centuries.

Kanaka epistemologies of expansive belonging provide a strategy of local and global alliance formation. Black residents, both locals and transplants, participate in the labor of creating alternative futures that bring further respite from the legacy of pain and oppression experienced by Black people around the world alongside their compatriots, who also contend with colonialism and a life contoured by White supremacy. They do this within the context of the Pacific, where Hawaiians, like the Kanaka feminist scholar Goodyear-Kaʻōpua, insist one does not have to be genealogically Hawaiian to remain. However, rather than exploit this refuge without giving back, we (all people in Hawaiʻi) must undertake our kuleana. This occurs through aloha ʻāina (restoration and love of the land that sustains), supporting Hawaiian self-determination, and collective processes of care.

Movements in these volcanic islands model Native and nonNative people working together based on Indigenous principles. Cultural revitalization is pivotal to envisioning new political futures. Black transplants view structural changes as necessary for new alignments of social, economic, and political power. But to truly change systems of domination, a much broader coalition of people is necessary. The scholar Chadwick Allen outlines, for instance, a "trans-Indigenous" method for a "global Native literacy" that moves "toward an intertribal or international approach and toward the possibility of a more global, trans-Indigenous approach."[121] This expansive orientation, similar to Du Bois's global outlook, recognizes the need for a coalition of oppressed people across the globe who face the effects of White supremacy. We can combine a transIndigenous approach with a racial analysis.

Some Black transplants reflect on their kuleana—aware of their positionality and, from that, attentive to living ethically—and offer a cross-racial, comparative, and translocal analysis of the world. This perspective echoes those of scholars who advance diasporic and relational outlooks unlimited by constructed colonial and racial boundaries. Bringing the local and comparative together explains the tentacles of historical processes of dispossession of multiple communities. It is attentive to how systems differentially affect specific populations. This same expansive yet nuanced worldview can also be the basis for challenging these interrelated systems. As one Black Hawaiian reflected, "When I was young, I always thought that everybody who wasn't Hawaiian should leave and just have the Hawaiians here. But as I got older, I realized that things have happened over a hundred years ago, and we can't go backwards. We can only go forwards. So what we need to do is concentrate on our future. Remember the past, learn from the past, but concentrate on the future." It signifies us collectively "backing into the future."[122]

In this chapter, I have illustrated Black residents' conceptions of the multivalent past, present, and future relationships between Black and Hawaiian people. Their analyses of sovereignty, land, and belonging highlight collaboration and contestation between two nonWhite groups within a nonWhite society in which neither occupies the status of the political elite. Most critically, in my view, this research illustrates models for mass-scale solidarity building from below. The "Black experience in America" has been forged through slavery, as a process co-constituted with settler colonialism and Native dispossession. However, the Middle Passage imprints unevenly on Black people living across the globe, whereby Black locals feel distant from the hegemonic "African American experience" but confront antiBlack racism within and outside the home. At the same time, Hawaiians have contended for centuries with the colonization and occupation of their land. As "two oppressed groups" who "have this history," Black and Hawaiian people are kin, even as their challenges and desires are not always shared.[123]

Black transplants come from across the United States and elsewhere to make these islands—which have accepted them for hundreds of years—their home. They learn about the dynamics of island life and, in many cases, about the struggles of Hawaiian people, which lead these transplants to reflect on their status and position. Younger arrivals represent the needs and skills of a generation of young Black people politicized by the Movement for Black Lives. They and other people I spoke with offered iterations of their kuleana to Hawai'i and Hawaiians. They considered—and mostly respected—Hawaiian desires for self-determination, seen as a goal also of Black social movements. Whether they felt at home in the Islands or felt that the Islands could never truly be their home, transplants and locals engaged the question of Hawaiian sovereignty through their positionality as Black people (or Black Hawaiians, in those cases) and a conscientiousness about their imprint on the Islands. Their analyses reframe considerations of land and independence beyond capitalist ownership and the nation-state. Rather, they align with those who feel that critical self-reflection, comprehending power, and forging alliances are key to living together. In their attempts to create community, they also confront tensions between Black and Hawaiian people as they work toward living more ethically away from the belly of the beast.

Conversely, Native Hawaiians have influenced—modeled, in fact—responses to current North American debates about land, resistance, cultural renaissance, and self-determination. People around the world are dialing in their support for the kia'i (protectors) of Maunakea against colonial entrenchments coded as "science" and progress. Kia'i are resuscitating Kanaka practices, forming refuge through classes, and practicing kapu aloha, which also embodies civil disobedience.

The links between Black and Hawaiian people, drawn by Black residents through shared historical oppression and reflections on accountability, highlight cross-fertilization. They illuminate how Blackness and Hawaiianness, race and indigeneity, native and settler, intersect, parallel, and overlap in ways that contest binary pairings. The histories of Black and Hawaiian politics and visions for shared futures transcend colonial categories and contest academic and political depictions of Black and Native communities as separate and distinct with political futures at odds. Rather, Black residents embody Kanaka principles of kuleana and connection with the ideas of self-determination and racial equality to imagine living ethically together in shared spaces. Now all of Hawai'i's residents must show our support to end state violence against Black people. The Movement for Black Lives is not an issue contained within the borders of the continental United States. Members of the African diaspora live in Hawai'i, including Black Hawaiian men and women, who confront police violence and other everyday and systemic forms of racism. Supporting Hawaiians' rights to land and self-determination and Black peoples' rights to live humanely and without violence must go hand in hand.

CONCLUSION

IDENTITY ↔ POLITICS ↔ KNOWLEDGE

> *I've always been outspoken, because I come from a proud family and a proud tradition, [from an] educated [African American] family for many generations, teachers. And so the fact that people [in Hawai'i] (sigh) were so uninformed was injurious. . . . People just didn't know who we were. And it was injurious to me. Because I knew that we had a proud history.*
>
> BLACK LONG-TERM RESIDENT

The ethnographic evidence unsettles hegemonic understandings of Black and Native people as *discrete groups* with *distinct histories* living in *different geographies* with *divergent political futures*. Furthermore, it adds a grounded portrait of the lives of contemporary people to what has largely been a historical, literary, and theoretical approach to Black and Native studies. Black residents in Hawai'i reveal how US Black/White racial thought intersects with—but does not neatly map onto—Hawaiian epistemologies of genealogy and orientation to others in ways that disrupt neat divisions of race and indigeneity. Black residents, both locals and transplants, expand our accepted notions of race, Blackness, and indigeneity. Black people in Hawai'i show us how to redefine our relationships with ourselves, acknowledge how others choose to be in the world, and fulfill our responsibilities to one another. In this conclusion, I suggest how to advance decolonization and antiracism simultaneously.

Hawai'i's Black civilians adopt Kanaka worldviews to develop what Angela Davis describes as the necessary expansive and inclusive community formations for revolutionary transformation, in contrast to identity-based com-

Figure 6.1 A group of Black women who are residents of Hawaiʻi display their banner with the message "Black Lives Matter in the Hawaiian Kingdom." Photo courtesy of Emilia Kandagawa.

munities, which can be exclusive and narrow.[1] The perspectives of Hawaiʻi's African-descended population are informed by histories of the African diaspora and the Pacific. They illuminate a Black Pacific worldview that weaves a racialized understanding of power with a conscientious understanding of place and people—and the connections among them. Hawaiʻi's alternative dynamics spark optimism and reveal possibility—a space to breathe, as it were, expressed in Barack Obama's own words and outlook—also embraced by most participants.

Transplants mentioned many ways that these islands offer Black people a refuge. Hawaiʻi is a majority nonWhite society where Black people experience "less pressure." They find opportunities to fulfill educational aspirations and achieve upward mobility while also enjoying peace and beauty. In a state voted the "healthiest . . . in the nation," Black people's closeness to death is mediated by an island culture that privileges nature, healing, spirituality, and communion. For people of African descent specifically, Hawaiʻi provides a sanctuary from strict and seemingly fixed and authenticating ideas of Blackness that are sedimented in US history. More compelling, the Islands offer a refuge from the racist violence Black people face across the continental United States. The Pacific offers expansive ways of being and belonging that embrace, cross, and exceed "race" and "indigeneity," ways that nonetheless consider historical and group specificity. However, Kanaka epistemologies also push against the more essentialist tendencies of movements today, such as the idea of a Hawaiian-only nation advocated by some sovereignty activists, or the Black-only spaces advocated by Afropessimists. In Hawai'i, we see people finding meaning in ancestral understandings of their identities along with broad ideological and political definitions of being together, or we-ness. This is a central component of what the Pacific offers people of African descent and what Black people bring to the Islands to help us understand current dynamics.

This book advances the theoretical and political work inspired more recently by the Movement for Black Lives. It calls for a reckoning with state-sanctioned police violence against Black people that *also* takes place in Hawai'i. While movement leaders are clear about their expansive conceptions of "Black," and their work crosses national boundaries, reductive iterations of Black life have taken shape in some academic discourse. We see the strength of the 1960s identity politics of the Black Power movement that influenced Hawaiian activists like Haunani-Kay Trask and Kihei "Soli" Niheu. However, this project contests divisive and reductive retrenchments of identity politics that advocate essentialist and exclusive notions of who "is" or "isn't" Black, Native, and so on. If we bring together an analysis of how race, indigeneity, and cultural practices commingle in people's daily lives with their material impacts, Hawai'i's Black residents trouble myopic and exclusionary intellectual engagements in at least three ways: through complex identifications *across* racialized and Indigenous communities, through understandings of the relationships between Black and Hawaiian histories and experiences with oppression, and through their political visions of the future. However, a lack of knowledge and acknowledgment of Black people fuels their invisibility and antiBlack racism, thereby diminishing life's full potential in Oceania.

In the Islands, race, indigeneity, and localness intersect to explain our relations to ourselves, to others, and to the land, the waters, and the skies. While US racial thinking informs locals, it does not determine their relationality. It coexists with the importance of 'ohana (family), kuleana (responsibility), and other practices of we-ness. When transplants arrive, they bring a Black/White lens, one informed by the Black Atlantic slave trade and systemic antiBlack racism. However, island dynamics, produced by a society that outlawed slavery, dispute this binary. Hawai'i's large mixed race population provides a context in which Black Hawaiians interrogate this binary and presumed monoracialism while expanding our understanding of multiracialism. An ethnographic portrait of Black Hawaiians, Black Okinawans, Black Sāmoans, Black Japanese,

Black Koreans, Black Mexicans, and Black Filipinos refutes simplistic dismissals of multiracialism as antiBlack. Their daily lives reveal complicated relationships with the various communities from which they emerge and the ancestors they call on.

Black people in the Pacific experience an expansive approach to Blackness while illustrating the limitations of the native/settler binary. First, this binary consolidates Black and White along with other nonNative people as settlers, enhanced through their shared participation in the US military. However, haole military personnel perpetuate a colonial relationship, a hierarchical relationship, to people of color. Black servicepeople are not pushed to join the armed forces by the same structural factors, and they also bring with them different orientations to themselves and their relationship to others. Second, military enlistees and nonmilitary civilians occupy different positions in the Islands. What of the growing population of Black civilians who have escaped the attention of scholars? Unlike haole in the military, Black transplants explain Black and Hawaiian comparative and historical *lateral* ties. Black people's perspectives on their relationships with Hawaiians, other local groups, and land provide a model for rights and responsibilities that acknowledge varied positionalities. Through informed solidarities, they articulate political visions of the future informed by Kanaka epistemologies.

The Pacific offers not only the possibility for, but also the clarity with which to understand, Black agency. The choices Black residents make here contest theories that posit Black abjection and the ongoing condition of slavery. Such theories prioritize the dehumanization of Black people and, therefore, their liberation before and over other groups. In Hawai'i, where Black people earn the highest incomes of any state (in part because of their work in the military), Black residents, along with Black visitors, have spending power. Black civilian residents, soldiers, and tourists, via their middle-class and nonlocal status, are accountable for their impacts on other groups, including Native Hawaiians.

Black residents, and particularly Black Hawaiians, understand Blackness and Hawaiianness relationally and highlight the racialization of Native Hawaiians. Colonialism and slavery inform their consideration of Hawai'i's status as illegally occupied by the United States. While categorizing Indigenous peoples only as racial or ethnic groups can be inaccurate, as such labels deny the specificity of their legal status and experiences with genocide and dispossession, "Hawaiian" is more than a legal and genealogical definition. It also represents identities, cultural practices, and resistant politics. Further, an indigeneity- or native-only analysis of Kānaka Maoli elides the historical racialization of

Native Hawaiians by early colonial agents and missionaries, some of whom transferred to them stereotypes of Black inferiority.[2]

I center a racial lens, but not to the extent of advocating a race-only analysis; similarly, there are limits to Indigenous-only or race-only framings of belonging. Black locals had to negotiate the meanings associated with Blackness in the absence of a Black community and Black family networks. Black transplants, on the other hand, had to discover modes of belonging in a site of racial invisibility, where Blackness had less salience than it had in the places they came from. This is also a place where multiracialism is a norm rather than exceptional, and where centuries-old methods exist for adopting, accepting, and understanding one's multiple ancestors. Monoracialism is contested by the attention to multiple ancestries and the question, "What are you?" It is in this context that Black transplants find themselves: in a place of "less pressure" that many arrivals end up considering their "haven," sanctuary, and refuge. In a place where ethnic identities are privileged, the specter of race—and racism—reveals different ways of performing localness and forces further examination of the category "settlers of color."

Black migrants import with them a racial lens that defines race and illuminates its functions and forms; it sheds light on persistent inequalities that unevenly affect island residents. Framed by a Black/White binary, this perspective is challenged by different hegemonies. With longer residencies, transplants learn how the colonial history of Hawai'i and Kanaka epistemological survivance—the ongoing influence of Hawaiian approaches to genealogy, people, places, and things—additionally inform island dynamics beyond its "diversity."[3] That this takes place within the context of Asian settler colonialism further refracts the Black/White binary. Nonetheless, settler colonialism is rooted in Native dispossession and racism, including the denigration of Blackness.

Why do Black people consider these islands their haven, their sanctuary, and refuge from life elsewhere? The answer lies in the long history of Black people in Hawai'i and the reception of Native Hawaiians to these arrivals. Coming to a place that outlawed slavery, offered citizenship, and viewed darkness as powerful, members of the African diaspora have long found the Islands a place of increased opportunities. Despite colonization and current military occupation, Hawai'i tempers White supremacist ideologies because of the survivance of Hawaiian ideologies and local practices that continue to inform daily life.

The Black Pacific is a place of possibility and site of accountability. Black people who make Hawai'i their home engage the world through their positionalities as racialized people. But they inhabit a heavily Indigenous place where they live among a host of people whose primary concerns may not include those of Black people. This leads to both invisibility and possibility—the possibility of, as one Black long-term resident from the US South says, "not just having to wake up and check every day" whether or not one is Black. With attention to the interconnectedness of people, places, and time, relationships in Hawai'i are central people's social lives. This orientation to life and the environs promotes communities that are not race based but relational, constructed through fictive kinship and one's responsibility to others. Yet rather than marking the irrelevance of race and Blackness, we see the specific ways race operates in a place without a Black Metropolis.

Histories of Black and Hawaiian exchanges predate the current moment and include the cross-fertilization of political ideologies and worldviews. If Black transplants provide us with a racial lens that illuminates how power operates across the spaces of the African diaspora, Kanaka worldviews teach us to prioritize responsibility and relationality. The prominence of Hawaiian activism encourages Black residents' self-reflexivity about their presence. At the same time, Hawaiian activism today emerges from a lineage of Kanaka resistance informed by Black political struggles that emanated from the continental United States and took flight across the Pacific. These political histories shape the lives of contemporary Black Hawaiians, who offer life lessons on both decolonization and antiracism that are not yet offered in the syllabi of Island schools.

Life Lessons

Black Hawaiians' knowledge of colonial history and racialist rules of engagement means that people engage Indigenous and racial logics through everyday strategies, often to their own ends. People have developed strategic responses not just to daily encounters with racism but to the policies and practices that structure their lives. This includes rearticulating blood quantum rules. Kauanui's study contrasts "Kanaka Maoli genealogical practices and kinship and how they differ from the U.S. colonial imposition of blood quantum."[4] Black Hawaiians contend with both of these logics simultaneously to access Home Lands set aside for Native Hawaiians while embracing Kanaka epistemologies that do not count belonging based on fractions.

Colin, a Black Hawaiian, explained, "Back in the day of Prince Kūhiō, my great grandfather used to be one of the leaders in our community. And him, along with Prince Kūhiō, had made a petition, gone to Washington, DC, to make [his area] part of the Hawaiian Homestead Act, which is kind of crazy because we weren't supposed to become a Homestead. So my community fought to become a Homestead, and we got included in the act." His great-grandfather had a Hawaiian and haole name, which, along with his visage and knowledge of White America, his community strategically called on:

> It's funny because, back then, Hawaiians felt that if you didn't have an English name or an American name, that you wouldn't be taken seriously. The fact that my great grandfather was Hawaiian haole, he looked like the White man, he spoke like the White man, and he had a White man's last name. So my community kind of figured that he would be the one that could speak the language and be able to get us to integrate with America.

While Colin sometimes uses blood quantum as fact, he simultaneously narrates his family's informed engagement with continental ideas of race (through looks) and culture (naming and language) to pursue their right to land. To get Hawaiian Home Lands, Colin has to return to quantifying ancestry: "I don't have 50 percent Hawaiian, I'm just shy—like 37.5 or something like that. So I can't get my own property, but I have 25 percent, which means that it can be willed to me."

"Hawaiian" may refer to blood quantum owing to federal policy. Yet when I asked Colin how he identified, he called himself a Black Hawaiian and later said, "It's kind of funny because I am part haole as well, Caucasian." I asked the backgrounds of his three children, and he said, "Okay. Ready? They're German, Dutch, Irish, English, French, Tahitian; Chinese, Japanese, Filipino; uh, Hawaiian, Puerto Rican, uh, and I think that's all I know (*laughs*) at that point." Colin's astute handling of various epistemologies of Hawaiianness highlights how "blood quantum can never account for the political nature and strategic positioning of genealogical invocation."[5] Yet what does it mean that Colin did not mention the African ancestry of his children, whom, he says, all identify as Hawaiian? By illustrating how people *live* and navigate political and conceptual terrains, we can see how the idea of having "Native blood" that does or does not "count" manifests in the lives of Hawaiians, and how being Black Hawaiian means facing antiBlack racism while also being recognized as Hawaiian. This is not about the imposition of ideas or legal strategies for self-determination. It is a depiction of life by people who straddle what we currently understand to be categories of race and indigeneity.

No study of Black Hawai'i should ignore its sizable hapa, or mixed race, population, which includes people with a world of experience navigating constructed boundaries of difference. Despite the obsession of sociologists and demographers who looked to Hawai'i as an exotic "interracial experiment" portending the future of mixed race America, most have overlooked Black multiracial people in the Islands.[6] Similarly, work in US-based mixed race studies tends to duplicate the Black/White (or Asian/White) binary. Instead, I hope to have illustrated the complexity of dual minority biracials. As a result, this project not only expands the literature on Hawai'i and refutes rifts between Black and Native studies but also contributes to debates within and between Black studies and critical mixed race studies.

Black Hawaiians in particular rupture easy discussions of "Black" and "Native" as discrete groups with divergent pasts and futures. Rather than simply being footnotes or dismissed as exceptional (or unreal, to those who discount the mixed race experience), they add to our understandings of race, indigeneity, ethnicity, and belonging. Throughout the book, we have seen how they, along with Black Asians and other Black hapas, unsettle native/settler binaries and the problematic framing of Black and Native studies as competitive, hierarchical, or unrelated.

Political Lessons

Yesterday at the #UHManoa [the University of Hawai'i at Mānoa] graduation two things stood out to me in the 3 hr-plus ceremony: first, a pair of African-American students raised their hands in a power salute as they reached the stage (like Tommie Smith and John Carlos in the 1968 Olympics). It seemed to be in solidarity with all the organizing and protest to recognize #blacklivesmatter. Second, one of the Hawai'inuiākea [School of Hawaiian Knowledge] grads stripped off his gown and received his diploma in his malo [loincloth], raising the diploma for the crowd to see (everyone cheered) and walked the full length of the floor to his seat triumphantly.

DR. FA'ANOFO LISACLAIRE (LISA) UPERESA, 2014

Dr. Fa'anofo Lisaclaire Uperesa, a former professor of ethnic studies at the University of Hawai'i, identified a political parallel in the actions of Black and Hawaiian students at their 2014 college graduation. Their performances demonstrated the race-conscious activism of the Black Power movement and the Hawaiian Renaissance that inspired pride in Kanaka cultural practices, such as wearing the malo, or loincloth. However, like Black Hawaiians, who themselves embody multiplicity, Black and Hawaiian freedom struggles do not just run parallel—they intersect. Despite characterizations of a recent "turn" in American studies toward conversations between Black and Native studies, we have evidence of a much longer genealogy of exchanges between Black and Indigenous academics, activists, and aesthetics. Fifty years ago, Black and Kānaka thinkers were engaging race and indigeneity across oceans while maintaining deeply local priorities through a global orientation to justice.

The Black Power movement inspired key figures in Hawaiian sovereignty and activism across the Pacific more broadly. Looking at contemporary debates in ethnic studies and Native and Indigenous studies, we see the influence of Pacific Islander women scholars like Haunani-Kay Trask and Teresia Teaiwa in our analyses of power and on our discussions of possible futures. The 1970s spotlighted race as a meaningful organizing structure and identity in Hawaiʻi. Valuations of Blackness and Hawaiianness changed owing to social movements like the Black Power movement. The race-conscious movements stemming from Oakland, California (the birthplace of the Black Panthers), swept across the Pacific to influence Indigenous Australians' identifications as Black and the rise of the Polynesian Panthers in Aotearoa/New Zealand. Black Power activists and thinkers also directly shaped players at the center of the emerging sovereignty movement in Hawaiʻi and the founding of ethnic studies at the flagship university. Black Power and American Indian movements contested the Americanization projects of the post–World War II period and encouraged the cultural resurgence of Hawaiian practices, ʻōlelo Hawaiʻi, the hula, and land-based practices that together encouraged pride in being Hawaiian.[7] These were the movements that inspired shifts from negative to positive valuations of Blackness and Hawaiianness that affected many of the Black locals who grew up in the 1970s and 1980s whose lives fill these pages.

Historical precedent confirms the influence of the civil rights and Black Power movements on Kānaka Maoli struggles on and off university campuses. Mary Choy, a local Korean activist for Korean women's rights and Kanaka supporter, recalls, "We studied Mao, liberalism, monopoly capitalism, etc. Our inspiration came from the Black and Puerto Rican movements. Leaders from the revolutionary Black Panthers and the Young Lords parties were invited by the Ethnic Studies Program to come to Hawaiʻi to share their experiences with us. What a consciousness raising time that was!"[8] Reflecting on this time, the Oakland-born Kanaka activist Terri Kekoʻolani (Auntie Terri) says, "Angela Davis and Eldridge Cleaver visited us in Hawaii and had a huge influence on our thinking and movement building at the time. We had to wrestle with our own contradictions, not appropriate black culture for our movement, but define our identity using our own culture and still be in solidarity with the black struggle."[9] The outcome of this parsing out is Auntie Terri's tireless work as an antinuclear and feminist activist across the Pacific, including her decolonial tours of Hawai'i.[10]

Young Hawaiians went to the continental United States in the 1960s and brought back what they learned. In college, Trask became inspired by the nationalist ideas of Black social movements. She recalls that when she "was an undergraduate and graduate student at the University of Wisconsin from the late 1960s through the mid-seventies, the Vietnam War focused a great deal of our organizing and protest. The Black Civil Rights Movement came also to define our resistance as did one of its offshoots, the fight for a Black Studies (now African American) studies program."[11] The activist Kihei "Soli" Niheu, who fought for Indigenous and local land rights, recollected both of these developments, citing his formative time in college in San Jose, California, during the 1960s. Just a few cities away from the birthplace of the Black Panthers, Niheu found himself where "there was a black students' union group," and he "made many friendships with people from the Black Panther Party."[12] This confluence, along with reading Martin Luther King Jr. and Mohandas Gandhi, helped to form Niheu's politics.[13] This was a heady time, preceded by anticolonial movements across Asia and Africa, including India's 1947 defeat of the British. The antiwar stance of the Muslim boxer Muhammad Ali went global and resonated in King's less celebrated excoriation of US involvement in Southeast Asia in his 1967 "Beyond Vietnam" speech. Upon his return to the Islands, Niheu joined the antiwar movement and linked it to local land struggles (particularly the fight to stop the eviction of farmers in Kalama Valley), both of which were central to the founding of ethnic studies in Hawai'i.[14] "This activity" in 1970, Niheu writes of the Kalama Valley struggle that included campus and community leaders, "initiated the renaissance of Hawaiian self-determination and, in a certain [respect], sovereignty, because we wanted the military out of Hawai'i."[15]

People who helped create Hawaiian studies and ethnic studies in Hawai'i were all influenced by Black social movements.[16] The development of ethnic studies and Hawaiian studies corresponds to Martha Biondi's illustration of the rise of Black studies across the nation, where students and community members were committed to exposing institutional power and increasing the numbers of underrepresented minority students.[17] Hawaiians constituted only 5 percent of the student body before the establishment of Hawaiian studies (they are now over three times that).[18] Trask went on to become the first tenured Hawaiian professor on campus.

Hawai'i's politics are not derivative or local versions of US ideas. Locally specific concerns and histories informed the burgeoning renaissance, and Hawaiian leaders have politically influenced those stateside. Haunani-Kay Trask is required reading across fields of ethnic studies as well as in Native and Indigenous studies, reminding people of the vast expanse of US domination. Her classic text *From a Native Daughter* places Trask among the great thinkers of our time. The Afropessimist scholar Frank Wilderson III describes the Kanaka professor as the "revolutionary from Hawaii," whose 1993 book continues to inform international debates on settler colonialism.[19] Whereas Wilderson's theories privilege Black liberation, Trask taught others, in the words of Joy Enomoto, "that although our struggles are distinctly different, we need solidarity to have true sovereignty."[20] Trask's work has significantly influenced not only Native and Indigenous studies across the Americas but also scholars in Black studies thinking through their relations with Native people. Tiffany King writes that "Trask's work is also a model for the ways that genocide and settlement could work in tandem with slavery and anti-black racism."[21] Trask did not see Black and Hawaiian concerns as entirely unrelated; she also drew parallels, stating, for instance:

> Women are at the forefront of our sovereignty movement. Women lead our Hawaiian Studies Center. Women represent most of our leadership in established organizations. In brief, women are on the front lines, the battle lines.... The reality is simply that women are there, where the action is, where the people live, where the nation resides.... This was true of the 1960s Black Civil Rights Movement in the South. Then, women and young people led the organizing efforts. The same is true for our sovereignty movement today. And the same is true for our campus organizing. Women lead.[22]

In "10 Reasons Black Lives Matter in the Hawaiian Kingdom," the Women's Voices, Women's Speak informational sheet lists at number 4: "There is a history of Kanaka Maoli and Black solidarity. Movements for black liberation have influenced the Hawaiian sovereignty movement."[23] The document quotes Trask, who wrote, "The evolution of my thinking owes a great debt to some of the most creative intellectuals and revolutionaries of the 20th century: Frantz Fanon, Malcolm X, and Ngugi wa Thiong'o."

These exchanges result from the global migration of the African and Hawaiian diasporas. The knowledge formation of Pacific Islander activists and scholars like Haunani-Kay Trask, Soli Niheu, and Teresia Teaiwa included their travels to the United States and elsewhere. In university, they studied leading Black anticolonial thinkers, who helped them theorize racial oppression, colonialism, and resistance and articulated the oppressive nature of global White supremacy and political domination. They then took these ideas and applied them to the Pacific context in ways deeply local (Trask focused on Hawai'i's sovereignty), communitarian (Niheu fought on behalf of workers), and Pan-Pacific (Teaiwa's work spans Oceania).

Questions about land prompted Trask, like the people I spoke with, to also link Hawaiians to Native Americans. She stated that "more akin to the American Indian Movement than to the black Civil Rights Movement, the Hawaiian Movement began as a battle for land rights but would evolve, by 1980, into a larger struggle for native Hawaiian autonomy."[24] The Black popular studies scholar Halifu Osumare, who earned her doctorate in American studies at the University of Hawai'i at Mānoa under the guidance of Trask's life partner and Hawai'i scholar David Stannard, adds that "no doubt the parallel between Native American and Native Hawaiian movements is close, but one has to acknowledge that fact that the Hawaiians' original *style* of protest and organizational strategy was a direct result of the Black Nationalist movement. Leaders of an early Hawaiian Movement organization, Kokua Hawai'i, attended Black Panther Party meetings on the mainland and adapted their organizational structure to the needs of the emerging *aloha aina* movement in Hawai'i.... Thus, at the onset a Black Nationalist *approach* undergirded the inchoate Hawaiian sovereignty movement."[25] Some activists, including those who attended the Black Panther conference in Washington, DC, linked the Black Power struggle and aesthetics to land struggles in Hawai'i. They returned to the Islands with "the idea of wearing berets."[26] The aesthetic symbolizes the political as Trask taught other Hawaiians about state violence against Black people. The scholar-activist Joy Enomoto recalls hearing how Trask "aligned the Hawaiian Sovereignty movement with Black Liberation."[27] Black social movements and thinkers thus had a multivalent influence on island activists, including on their aesthetics, understanding of systemic processes, and strategies.

In her courses, Trask paid homage to those who helped form her ideas, integrating political and intellectual Black thinkers into her syllabi. Trask's former student and Pacific Islands studies scholar Teresia Teaiwa notes that "Trask assigned readings by revolutionary writers from outside the Pacific, such as Frantz Fanon and Malcolm X," in her "first ever decolonization seminar."[28] Teaiwa is a Hawai'i-born, Fiji-raised scholar and poet who tragically passed away much too young in 2017. The daughter of an I-Kiribati father and African

American mother, Teaiwa developed some of the most influential conceptions of the Pacific, decentering Hawaiʻi's hegemony, and that of Polynesia in Oceania more broadly, to analyze the effects of militarism. Like Trask, Teaiwa earned her PhD in the continental United States, at the University of California, Santa Cruz's, History of Consciousness Department (where the Pacific Islands studies scholar Vicente Diaz earned his PhD). There she worked under the anthropologist James Clifford and developed her concept of militourism.[29] The influence of Teaiwa's other mentor, former Black Panther and professor Angela Davis, is clear. In return, Davis notes how much she learned about the Pacific from Teaiwa, her mentee who went on to direct Pacific studies and Sāmoan studies at Victoria University in Aotearoa.[30]

Teaiwa's scholarly and literary work brought together Black and Pacific Islands studies, illustrated in the poem "Black in the Blue Pacific (for Mohit and Riyad)." It begins with the following lines:

a hawaiian nationalist / idealizes malcolm x /
wishes white people / would fear hawaiians
the way they fear blacks[31]

This is one of the so few writings on Black and Hawaiian people within the Pacific, coming unsurprisingly, like many of the local participants I interviewed, from someone with African and Pacific Islander ancestry. She lists the names used to call Black people (pōpolo/meauli) in her consideration of Pacific Islanders:

in melanesia / the islands are not / black /
but / the people are / unlike Polynesians[32]

Teaiwa gets to the root of colonial divisions of Oceania while also noting the division between Melanesians and African Americans. Teaiwa's family history and scholarly trajectory, including her postgraduate work at the University of Hawaiʻi, developed her Oceanic consciousness. She urges us to address colonial and racial divisions and to be cautious of the ways that people in the Pacific, Native and not, have adopted them. Teaiwa ends with the assessment of Black as a politics, Black as a "state of mind." She emerges from an intellectual and political genealogy that includes the Black and Hawaiian feminist activists Angela Davis and Haunani-Kay Trask.

In 2019, Haunani-Kay Trask earned the American Studies Association Angela Y. Davis Prize, awarded to those who have developed scholarship for the public good. Fittingly, the conference was held that year in Honolulu, and Angela Davis commended Trask, stating, "I see the prize as symbolizing the comradeship and the solidarity and the way in which we have worked as a community." Like Davis, Trask's political awareness combines with her work as a professor to school people within and outside of campus—and not just locally. For instance, an old video of Trask resurfaced recently on the internet through the Facebook feeds of many people—some of whom had never heard of this Hawaiian revolutionary. The one-and-a-half-minute video, titled "Native Hawaiian Woman Responds to Racist Caller," shows her as a panel member who educates a haole caller questioning why White people are blamed for taking Native land. Trask calls the woman "woefully ignorant" and discusses the colonization of Hawai'i.[33] This video, which always earns claps, finger snaps, and calls of "ooooh, you go, girl," gained broad circulation in the continental United States in 2016 because Trask's quick lesson cited a global history of land loss that resonated not just with Native Americans but also with anyone affected by Europeans. The Kanaka activist's global understanding of race, colonialism, and land dispossession reveals the cross-circulation of movements for self-determination that resonate with Black people around the world. *Hawai'i Is My Haven* is my attempt to make this knowledge more widely known—knowledge that should be included in school curricula.

Lessons for the Syllabus

There's an existent piece of the historical pie in Hawai'i that needs to be taught, not just during the month of February. This is Hawai'i history, and all kids need to know about this, but it's especially for African American kids, for Black kids, because in many ways they have no anchors that are rooted in Hawai'i. But there's history. It's just underrepresented, right? So that needs to happen within the school system. You need to be teaching this just as much as you teach about [James] Cook, just as much as you teach about King Kamehameha, just as much as you teach about Kalākaua, Lili'uokalani, the Great Māhele, all those things.

LOCAL BLACK SĀMOAN

Black people in Hawai'i, local and transplant, suggest the need for educating residents about the history of the Black diaspora, including the United States, the Pacific, and Hawai'i. K–12 schools and institutions of higher learning should serve rather than discriminate against Black students, teachers, and staff. Weaving existing syllabi with Black studies scholarship to address the

African diaspora would provide students with the analytics of race necessary for understanding its global force and how it shapes life in the Islands. Just as Hawaiians are not just another ethnic group owing to their indigeneity, so Black residents too are not just another ethnic group. We cannot understand the Black experience outside a racial framework, although it alone does not suffice.

Institutions of early education and higher learning can incorporate the contributions of Black residents *to benefit local students*. Some models already exist. For instance, the Ke Kaulike He Haʻawina Kiwila High School Curriculum, designed with Kanaka principles in mind, offers a section titled "Civics Hawaiian Style."[34] Lesson 6, "Social Injustice in Hawaiʻi," centers the Massie cases of the 1930s. It first asks students to "develop a timeline of contributions by people of African ancestry in Hawaiʻi."[35] The students are provided some background information, including an article by participant Kathryn Takara ("African Americans in Hawaiʻi") and another by the American studies professor David Stannard on the Massie case, and a news article on the discrimination Obama faced growing up. These readings provide the "little known history of people of African heritage in Hawaiʻi, a group whose presence and contributions preceded racial intolerance toward individuals with dark skin. These materials serve as excellent resources for Black History Month held each February."[36] Students are asked to address why the status of people of African ancestry shifted from being held in high regard (it doesn't say *to what*). This backward- and forward-looking and politically relevant lesson plan links a historical case of lynching against a Hawaiian man, Joseph Kahahawai, to the existence and experience of Black people in Hawaiʻi, including the former US president. The lesson plan summarizes the goal:

> These activities were created to help students develop a deeper understanding of how people at the time of the Massie Trial were swept up in the foreign turmoil of racial hatred and injustice. It is also hoped that by exploring these social injustices, students will gain more empathy toward oppressed ethnic groups in Hawaiʻi today. With this understanding of past and present issues, students are then [asked] to voice their visions for a future of Hawaiʻi based on justice and doing what is *pono* or right, for the land and its people.[37]

This curriculum offers an example of the kinds of expansive, cross-temporal, and cross-group linkages that emerge out of a Kanaka-centered education that is attendant to race, African Americans, and the discrimination faced by Micronesians. Incorporating Black studies theories about race could sharpen and expand this lesson. It would counter its reduction of Blackness to the United States and race to a matter of skin color. A racial lens would also insert the appropriate *racial* analysis that is subsumed by the term "ethnic groups." The lesson plan asks students to learn about slavery and the social injustice faced by African Americans, which they then tie to the "association of skin color with social acceptance and economic growth. This stigma of skin color was at the heart of the Massie trial," revealing how the Massies transposed supremacist notions onto Kahahawai.[38] The lesson plan then makes the critical turn to calling up "the challenges of Micronesians in Hawai'i" as relevant to this discussion of race, denigration, skin color, and the US military in the Pacific.[39]

Bringing a racial analysis to our study of life illuminates the politics of race more broadly. This includes the task of being more specific in disarticulating the concepts of ethnicity, indigeneity, race, and culture. Correcting the dominant and official state-level tendency to call haole "Caucasian" instead of White would encourage haole accountability for power relations and their positionality in the Islands while acknowledging their denigrated social status. It would also allow Black locals to understand how they are simultaneously part of multiple communities of belonging while recognizing that Black and African American are racialized categories, rather than apolitical ethnicities or cultures.

I interviewed Black educators who were also developing curricula. Black Sāmoan local Walt is inspired to implement his plan to educate residents about Black people in Hawai'i because "I think it's a stunted type of growth.... This program [is] designed for kids from the age of fourteen to the age of eighteen. That's our target, but I've had grown men that have been like, 'Can I come?'" The passionate social worker links this untold history to militarism and Black residents who feel a sense of rootlessness, without a place in nearby physical and imagined Black communities.

At the college level, support for resurrecting the University of Hawai'i's Faculty of African Descent (FAD) group could lead to the output of more information on the status of Black members of the university.[40] The East-West Center has also hosted four biennial Winter Institutes on Black Studies convened by former Black UH ethnic studies professors Kathryn Takara and Elisa Joy White. The institutes' themes included "Lifestyle Changes: Keys to Reducing Health Disparities among People of Color" (2005), "Telling the Story: Blacks in America and the Pacific" (2007), "The 'Alternative' African Diaspora: Interdisciplinary Roundtables on Emergent, Oppositional and New Discourses in the Field" (2009), and "When Then Is Now: A Mediation on Social Justice, Activism and Political Change" (2011).⁴¹ The burden of our education should not fall only on Black faculty, who are themselves overburdened as racial representatives. As a result, organizations on and off campus can invite and compensate off-Island Black speakers like Patrisse Khan-Cullors as well as local Black performers and activists who can articulate what Black residents know: "that this pain is serious in the context of the continent, so it means something," as one professor put it. While the Faculty of African Descent group and the Winter Institutes may no longer exist, recent initiatives outside the university are highlighting Hawai'i's Black experience and focusing on Black and Kānaka Maoli relations and politics. Pōpolo Project cofounder Akiemi Glenn and professors Charles Lawrence and Kathryn Takara have created well-received conversations about the Movement for Black Lives and collected and made available the stories of Black residents.

Education at the college level about concepts of race is crucial for both locals and out-of-state students. Some local college students "are surprised" by what they learn in their Black studies classes. A Black professor said, "That's what always interests me, those who are surprised who are local, because that's really an opportunity to really dig in there and change their whole worldview. But the others are just processing something they already knew and starting to be able to understand that it's okay to articulate it as negative." This process of understanding shapes the ways we interact and live in the world—the stakes are no lower than that.

Truly integrating our education with the knowledge about the past *and* present, the global *and* local conditions and experiences of people of African descent within Hawai'i's early and secondary education would heighten locals' understanding of Black neighbors and deepen our appreciation for Black cultural formations. This would further explain why Black protests, like those rocking the United States at unprecedented levels, are necessary rather than "rude" or simply the result of an unrelieved "chip on your shoulder" owing to events long past.⁴² Locals are unfamiliar, and possibly unconcerned, with persistent forms of racism that lead to Black death. This new information may convince students and administrators of the need for greater numbers of Black faculty and courses on race and racism. How would this exposure, appreciation, and acknowledgment change the experiences of young Black people, from Papakōlea to Pūpūkea, from Mānoa to Makawao?

What compels this project is a sense of responsibility—to one another and to ourselves. It explains my focus on the daily lives of people and why I draw heavily from the Hawaiian notion of kuleana as a central framework. This is the conception of critical self-reflection that accounts for our positionalities but does not stop there—at only a consideration of our given identities. It must do the work of accounting for our positions vis-à-vis structures to craft—and act on—our responsibilities. It is the kuleana of each of us to reckon with ongoing systems of oppression that we are implicated within. How are we located in these systems, and are we working to advance or dismantle them? What can motivate us to take up this challenge? The impetus for critical self-reflection on our accountability is modeled also in the development of ethnic studies and Native and Indigenous studies, including works on the Pacific. These fields analyze the conditions of nonWhite people, forged in the crucible of colonialism, slavery, genocide, and exploitation, all supported by White supremacy. Race studies and Indigenous studies scholars, however, do not only analyze the relationships of various groups to White people; they also look at the relations within and across communities of color. Such analyses foreground the deep desire to understand the conditions of life as we develop the possibilities that the world holds for all its people.

NOTES

Introduction: Hawai'i Is My Haven

1. "Jury Awards Former Queen's Nurse."
2. Rucker, "Hawai'i's Influence on Barack Obama."
3. Obama, in Glauberman and Burris, *Dream Begins*, 4.
4. Obama, *Dreams from My Father*.
5. "Demographic, Social, Economic, and Housing Characteristics," 28. Forty-one percent were "Black in combination with another race" between 2011 and 2015.
6. Lee, "Thousands Show Up across Hawaii."
7. Tsai, "All We Want."
8. Hofschneider, "Many in Hawaii Grieve."
9. Glenn, "African American Solidarity."
10. Glenn, "African American Solidarity."
11. Mahalo nui loa to Hiʻilei Hobart for this important framing.
12. Glenn, "African American Solidarity"; Hofschneider, "Many in Hawaii Grieve."
13. Patrisse Khan-Cullors, interview with Pōpolo Project, June 2018. In the same interview, she stated, "But, that doesn't mean that there aren't very important conversations that Black Lives Matter has initiated that can happen everywhere. We *have* to talk about Blackness. We *have* to talk about how many Indigenous Hawaiians are actually Black! What does it mean to claim Blackness? What does it mean to have a Black politic? And this idea that Black Lives Matter isn't a separate struggle for Black people to take on. It's actually a struggle for every single one of us. Because *really* and *truly* when Black people get free, everybody else gets free."
14. https://patrissecullors.com/about.
15. Khan-Cullors, "Interview with Pōpolo Project," pt. 2.
16. Hobart, "At Home on the Mauna." "Thirty Meter" refers to the diameter of the telescope's lens.
17. Casumbal-Salazar, "Where Are Your Sacred Temples?"
18. Casumbal-Salazar, "Where Are Your Sacred Temples?"
19. Hofschneider, "Many in Hawaii Grieve."
20. Hofschneider, "Many in Hawaii Grieve."
21. Hofschneider, "Many in Hawaii Grieve."
22. Puʻuhonua o Puʻuhuluhulu and Hawaiʻi Unity and Liberation Institute (HULI), "Joint Statement of Solidarity for the Protection of Black Lives," June 5, 2020.
23. Glenn, "African American Solidarity."
24. Gilroy, *Black Atlantic*.

25 Epigraph: Professor Goodyear-Kaʻōpua was describing the history of Hawaiian independence. On a Wednesday in 2018, people gathered at the ʻIolani Palace in Honolulu to commemorate the 125th anniversary of the overthrow of the Hawaiian Kingdom.
26 King, "Address to the House of Representatives," 278.
27 "The Population of Hawaiʻi by Race/Ethnicity: U.S. Census 1900–2010," Bureau of the Census 2010 Summary File (SF1), June 16, 2011; Stannard, "The Hawaiians"; United Status Census Bureau, FactFinder, http://factfinder.census.gov. Asians, who are not generally lumped together as one racial demographic in Hawaiʻi, do not form a majority because of key ethnic group distinctions.
28 The Hawaiʻi journalist Eric Stinton's excellent eight-part series on Black people, history, and culture in Hawaiʻi celebrating Black History Month in 2020 is a notable exception. Stinton, "Black History in Hawaii."
29 The 2010 Census counted 38,820 Black or African Americans, alone or in combination, while, for instance, Sāmoans were counted at 37,463. State of Hawaiʻi, "Sāmoan Population by County," 5.
30 Ikeda, foreword, n.p.; Nitasha Sharma, "Pacific Revisions of Blackness."
31 "Hawaii Facts and Trivia," https://www.50States.com/facts/hawaii.htm.
32 Tengan, *Native Men Remade*, 2.
33 "Grover Cleveland on the Overthrow."
34 For more on these sociologists' work on race in Hawaiʻi, see Pierce, "Creating a Racial Paradise."
35 Lee and Baldoz, "A Fascinating Interracial Experiment Station," 88. For critiques of these early sociologists, see Okamura, "Illusion of Paradise"; Pierce, "Creating a Racial Paradise."
36 Initially referring to any foreigner to Hawaiʻi, "haole" today refers to White people, whether they come from the Islands or elsewhere. I use the term interchangeably with "White."
37 "Demographic, Social, Economic, and Housing Characteristics," 2; Okamura, *Ethnicity and Inequality*, 22–23.
38 "Demographic, Social, Economic, and Housing Characteristics," 2. These numbers include people who selected Black or African American alone or in combination.
39 Clark, "10 Best States for Black Household Wealth."
40 Their high school graduation rate was listed at 97.48 percent, while Black people in Hawaiʻi were 8.57 percent below the poverty level. World Population Review, "Honolulu, Hawaii," http://worldpopulationreview.com/us-cities/honolulu-population. Sources on Hawaiʻi that provide demographic data do not usually include Black people; I was unable to confirm the statistics in this source. Okamura explains that Hawaiʻi has the only statewide (public) school system in the United States; thus the funding system does not have the imbalances of other states with multiple school districts. Okamura, *Ethnicity and Inequality*, 65.
41 World Population Review, 22. Compared with less than 6 percent each for Asians and Hawaiians, according to World Population Review, "Honolulu, Hawaii."
42 "Demographic, Social, Economic, and Housing Characteristics," 9.

43 Belton, "5 Best States for Black People."
44 "Demographic, Social, Economic, and Housing Characteristics," 19. Almost 80 percent of Black people in Hawaiʻi work more than thirty-five hours per week (11).
45 For another explication of the concept of "otherwise," see Crawley, *Blackpentacostal Breath*.
46 Drake and Cayton, *Black Metropolis*.
47 See Lee and Baldoz, "Fascinating Interracial Experiment Station."
48 Teaiwa, "Black and Blue in the Pacific"; Andrews, "'Something within Me'"; Enomoto, "These Could Be Evidence." See also an important discussion about Hawaiian and Black relations in Jamaica Osorio, "E Iho ana ʻo Luna."
49 Beamer, *No Mākou Ka Mana*; Arista, *Kingdom and the Republic*; Malo, *Moʻolelo Hawaiʻi*.
50 Wright, *Physics of Blackness*.
51 Many thanks to Vicente Diaz for a deeply generative conversation about layers of Blackness in the Pacific.
52 Arvin, *Possessing Polynesians*; Warren, "Theorizing Pō."
53 "Kanaka" was a term that haole colonizers used derogatorily to refer to a Hawaiian person and has since been adopted by Hawaiians as a way to refer to themselves. "Kanaka Maoli" means real or true person; "Kānaka Maoli" (plural) means real or true people. "Hawaiian" does not refer to someone from Hawaiʻi (e.g., it is not like "Californian") but refers specifically to someone with native ancestry. The Hawaiian language scholar Charles Langlas, personal communication, May 4, 2020. See D. Chang, *World and All the Things*, 263.
54 D. Chang, *World and All the Things*; See Kim and Sharma, "Interventions in Pacific Islands Studies."
55 By "race" I refer to the process of racialization in the United States, or the ideological processes by which dominant groups categorize others based on phenotype and develop ideas that are imputed on those Others, who are de/valued within a hierarchy. This process is amplified by racism, in which the ideologies of racialized Others are then called on to justify their exploitation and decimation (genocide, slavery, indentured servitude) for the material benefit of those in power. This notion of race is constructed over time, and sometimes quickly, through systemic dispossession (such as access to land rights) and exclusion (from the nation, from the right to live, from accessing health care, for example). However, people engage the process of race-making, contesting the devaluation of nonWhite identities.
56 See, e.g., Horne, *White Pacific*; Taketani, *Black Pacific Narrative*; Smyth, "Black Atlantic Meets"; Okihiro, "Afterword."
57 Schleitwiler, *Strange Fruit*; Lucious, "In the Black Pacific"; Cloyd, *Dream of the Water Children*.
58 Lyons and Tengan, "Pacific Currents."
59 Gilroy, *Black Atlantic*.
60 Shilliam, *Black Pacific*; Webb-Binder, "Affinities and Affiliations"; Solis, "Black Pacific."
61 Rokolekutu, "Heterogeneity."

62 Kabutaulaka, "Re-presenting Melanesia," 112.
63 Rokolekutu, "Heterogeneity."
64 Kabutaulaka, "Re-presenting Melanesia," 113–15; Arvin, *Possessing Polynesians*.
65 Du Bois, "Color Line."
66 Solis, "Black Pacific."
67 Walcott in Spady, "Reflections on Late Identity," 102.
68 Sexton, *Amalgamation Schemes*.
69 Ledward, "Inseparably Hapa," 20. See also Ledward, "On Being Hawaiian Enough." "Hapa" is a Hawaiian term meaning "part" and is used to mean "of mixed blood" in Hawaiian Creole English or pidgin English. While Ledward uses it to refer to Hawaiians, many people in Hawai'i, as well as across the United States, have erroneously adopted the term to only refer to Asian and White multiracial individuals and without acknowledging Hawaiians or the word's etymology. Dariotis, "Hapa."
70 Ledward, "Inseparably Hapa," 35.
71 Ledward, "Inseparably Hapa," 47.
72 Ledward, "Inseparably Hapa," 8.
73 Ledward, "Inseparably Hapa," 10.
74 Wolfe, "Settler Colonialism."
75 Glenn, "Settler Colonialism as Structure," 52.
76 K. Chang, *Pacific Connections*; Shah, *Stranger Intimacy*; Mawani, *Across Oceans of Law*; Leong and Carpio, "Carceral States." See also J. Chang, *Chino*.
77 Miles and Holland, *Crossing Waters*, 2–3. This important volume includes a chapter on Hawai'i.
78 S. Jackson, *Creole Indigeneity*; see also Newton, "Returns to a Native Land."
79 "Latest Census Data."
80 "Demographics, Social, Economic, and Housing Characteristics," 12, 14.
81 Okamura, *Ethnicity and Inequality*, 57.
82 Fujikane and Okamura, *Asian Settler Colonialism*.
83 Okamura, "Why There Are No Asian Americans."
84 Leong and Carpio, "Carceral States," vii; Karuka, *Empire's Tracks*.
85 Callis, "Kim Finalizing Maunakea Committee."
86 Kauanui, *Hawaiian Blood*, 75.
87 Trask, *From a Native Daughter*; Saranillio, *Unsustainable Empire*; Fujikane, "Mapping Wonder."
88 Tuck, Guess, and Sultan, "Not Nowhere."
89 Tuck, Guess, and Sultan, "Not Nowhere."
90 Tuck, Guess, and Sultan, "Not Nowhere."
91 Tuck, Guess, and Sultan, "Not Nowhere."
92 Tuck, Guess, and Sultan, "Not Nowhere."
93 Aikau et al., "Indigenous Feminisms Roundtable," 86–87.
94 Aikau et al., "Indigenous Feminisms Roundtable," 87.
95 Aikau et al., "Indigenous Feminisms Roundtable," 88.
96 Glenn, "Settler Colonialism," 67.
97 Aikau et al., "Indigenous Feminisms Roundtable."

98 Jay-Z, "Girls, Girls, Girls."
99 Davis, "Grace Lee Boggs in Conversation with Angela Davis."
100 Wilderson, *Afro-pessimism*.

Chapter 1. Over Two Centuries

1 Arvin, *Possessing Polynesians*.
2 Gilroy, *Black Atlantic*.
3 David Chang's analysis of nineteenth-century Hawai'i highlights the agency of influential commoners who cultivated their knowledge and alliances. D. Chang, *World and All the Things*, 31–32.
4 Stannard, *Before the Horror*.
5 Osorio, *Dismembering Lāhui*, 10.
6 Osorio, *Dismembering Lāhui*, 15; Beamer, *No Mākou Ka Mana*.
7 Elisa Joy White, in Okino, *Holding Fast the Dream*. This is the only full-length documentary on Black people in Hawai'i.
8 White, in Okino, *Holding Fast the Dream*.
9 J. Kēhaulani Kauanui charts how quantification of Hawaiian ancestry, or blood quantum eligibility for lands, became lodged into policy through the 1921 Hawaiian Homes Commission Act. Kauanui, *Hawaiian Blood*.
10 Kauai, "Color of Nationality," 102.
11 Beamer, *No Mākou Ka Mana*; see also Arista, *Kingdom and the Republic*. These scholars contest narratives that overstate the missionary influence by drawing on Hawaiian-language sources that highlight Kānaka adaption and negotiation, rather than just reactive resistance. Arista notes how the 1825 kapu (chiefly legal pronouncement) enacted by Hawaiian ali'i restricting Hawaiian women from going on board ships for sexual relations was *not* simply their enforcement of Christian influence. Rather, it reflected the ongoing influence of ali'i over Hawaiians and foreigners alike.
12 Silva, *Aloha Betrayed*.
13 Lili'uokalani, *Hawaii's Story by Hawaii's Queen*.
14 Pro-annexation forces brought forth the Newlands Resolution requiring a majority rather than two-thirds vote to pass. This resolution was mentioned in the 1993 Congressional Joint Resolution "to offer an apology to Native Hawaiians on behalf of the United States for the overthrow of the Kingdom of Hawaii," https://www.hawaii-nation.org/publawall.html. See Kauanui's critique of this apology in *Paradoxes of Hawaiian Sovereignty*.
15 Osorio, *Dismembering Lāhui*, 244.
16 Osorio, *Dismembering Lāhui*, 244.
17 Arvin, *Possessing Polynesians*.
18 Merriam-Webster Dictionary, https://www.merriam-webster.com/dictionary/pacific#other-words.
19 Du Bois, in Bolden, *W. E. B. Du Bois*, 163; M. Jackson, introduction, xv.
20 Horne, *White Pacific*, 10.
21 Nitasha Sharma, "Over Two Centuries."
22 I discuss the history and politics of the term "local" in chapter 2.

23 R. Adams, "Census Notes," 25.
24 Nordyke, "Blacks in Hawai'i."
25 Pukui and Elbert, *Hawaiian Dictionary*, 40
26 "N-1495—Woodcuts of animals: Bea Eleele & Leopadi (black bear & leopard). Photograph," Hawaiian Mission Houses Digital Archive, https://hmha.missionhouses.org/items/show/4665.
27 Pukui and Elbert, *Hawaiian Dictionary*, 298. Also in Lorrin Andrews's dictionary, *A Dictionary of the Hawaiian Language* (1922), prepared under the direction of the Board of Commissioners of Public Archives of the Territory of Hawaii, Honolulu, and published by the Board.
28 An article dated April 25, 1834, in the newspaper *Ka Lama Hawaii* has "O ke kanaka eleele i kapaia he nika ia makou, he negero, i ka haole." *Ka Lama Hawaii* was the first Hawaiian-language newspaper (1834–1841) by seminary students in Lahainaluna, Maui, under missionary editor Lorrin Andrews. See http://nupepa.org.
29 Armstrong, journal entry, August 21, 1835.
30 Such adoption reflects the problems of decontextualized appropriations of Black culture emerging from the popularity of hip hop since the late 1980s. However, some forms of adoption of Black culture can signify deep political and social identification with Black people as people of color. For more on appropriation, see Nitasha Sharma, *Hip Hop Desis*.
31 Charles Langlas, personal communication, May 10, 2020. Lili'uokalani, *Kumulipo*.
32 "The Polynesian Chant of Creation," http://www.sacred-texts.com/pac/ku/ku27.htm; Warren, "Theorizing Pō," 1.
33 Pukui and Elbert, *Hawaiian Dictionary*, 333.
34 Pukui and Elbert, *Hawaiian Dictionary*, 343.
35 Takara, "African Diaspora," 2.
36 McGhee, "Hidden History," 2.
37 M. Jackson, "Introduction," xvi; Knowlton, "Notes on the Cape Verde Diaspora." Cape Verde is an African island country in the Atlantic that was colonized by the Portuguese. It played an important role in the Atlantic slave trade, with a large maritime industry that connected Cape Verdeans to the port of New Bedford in Massachusetts, where a number of freed and enslaved Black people began seafaring.
38 Knowlton, "Notes on the Cape Verde Diaspora." "Marriages occurred with Hawaiians and these people and their children became classified in censuses as Portuguese or Part-Hawaiian." Nordyke, "Blacks in Hawai'i," 243.
39 The first official census in Hawai'i was in 1860. Kauai, "Color of Nationality," 32.
40 Kauanui, *Hawaiian Blood*, 3.
41 Smallwood, *Saltwater Slavery*.
42 Takara, *Oral Histories of African Americans*.
43 Bandy, "Bandmaster Henry Berger."
44 Amos Starr Cooke, journal entry, July 11, 1848, 160.
45 Hawkins and Hawkins, "Blacks," 223; M. Jackson, introduction, xv; Horne, *White Pacific*, 130.

46 For a more complete history that offers details on the eighteenth century as well, see Nitasha Sharma, "Over Two Centuries"; Takara, "African Diaspora"; M. Jackson, *They Followed the Trade Winds*.
47 Scruggs, "There Is One Black Man," 34.
48 Betsey Stockton journal. David Wills and Albert Raboteau state that this version of Stockton's diary comes from "versions published in installments by Ashbel Green" in *Christian Advocate*, and so I cannot say what has been edited from it.
49 Takara, "African Diaspora," 15; Nitasha Sharma, "Pacific Revisions of Blackness." Stockton may be the "one female 'negro' assistant" of the Sandwich Islands Mission in October 1825 in Arista, *Kingdom and the Republic*, 170; A. Adams, *African Americans in Hawai'i*. On schooling developed for Native Americans, see Okihiro, *Island World*. General Samuel Armstrong, the founder of the Hampton Institute, was born on Maui to missionary parents and attended the Punahou School in Honolulu. Initially founded for the children of missionaries, the school now gives the Samuel Chapman Armstrong Humanitarian Award to "Punahou alumni who have made outstanding contributions to society, garnering national or international recognition." "Punahou Alumni, PAA Awards, Samuel Chapman Armstrong Humanitarian Award," https://www.punahou.edu/alumni/recognition/paa-awards.
50 Arista, *Kingdom and the Republic*.
51 Kauanui, *Hawaiian Blood*, 15–16.
52 Fred McGhee, personal communication; McGhee, "Hidden History," 6.
53 McGhee, "Hidden History."
54 On legal and cultural changes to society, see Merry, *Colonizing Hawai'i*; Arista, *Kingdom and the Republic*; Silva, "Political Economy of Banning the Hula."
55 Byrd, *Transit of Empire*, 26.
56 Gast, *Don Francisco de Paula Marin*.
57 Lili'uokalani, *Hawaii's Story by Hawaii's Queen*, 369.
58 Kānaka debate their status, including their political and legal relationship to the United States, relative to and distinct from Native Americans. This emerged in debates over the unsuccessfully proposed Akaka Bill. See Byrd, *Transit of Empire*; Kauanui, "Resisting the Akaka Bill"; Rohrer, "Got Race?"
59 D. Chang, *World and All the Things*, 227.
60 Dominguez, "Exporting U.S. Concepts of Race."
61 Betsey Stockton journal.
62 Interracial marriage prohibitions were in effect in some states until the 1967 *Loving v. Virginia* case.
63 Kauanui, *Hawaiian Blood*, 15.
64 Horne, *White Pacific*, 30.
65 See also Rosenthal, *Beyond Hawai'i*. For more on Hawaiians circulating overseas, see Imada, *Aloha America*.
66 D. Chang, *World and All the Things*; Okihiro, *Island World*.
67 Aikau, "Indigeneity in the Diaspora"; Hall, "Hawaiian at Heart"; Imada, *Aloha America*.
68 Adler, "King Kamehameha IV's Attitude"; D. Chang, *World and All the Things*, 162.

69 Love, *Race over Empire*, 81.
70 D. Chang, *World and All the Things*.
71 Knowlton, "Notes on the Cape Verde Diaspora."
72 Dominguez, "Exporting U.S. Concepts of Race," 372.
73 Kauai, "Color of Nationality," 131. Jon Osorio discusses petitions signed by hundreds of Kānaka in the 1830s urging the rulers not to grant citizenship to foreigners. Osorio, *Dismembering Lāhui*.
74 *The Penal Code of the Hawaiian Kingdom*, 370. See also Kauai, "Color of Nationality," 130; personal communication with Willy Kauai, September 16, 2019.
75 Kauai, "Color of Nationality," vii.
76 David Keanu Sai, "Registry of Naturalized Subjects in the Hawaiian Kingdom (circ. 1840–1893)," *Hawaiian Kingdom* (blog), https://www.hawaiiankingdom.org/info-registry.shtml.
77 Dominguez, "Exporting U.S. Concepts of Race," 372.
78 Kent, *Hawaii*, 28; Tengan, *Native Men Remade*, 44; Arvin, *Possessing Polynesians*. For an expansive analysis of empire, plantation economies, and racial ideologies, see Okihiro, *Pineapple Culture*.
79 Enomoto, "Where Will You Be?"
80 Takara, "African Diaspora," 18.
81 Horne, *White Pacific*, 129; Bishop, in Silva, *Aloha Betrayed*, 173.
82 Silva, *Aloha Betrayed*, 176–77; Nitasha Sharma, "Pacific Revisions of Blackness," 50–51. See also Horne, *White Pacific*. On the "layering of racial expectation of Southern plantations and blackness into Hawai'i," see Byrd, *Transit of Empire*, 24.
83 Silva, *Aloha Betrayed*, 178–79.
84 Journal of Rev. D. Baldwin, 1830–1831, Hawaiian Mission Houses Digital Archives, 166.
85 Leroy, "Black History in Occupied Territory," n.p.
86 Journal of Rev. D. Baldwin, 161.
87 Dye, *Merchant Prince*, 48.
88 "Historical Collections of the Hawaiian Islands—Kamehameha IV—(Part 2)," http://files.usgwarchives.net/hi/keepers/koc51.txt.
89 Leroy, "Black History in Occupied Territory," n.p.
90 Lili'uokalani, *Hawaii's Story by Hawaii's Queen*, 368.
91 D. Chang, *The World*; Rosenthal, *Beyond Hawai'i*.
92 Nordyke, "Blacks in Hawai'i," 241–42; see Okamura, *Ethnicity and Inequality*.
93 Gaylord Kubota, in Okino, *Holding Fast the Dream*.
94 M. Jackson, "Prelude to a New Century," 63; Nordyke, "Blacks in Hawai'i," 245.
95 Takara, "African Diaspora," 7.
96 Nordyke, "Blacks in Hawai'i," 244; Takara, "The African Diaspora," 7; M. Jackson, "Prelude to a New Century," 60–63. Miles Jackson Jr., personal communication.
97 Jung, *Coolies and Cane*; Bow, *Partly Colored*.
98 Takaki, *Pau Hana*, xi.
99 They also imported new commodities, including those, like ice, that changed—or colonized—culinary tastes in Hawai'i. Hobart, "Snowy Mountaineers and Soda Waters."

100   The Hawai'i-raised historian Ronald Takaki tracks its beginnings in 1835 to the start of its decline in 1920 in *Pau Hana*. Local KITV News cites 2016 as the year "the sugar industry is shutting down" with the close of the last plantation, Maui's Hawaiian Commercial and Sugar Company. (Hawai'i is still home to other plantations, including coffee.) Awa, "End of the Sugar Cane Era."
101   "History of Labor in Hawai'i."
102   "History of Labor in Hawai'i."
103   Lili'uokalani, *Hawaii's Story by Hawaii's Queen*, 78. The Queen writes of her brother, the King: "By his investigations and solution of the problem of labor he gave [those of American birth] the opportunity to raise sugar at an enormous profit; and he thus devoted the earlier part of his reign to the aggrandizement of the very persons, who, as soon as they had become rich and powerful, forgot his generosity, and plotted a subversion of his authority, and an overthrow of the constitution."
104   Miyares, "Expressing 'Local Culture' in Hawai'i."
105   See Okamura, "Why There Are No Asian Americans."
106   See chapter 2 for an analysis of the term "local" and chapter 3 for an extended discussion of Asian settler colonialism.
107   Das Gupta and Haglund, "Mexican Migration to Hawai'i"; Guevarra, "Latino Threat in the 808?"
108   Wynes, "T. McCants Stewart," 311.
109   Barbee-Wooten, *African American Attorneys in Hawai'i*, 3.
110   C. Smith, *Emancipation*, 492.
111   "Thomas McCants Stewart," reprint from *Negro Times*, 4.
112   Wooten, in Barbee-Wooten, *African American Attorneys*, iv, 3.
113   Referring to the 1886 exclusion act against Chinese arrivals. Barbee-Wooten, *African American Attorneys*, 3. An advocate of repatriation to Africa, Stewart moved to Liberia, where he taught and went on to become an associate Justice of the Liberian Supreme Court (5–6).
114   Stewart's contemporary was the Black lawyer William F. Crockett, who arrived a few years later and represented Black plantation workers on Maui, where Crockett's grandson, William F. Crockett, also practiced law and was once married to former Republican governor Linda Lingle. Pignataro, "Maui County Finally Honors."
115   Part of the difficulty in tracing the history of nineteenth-century Black women in Hawai'i is due to the high rates of intermarriage and thus their Asian and Hawaiian surnames.
116   P. Young, "Carlotta."
117   In Barbee-Wooten, *African American Attorneys*, 7.
118   M. Jackson, "Ball, Alice Augusta."
119   Guttman, "History of African Americans in Hawaii"; Gugliotta, *Nolle Smith*. The legal scholar Lani Guinier was named after Nolle Smith's eldest daughter, Iwalani. Guinier, *Lift Every Voice*, 66.
120   Hale was Bunche's niece through marriage; Bishop, "Oregon Niece Adds."

121 Obama called his grandmother "Toot," a shortened version of this Hawaiian word.
122 *Ka Hoku o Hawaii* (Star of Hawaiʻi) 34, no. 11 (July 12, 1939), 6.
123 Burnett, "Helen Hale Remembered."
124 "Hawaii's Top Woman Politician," *Ebony*, April 1963, 51.
125 Burnett, "Helen Hale Remembered."
126 Bishop, "Oregon Niece Adds"; Burnett, "Helen Hale Remembered."
127 The Pōpolo Project is expanding depictions of Black people in Hawaiʻi by representing Black transplants and locals.
128 Guttman, "History of African Americans in Hawaiʻi."
129 R. Adams, "Census Notes," 25.
130 James Lane, Miles Shishido, and Kimie Lane, editor's note in R. Adams, "Census Notes," 25, footnote.
131 See Pierce, "Creating a Racial Paradise."
132 Nordyke, "Blacks in Hawaiʻi," 249.
133 Horne, *White Pacific*, 30.
134 Horne, *White Pacific*, 30.
135 Takara, in Nordyke, "Blacks in Hawaiʻi," 246.
136 This includes the Hawaiian Homes Commission Act of 1921, which instituted a blood ratio requirement for Hawaiians to access reserved lands, and the founding of "English Standard Schools" as a form of segregated schooling for haole children. Kauanui, *Hawaiian Blood*; Tamura, "English-Only Effort."
137 Takara, "African Diaspora," 19.
138 Teaiwa, "bikinis and other s/pacific n/oceans"; Gonzalez, *Securing Paradise*. See also Teaiwa, "Black in the Blue Pacific (for Mohit and Riyad)"; Teaiwa and Husband, "You Can't Paint the Pacific."
139 Among them was also Corporal George Schuyler, whose time in this multiracial society informed his later writings as a Black conservative journalist. See Ferguson, *Sage of Sugar Hill*.
140 Hoverson, "Buffalo Soldiers at Kilauea," 74, 83, 88.
141 Hoverson, "Buffalo Soldiers at Kilauea," 76.
142 Bailey and Farber, "'Double-V' Campaign," 820.
143 Bailey and Farber, "'Double-V' Campaign," 820.
144 For more on these tours, see Kajihiro and Kekoʻolani, "Hawaiʻi DeTour Project."
145 Formerly called United States Pacific Command. https://www.pacom.mil/About-USINDOPACOM/History.
146 Bailey and Farber, "'Double-V' Campaign," 818.
147 Kajihiro, "Militarizing of Hawaiʻi," 174–75; Kiersz, "Here's How Much Land Military Bases Take Up."
148 "Native Hawaiian Health Fact Sheet 2015, Volume 1: Chronic Diseases," Office of Hawaiian Affairs, Research Division, 1–12.
149 Department of Defense Manpower Data Center, https://www.governing.com/gov-data/public-workforce-salaries/military-civilian-active-duty-employee-workforce-numbers-by-state.html.
150 See also Data USA: Hawaii, https://datausa.io/profile/geo/hawaii.

151 Farber and Bailey, "'Double-V' Campaign," 818.
152 S. Johnson, *African American Religions*, 160.
153 S. Johnson, *African American Religions*, 184.
154 The historian Guy Emerson Mount suggests that there were "concrete plans after emancipation for a massive state-funded colonization program that promised to relocate over five million formerly enslaved peoples to America's nascent empire in Hawai'i and the Philippines." https://cla.auburn.edu/history/people/faculty/guy-e-mount.
155 US Census Bureau, "Ranking of Selected Races for the State of Hawaii: 2010," https://files.hawaii.gov/dbedt/census/Census_2010/SF2/2010_race_ranking_from_SF2_final.pdf.
156 Nordyke, "Blacks in Hawai'i," 245, 247–48; Okamura, *Ethnicity and Inequality*.
157 Livingston and Brown, "Intermarriage in the U.S."
158 http://factfinder2.census.gov/faced/tableservices/jsf/pages. Accessed September 6, 2011. (American FactFinder has been decommissioned; link no longer available.)
159 Richards, "Hawai'i," 104–5.
160 Of course, my sample is not comprehensive. There are Black Hawaiians whose mothers are Black and whose fathers are Hawaiian, but their numbers are much smaller.
161 "Native Hawaiian Health Fact Sheet 2015, Volume 1: Chronic Diseases," Office of Hawaiian Affairs, Research Division, 1–12.
162 "2011 State of Hawaii Data Book," 61.
163 "2011 State of Hawaii Data Book," 61, 585.
164 Rucker, "Hawaii's Still Waters Run Deep."
165 Walsh, "Obama's Hawaiian Roots."
166 Hattenstone, "Janet Mock"; see Mock, *Redefining Realness*.
167 Okino, "Holding Fast the Dream."
168 "Dwayne Johnson Recalls Hard Times."
169 Kumu Hinaleimoana Wong (who supported the actor's decision), in "Reaction Is Mixed."
170 The Puerto Rican Filipino Jewish pop sensation Bruno Mars also comes from Hawai'i and graduated from Roosevelt High School.
171 Irie Love, interview on Fresh, https://www.thecoconet.tv/fresh-series/inspiring-islanders/my-world-irie-love. For more, see https://www.thisisirielove.com.
172 Caldwell, "Blackness at the Margins of Empire." For an extraordinary and comprehensive story of the children of World War II American soldiers across the Pacific Islands, see Bennett and Wanhalla, *Mothers' Darlings*.

Chapter 2. "Saltwater Negroes"

1 "Applying for Hawaiian Home Lands," Department of Hawaiian Home Lands, https://dhhl.hawaii.gov/applications/applying-for-hawaiian-home-lands.
2 Warren, "Theorizing Pō"; Teaiwa, "Ancestors We Get to Choose"; Teaiwa, "Black in the Blue Pacific (for Mohit and Riyad)"; Teaiwa, "Black and Blue in the Pacific: Afro-Diasporic Women Artists."

3. Sundstrom, "Being and Being Mixed Race," 307.
4. Coates, "When My President Was Black."
5. Barack Obama, "Interview with President Obama," interview by Steve Kroft, *60 Minutes*, CBS, December 10, 2011.
6. Coates, "When My President Was Black."
7. Coates, "When My President Was Black." Coates also discusses Obama's relatively conservative racial stances.
8. Keel, "Neanderthal-Human Hybridity," 213.
9. Sundstrom, "Being and Being Mixed Race," 299–300.
10. Keel, "Neanderthal-Human Hybridity," 214.
11. Makalani, "Biracial Identity," 95. This movement is also known as the Multiracial Movement. They advanced two outcomes: some argued for a "multiracial" box; the other option, which ultimately won out in the 2000 Census, was for people to select more than one racial category. This is an important victory, as it allows us to collect racial data on the complicated and diverse ancestries of multiracial people, telling us about racial and gendered patterns of intermarriage and informing the distribution of federal funds. Additionally, it allows people to identify as Black as well as other categories, or Black alone.
12. Makalani, "Biracial Identity," 95.
13. Makalani, "Biracial Identity," 95.
14. Makalani, "Biracial Identity," 95.
15. Trask, "Feminist and Indigenous Hawaiian Nationalism," 906.
16. Kauanui, *Hawaiian Blood*, 15.
17. Sexton, *Amalgamation Schemes*.
18. Sundstrom, "Being and Being Mixed Race."
19. Gaither, "I Study Biracial Identity."
20. Gaither, "I Study Biracial Identity."
21. Fujikane and Okamura, *Asian Settler Colonialism*; Labrador, *Building Filipino Hawai'i*; Saranillio, *Unsustainable Empire*; Compoc, "Emergent Allies"; Trask, "Settlers of Color"; Rohrer, *Haoles in Hawai'i*.
22. Saranillio, "Why Asian Settler Colonialism Matters," 288.
23. Saranillio, "Why Asian Settler Colonialism Matters," 288.
24. Geertz, "Thick Description."
25. Kekuewa Kikiloi's careful genealogical and geological research on the northern Hawaiian Islands argues that Hawaiians' ancestors, Papahānaumoku and Wākea, birthed both the islands of the archipelago and the Hawaiian people. Kikiloi, "Rebirth of an Archipelago," 2010.
26. Saranillio, "Why Asian Settler Colonialism Matters."
27. Saranillio, "Why Asian Settler Colonialism Matters," 280.
28. Saranillio, "Why Asian Settler Colonialism Matters," 281.
29. Zack, *Race and Mixed Race*; Williams-Leon and Nakashima, *Sum of Our Parts*.
30. Dariotis, "Hapa."
31. Pukui and Elbert, *Hawaiian Dictionary*, 58.

32 I expect that this will change generationally, as the locals I interviewed include Black Hawaiians and Black Asians who are fathers of Hawai'i-born young children.
33 These couples were Black Mexican, Black Hawaiian, and Black Okinawan, as well as African American.
34 While this individual's story, discussed throughout the book, reveals the slippage between race and indigeneity, Blackness and Hawaiianness, and race and culture, I categorize him here as a Black local.
35 This was also the case for a graduate student who was raised by his African American father in the Midwest and had never met his Korean mom.
36 Walker, "Hui Nalu," 90.
37 See Anderson, *Black and Indigenous*; Jayawardene, "Pushing the Paradigm."
38 See Hall, "'Hawaiian at Heart.'"
39 Aikau et al., "Indigenous Feminisms Roundtable," 97.
40 Some multiracial people reject this logic and assert that they are not "half and half" but rather "fully Black and Japanese," for example, or "100 percent Mexican and 100 percent Filipino."
41 Kiel, "Bleeding Out," 80.
42 Aikau et al., "Indigenous Feminisms Roundtable," 90.
43 Rosa, *Local Story*.
44 Stinton, "Black Identity in Hawaii."
45 Kauanui, *Hawaiian Blood*.
46 Wolfe, "Settler Colonialism."
47 Goo, "After 200 Years."
48 Ledward, "Inseparably Hapa," 60.
49 This is also a theme in trans studies. See Snorton, *Black on Both Sides*.
50 Note that people say "be local" rather than "be a local"; it is more expansive than a noun and is usually used as an adjective: "local Japanese" rather than "Japanese local." However, I say "Black local" because Black is also expansive and descriptive rather than an object.
51 Obama, *Dreams from My Father*, 69.
52 Hall, "Hawaiian at Heart," 407.
53 See Brunsma's summary of the literature, "Interracial Families," 1133.
54 Brundage, in Nordyke, "Blacks in Hawai'i," 246.
55 Ledward, "Inseparably Hapa," 40. To be sure, not all Black locals feel racially ambivalent, just as not all transplants express racial pride. A fair-skinned professional from the US South feels that Blackness holds no positive meaning for her, and she prefers not to identify only along the lines of race.
56 Leonard, "High Tech Blackface."
57 Nitasha Sharma, "Rap, Race, Revolution."
58 Frank Anton, "Rock Fever Is Common for Non Islanders," Ezine Articles, June 6, 2010, https://ezinearticles.com/?Rock-Fever-Common-For-Non-Islanders&id=4431172.

59 Paul Gilroy writes about the hegemony of American Blackness through this concept of Americocentrism. Gilroy, "It's a Family Affair."
60 E. Johnson, *Appropriating Blackness*, 12.
61 Other locals and multiracial Black transplants say they experienced a similar racial gatekeeping (although with different class articulations) in their interactions with Black old-timers.

Chapter 3. "Less Pressure"

1 "Success Story of One Minority."
2 However, Japanese experienced slower upward mobility compared with Chinese soon after the end of the plantation era. Okamura, "Race Relations in Hawaiʻi."
3 "Militourism," a term coined by Teresia Teaiwa and further expanded by Vernadette Gonzalez, combines militarism and tourism. I elaborate on this term in the next two chapters. Teaiwa, "Militarism, Tourism, and the Native"; Gonzalez, *Securing Paradise*.
4 Okamura, "Aloha Kanaka Me Ke Aloha ʻAina"; Yamamoto, "Significance of Local"; Chock, "Neocolonization of Bamboo Ridge."
5 Okamura, "Aloha Kanaka Me Ke Aloha ʻAina," 131.
6 Rosa, *Local Story*, 12.
7 Rosa, *Local Story*, 12; Okamura, "Aloha Kanaka Me Ke Aloha ʻAina."
8 Trask, "Settlers of Color," 6. Hōkūlani Aikau's work on Pacific Islanders in Utah further unsettles the White/Native binary through an important critique of "indigenous settler colonialism." Aikau, "Indigeneity in the Diaspora."
9 Trask, "Settlers of Color," 2, 6–7; Trask is referring to Fujikane, "Between Nationalisms."
10 Saranillio, *Unsustainable Empire*, 17.
11 Fujikane and Okamura, *Asian Settler Colonialism*; see also Fujikane, "Sweeping Racism under the Rug."
12 Thomas, "Who Is a Settler."
13 Thomas, "Who Is a Settler."
14 See K. Chang, *Pacific Connections*; Shah, *Stranger Intimacy*; Day, *Alien Capital*; J. Chang, *Chino*.
15 Thomas, "Who Is a Settler."
16 Sexton, "Vel of Slavery." When asked about his relationship to his White wife, Frank Wilderson responds that "the reality is that I'm her slave." Wilderson, "Blacks and the Master/Slave Relation," 28.
17 T. King, *Black Shoals*; Rifkin, *Fictions of Land and Flesh*.
18 T. King, "New World Grammars," n.p.
19 T. King, "New World Grammars," n.p.
20 Fujikane, *Mapping Abundance*; Byrd, *Transit of Empire*; Rohrer, *Staking Claim*.
21 L. Simpson, *As We Have Always Done*; Karuka, *Empire's Tracks*. Some stark definitions of peoplehood and private property also animate problematic expressions of nationalism explicated in Kauanui, *Paradoxes of Hawaiian Sovereignty*.
22 Goodyear-Kaʻōpua, *Seeds We Planted*, 150.

23 Goodyear-Kaʻōpua, *Seeds We Planted*, 149.
24 Goodyear-Kaʻōpua, *Seeds We Planted*, 133.
25 Goodyear-Kaʻōpua, *Seeds We Planted*, 134.
26 In Lowe, "Angela Davis."
27 Wallace, "Hawaiʻi Football Is Hot Right Now."
28 See Tengan and Markham, "Performing Polynesian Masculinities." Some critics viewed this performance both as appropriating the Maori practice from Aotearoa/New Zealand and as being overly intimidating. Under Coach Rolovich, the team shifted to performing a haʻa, or Hawaiian chant, which Hawaiian players felt was more meaningful to them. Afualo, "New Haʻa."
29 See Faʻanofo Lisaclaire (Lisa) Uperesa's work on the Sāmoan NFL diaspora. Uperesa, "Fabled Futures and Gridiron Dreams."
30 Mullen, *Afro-Orientalism*.
31 Center for Oral History, UH Ethnic Studies Department. See also A. Adams, *African Americans in Hawaiʻi* and *Kwanzaa in Hawaiʻi*; Guttman and Golden, *African Americans in Hawaiʻi*; Barbee-Wooten, *African American Attorneys in Hawaii*.
32 Oiyan Poon, personal communication, July 12, 2018.
33 Obama, *Dreams from My Father*, 23.
34 For a critique of the hailed aloha spirit, see Guevarra's introduction in Fojas, Guevarra, and Sharma, *Beyond Ethnicity*.
35 Okamura and Fujikane, *Asian Settler Colonialism*; Saranillio, *Unsustainable Empire*; Rohrer, *Staking Claim*; Goodyear-Kaʻōpua, Hussey, and Wright, *Nation Rising*.
36 Rohrer, *Haoles in Hawaiʻi*, 2.
37 Rohrer, *Haoles in Hawaiʻi*, 3.
38 Rohrer, *Haoles in Hawaiʻi*, 3.
39 Rohrer, *Haoles in Hawaiʻi*, 2.
40 Democrat Abercrombie (who was the hānai [adoptive] parent of a Zimbabwean student I interviewed) beat Hannemann to become governor in 2010.
41 Black people may wish to distinguish themselves from White people as a result, as well, of the racist White constructs of Blackness as inferior and dehumanized developed to "justify" Europeans' colonization of Africa, the enslavement of West Africans.
42 Pierre, "Black Immigrants."
43 Racialized visibility is gendered, however; Black feminist scholars analyze Black women's invisibility compared with Black men. We see the relative visibility of Black men and women in the prominent stories of the murders of Black men, for instance, compared with less attention granted to violence faced by Black women, including queer and especially trans women. Black women become hypervisible and sexualized, however, in representations of leisure and popular culture. Mowatt and French, "Black/Female/Body Hypervisibility"; see Nash, *Black Body in Ecstasy*.
44 Abe, "Violations of the Racial Code," 34.
45 Broussard, "Honolulu NAACP," 116.
46 For more on racial scripts, see Molina, *How Race Is Made*.

47 Honolulu NAACP Facebook page, https://www.facebook.com/HonoluluHawaiiNaacp.
48 Saranillio, "Why Asian Settler Colonialism Matters," 282–83.
49 Saranillio, "Why Asian Settler Colonialism Matters," 282–83.
50 Okino and Jackson, *Holding Fast the Dream*.
51 Laulani Teale recounts tensions that emerged as a result of the parade format—frontlined by US military personnel—leading to calls to boycott the march because of what one person cited as "their extreme abuse of the kanaka movement." Teale, "Why I Am Boycotting."
52 These authors tend to use the term "African American" in their publications rather than the more expansive—or political—term "Black."
53 Pōpolo Project, https://www.thepopoloproject.org.
54 "Community Talk Story: Charles Lawrence," Pōpolo Project, https://www.facebook.com/ThePopoloProject/videos/887607208278904.
55 "Saltwater People," Eventbrite, https://www.eventbrite.com/e/saltwater-people-tickets-62457643493. Chicago transplant David Nala hosts a newer party in Kaimuki.
56 "Saltwater People," Eventbrite.
57 "Free Black Women's Library Pop-Up," Pōpolo Project. For recent events, see https://www.thepopoloproject.org/events-2021.
58 Shangri La, https://www.shangrilahawaii.org; Mana Ai, www.manaai.com.

Chapter 4. Racism in Paradise

1 Karen Rose, "Pick Your Paradise!" Hawaii.com, https://www.hawaii.com/discover/pick-your-paradise-islands-in-hawaii.
2 Hawaii Tourism Authority, "The Hawaiian Islands," https://www.gohawaii.com.
3 Kent, *Hawaii*.
4 *Ebony*, January 1981, 122.
5 See Akiemi Glenn's excellent response to the *New York Times* opinion article, in which she explains "why the *Times* article's tongue-in-cheek exhortation to move to Hawaiʻi where many of the most marginalized struggle to remain and thrive was felt by many in our community as an affront." Glenn, "Want to Explore Race in Hawaiʻi?," https://akiemiglenn.net/blog/2019/7/2/2po1kxsurmc9fzkx8jvme7pwozo3bf.
6 M. Jackson, "They Followed the Trade Winds"; A. Adams, *African Americans in Hawaiʻi*; Kubo, "Negro Soldier in Kahuku"; Lloyd, "A Brief Analysis." See also Farber and Bailey, *First Strange Place*; Nordyke, "Blacks in Hawaiʻi"; "African Americans in Hawaiʻi Reading List"; and more comprehensive is #pōpoloSyllabus, https://www.thepopoloproject.org/popolosyllabus.
7 Vinacke, "Stereotyping among National-Racial Groups"; Abe, "Violations of the Racial Code"; Broussard, "Honolulu NAACP"; Richards, "Hawaiʻi"; Kalish, "Comparison of Hawaiian and Mainland."
8 Abe, "Violations of the Racial Code," 34.
9 Ransby, *Making All Black Lives Matter*; Pattillo, *Black Picket Fences*; Lipsitz, *Possessive Investment in Whiteness*; Taylor, *Race for Profit*.
10 Brown, *Dark Matters*, 20.
11 Beutin, "Racialization," 5.

12 Brown, "Everybody's Got a Little Light," 545.
13 Brown, "Everybody's Got a Little Light," 545–46.
14 Brown, "Everybody's Got a Little Light," 546.
15 Mahtani, *Mixed Race Amnesia*, 14.
16 Miles, *Ties That Bind*; Miles and Holland, *Crossing Waters*; Miles, *Dawn of Detroit*.
17 Sexton, "Vel of Slavery"; Wilderson, *Red, White and Black*.
18 Amadahy and Lawrence, "Indigenous Peoples"; Smallwood, "Reflections on Settler Colonialism"; T. King, "Into the Clearing"; T. King, "Black Shoals"; Tuck, Guess, and Sultan, "Not Nowhere"; Garba and Sorentino, "Slavery Is a Metaphor."
19 See Klopotek, *Recognition Odysseys*.
20 Leroy, "Black History in Occupied Territory," n.p.
21 Leroy, "Black History in Occupied Territory."
22 Miles, *Ties That Bind*, xiii, preface to the 2nd ed.
23 Alexander, *New Jim Crow*.
24 Leong and Carpio, "Carceral States," vii.
25 See Lacy, *Out of State*.
26 "50 State Incarceration Profiles."
27 "50 State Incarceration Profiles."
28 Sexton, "Vel of Slavery," 11.
29 Miles, *Ties That Bind*, xvii.
30 Sexton, "Vel of Slavery," 9.
31 Leroy, "Black History in Occupied Territory," n.p.; A. Smith, "Colonialism That Is Settled," n.p.
32 Leroy, "Black History in Occupied Territory."
33 Miles and Holland, *Crossing Waters*; T. King, "Into the Clearing"; Leroy, "Black History in Occupied Territory."
34 Okamura, *Ethnicity and Inequality in Hawaiʻi*; McDermott and Andrade, *People and Cultures of Hawaiʻi*. Cf. Rohrer, *Haoles in Hawaiʻi*.
35 Okamura, *From Race to Ethnicity*, 4.
36 Yuen, "Which Ethnic Group."
37 For a longer critique of the ethnicity paradigm, see Nitasha Sharma, "Racial Imperative."
38 Ledward, "Inseparably Hapa," xiii.
39 S. Jackson, *Creole Indigeneity*, 25.
40 hooks, in Byrd, *Transit of Empire*, 42; Byrd, "Been to the Nation."
41 Byrd, *Transit of Empire*, 134.
42 S. Jackson, *Creole Indigeneity*, 3. This is also detailed in Fujikane and Okamura's seminal 2008 book, *Asian Settler Colonialism*. See also Day, *Alien Capital*.
43 Guevarra, *Aloha Compadre*.
44 S. Chang, *Raising Mixed Race*, 104, 154.
45 Moreton-Robinson, *White Possessive*; Arvin, *Possessing Polynesians*.
46 A Black Asian woman recalls another term: "Me and my sister would be called 'toads' every time we'd go down to the pool. There was this old guy in the Jacuzzi, and he was like, 'Oh, the toads are coming,' talking to himself."

47 "Moke" is a term used in England as slang for "donkey," and in Australia it refers to a nag or inferior horse. People in Hawai'i use the word to derogatorily describe segments of the local Polynesian population. "Going moke" can refer to being aggressive or physical, calling on stereotypes of Polynesian male excess.

48 Sāmoan masculinity is racialized in ways that overlap with Black masculinity through conceptions of physical excess. This stems from colonization of the Pacific and the articulation of Polynesian men as warriors, but it extends through the dominant representation of Sāmoan men as college and professional football players. See Henderson, "Fleeting Substantiality"; Uperesa, *Fabled Futures*; Tengan, *Native Men Remade*; Diaz, "Fight Boys."

49 Roderick Labrador analyzes this role of humor in the Islands, as well as its serious underside of buttressing difference and hierarchy. Labrador, "We can laugh at ourselves." See also Labrador, "I no eat dog, k."

50 Frank De Lima, https://www.frankdelima.com/about.

51 For a genealogy of the term "pōpolo," see https://www.thepopoloproject.org/history-blog/2017/4/20/popolo-a-taxonomy.

52 "Saltwater People Pool Party."

53 Kennedy, *Nigger*, xi–xii.

54 Feagin, "Editor's Preface," in S. Chang, *Raising Mixed Race*, xiii.

55 Beltran and Fojas, *Mixed Race Hollywood*; Elam, *Souls of Mixed Folk*.

56 Labrador, "I no eat dog, k," 68.

57 Labrador, "I no eat dog, k," 68; Guevarra, "Latino Threat in the 808?"; Nitasha Sharma, "Racial Imperative."

58 Ledward, "Inseparably Hapa."

59 See Tengan, *Native Men Remade*, xi; Sato, "Linguistic Inequality"; Sakoda and Siegal, *Pidgin Grammar*; Hisatake, "Hawaiian Hospitality and Hostility."

60 Kara Hisatake, https://karahisatake.com. See the Charlene Junko Sato Center for Pidgin, Creole, and Dialect Studies, https://www.hawaii.edu/satocenter.

61 Balibar, "Is There a 'Neo-Racism'?," 21.

62 For an examination of intersectionality as part of Black feminist theorizing, see Nash, *Black Feminism Reimagined*.

63 A. Smith, "Heteropatriarchy and the Three Pillars," 67.

64 On Japan, see Gomez, "Politics of Afro-Asian Intimacies."

65 Rondilla and Spickard, *Is Lighter Better*; Jha, *Global Beauty Industry*.

66 Dolgin, "Daughter from Danang."

67 Trenka, Oparah, and Shin, *Outsiders Within*.

68 Teves, *Defiant Indigeneity*, 53.

69 See my book on (South) Asian antiBlack racism, *Hip Hop Desis*.

70 Nitasha Sharma, *Hip Hop Desis*.

71 "Programme for Patriotic Exercises in the Public Schools."

72 Sato, "Linguistic Inequality"; Tamura, "The English-Only Effort."

73 Samuel Armstrong, a Maui-born missionary, founded the Hampton Normal and Industrial Institute, believing that such schools would lead to racial uplift for Black people. The Bishops, founders of the Kamehameha Schools, consulted with

General Armstrong in Virginia to model the industrial education system. *Southern Workman and Hampton School Record*, 452–53. See also Goodyear-Kaʻōpua, "Domesticating Hawaiians."

74 Labrador, "I no eat dog, k," 68.
75 Labrador, "I no eat dog, k," 68.
76 Kubota, "Racism at Wailuku."
77 Wooten, "Slavery Still Haunts Us."
78 Ingram, "Blacks Must Stop Using Slavery."
79 Ingram, "Blacks Must Stop Using Slavery."
80 Robertson, "Storm at Kalaheo."
81 Robertson, "Storm at Kalaheo."
82 Robertson, "Storm at Kalaheo."
83 On racism, inequality, and Americanization in schooling, see Kaʻomea, "Reading Erasures"; Tamura, "English-Only Effort."
84 On outmarriage rates, including for African Americans in Hawaiʻi, see Okamura, *Ethnicity and Inequality in Hawaiʻi*, 31–32.
85 Takara, "Who Is the Black Woman," 91.
86 Pattillo, *Black Picket Fences*. (Epigraph to section: An email to the *Honolulu Civil Beat*, "Racism in Hawaiʻi toward African Americans has always gotten a pass," in response to an article by journalist Chad Blair is the source of this quotation. Blair, "Harry Kim.")
87 "Betrayal of a Community."
88 "Betrayal of a Community." Persistent in exposing problems of unequal access to resources, Cox was once beaten by two masked men for his reporting on illegal dumping on Hawaiian Home Lands.
89 "Betrayal of a Community."
90 Linda Lingle was the first Jewish and woman (Republican) governor in the state of Hawaiʻi. Her former husband was William Crockett—part of three generations of Black attorneys on the island. McAvoy, "Disgraced Hawaiʻi Tourism Leader."
91 David, "Hawaiʻi Tourism Authority."
92 Gilmore, *Golden Gulag*, 247; Howard, "Hawaii Named Healthiest State."
93 "Betrayal of a Community."
94 See Reddy and Sudhakar, "Feminist and Queer Afro-Asian Formations," for an excellent overview and critique of the masculinist focus of Afro-Asian Studies.
95 Gutierrez, "Nurse Who Found Photo." Notably, the lawyer in this case, Carl Varady, also represented clients in a class action lawsuit arguing that "the DHHL (Department of Hawaiian Home Lands) and the state breached their trust obligations to Native Hawaiians by failing to place them on homesteads in a prompt manner." Pang, "Home Lands Suit to Proceed."
96 Callis, "Kim Finalizing Maunakea Committee."
97 Lauer, "No Regrets from Kim."
98 "Betrayal of a Community."
99 Hiller, "Jury Backs Teacher."
100 Lawrence, "Local Kine Implicit Bias," 499.

101   Alexander, *New Jim Crow*, 13.
102   Lawrence, "Local Kine Implicit Bias," 499–500.
103   Black, Kidd, and Thom, "Kōti Rangatahi"; Arvin, "Mauna Kea Protests Aren't New."
104   This is the second-lowest number, after "American Indian or Alaska Native" at 0.2 percent. "University of Hawaii at Mānoa Undergraduate Ethnic Diversity Breakdown," College Factual, https://www.collegefactual.com/colleges/university-of-hawaii-at-manoa/student-life/diversity/chart-ethnic-diversity.html.
105   "Mānoa's Racial and Ethnic Diversity Profile," March 30, 2016, 6. University of Hawai'i at Mānoa Office of Student Equity, Excellence and Diversity.
106   The fall 2020 undergraduate population at the University of Hawai'i at Mānoa was "Asian: 35.9%, *Caucasian*: 24.9%, Native Hawaiian or other Pacific Islander: 18.6%, Multiracial: 16.4%, International: 6%, Hispanic: 1.8%, African American: 1.6%, American Indian or Alaska Native: 0.4%" (italics mine). "2020 Fast Facts," https://manoa.hawaii.edu/miro/quick-facts/.
107   painlessrisen, "What's It Like." The first epigraph in this section is also from this source.
108   Yin, "Mothers Against Senseless Killings."
109   Honolulu Police Department 2017 Annual Report, 36.
110   Mike Maciag, "Where Police Don't Mirror Communities and Why It Matters," in *Governing: The Future of States and Localities*, "A Governing Special Report," 8. https://www.governing.com/archive/gov-police-department-diversity.html.
111   "Where Police Don't Mirror."
112   "Where Police Don't Mirror"; "Police Department Race and Ethnicity Demographic Data," Honolulu County Police Department.
113   Pōpolo Project, "Community Profile: Charles Lawrence," YouTube, September 3, 2019, https://www.youtube.com/watch?v=iHTNsxNbuKs.
114   Lawrence, "Local Kine Implicit Bias."
115   "Remark about Ethnicity Wins Convict Resentencing Hearing," *Honolulu Star Advertiser*, December 17, 2014, in Lawrence, "Local Kine Implicit Bias," 459.
116   For more on Micronesians, see Peter, Tanaka, and Yamashiro, "Reconnecting Our Roots."
117   See the poet and activist Kathy Jetñil-Kijiner's phenomenal work, including her poem "Lessons from Hawaii," https://jkijiner.wordpress.com/2011/04/13/micronesia-i-lessons-from-hawaii.
118   Lyons, "#BeingMicronesian."
119   Structural racism also includes housing discrimination. A 2018 report from the state of Hawai'i listed Black people as being among those facing the highest median gross rents—paying over $300 a month more than what haole pay in Hawai'i. "Demographic, Social, Economic, and Housing Characteristics," 15.
120   The organization also hosted a virtual meeting, "Darker than Blue." The email explains, "We invite our Local Black community to join us—no allies this time,

thank you—to gather virtually, to check in with each other, to grieve, and to build." Email communication, May 28, 2020.
121 Epigraph: Akiemi Glenn is quoted in Blair, "Harry Kim."
122 There are many examples of this type of activism. See #Asians4BlackLives, https://a4bl.wordpress.com; and on Asian Americans in support of affirmative action, see the work of Oiyan Poon and Janelle Wong: Poon et al., "Asian Americans, Affirmative Action."
123 Blair, "Harry Kim"; AF3IRM, a transnational feminist organization, http://www.af3irm.org/af3irm/chapters/hawaii.

Chapter 5. Embodying Kuleana

1 Larry Kimura and Doug Simons, "Physics of Pō," talk sponsored by Association of Universities for Research in Astronomy, 235th Meeting of the American Astronomical Society, Hawai'i Convention Center, January 6, 2020. See Warren, "Theorizing Pō."
2 Lowe, *Intimacies of Four Continents*; Gilmore, *Golden Gulag*, 28.
3 Wolfe, "Settler Colonialism."
4 Kauanui, *Hawaiian Blood*.
5 Veracini, in E. Glenn, "Settler Colonialism as Structure," 61.
6 See Hannah-Jones, "1619 Project."
7 E. Glenn, "Settler Colonialism as Structure," 59.
8 Moreton-Robinson, *White Possessive*, 51.
9 E. Glenn, "Settler Colonialism as Structure," 60.
10 T. King, *Black Shoals*; Rifkin, *Fictions of Land and Flesh*. See also Tuck and Wang, "Decolonization Is Not a Metaphor," and the response piece it engendered, Garba and Sorentino, "Slavery Is a Metaphor."
11 Sexton, "Vel of Slavery."
12 Kelley, "Rest of Us."
13 Cf. Arvin, *Possessing Polynesians*.
14 Kauanui, *Hawaiian Blood*.
15 Wolfe, "Settler Colonialism."
16 Moreton-Robinson, "Race and Cultural Entrapment," 114.
17 Moreton-Robinson, "Race and Cultural Entrapment," 114.
18 Wilderson, *Afro-pessimism*; Wilderson, *Afropessimism*.
19 Hannah-Jones, "1619 Project."
20 Twitter, accessed August 19, 2019.
21 Twitter, accessed August 20, 2019.
22 Regarding the military troops that Trump called in to quell the protests in DC in June 2020, Hannah-Jones tweeted, "Whew, I feel for our black servicemen being called out to suppress protesters marching for THEIR lives, too. The dual role we've always forced upon our black soldiers. Fighting for democracy abroad while often being denied it at home." Twitter, June 6, 2020.
23 See "IndiVisible: African-Native American Lives in the Americas," a symposium hosted by the National Museum of the American Indian. It "aimed to bring visibility

to African-Native American lives and initiate a healing dialogue on African-Native American experiences for people of all backgrounds."

24 See also T. King, "Into the Clearing."
25 Miles, *Ties That Bind*; Dineen-Wimberly, "Being Mixed Race."
26 Dineen-Wimberly, "Being Mixed Race," 110.
27 Dineen-Wimberly, "Being Mixed Race," 110.
28 Klopotek, *Recognition Odysseys*, 213–214.
29 Goodyear-Kaʻōpua, "Indigenous Oceanic Futures," 95.
30 Goodyear-Kaʻōpua, "Indigenous Oceanic Futures," 95.
31 Bowman, "Lloyd Austin."
32 Beamer, *No Mākou Ka Mana*; Arista, *Kingdom and the Republic*; Silva, *Power of the Steel-Tipped Pen*.
33 Teaiwa, "Postscript."
34 Gonzalez, *Securing Paradise*.
35 Kajihiro, "Militarizing of Hawaiʻi," 174; Kajihiro and Kekoʻolani, "Hawaiʻi DeTour Project."
36 Kathy Ferguson and Phyllis Turnbull also used the phrase "hidden in plain sight" with regard to the US military in Hawaiʻi. Ferguson and Turnbull, *Oh, Say, Can You See?*, xiii.
37 See Man, "Aloha, Vietnam."
38 For more on the racial dimensions of the Massie and Deedy cases, see Fojas, Guevarra, and Sharma, introduction. See also the 1920s Fukunaga case, analyzed in Okamura, *Raced to Death*.
39 Rosa, *Local Story*.
40 Rosa, *Local Story*, 32. See also David Stannard's excellent account, *Honor Killing*.
41 Terrell, "OffShore."
42 Associated Press, "Jury Acquits Fed Agent."
43 Associated Press, "Prosecutors Keep Up Manslaughter Quest."
44 Stone, "Tragic Killing of Kollin Elderts."
45 Terrell, "OffShore."
46 Chamber of Commerce Hawaiʻi, accessed June 29, 2018, http://cochawaii.com/hawaii-military-appreciation-m.asp.
47 For more on Hawaiians in/and the military, see Tengan, "Re-membering Panalāʻau" and "Embattled Stories of Occupied Hawaiʻi."
48 Blair, "No Aloha for Micronesians"; Lang, "Beer Named after Nuclear Testing Site."
49 Alexander, *New Jim Crow*; Davis, *Are Prisons Obsolete?*
50 Moskos, "Success Story."
51 Belton, "5 Best States."
52 Reynolds and Shendruk, "Demographics of the U.S. Military."
53 Abe, "Violations of the Racial Code," 36; Broussard, "Honolulu NAACP."
54 "Hawaiians hating blacks" forum, topix.com, accessed November 15, 2010 (now defunct), http://www.topix.com/forum/afam/TU88QRAVS8TSUP1NF.
55 Abe, "Violations of the Racial Code."

56 Tengan, "Mana of Kū."
57 Caldwell, "Blackness at the Margins."
58 Wilderson, *Afro-pessimism*.
59 Deniz, "Bombing of Kahoʻolawe."
60 Hofschneider, "Missile Scare Motivates Activists."
61 Goodyear-Kaʻōpua, *Seeds We Planted*, 149.
62 Goodyear-Kaʻōpua, *Seeds We Planted*, 150, 154.
63 Black scholars at the University of Hawaiʻi whose work centers on race include former faculty members Kathryn Takara and Elisa Joy White in ethnic studies and current faculty Ngoroge Ngoroge (history), Ethan Caldwell (ethnic studies), Charles Lawrence (political science and law), and a newly appointed dean of the Law School, Camille Nelson. This list is not comprehensive.
64 Aikau et al., "Indigenous Feminisms Roundtable," 90.
65 Karuka, "Black and Native Visions," 84.
66 Karuka, "Black and Native Visions," 84.
67 Aikau et al., "Indigenous Feminisms Roundtable," 96.
68 Aikau et al., "Indigenous Feminisms Roundtable," 96.
69 Aikau et al., "Indigenous Feminisms Roundtable," 96.
70 Aikau et al., "Indigenous Feminisms Roundtable," 94.
71 Cerizo, "Kapu Aloha March."
72 Cerizo, "Kapu Aloha March."
73 Fox and Prescod-Weinstein, "Fight for Mauna Kea."
74 "HULI Statement."
75 Diaz, "Expanding Worlds."
76 "Protectors of the Future" is the title of an article by Goodyear-Kaʻōpua.
77 Nandita Sharma, review of *Asian Settler Colonialism*. For a rebuttal, see Wolfe, "Recuperating Binarism."
78 Smallwood, "Reflections on Settler Colonialism," 414–15.
79 Saranillio, *Unsustainable Empire*, xviii.
80 Mary Choy, in P. Choy, "Anatomy of a Dancer," 245.
81 Trask, "Settlers of Color," 11.
82 Lipsitz, *Possessive Investment in Whiteness*; Taylor, *From #BlackLivesMatter to Black Liberation*; Taylor, *Race for Profit*.
83 Kamehameha Schools, https://www.ksbe.edu/our_land_kuleana.
84 A. Smith, "Native Studies Workshop."
85 Kelley, "Rest of Us."
86 A. Smith, "Native Studies Workshop." To be clear, in arguing for expansive connections across groups, I am not advocating the view that anyone can claim Indigenous ancestry.
87 "The Fishpond," Paepae o Heʻeia, https://paepaeoheeia.org/the-fishpond. For more on fishponds, see Kawelo, "Fishponds, Food, and the Future."
88 Anthony's farm, Mana Ai, https://www.facebook.com/ManaAiPaiai/.
89 Du Bois wrote this in 1906; in Mullen and Watson, *W. E. B. Du Bois on Asia*, 1–6.
90 See Allen, *Trans-Indigenous*.

91 Saranillio, *Unsustainable Empire*; Kauanui, *Hawaiian Blood*.
92 See Rohrer, *Staking Claim*.
93 Wolfe, "Recuperating Binarism," 265.
94 Lawrence and Matsuda, "Civil Disobedience."
95 Lawrence and Matsuda, "Civil Disobedience."
96 Lawrence and Matsuda, "Civil Disobedience."
97 Obama, *Dreams from My Father*, 76.
98 Obama, *Dreams from My Father*, 90.
99 Du Bois, *Souls of Black Folk*; hooks, "marginality as a site of resistance."
100 Takara, "Frank Marshall Davis in Hawai'i," 126.
101 Takara, "Frank Marshall Davis in Hawai'i," 132; see Takara, *Frank Marshall Davis*.
102 Takara, "Frank Marshall Davis in Hawai'i," 132; Davis, "Africa Is Next Door."
103 Kauanui, *Paradoxes of Hawaiian Sovereignty*, 1; Byrd, *Transit of Empire*, chap. 5.
104 "Our Future, Our Way: Directions in Oceanic Ethnic Studies," Department of Ethnic Studies, University of Hawai'i at Mānoa, March 12–14, 2015. This represents a global Indigenous movement discussed at an ethnic studies conference hosted by the University of Hawai'i that frames local issues within international lateral experiences and resistances. https://www.facebook.com/events/1405633346403494.
105 For a critical set of readings on these and broader questions of Native history, colonialism, land, and rights, see Erdrich, *Night Watchman*; A. Simpson, *Mohawk Interruptus*; Stark, "Criminal Empire"; Coulthard, *Red Skin, White Masks*; Byrd, *Transit of Empire*; Moreton-Robinson, *White Possessive*; Goldstein, *Formations of United States Colonialism*.
106 Arvin, *Possessing Polynesians*.
107 Fujikane, "Mapping Wonder"; Saranillio, *Unsustainable Empire*.
108 Circulated on the Department of Ethnic Studies Facebook page, June 4, 2020.
109 "Representative Kaniela Ing," Hawaii State Legislature, https://www.capitol.hawaii.gov/memberpage.aspx?member=ing. Accessed April 27, 2017.
110 Harmon, "Conversation with Black Lives Matter Co-founder."
111 See *Flux* magazine's photo-essay on Black people in Hawai'i. *Flux* has a few stories focused on this population. Pualoa, "Lineage of Language."
112 See also Shilliam, *Black Pacific*, for Blackness in Aotearoa/New Zealand; Solis, "Black Pacific."
113 Patrisse Khan-Cullors, personal communication. Event hosted by Kaplan Institute for the Humanities, Norris Center, Northwestern University, January 24, 2019.
114 Aikau et al., "Indigenous Feminisms Roundtable," 100.
115 Enomoto, "Where Will You Be?"
116 "Closing Thoughts," Expanding Oceanic Ethnic Studies Conference, Department of Ethnic Studies, University of Hawai'i at Mānoa, March 13, 2015, https://www.youtube.com/watch?v=1-ZWA_qr7mo.
117 Enomoto, "Where Will You Be?"
118 Enomoto, "Where Will You Be?"

119 Enomoto, "Where Will You Be?"
120 See *American Quarterly* 69, no. 2 (June 2017).
121 Allen, *Trans-Indigenous*, xxix.
122 Diaz, "Expanding Worlds."
123 For Black and Asian people as kin, see Okihiro, "Is Yellow Black or White?"

Conclusion: Identity ⟷ Politics ⟷ Knowledge

1 Davis, "Grace Lee Boggs in Conversation."
2 Silva, *Aloha Betrayed*.
3 Vizenor, *Survivance*.
4 Kauanui, *Hawaiian Blood*, 3.
5 Kauanui, *Hawaiian Blood*, 13.
6 See Lee and Baldoz, "Fascinating Interracial Experiment Station."
7 Tengan, *Native Men Remade*.
8 In Choy, "Anatomy of a Dancer," 243.
9 Enomoto et al., "10 Reasons Black Lives Matter." For more on Kekoʻolani, see Akaka et al., *Nā Wāhine Koa*. Jamaica Osorio discusses this history in "E Iho ana ʻo Luna."
10 See Kajihiro and Kekoʻolani, "Hawaiʻi DeTour Project."
11 Trask, *From a Native Daughter*, 187.
12 Niheu, "Huli," 43.
13 Niheu, "Huli," 43.
14 Niheu, "Huli," 44–45. My mother, Dr. Miriam Sharma, was the first director of ethnic studies at UH. M. Sharma, "Ethnic Studies and Ethnic Identity."
15 Niheu, "Huli," 45. Mahalo nui loa to Davianna McGregor for pointing me in this direction.
16 For a chronology of Hawaiian studies, see Hawaiʻinuiākea School of Hawaiian Knowledge, "KCHS Timeline," https://manoa.hawaii.edu/hshk/kamakakuokalani/history-op/kchs-history-timeline.
17 Biondi, *Black Revolution on Campus*.
18 Trask, *From a Native Daughter*, 191.
19 Wilderson, "Blacks and the Master/Slave Relation"; Wilderson, *Red, White & Black*.
20 Enomoto, "Where Will You Be?"
21 T. King, "New World Grammars."
22 Trask, *From a Native Daughter*, 191.
23 Enomoto et al., "10 Reasons Black Lives Matter."
24 Trask, "Birth of the Modern Hawaiian Movement," 126.
25 Osumare, *Africanist Aesthetic*, 141.
26 Niheu, "Huli," 49.
27 Enomoto, "Where Will You Be?"
28 Teaiwa, "Ancestors We Get to Choose," 46.
29 Teaiwa, "Militarism, Tourism, and the Native."
30 Jutel, "Remembering Dr. Teresia Teaiwa."

31 Teaiwa, "Black in the Blue Pacific," 13.
32 Teaiwa, "Black in the Blue Pacific," 13.
33 "Native Hawaiian Woman Responds to Racist Caller," YouTube, June 3, 2016, https://www.youtube.com/watch?v=74u8KzxyzRM.
34 The online manuscript does not provide the names of the curriculum's creators, but they describe its purpose and draw from guidelines created by the Native Hawaiian Education Council and the Ka Haka ʻUla O Keʻilikōlani College of Hawaiian Language at the University of Hawaiʻi at Hilo. "Ke Kaulike He Haʻawina Kiwila," 1.
35 "Lesson #6: Social Injustice in Hawaiʻi," 1, http://ulukau.org/gsdl2.81/cgi-bin/cbkiwila?a=pdf&d=D0.3&aurl=/gsdl2.81/collect/cbkiwila/index/assoc.
36 "Lesson #6," 1.
37 "Lesson #6," 1.
38 "Lesson #6," 3.
39 "Lesson #6," 4.
40 The Faculty of African Descent was created in 2003 and consisted of faculty and staff throughout the University of Hawaiʻi system across fields. "Second Winter Institute on Black Studies to Feature African American Museum Director from Smithsonian Institute," https://manoa.hawaii.edu/news/article.php?aId=1634.
41 The end of the institutes may have coincided with the loss of the University's African Americanist, who took a position elsewhere in 2013.
42 Ransby, *Making All Black Lives Matter*.

BIBLIOGRAPHY

Abe, Shirley. "Violations of the Racial Code in Hawaii." *Social Process in Hawaii* 9–10 (July 1945): 33–38.
Adams, Ayin. *African Americans in Hawai'i: A Search for Identity*. Ka'a'awa, HI: Pacific Raven Press, 2010.
Adams, Ayin. *Kwanzaa in Hawaii*. Ka'a'awa, HI: Pacific Raven Press, 2012.
Adams, Romanzo. "Census Notes on the Negroes in Hawaii Prior to the War." *Social Process in Hawai'i* 9–10 (1945): 25–27.
Adler, Jacob. "King Kamehameha IV's Attitude towards the United States." *Journal of Pacific History* 3 (1968): 107–115.
"African Americans in Hawai'i Reading List." Compiled by the Hawai'i State Library, Hawai'i and Pacific Section, African American History Month 2018. https://www.librariesHawaii.org/2018/02/01/february-is-african-american-history-month.
Afualo, Drew. "The New Ha'a: UH Football Presents a New Culture on the Field." *Ka Leo*, October 3, 2016. http://www.manoanow.org/kaleo/special_issues/the-new-haa/article_04e4e8c0-891f-11e6-98bb-2b009ea4436f.html.
Aikau, Hōkūlani. "Indigeneity in the Diaspora: The Case of Native Hawaiians at Iosepa, Utah." *American Quarterly* 62, no. 3 (September 2010): 477–500.
Aikau, Hōkūlani, Maile Arvin, Mishuana Goeman, and Scott Morgensen. "Indigenous Feminisms Roundtable." *Frontiers* 36, no. 3 (2015): 84–106.
Aikau, Hōkūlani, and Vernadette Gonzalez, eds. *Detours: A Decolonial Guide to Hawai'i*. Durham, NC: Duke University Press, 2019.
Akaka, Moanike'ala, Maxine Kahaulelio, Terrilee Keko'olani-Raymond, and Loretta Ritte. *Nā Wāhine Koa: Hawaiian Women for Sovereignty and Demilitarization*. Edited by Noelani Goodyear-Ka'ōpua. Honolulu: University of Hawai'i Press, 2018.
Alexander, Michelle. *The New Jim Crow: Mass Incarceration in the Age of Colorblindness*. New York: New Press, 2012.
Allen, Chadwick. *Trans-Indigenous: Methodologies for Global Native Literary Studies*. Minneapolis: University of Minnesota Press, 2012.
Amadahy, Zainab, and Bonita Lawrence. "Indigenous Peoples and Black People in Canada: Settlers or Allies?" In *Breaching the Colonial Contract*, edited by Arlo Kemp, 105–136. Dordrecht, Netherlands: Springer, 2009.
Anderson, Mark. *Black and Indigenous: Garifuna Activism and Consumer Culture in Honduras*. Minneapolis: University of Minnesota Press, 2009.
Andrew, Lorrin. "Lorrin Andrew's Pocket Diary Written in Pencil on Board the Ship *Parthian* Voyage to Sandwich Islands in 1837–1838."

Andrews, Courtney-Savali. "'Something within Me': A Performative Exploration of Afro-Pacific Identity and Refrain of Black Lives Matter." *Amerasia Journal* 43, no. 1 (2017): 163–168.

Arista, Noelani. *The Kingdom and the Republic: Sovereign Hawaiʻi and the Early United States*. Philadelphia: University of Pennsylvania Press, 2019.

Armstrong, Clarissa. "Armstrong, Clarissa—Journal—1831–1838." Hawaiian Mission Houses Digital Archive 17. https://hmha.missionhouses.org/items/show/11.

Arvin, Maile. "Mauna Kea Protests Aren't New. They're Part of a Long Fight against Colonialism." Op-ed. Truthout.org, July 27, 2019. https://truthout.org/articles/mauna-kea-protests-are-part-of-a-long-fight-against-colonialism.

Arvin, Maile. "Polynesia Is a Project, Not a Place: Polynesian Proximities to Whiteness in *Cloud Atlas* and Beyond." In *Beyond Ethnicity: New Politics of Race in Hawaiʻi*, edited by Camilla Fojas, Rudy Guevarra Jr., and Nitasha Sharma, 21–47. Honolulu: University of Hawaiʻi Press, 2018.

Arvin, Maile. *Possessing Polynesians: The Science of Settler Colonial Whiteness in Hawaiʻi*. Durham, NC: Duke University Press, 2019.

Arvin, Maile. "Possessions of Whiteness: Settler Colonialism and Anti-Blackness in the Pacific." *Decolonization: Indigeneity, Education and Society*, June 2, 2014. https://decolonization.wordpress.com/2014/06/02/possessions-of-whiteness-settler-colonialism-and-anti-blackness-in-the-pacific.

Associated Press. "Jury Acquits Fed Agent from Arlington of Murder in Hawaii Shooting." WJLA, August 14, 2014. https://wjla.com/news/local/jury-acquits-federal-agent-from-arlington-of-murder-in-hawaii-shooting-106103.

Associated Press. "Prosecutors Keep Up Manslaughter Quest against U.S. Agent Christopher Deedy." *Star Advertiser*, December 24, 2019. https://www.staradvertiser.com/2019/12/24/hawaii-news/prosecutors-keep-up-manslaughter-quest-against-u-s-agent-christopher-deedy.

Awa, Brenton. "The End of the Sugar Cane Era in Hawaii." *KITV Island News*, January 6, 2016. https://www.kitv.com/story/30905681/the-end-of-the-sugar-cane-era-in-hawaii.

Bailey, Beth, and David Farber. "The 'Double-V' Campaign in World War II Hawaii: African Americans, Racial Ideology, and Federal Power." *Journal of Social History* 26, no. 4 (Summer 1993): 817–843.

Bailey, Beth, and David Farber. *The First Strange Place: The Alchemy of Race and Sex in World War II Hawaii*. New York: Free Press, 2012.

Baldwin, D. Journal of Rev. D. Baldwin, 1830–1831. Hawaiian Mission Houses Digital Archives, 166.

Balibar, Étienne. "Is There a 'Neo-Racism'?" In *Race, Nation, Class: Ambiguous Identities*, edited by Étienne Balibar and Immanuel Wallerstein. London: Verso, 1991.

Bandy, David. "Bandmaster Henry Berger and the Royal Hawaiian Band." *Hawaiian Journal of History* 24 (1990): 69–90.

Barbee-Wooten, Daphne. *African American Attorneys in Hawaiʻi*. Kaʻaʻawa, HI: Pacific Raven Press, 2010.

Beamer, Kamanamaikalani. *No Mākou Ka Mana: Liberating the Nation*. Honolulu: Kamehameha Press, 2014.

Belton, Danielle. "The 5 Best States for Black People." The Root, November 19, 2014. https://www.theroot.com/the-5-best-states-for-black-people-1790877760.

Beltran, Mary, and Camilla Fojas, eds. *Mixed Race Hollywood*. New York: New York University Press, 2008.

Bennett, Judith, and Angela Wanhalla, eds. *Mothers' Darlings of the South Pacific: The Children of Indigenous Women and U.S. Servicemen, World War II*. Honolulu: University of Hawai'i Press, 2016.

"Betrayal of a Community." News and Commentary. *The Carroll Cox Show*, May 5, 2016. http://www.carrollcox.com/RexJohnson.htm.

Beutin, Lyndsey. "Racialization as a Way of Seeing: The Limits of Counter-surveillance and Police Reform." *Surveillance and Society* 15, no. 1 (2017): 5–20.

Bingham, Sybil Moseley. Journal, 41–43, November 8, 1819–July 24, 1820. Collections of the Hawaiian Children's Mission Society Library.

Biondi, Martha. *The Black Revolution on Campus*. Berkeley: University of California Press, 2014.

Bishop, Hunter. "Oregon Niece Adds to Helene Hale's Scholarship Fund." *Big Island Now*, August 4, 2014. http://bigislandnow.com/2014/08/04/oregon-niece-adds-to-helene-hales-scholarship-fund.

Black, Stella, Jacquie Kidd, and Katey Thom. "Kōti Rangatahi: Whanaungatanga Justice and the 'Magnificence of the Connectedness.'" In *Reppin': Pacific Islander Youth and Native Justice*, edited by Keith L. Camacho, 33–54. Seattle: University of Washington Press, 2021.

Blair, Chad. "Harry Kim Shouldn't Get a Pass on Racist Comment." *Honolulu Civil Beat*, May 18, 2018. https://www.civilbeat.org/2018/05/chad-blair-harry-kim-shouldnt-get-a-pass-on-racist-comment.

Blair, Chad. "No Aloha for Micronesians in Hawaii." *Honolulu Civil Beat*, June 10, 2011. https://www.civilbeat.org/2011/06/no-aloha-for-micronesians-in-hawaii.

Bolden, Tanya. *W. E. B. Du Bois: A Twentieth-Century Life (Up Close)*. New York: Viking, 2008.

Bow, Leslie. *Partly Colored: Asian Americans and Racial Anomaly in the Segregated South*. New York: New York University Press, 2010.

Bowman, Tom. "Lloyd Austin: A Man 'of the Highest Integrity,' but Still Unknown to Many," npr.com, December 8, 2020. https://www.npr.org/2020/12/08/944321280/lloyd-austin-a-man-of-the-highest-integrity-but-still-unknown-to-many.

Broussard, Albert. "The Honolulu NAACP and Race Relations in Hawai'i." *Hawaiian Journal of History* 39 (2005): 115–133.

Brown, Simone. *Dark Matters: On the Surveillance of Blackness*. Durham, NC: Duke University Press, 2015.

Brown, Simone. "Everybody's Got a Little Light under the Sun." *Cultural Studies* 26, no. 4 (2012): 542–564.

Brundage, Kay. *See* Kathryn Takara.

"Bruno Mars Opens Up about Race, Discrimination, and Loss of His Mother." *Rap-Up*, January 30, 2017. https://www.rap-up.com/2017/01/30/bruno-mars-opens-up-about-race-discrimination-loss-of-mother.

Brunsma, David. "Interracial Families and the Racial Identification of Mixed-Race Children: Evidence from the Early Childhood Longitudinal Study." *Social Forces* 84, no. 2 (December 2005): 1131–1157.

Burnett, John. "Helen Hale Remembered as Amazing Woman." *Hawaii Tribune Herald*, February 3, 2013. https://www.hawaiitribune-herald.com/2013/02/03/hawaii-news/helen-hale-remembered-as-amazing-woman.

Byrd, Jodi. "'Been to the Nation, Lord, but I Couldn't Stay There.'" *Interventions: International Journal of Postcolonial Studies* 13, no. 1 (2011): 31–52.

Byrd, Jodi. *The Transit of Empire: Indigenous Critiques of Colonialism*. Minneapolis: University of Minnesota Press, 2011.

Caldwell, Ethan. "Blackness at the Margins of Empire: African American Soldier–Okinawan Civilian Relations and the Colonized-Colonizer Paradox." PhD diss., African American Studies, Northwestern University, 2017.

Callis, Tom. "Kim Finalizing Maunakea Committee: Mission Statement Emphasizes Native Hawaiians' Connection to Mountain Exploration." *Hawaiʻi Tribune Herald*, June 26, 2019. https://www.hawaiitribune-herald.com/2018/02/11/hawaii-news/kim-finalizing-maunakea-committee-mission-statement-emphasizes-native-hawaiians-connection-to-the-mountain-exploration.

Casumbal-Salazar, Iokepa. "'Where Are Your Sacred Temples?': Notes on the Struggle for Manua a Wākea." In *Detours: A Decolonial Guide to Hawaiʻi*, edited by Hōkūlani Aikau and Vernadette Gonzalez, 200–210. Durham, NC: Duke University Press, 2019.

Cerizo, Kehaulani. "Kapu Aloha March Displays 'Power of a Unified People.'" *Maui News*, August 12, 2019. https://www.mauinews.com/news/local-news/2019/08/kapu-aloha-march-displays-power-of-a-unified-people.

Chamberlain, Levi. Chamberlain Levi Journal, 6–20, June 21, 1826–November 10, 1836. Hawaiian Mission Houses Digital Archives. https://hmha.missionhouses.org/collections/show/173.

Chang, David. *The World and All the Things upon It: Native Hawaiian Geographies of Exploration*. Minneapolis: University of Minnesota Press, 2016.

Chang, Jason. *Chino: Anti-Chinese Racism in Mexico, 1880–1940*. Champaign: University of Illinois Press, 2017.

Chang, Kornel. *Pacific Connections: The Making of the U.S.-Canadian Borderlands*. Berkeley: University of California Press, 2012.

Chang, Sharon. *Raising Mixed Race: Multiracial Asian Children in a Post-racial World*. New York: Routledge, 2016.

Chock, Eric. "The Neocolonization of Bamboo Ridge: Repositioning Bamboo Ridge and Local Literature in the 1990s." *Bamboo Ridge: A Hawaiʻi Writers Quarterly* 69 (1996): 11–25.

Choy, Peggy. "Anatomy of a Dancer: Place, Lineage and Liberation." *Amerasia Journal* 26, no. 2 (2000): 234–252.

Clark, Kevin. "10 Best States for Black Household Wealth." *Black Enterprise*, September 29, 2014. https://www.blackenterprise.com/the-10-best-states-with-top-black-household-incomes/11.

Cloyd, Fredrick. *Dream of the Water Children: Memory and Mourning in the Black Pacific*. New York: 2Leaf Press, 2019.

Coates, Ta-Nehisi. "When My President Was Black." *The Atlantic*, September 2012. https://www.theatlantic.com/magazine/archive/2012/09/fear-of-a-black-president/309064.

Coleman, Arica. *That the Blood Stay Pure: African Americans, Native Americans, and the Predicament of Race and Identity in Virginia*. Bloomington: Indiana University Press, 2013.

Collins, Patricia Hill. *Black Feminist Thought: Knowledge, Consciousness, and the Politics of Empowerment*. New York: Routledge, 2000.

Compoc, Kimberly. "Emergent Allies: Decolonizing Hawaiʻi from a Filipin@ Perspective." PhD diss., English, University of Hawaiʻi, 2017.

Condry, Ian. *Hip-Hop Japan: Rap and the Paths of Cultural Globalization*. Durham, NC: Duke University Press, 2006.

Cooke, Amos Starr. Journal entry, July 11, 1848, 160. Hawaiian Mission Houses Digital Archives. https://hmha.missionhouses.org/items/show/432.

Coulthard, Glen. *Red Skin, White Masks: Rejecting the Colonial Politics of Recognition*. Minneapolis: University of Minnesota Press, 2014.

Crawley, Ashon. *Blackpentacostal Breath: The Aesthetics of Possibility*. New York: Fordham University Press, 2017.

Crenshaw, Kimberlé. "Demarginalizing the Intersection of Race and Sex: A Black Feminist Critique of Antidiscrimination Doctrine, Feminist Theory and Antiracist Politics." *University of Chicago Legal Forum* 1989, no. 1, article 8 (1989): 139–167.

Crowninshield, Benj. *An Account of the Yacht Cleopatra's Barge Built at Salem in 1816*. Historical Collections of the Essex Institute. Salem, MA: Salem Publishing and Printing, 1889.

Crowninshield, Francis, comp. *The Story of George Crowninshield's Yacht, Cleopatra's Barge, on a Voyage of Pleasure to the Western Islands and the Mediterranean, 1816-1817*. Boston: privately printed, 1918.

Dariotis, Wei Ming. "Hapa: The Word of Power." *Multiracial America: An Emerging Voice*. Mixed Heritage Center, 2007.

Das Gupta, Monisha, and Sue Haglund. "Mexican Migration to Hawaiʻi and US Settler Colonialism." *Latino Studies* 13, no. 4 (December 2015): 455–480.

David, Mari-Ela. "Hawaiʻi Tourism Authority CEO Rex Johnson Resigns." *Hawaiʻi News Now*, October 8, 2008. https://www.hawaiinewsnow.com/story/9149996/hawaii-tourism-authority-ceo-rex-johnson-resigns.

Davis, Angela. "Angela Davis: Reflections on Race, Class, and Gender in the USA." Interview with Lisa Lowe. In *The Politics of Culture in the Shadow of Capital*, edited by Lisa Lowe and David Lloyd, 303–323. Durham, NC: Duke University Press, 1997.

Davis, Angela. *Are Prisons Obsolete?* New York: Seven Stories Press, 2003.

Davis, Angela. "Grace Lee Boggs in Conversation with Angela Davis." Making Contact: Radio Stories and Voices to Take Action, February 20, 2012. https://www.radioproject.org/2012/02/grace-lee-boggs-berkeley.

Davis, Frank Marshall. "Africa Is Next Door." Frank-ly Speaking. *Honolulu Record*, January 12, 1950. http://www.hawaii.edu/uhwo/clear/HonoluluRecord1/frankblog1950.html.

Day, Iyko. *Alien Capital: Asian Racialization and the Logic of Settler Colonial Capitalism.* Durham, NC: Duke University Press, 2016.

"Demographic, Social, Economic, and Housing Characteristics for Selected Race Groups in Hawaii." Research and Economic Analysis Division, Department of Business, Economic Development and Tourism, State of Hawaii, March 2018. https://census.hawaii.gov/home/data-products.

Deniz, Lacy. "The Bombing of Kahoʻolawe Went on for Decades. The Clean-Up Will Last Generations." *Hawaii News Now*, February 27, 2018.

Denning, Michael. *Noise Uprising: The Audiopolitics of a World Musical Revolution.* New York: Verso, 2015.

Diaz, Vicente. "Back to the Future: Navigating Micronesian Seas through Dakota Skyways." Public lecture delivered at "Pacific Island Studies Now!" Asian American Studies Program, Northwestern University, May 4, 2018.

Diaz, Vicente. "Expanding Worlds." Paper delivered at "Our Future, Our Way: Directions in Oceanic Ethnic Studies." Department of Ethnic Studies, University of Hawaiʻi at Mānoa, March 13, 2015.

Diaz, Vicente. "'Fight Boys, 'Til the Last . . .': Islandstyle Football and the Remasculinization of Indigeneity in the Militarized American Pacific Islands." In *Pacific Diaspora: Island Peoples in the United States and across the Pacific*, edited by Paul Spickard, Joanne Rondilla, and Debbie Wright, 169–194. Honolulu: University of Hawaiʻi Press, 2002.

Diaz, Vicente, and J. Kēhaulani Kauanui. "Native Pacific Cultural Studies on the Edge." *Contemporary Pacific* 13, no. 2 (Fall 2001): 315–342.

Dineen-Wimberly, Ingrid. "Being Mixed Race in the Makah Nation." In *Red and Yellow, Black and Brown: Decentering Whiteness in Mixed Race Studies*, edited by Joanne Rondilla, Rudy Guevarra Jr., and Paul Spickard, 109–126. New Brunswick, NJ: Rutgers University Press, 2017.

Dolgin, Gail, and Vicente Franco, dirs. *Daughter from Danang.* Alexandria, VA: WGBH, 2003. Distributed by PBS Home Video. DVD.

Dominguez, Virginia. "Exporting U.S. Concepts of Race: Are There Limits to the U.S. Model?" *Social Research* 65, no. 2 (Summer 1998): 369–399.

Drake, St. Clair, and Horace Cayton. *Black Metropolis: A Study of Negro Life in a Northern City.* 1945. Reprint, Chicago: University of Chicago Press, 2015.

Du Bois, W. E. B. "The Color Line Belts the World." October 20, 1906. W. E. B. Du Bois Papers (MS 312). Special Collections and University Archives, University of Massachusetts Amherst Library. https://credo.library.umass.edu/view/full/mums312-b207-i148.

Du Bois, W. E. B. *The Souls of Black Folk.* Chicago: A. C. McClurg, 1903.

"Dwayne Johnson Recalls Hard Times in Hawaii." *Star Advertiser*, July 11, 2016. https://www.staradvertiser.com/2016/07/11/breaking-news/dwayne-johnson-recalls-hard-times-in-hawaii.

Dye, Bob. *Merchant Prince of the Sandalwood Mountains: Afong and the Chinese in Hawaiʻi.* Honolulu: University of Hawaiʻi Press, 1997.

Elam, Michele. *The Souls of Mixed Folk: Race, Politics, and Aesthetics in the New Millennium.* Palo Alto, CA: Stanford University Press, 2011.

Enomoto, Joy. "These Could Be Evidence: A Response Work to *Write for Ferguson: Protest Poetry from Hawai'i Review*." *Amerasia Journal* 43, no. 1 (2017): 157–162.
Enomoto, Joy. "Where Will You Be? Why Black Lives Matter in the Hawaiian Kingdom." Blog, February 1, 2017. https://hehiale.wordpress.com/2017/02/01/where-will-you-be-why-black-lives-matter-in-the-hawaiian-kingdom.
Enomoto, Joy, Bryan Kuwada, Aiko Yamashiro, Jamaica Osorio, Caitlin Kee Jeonghye, Kelsey Amos, Jennifer Vehis Wheeler, Ilima Long, and Reyna Ramolete Hayashi. "10 Reasons Black Lives Matter in the Hawaiian Kingdom." Women's Voices Women Speak. http://wvws808.blogspot.com/2016/11/many-of-you-have-asked-for-link-to-info.html.
Erdrich, Louise. *The Night Watchman*. New York: Harper, 2020.
Ferguson, Jeffrey. *The Sage of Sugar Hill: George S. Schuyler and the Harlem Renaissance*. New Haven, CT: Yale University Press, 2005.
Ferguson, Kathy, and Phyllis Turnbull. *Oh, Say, Can You See? The Semiotics of the Military in Hawai'i*. Minneapolis: University of Minnesota Press, 1999.
"50 State Incarceration Profiles, Hawaii Profile." Prison Policy Initiative. http://www.prisonpolicy.org/profiles/HI.html.
Finn's Leinster Journal, March 1, 1778. Irish Newspaper Archives. https://www.irishnewsarchive.com.
Fojas, Camilla, Rudy Guevarra Jr., and Nitasha Sharma, eds. *Beyond Ethnicity: New Politics of Race in Hawai'i*. Honolulu: University of Hawai'i Press, 2018.
Fojas, Camilla, Rudy Guevarra Jr., and Nitasha Sharma. "Introduction: New Politics of Race in Hawai'i." In *Beyond Ethnicity: New Politics of Race in Hawai'i*, edited by Camilla Fojas, Rudy Guevarra Jr., and Nitasha Sharma, 1–18. Honolulu: University of Hawai'i Press, 2018.
Fornander, Abraham. *An Account of the Polynesian Race: Its Origin and Migrations, and the Ancient History of the Hawaiian People to the Times of Kamehameha I*. English and Foreign Philosophical Library Extra Series. London: Trench K. Paul, 1880.
Fox, Keolu, and Chanda Prescod-Weinstein. "The Fight for Mauna Kea Is a Fight against Colonial Science." *The Nation*, July 24, 2019. https://www.thenation.com/article/mauna-kea-tmt-colonial-science.
Franklin, Cynthia, and Laura Lyons. "Remixing Hybridity: Globalization, Native Resistance, and Cultural Production in Hawai'i." *American Studies* 45, no. 3 (Fall 2004): 49–80.
Fujikane, Candace. "Between Nationalisms: Hawaii's Local Nation and Its Troubled Racial Paradise." *Critical Mass: A Journal of Asian American Cultural Criticism* 1, no. 2 (Spring–Summer 1994): 23–58.
Fujikane, Candace. *Mapping Abundance for a Planetary Future: Kanaka Maoli and Critical Settler Cartographies in Hawai'i*. Durham, NC: Duke University Press, 2021.
Fujikane, Candace. "Mapping Wonder in the Māui Mo'olelo on the Mo'o'āina: Growing Aloha 'Āina through Indigenous and Settler Affinity Activism." *Marvels and Tales* 30, no. 1 (2016): 45–69.
Fujikane, Candace. "Sweeping Racism under the Rug of 'Censorship': The Controversy over Lois-Ann Yamanaka's *Blu's Hanging*." *Amerasia Journal* 26, no. 2 (2000): 158–194.

Fujikane, Candace, and Jonathan Okamura, eds. *Asian Settler Colonialism: From Local Governance to the Habits of Everyday Life in Hawaiʻi*. Honolulu: University of Hawaiʻi Press, 2008.

Gaines, Kevin. *Uplifting the Race: Black Leadership, Politics, and Culture in the Twentieth Century*. 2nd ed. Chapel Hill: University of North Carolina Press, 1996.

Gaither, Sarah. "I Study Biracial Identity in America. Here's Why the Royal Baby Is a Big Deal." *Vox*, May 7, 2019. https://www.vox.com/first-person/2018/5/14/17345162/meghan-markle-royal-baby-prince-harry.

Garba, Tapji, and Sara-Maria Sorentino. "Slavery Is a Metaphor: A Critical Commentary on Eve Tuck and K. Wayne Yang's 'Decolonization Is Not a Metaphor.'" *Antipode* 52, no. 3 (2020): 764–782.

Gast, Ross. *Don Francisco de Paula Marin: A Biography by Ross H. Gast*. Honolulu: University of Hawaiʻi Press, 2003.

Geertz, Clifford. "Thick Description: Toward an Interpretive Theory of Culture." In *The Interpretation of Cultures: Selected Essays*, by Clifford Geertz, 3–30. New York: Basic Books, 1973.

Gilmore, Ruth Wilson. *Golden Gulag: Prisons, Surplus, Crisis, and Opposition in Globalizing California*. Oakland: University of California Press, 2007.

Gilroy, Paul. *The Black Atlantic: Modernity and Double Consciousness*. London: Verso, 1993.

Gilroy, Paul. "It's a Family Affair." In *Black Popular Culture*, edited by Gina Dent. Seattle, WA: Bay Press, 1992.

Glauberman, Stu, and Jerry Burris. *The Dream Begins: How Hawaiʻi Shaped Barack Obama*. Honolulu: Watermark, 2009.

Glenn, Akiemi. "African American Solidarity." *Hawaiʻi Public Radio*, June 4, 2020. https://hawaiipublicradio.org/post/conversation-african-american-community-stands-solidarity#stream/0.

Glenn, Akiemi. "Want to Explore Race in Hawaiʻi? Center Those Most Impacted by It." Blog, July 2, 2019. https://akiemiglenn.net/blog/2019/7/2/2p01kxsurmc9fzkx8jvme7pwoz03bf.

Glenn, Evelyn Nakano. "Settler Colonialism as Structure: A Framework for Comparative Studies of U.S. Race and Gender Formation." *Sociology of Race and Ethnicity* 1, no. 1 (2015): 52–72.

Goldsmith, Elizabeth. "Captain Cook's Cook." Wonders and Marvels, May 2016. http://www.wondersandmarvels.com/2016/05/captain-cooks-cook.html.

Goldstein, Alyosha. *Formations of United States Colonialism*. Durham, NC: Duke University Press, 2014.

Gomez, Sonia. "The Politics of Afro-Asian Intimacies in Jim Crow Tokyo." *Journal of American Ethnic History* 39, no. 1 (2019): 35–65.

Gonzalez, Vernadette. *Securing Paradise: Tourism and Militarism in Hawaiʻi and the Philippines*. Durham, NC: Duke University Press, 2013.

Goo, Sara Kehaulani. "After 200 Years, Native Hawaiians Make a Comeback." Pew Research Center, April 6, 2015. https://www.pewresearch.org/fact-tank/2015/04/06/native-hawaiian-population.

Goodyear-Kaʻōpua, Noelani. "Domesticating Hawaiians: Kamehameha Schools and the 'Tender Violence' of Marriage." *Indian Subjects: Hemispheric Perspectives on the History of Indigenous Education*, 2014, 16–47.

Goodyear-Kaʻōpua, Noelani. "Indigenous Oceanic Futures: Challenging Settler Colonialisms and Militarization." In *Indigenous and Decolonizing Studies in Education: Mapping the Long View*, edited by Linda Tuhiwai Smith, Eve Tuck, and Wayne Yang, 82–102. New York: Routledge, 2019.

Goodyear-Kaʻōpua, Noelani. "Protectors of the Future, Not Protesters of the Past: Indigenous Pacific Activism and Mauna a Wākea." *South Atlantic Quarterly* 116, no. 1 (2017): 184–194.

Goodyear-Kaʻōpua, Noelani. *The Seeds We Planted: Portraits of a Native Hawaiian Charter School*. Minneapolis: University of Minnesota Press, 2013.

Goodyear-Kaʻōpua, Noelani, Ikaika Hussey, and Erin Kahunawaikaʻala Wright, eds. *A Nation Rising: Hawaiian Movements for Life, Land, and Sovereignty*. Durham, NC: Duke University Press, 2014.

"Grover Cleveland on the Overthrow of Hawaii's Royal Government." President Cleveland to the Senate and House of Representatives, 1893. Digital History ID 1283. http://www.digitalhistory.uh.edu/disp_textbook.cfm?smtID=3&psid=1283.

Guevarra, Rudy, Jr. *Aloha Compadre: Latinx in Hawaiʻi, 1832–2010*. New Brunswick, NJ: Rutgers University Press, forthcoming.

Guevarra, Rudy, Jr. "'Latino Threat in the 808?': Mexican Migration and the Politics of Race in Hawaiʻi." In *Beyond Ethnicity: New Politics of Race in Hawaiʻi*, edited by Camilla Fojas, Rudy Guevarra Jr., and Nitasha Sharma, 152–177. Honolulu: University of Hawaiʻi Press, 2018.

Gugliotta, Bobette. *Nolle Smith, Cowboy, Engineer, Etc.* New York: Dodd Mead, 1971.

Guinier, Lani. *Lift Every Voice: Turning a Civil Rights Setback into a New Vision of Social Justice*. New York: Simon and Schuster, 1998.

Gutierrez, Ben. "Nurse Who Found Photo of Noose on Locker Gets $3.8M Payout." *Hawaiʻi News Now*, March 1, 2018. http://www.hawaiinewsnow.com/story/37619986/jury-awards-former-queens-nurse-38-million-in-racial-discrimination-lawsuit.

Guttman, Deloris. "The History of African Americans in Hawaiʻi, Part I, Part II." African American Diversity Cultural Center Hawaii (AADCCH). https://aadcch.org.

Guttman, D. Molentia, and Ernest Golden. *African Americans in Hawaiʻi*. Charleston, SC: Arcadia, 2011.

Hall, Lisa Kahaleole. "'Hawaiian at Heart' and Other Fictions." *Contemporary Pacific* 17, no. 2 (2005): 404–413.

Hamako, Eric. "Improving Anti-racist Education for Multiracial Students." PhD diss., Social Justice Education, University of Massachusetts, Amherst, 2014.

Hannah-Jones, Nikole. "The 1619 Project." *New York Times Magazine*, https://www.nytimes.com/interactive/2019/08/14/magazine/1619-america-slavery.html.

Harmon, Anna. "A Conversation with Black Lives Matter Co-founder Patrisse Khan-Cullors." *Flux*, February 8, 2017. http://fluxhawaii.com/black-lives-matter-in-hawaii.

Hattenstone, Simon. "Janet Mock: 'I'd Never Seen a Young Trans Woman Who Was Thriving in the World—I Was Looking for That.'" *The Guardian*, April 15, 2018.

Hauʻofa, Epeli. "Our Sea of Islands." *Contemporary Pacific* 6, no. 1 (Spring 1994): 147–161.

"Hawaii's Top Woman Politician." *Ebony*, April 1963.

Hawaiian Mission Houses Digital Archive. https://hmha.missionhouses.org.

Hawkins, John, and Emily Hawkins. "The Blacks." In *People and Cultures of Hawaiʻi: The Evolution of Culture and Ethnicity*, edited by John McDermott and Naleen Naupaka Andrade, 220–239. Honolulu: University of Hawaiʻi Press, 2011.

Henderson, April. "Fleeting Substantiality: The Samoan Giant in US Popular Discourse." *Contemporary Pacific* 23, no. 2 (2011): 269–302.

Hiller, Jennifer. "Jury Backs Teacher in Discrimination Case." *Honolulu Advertiser*, December 5, 2002. http://the.honoluluadvertiser.com/article/2002/Dec/05/ln/ln07a.html.

Hisatake, Kara. "Hawaiian Hospitality and Hostility: Camp in Rap Reiplinger's Pidgin Comedy." *Amerasia Journal* 44, no. 3 (2018): 27–48.

"History of Labor in Hawaiʻi." Center for Labor Education and Research, University of Hawaiʻi–West Oʻahu. https://www.hawaii.edu/uhwo/clear/home/HawaiiLaborHistory.html.

Hobart, Hiʻilei. "At Home on the Mauna: Ecological Violence and Fantasies of Terra Nullius on Maunakea Summit." *Native American and Indigenous Studies* 6, no. 2 (Fall 2019): 30–50.

Hobart, Hiʻilei. *Cooling the Tropics: Ice, Indigeneity, and Hawaiian Refreshment.* Durham, NC: Duke University Press, forthcoming.

Hobart, Hiʻilei. "Snowy Mountaineers and Soda Waters: Honolulu and Its Age of Ice Importation." *Food, Culture and Society* 19, no. 3 (2016): 461–483.

Hobart, Hiʻilei. "Tropical Necessities: Ice, Taste, and Territory in Settler Colonial Hawaiʻi." PhD diss., Program in Food Studies, New York University, 2016.

Hofschneider, Anita. "Many in Hawaii Grieve—and Protest—the Police Killing of George Floyd." *Honolulu Civil Beat*, June 3, 2020. https://www.civilbeat.org/2020/06/many-in-hawaii-grieve-and-protest-the-police-killing-of-george-floyd.

Hofschneider, Anita. "Missile Scare Motivates Activists Who Fear Military's Presence." *Civil Beat*, January 17, 2018. https://www.civilbeat.org/2018/01/missile-scare-motivates-activists-who-fear-militarys-presence.

hooks, bell. "marginality as a site of resistance." In *Out There: Marginalization and Contemporary Culture*, edited by Russell Ferguson, Martha Gever, Trinh T. Minh-ha, and Cornel West, 341–343. Cambridge, MA: MIT Press, 1992.

hooks, bell. *We Real Cool: Black Men and Masculinity*. New York: Routledge, 2004.

Hormann, Bernard L. *Community Forces in Hawaii: A Book of Readings*. Honolulu: University of Hawaiʻi, 1968.

Horne, Gerald. *The White Pacific: U.S. Imperialism and Black Slavery in the South Seas after the Civil War*. Honolulu: University of Hawaiʻi Press, 2007.

Hoverson, Martha. "Buffalo Soldiers at Kilauea, 1915–1917." *Hawaiian Journal of History* 49 (2015): 73–90.

Howard, Jacqueline. "Hawaii Named Healthiest State, Louisiana Ranks Last in New Report." CNN.com, December 20, 2018. https://www.cnn.com/2018/12/20/health/healthiest-states-2018-study/index.html.

"HULI Statement: 'We Will Stand in Kapu Aloha.'" *Big Island News*, July 11, 2019. https://www.bigislandvideonews.com/2019/07/11/huli-we-will-stand-in-kapu-aloha.

Ikeda, Kiyoshi. Foreword to "They Followed the Trade Winds: African Americans in Hawai'i." In Miles Jackson, "They Followed the Trade Winds," n.p.

Imada, Adria. *Aloha America: Hula Circuits through the U.S. Empire*. Durham, NC: Duke University Press, 2013.

Ingram, Rueben A. "Blacks Must Stop Using Slavery as a 'Crutch.'" Letters. *Honolulu Star-Bulletin*, August 29, 1997. http://archives.starbulletin.com/97/08/29/editorial/letters.html.

Jackson, Miles. "Ball, Alice Augusta (1892–1916)." http://www.blackpast.org/aaw/ball-alice-augusta-1892-1916.

Jackson, Miles. "Introduction." Miles Jackson, guest ed. "They Followed the Trade Winds: African Americans in Hawai'i." Special issue, *Social Process in Hawai'i* 43 (2004): xii–xxi.

Jackson, Miles. "Prelude to a New Century." Miles Jackson, guest ed. "They Followed the Trade Winds: African Americans in Hawai'i." Special issue, *Social Process in Hawai'i* 43 (2004): 53–69.

Jackson, Miles, ed. "They Followed the Trade Winds: African Americans in Hawai'i." Special issue, *Social Process in Hawai'i* 43 (2004).

Jackson, Shona. *Creole Indigeneity: Between Myth and Nation in the Caribbean*. Minneapolis: University of Minnesota Press, 2012.

Jayawardene, Sureshi. "Pushing the Paradigm: Locating Scholarship on the Siddis and Kaffirs." *Journal of Black Studies* 44, no. 7 (October 2013): 687–705.

Jay-Z. "Girls, Girls, Girls." On *The Blueprint*. New York: Def Jam and Roc-A-Fella, 2001.

Jha, Meeta Rani. *The Global Beauty Industry: Colorism, Racism, and the National Body*. New York: Routledge, 2016.

Johnson, E. Patrick. *Appropriating Blackness: Performance and the Politics of Authenticity*. Durham, NC: Duke University Press, 2003.

Johnson, E. Patrick. *Sweet Tea: Black Gay Men of the South*. Chapel Hill: University of North Carolina Press, 2008.

Johnson, Sylvester. *African American Religions, 1500–2000: Colonialism, Democracy, and Freedom*. New York: Cambridge University Press, 2015.

Johnston, Paul. "A Million Pounds of Sandalwood: The History of *Cleopatra's Barge* in Hawaii." *American Neptune* 62, no. 1 (2002): 5–45.

Jordan, Winthrop. "Historical Origins of the One-Drop Racial Rule in the United States." *Journal of Critical Mixed Race Studies* 1, no. 1 (2014). Edited by Paul Spickard. http://escholarship.org/uc/item/91g761b3.

Joseph, Peniel, ed. *The Black Power Movement: Rethinking the Civil Rights–Black Power Era*. New York: Routledge, 2006.

Joseph, Ralina. *Transcending Blackness: From the New Millennium Mulatta to the Exceptional Multiracial*. Durham, NC: Duke University Press, 2012.

Jung, Moon-Ho. *Coolies and Cane: Race, Labor, and Sugar in the Age of Emancipation.* Baltimore, MD: Johns Hopkins University Press, 2008.

"Jury Awards Former Queen's Nurse $3.8 Million in a Lawsuit." *KITV Island News.* https://www.kitv.com/story/37620573/jury-awards-former-queens-nurse-38-millionin-lawsuit.

Jutel, Olivier. "Remembering Dr. Teresia Teaiwa." *Wansolwara*, March 29, 2017. http://www.wansolwaranews.com/2017/03/29/remembering-dr-teresia-teaiwa.

Kabutaulaka, Tarcisius. "Re-presenting Melanesia: Ignoble Savages and Melanesian Alter-Natives." *Contemporary Pacific* 27, no. 1 (2015): 110–145.

Kajihiro, Kyle. "The Militarizing of Hawai'i: Occupation, Accommodation, and Resistance." In *Asian Settler Colonialism: From Local Governance to the Habits of Everyday Life in Hawai'i*, edited by Candace Fujikane and Jonathan Okamura, 170–194. Honolulu: University of Hawai'i Press, 2008.

Kajihiro, Kyle, and Terrilee Keko'olani. "The Hawai'i DeTour Project: Demilitarizing Sites and Sights on O'ahu." In *Detours: A Decolonial Guide to Hawai'i*, edited by Hōkūlani Aikau and Vernadette Gonzalez, 249–260. Durham, NC: Duke University Press, 2019.

Kalish, Richard. "A Comparison of Hawaiian and Mainland Attitudes towards the Negro." *Social Process in Hawai'i* 20 (1956): 16–22.

Ka'omea, Julie. "Reading Erasures and Making the Familiar Strange: Defamiliarizing Methods for Research in Formerly Colonized and Historically Oppressed Communities." *Educational Researcher* 32, no. 2 (2003): 14–23.

Karuka, Manu. "Black and Native Visions of Self-Determination." *Critical Ethnic Studies* 3, no. 2 (Fall 2017): 77–98.

Karuka, Manu. *Empire's Tracks: Indigenous Nations, Chinese Workers, and the Transcontinental Railroad.* Berkeley: University of California Press, 2019.

Kauai, Willy. "The Color of Nationality: Continuities and Discontinuities of Citizenship in Hawai'i." PhD diss., Political Science, University of Hawai'i at Mānoa, 2014.

Kauanui, J. Kēhaulani. "Colonialism in Equality: Hawaiian Sovereignty and the Question of U.S. Civil Rights." *South Atlantic Quarterly* 107, no. 4 (2008): 635–650.

Kauanui, J. Kēhaulani. "Diaspora Deracination and 'Off-Island' Hawaiians." *Contemporary Pacific* 19, no. 1 (2007): 137–160.

Kauanui, J. Kēhaulani. *Hawaiian Blood: Colonialism and the Politics of Sovereignty and Indigeneity.* Durham, NC: Duke University Press, 2008.

Kauanui, J. Kēhaulani. *Paradoxes of Hawaiian Sovereignty: Land, Sex, and the Colonial Politics of State Nationalism.* Durham, NC: Duke University Press, 2018.

Kauanui, J. Kēhaulani. "Resisting the Akaka Bill." In *A Nation Rising: Hawaiian Movements for Life, Land, and Sovereignty*, edited by Noelani Goodyear-Ka'ōpua, Ikaika Hussey, and Erin Kahunawaika'ala Wright, 312–330. Durham, NC: Duke University Press, 2014.

Kawelo, Hi'ilei. "Fishponds, Food, and the Future in Our Past." In *The Value of Hawai'i 2: Ancestral Roots, Oceanic Visions*, edited by Aiko Yamashiro and Noelani Goodyear-Ka'ōpua, 163–172. Honolulu: University of Hawai'i Press, 2014.

Keel, Terence. "Neanderthal-Human Hybridity and the Frontier of Critical Mixed Race Studies." In *Red and Yellow, Black and Brown: Decentering Whiteness in Mixed Race Studies*, edited by Joanne Rondilla, Rudy Guevarra Jr., and Paul Spickard, 201–218. New Brunswick, NJ: Rutgers University Press, 2017.

"Ke Kaulike He Haʻawina Kiwila—Civics, Hawaiian Style Curriculum." Ulukau.org, 1–109. http://ulukau.org.

Kelley, Darlene. "Keepers of the Culture, a Study in Time of the Hawaiian Islands, African Americans in Hawaiʻi." Statewide County HI Archives News, African Americans in Hawaiʻi, May 29, 2008.

Kelley, Robin. "The Rest of Us: Rethinking Settler and Native." *American Quarterly* 69, no. 2 (2017): 267–276.

Kennedy, Randall. *Nigger: The Strange Career of a Troublesome Word*. New York: Vintage Books, 2003.

Kent, Noel. *Hawaii: Islands under the Influence*. Honolulu: University of Hawaiʻi Press, 1993.

Khan-Cullors, Patrisse. "Interview with Pōpolo Project." Pōpolo Project, June 2018. Part 1, video posted to YouTube, September 2019, https://www.youtube.com/watch?v=2C2Kv6-8qJ8. Part 2, posted September 14, 2019, https://www.youtube.com/watch?v=Cr7_4oyrOO4.

Kiel, Doug. "Bleeding Out: Histories and Legacies of 'Indian Blood.'" In *The Great Vanishing Act: Blood Quantum and the Future of Native Nations*, edited by Kathleen Ratteree and Norbert Hill, 80–97. Golden, CO: Fulcrum, 2017.

Kiersz, Andy. "Here's How Much Land Military Bases Take Up in Each State." *Business Insider*, November 10, 2014. http://www.businessinsider.com/how-much-land-military-bases-take-up-in-each-state-2014-11.

Kikiloi, Kekuewa. "Rebirth of an Archipelago: Sustaining a Hawaiian Cultural Identity for People and Homeland." *Hūlili* 6 (2010): 73–115.

Kim, Jinah, and Nitasha Sharma, eds. "Interventions in Pacific Islands Studies and Trans-Pacific Studies." Special issue, *Critical Ethnic Studies* 7, no. 2 (November 2021).

King, Martin Luther, Jr. "Address to the House of Representatives of the First Legislature, State of Hawaii, on 17 September 1959." Honolulu, HI. Speech. The Martin Luther King Jr. Papers Project, Stanford University, 1959, 277–281.

King, Tiffany Lethabo. *The Black Shoals: Offshore Formations of Black and Native Studies*. Durham, NC: Duke University Press, 2019.

King, Tiffany Jeannette. "In the Clearing: Black Female Bodies, Space and Settler Colonial Landscapes." PhD diss., American Studies, University of Maryland, College Park, 2013.

King, Tiffany Lethabo. "New World Grammars: The 'Unthought' Black Discourses of Conquest." *Theory and Event* 19, no. 4 (2016). https://muse.jhu.edu/article/633275.

Klopotek, Brian. *Recognition Odysseys: Indigeneity, Race, and Federal Tribal Recognition Policy in Three Louisiana Indian Communities*. Durham, NC: Duke University Press, 2011.

Knowlton, Edgar, Jr. "Cabo Verde and Hawaiʻi." http://www.medesign.org/cv/Brava.html.

Knowlton, Edgar, Jr. "Notes on the Cape Verde Diaspora in Hawai'i." http://www.medesign.org/cv/Brava.html.

Kubo, Judy. "The Negro Soldier in Kahuku." *Social Process in Hawai'i* 9–10 (July 1945): 28–31.

Kubota, Gary. "Racism at Wailuku 'Really Wrong.'" *Honolulu Star-Bulletin*, December 17, 1998.

Labrador, Roderick. *Building Filipino Hawai'i*. Champaign: University of Illinois Press, 2015.

Labrador, Roderick. "'I no eat dog, k': Humor, Hazing, and Multicultural Settler Colonialism." In *Beyond Ethnicity: New Politics of Race in Hawai'i*, edited by Camilla Fojas, Rudy Guevarra Jr., and Nitasha Sharma, 61–77. Honolulu: University of Hawai'i Press, 2018.

Labrador, Roderick. "'We can laugh at ourselves': Hawai'i Ethnic Humor, Local Identity and the Myth of Multiculturalism." *Pragmatics* 14, nos. 2–3 (January 2004): 291–316.

Lacy, Ciara, dir. *Out of State*. United States: Strongman Films, 2017. DVD.

Lang, Cady. "Beer Named after Nuclear Testing Site Bikini Atoll Gets Called Out for Insensitivity." *Time*, August 16, 2019. https://time.com/5654254/bikini-atoll-manhattan-project-beer-company-controversy.

"Latest Census Data Looks at Hawaii's Racial Makeup: Aging Population." *Hawaii News Now*, June 25, 2015. https://www.hawaiinewsnow.com/story/29411958/latest-census-data-looks-at-hawaiis-racial-makeup-aging-population.

Lauer, Nancy Cook. "No Regrets from Kim after Questionable Comment." *Hawai'i Tribune Herald*, June 26, 2019. https://www.hawaiitribune-herald.com/2018/05/19/hawaii-news/no-regrets-from-kim-after-questionable-comment.

Lawrence, Charles, III. "Local Kine Implicit Bias: Unconscious Racism Revisited (Yet Again)." *University of Hawai'i Law Review* 37 (2015): 457–500.

Lawrence, Charles, and Mari Matsuda. "Column: Civil Disobedience Has Changed the Law." *Star Advertiser*, August 18, 2019. https://www.staradvertiser.com/2019/08/18/editorial/island-voices/civil-disobedience-has-changed-the-law.

Ledward, Brandon. "Inseparably Hapa: Making and Unmaking a Hawaiian Monolith." PhD diss., Anthropology, University of Hawai'i, 2007. ProQuest (663426640).

Ledward, Brandon. "On Being Hawaiian Enough: Contesting American Racialization with Native Hybridity." *Hūlili* 4, no. 1 (2007): 107–143.

Lee, Shelley, and Rick Baldoz. "'A Fascinating Interracial Experiment Station': Remapping the Orient-Occident Divide in Hawai'i." *American Studies* 49, nos. 3–4 (Fall–Winter, 2008): 87–109.

Lee, Suevon. "Thousands Show Up across Hawaii to Protest Racial Injustice." *Honolulu Civil Beat*, June 6, 2020. https://www.civilbeat.org/2020/06/thousands-show-up-across-hawaii-to-protest-racial-injustice.

Leonard, David. "High Tech Blackface: Race, Sports Video Games and Becoming the Other." In *Intelligent Agent* 4, no. 2 (2004): n.p. http://www.intelligentagent.com/archive/IA4_4gamingleonard.pdf.

Leonard, David. "It's Gotta Be the Body: Race, Commodity, and Surveillance of Contemporary Black Athletes." In *Studies in Symbolic Interaction*, edited by Norman Denzin, 165–190. Bingley, UK: Emerald Group, 2009.

Leong, Karen, and Myla Carpio. "Carceral States: Converging Indigenous and Asian Experiences in the Americas." Special issue, *Amerasia Journal* 42, no. 1 (2016): vii–xviii.

Leroy, Justin. "Black History in Occupied Territory: On the Entanglements of Slavery and Settler Colonialism." *Theory and Event* 19, no. 4 (2016). https://muse.jhu.edu/article/633276.

Liliʻuokalani. *Hawaii's Story by Hawaii's Queen*. 1898. Reprint, Honolulu: Mutual Publishing, 1991.

Liliʻuokalani, trans. *The Kumulipo: An Hawaiian Creation Myth*. Honolulu: Pueo Press, 1978.

Lipsitz, George. *The Possessive Investment in Whiteness: How White People Benefit from Identity Politics*. Philadelphia: Temple University Press, 2006.

Livingston, Gretchen, and Anna Brown. "Intermarriage in the U.S. 50 Years after *Loving v. Virginia*." *Pew Social Trends*, May 18, 2017. https://www.pewsocialtrends.org/2017/05/18/1-trends-and-patterns-in-intermarriage.

Lloyd, Lee. "A Brief Analysis of the Role and Status of the Negro in the Hawaiian Community." *American Sociological Review* 13, no. 4 (August 1948): 419–437.

Love, Eric. *Race over Empire: Racism and U.S. Imperialism, 1865–1900*. Chapel Hill: University of North Carolina Press, 2004.

Lowe, Lisa. *The Intimacies of Four Continents*. Durham, NC: Duke University Press, 2015.

Lucious, Bernard. "In the Black Pacific: Testimonies of Vietnamese Afro-Amerasian Displacements." In *Displacements and Diasporas: Asians in the Americas*, edited by Wanni Anderson and Robert Lee, 122–156. New Brunswick, NJ: Rutgers University Press, 2005.

Lyons, Kate. "#BeingMicronesian: Online Hatred Spurs Positive Fightback." *The Guardian*, October 6, 2018. https://www.theguardian.com/world/2018/oct/06/beingmicronesian-online-hatred-spurs-positive-fightback.

Lyons, Paul, and Ty Tengan. "Introduction: Pacific Currents." Special issue, *American Quarterly* 67, no. 3 (September 2015): 545–574.

Mahtani, Minelle. *Mixed Race Amnesia: Resisting the Romanticization of Multiraciality*. Vancouver, Canada: UBC Press, 2015.

Makalani, Minkah. "A Biracial Identity or a New Race? The Historical Limitations and Political Implications of a Biracial Identity." *Souls* 3, no. 4 (Fall 2001): 83–112.

Malo, Davida. *The Moʻolelo Hawaiʻi of Davida Malo: Ka ʻŌlelo Kumu*. Edited by Charles Langlas and Jeffrey Lyon. Honolulu: University of Hawaiʻi Press, 2020.

Man, Simeon. "Aloha, Vietnam: Race and Empire in Hawaiʻi's Vietnam War." *American Quarterly* 67, no. 4 (December 2015): 1085–1108.

Mawani, Renisa. *Across Oceans of Law: The Komagata Maru and Jurisdiction in the Time of Empire*. Durham, NC: Duke University Press, 2018.

McAvoy, Audrey. "Disgraced Hawaiʻi Tourism Leader Gets $290,000 Payout." *Seattle Times*, November 4, 2008. https://www.seattletimes.com/life/travel/disgraced-Hawai'i-tourism-leader-gets-290000-payout.

McDermott, John, and Naleen Naupaka Andrade. *People and Cultures of Hawaiʻi: The Evolution of Culture and Ethnicity*. Honolulu: University of Hawaiʻi Press, 2011.

McGhee, Fred L. "The Hidden History of the African Diaspora in Hawai'i." Paper presented at the Thirteenth Annual Symposium on Maritime Archaeology and History of Hawai'i and the Pacific, Hawai'i Maritime Center, Honolulu, Hawai'i, February 17–19, 2001.

Merry, Sally Engle. *Colonizing Hawai'i: The Cultural Power of Law*. Princeton, NJ: Princeton University Press, 2000.

Miles, Tiya. *The Dawn of Detroit: A Chronicle of Slavery and Freedom in the City of the Straits*. New York: New Press, 2019.

Miles, Tiya. *Ties That Bind: The Story of an Afro-Cherokee Family in Slavery and Freedom*. 2nd ed. Berkeley: University of California Press, 2015.

Miles, Tiya, and Sharon Holland. *Crossing Waters, Crossing Worlds: The African Diaspora in Indian Country*. New ed. Durham, NC: Duke University Press, 2006.

Miyares, Ines. "Expressing 'Local Culture' in Hawai'i." *Geographical Review* 98, no. 4 (2010): 513–533.

Mock, Janet. *Redefining Realness: My Path to Womanhood, Identity, Love and So Much More*. New York: Atria Books, 2014.

Moffett, Eileen. "Betsey Stockton: Pioneer American Missionary." *International Bulletin of Missionary Research* 19, no. 2 (April 1, 1995): 71–76.

Molina, Natalia. *How Race Is Made in America: Immigration, Citizenship, and the Historical Power of Racial Scripts*. Berkeley: University of California Press, 2014.

Moreton-Robinson, Aileen. "Race and Cultural Entrapment: Critical Indigenous Studies in the Twenty-First Century." In *Critical Indigenous Studies: Engagements in First World Locations*, edited by Aileen Moreton-Robinson, 102–118. Phoenix: University of Arizona Press, 2016.

Moreton-Robinson, Aileen. *The White Possessive: Property, Power, and Indigenous Sovereignty*. Minneapolis: University of Minnesota Press, 2015.

Moskos, Charles. "Success Story: Blacks in the Military." *The Atlantic*, May 1986. https://www.theatlantic.com/magazine/archive/1986/05/success-story-blacks-in-the-military/306160.

Mount, Guy. "Slavery, Migration, and Narratives of the Black Pacific." *Black Perspectives*, October 28, 2016. https://www.aaihs.org/slavery-migration-and-narratives-of-the-black-pacific.

Mowatt, Rasul, and Bryana French. "Black/Female/Body Hypervisibility and Invisibility: A Black Feminist Augmentation of Feminist Leisure Research." *Journal of Leisure Research* 45, no. 5 (Winter 2013): 644–660.

Mullen, Bill. *Afro-Orientalism*. Minneapolis: University of Minnesota Press, 2004.

Mullen, Bill, and Cathryn Watson, eds. *W. E. B. Du Bois on Asia: Crossing the World Color Line*. Jackson: University Press of Mississippi, 2005.

Nakamura, Tadashi, dir. *Mele Murals*. San Francisco: Center for Asian American Media, 2016. DVD.

Nash, Jennifer. *The Black Body in Ecstasy: Reading Race, Reading Pornography*. Durham, NC: Duke University Press, 2014.

Nash, Jennifer. *Black Feminism Reimagined: After Intersectionality*. Durham, NC: Duke University Press, 2019.

National Museum of the American Indian. "IndiVisible: African–Native American Lives in the Americas." November 13, 2009. https://americanindian.si.edu/exhibitions/indivisible/symposium.html.
Newton, Melanie. "Returns to a Native Land: Indigeneity and Decolonization in the Anglophone Caribbean." *Small Axe* 17, no. 2 (July 2013): 108–122.
Niheu, Soli Kihei. "Huli: Community Struggles and Ethnic Studies." Ibrahim Aoudé, guest ed. "The Ethnic Studies Story: Politics and Social Movements in Hawai'i." Special issue, *Social Process in Hawai'i* 39 (1999): 43–59.
Nordyke, Eleanor. "Blacks in Hawai'i: A Demographic and Historical Perspective." *Hawaiian Journal of History* 22 (1988): 241–255.
Obama, Barack. *Dreams from My Father: A Story of Race and Inheritance*. New York: Three Rivers Press, 2004.
Obama, Barack. "Interview with President Obama." Interview by Steve Kroft, *60 Minutes*, CBS News, December 10, 2011. https://www.cbsnews.com/news/interview-with-president-obama-the-full-transcript/.
Okamura, Jonathan. "Aloha Kanaka Me Ke Aloha 'Āina: Local Culture and Society in Hawaii." *Amerasia* 7, no. 2 (1980): 119–137.
Okamura, Jonathan. *Ethnicity and Inequality in Hawai'i*. Philadelphia: Temple University Press, 2008.
Okamura, Jonathan. *From Race to Ethnicity: Interpreting Japanese American Experiences in Hawai'i*. Honolulu: University of Hawai'i Press, 2014.
Okamura, Jonathan. "The Illusion of Paradise: Privileging Multiculturalism in Hawaii." In *Making Majorities: Constituting the Nation in Japan, Korea, China, Malaysia, Fiji, Turkey, and the United States*, edited by Dru Gladney, 264–284. Palo Alto, CA: Stanford University Press, 1998.
Okamura, Jonathan. "Race and/or Ethnicity in Hawai'i: What's the Difference and What Difference Does It Make?" In *Beyond Ethnicity: New Politics of Race in Hawai'i*, edited by Camilla Fojas, Rudy Guevarra Jr., and Nitasha Sharma, 94–113. Honolulu: University of Hawai'i Press, 2018.
Okamura, Jonathan. *Raced to Death in 1920s Hawai'i: Injustice and Revenge in the Fukunaga Case*. Champaign: University of Illinois Press, 2019.
Okamura, Jonathan. "Race Relations in Hawai'i during World War II: The Noninternment of Japanese Americans." *Amerasia Journal* 26, no. 2 (2000): 117–141.
Okamura, Jonathan. "Why There Are No Asian Americans in Hawai'i: The Continuing Significance of Local Identity." *Social Process in Hawai'i* 35 (1994): 161–178.
Okihiro, Gary. "Afterword: Toward a Black Pacific." In *AfroAsian Encounters: Culture, History, Politics*, edited by Heike Raphael-Hernandez and Shannon Steen, 313–330. New York: New York University Press, 2006.
Okihiro, Gary. *Island World: A History of Hawai'i and the United States*. Berkeley: University of California Press, 2008.
Okihiro, Gary. "Is Yellow Black or White?" In *Mainstreams: Asians in American History and Culture*. Seattle: University of Washington Press, 1994.
Okihiro, Gary. *Pineapple Culture: A History of the Tropical and Temperate Zones*. Berkeley: University of California Press, 2009.

Okino, Steve, dir. *Holding Fast the Dream: Hawai'i's African American Experience*. Produced by Lisa Altieri and presented by Miles Jackson. Honolulu: Wallace Alexander Gerbode Foundation; Hawai'i Council for the Humanities, 2010. Videodisc.

Omi, Michael, and Howard Winant. *Racial Formation in the United States: From the 1960s to the 1990s*. 2nd ed. New York: Routledge, 1994.

Ongiri, Amy. *Spectacular Blackness: The Cultural Politics of the Black Power Movement and the Search for a Black Aesthetic*. Charlottesville: University of Virginia Press, 2010.

Osorio, Jamaica. "E Iho ana 'o Luna, E Pi'ana 'o Lalo." Empowering Pacific Islander Communities. Public Zoom conversation, June 5, 2020.

Osorio, Jonathan Kamakawiwo'ole. *Dismembering Lāhui: A History of the Hawaiian Nation to 1887*. Honolulu: University of Hawai'i Press, 2002.

Osumare, Halifu. *The Africanist Aesthetic in Global Hip-Hop: Power Moves*. New York: Palgrave Macmillan, 2008.

painlessrisen. "What's It Like to Be a Black Man in Hawaii?" YouTube, August 12, 2012. Accessed 2013. http://www.youtube.com/watch?v=NNdYqHjaMpU.

Pang, Gordon. "Home Lands Suit to Proceed." *Honolulu Advertiser*, April 13, 2007. http://the.honoluluadvertiser.com/article/2007/Apr/13/ln/FP704130362.html.

Pattillo, Mary. *Black on the Block: The Politics of Race and Class in the City*. Chicago: University of Chicago Press, 2007.

Pattillo, Mary. *Black Picket Fences: Privilege and Peril among the Black Middle Class*. 2nd ed. Chicago: University of Chicago Press, 2013.

Penal Code of the Hawaiian Kingdom, Compiled from the Penal Code of 1850: And the Various Penal Enactments since Made, Pursuant to Act of the Legislative Assembly, The, June 22, 1868. Ebook. https://books.google.com.

Perry, Marc. *Negro Soy Yo: Hip Hop and Raced Citizenship in Neoliberal Cuba*. Durham, NC: Duke University Press, 2015.

Peter, Joakim, Wayne Tanaka, and Aiko Yamashiro. "Reconnecting Our Roots: Navigating the Turbulent Waters of Health-Care Policy for Micronesians in Hawai'i." In *Beyond Ethnicity: New Politics of Race in Hawai'i*, edited by Camilla Fojas, Rudy Guevarra Jr., and Nitasha Sharma. Honolulu: University of Hawai'i Press, 2018.

Pierce, Lori. "Creating a Racial Paradise: Citizenship and Sociology in Hawaii." In *Race and Nation: Ethnic Systems in the Modern World*, edited by Paul Spickard, 69–86. New York: Routledge, 2004.

Pierre, Jemima. "Black Immigrants in the United States and the 'Cultural Narratives' of Ethnicity." *Identities* 11, no. 2 (2004): 141–170.

Pignataro, Anthony. "Maui County Finally Honors Its African-American History." *Maui Time*, July 1, 2015. https://mauitime.com/culture/history/maui-county-finally-honors-its-african-american-history.

Poon, Oiyan, Megan Segoshi, Lilianne Tang, Kristen Surla, Caressa Nguyen, and Dian Squire. "Asian Americans, Affirmative Action, and the Political Economy of Racism: A Multidimensional Model of Raceclass Frames." *Harvard Educational Review* 89, no. 2 (Summer 2019): 201–226.

Pōpolo Project. "#PōpoloSyllabus." https://www.thepopoloproject.org/popolosyllabus.

Porter, Kenneth. "Notes on Negroes in Early Hawaii." *Journal of Negro History* 19, no. 2 (April 1934): 193–197.

"Programme for Patriotic Exercises in the Public Schools, Territory of Hawaii, Adopted by the Department of Public Instruction," 1906. *Hawaiian Kingdom* (blog), July 24, 2015. https://hawaiiankingdom.org/blog/denationalization-through-americanization.

Pualoa, Kelsie. "The Lineage of Language." *Flux*, October 2, 2018. https://fluxhawaii.com/the-lineage-of-language.

Pukui, Mary Kawena, and Samuel Elbert. *Hawaiian Dictionary: Hawaiian-English, English-Hawaiian*. Rev. ed. Honolulu: University of Hawai'i Press, 1986.

Ransby, Barbara. *Making All Black Lives Matter: Reimagining Freedom in the Twenty-First Century*. Oakland: University of California Press, 2018.

Raphael-Hernandez, Heike, and Shannon Steen, eds. *AfroAsian Encounters: Culture, History, Politics*. New York: New York University Press, 2006.

"Reaction Is Mixed to 'The Rock's' New Role as King Kamehameha." *Hawai'i News Now*, August 29, 2018. https://www.hawaiinewsnow.com/story/38988098/the-rock-to-the-king-dwayne-johnson-to-play-kamehameha-in-new-film.

Reddy, Vanita, and Anantha Sudhakar, eds. "Feminist and Queer Afro-Asian Formations." *S&F Online* 14, no. 3 (2018). http://sfonline.barnard.edu/feminist-and-queer-afroasian-formations.

Reed, Ishmael. "Ishmael Reed Interviews Kathryn Takara: Part 1 and Part 2." *Konch Magazine: An Ishmael Reed and Tennessee Reed Publication*, May 18–19, 2018. https://www.ishmaelreedpub.com.

Reynolds, George, and Amanda Shendruk. "Demographics of the U.S. Military." Council on Foreign Relations, April 24, 2018. https://www.cfr.org/article/demographics-us-military.

Richards, Leon. "Hawai'i: A Multicultural-Multiracial Society or a Fragile Myth? A Look at Contemporary Hawai'i from a Black Perspective Based on 2000 U.S. Census." In Miles Jackson, "They Followed the Trade Winds," 95–122.

Rifkin, Mark. *Fictions of Land and Flesh: Blackness, Indigeneity, and Speculation*. Durham, NC: Duke University Press, 2019.

Robertson, Martha L. "Storm at Kalaheo." *Honolulu Star-Bulletin*, August 25, 1997. http://archives.starbulletin.com/97/08/25/editorial/story1.html.

Rohrer, Judy. "'Got Race?': The Production of Haole and the Distortion of Indigeneity in the Rice Decision." *Contemporary Pacific* 18, no. 1 (2006): 1–31.

Rohrer, Judy. *Haoles in Hawai'i*. Honolulu: University of Hawai'i Press, 2010.

Rohrer, Judy. *Staking Claim: Settler Colonialism and Racialization in Hawai'i*. Tucson: University of Arizona Press, 2017.

Rokolekutu, Ponipate. "Heterogeneity, Race and Genealogical Connection of Spiritual Hinterlands." In "The Black Pacific: Forum, Critiques, Responses." Robbie Shilliam, February 7, 2016. https://robbieshilliam.wordpress.com/2016/02/07/the-black-pacific-forum-critiques-responses.

Rondilla, Joanne, Rudy Guevarra, and Paul Spickard, eds. *Red and Yellow, Black and Brown: Decentering Whiteness in Mixed Race Studies*. New Brunswick, NJ: Rutgers University Press, 2017.

Rondilla, Joanne, and Paul Spickard. *Is Lighter Better? Skin-Tone Discrimination among Asian-Americans*. New York: Rowman and Littlefield, 2017.

Rosa, John. *Local Story: The Massie-Kahahawai Case and the Culture of History*. Honolulu: University of Hawai'i Press, 2014.

Rosenthal, Gregory. *Beyond Hawai'i: Native Labor in the Pacific World*. Berkeley: University of California Press, 2018.

Rucker, Philip. "Hawaii's Influence on Barack Obama." *Washington Post*, January 2, 2009. https://www.washingtonpost.com/wp-dyn/content/article/2009/01/01/AR2009010102035.html.

Sai, Keanu. "The American Occupation of the Hawaiian Kingdom: Beginning the Transition from Occupied to Restored State." PhD diss., Political Science Department, University of Hawai'i, 2008.

Sakoda, Kent, and Jeff Siegel. *Pidgin Grammar: An Introduction to the Creole English of Hawaii*. Honolulu: Bess Press, 2003.

"Saltwater People Pool Party at the Hyatt Centric Waikiki." Photographs by Kat Wade, special to the *Star-Advertiser*, June 24, 2019. https://www.staradvertiser.com/out-and-about/saltwater-people-pool-party-hyatt-centric-waikiki.

"Samoan Population by County, Island and Census Tract in the State of Hawai'i: 2010." State of Hawai'i: Department of Business, Economic Development and Tourism Research and Economic Division Data Center, February 2012.

Saranillio, Dean. "Reflections on Late Identity: In Conversation with Melanie J. Newton, Nirmala Erevelles, Kim TallBear, Rinaldo Walcott, and Dean Itsuji Saranillio." Edited by Sam Spady. *Critical Ethnic Studies* 3, no. 1 (Spring 2017): 90–115.

Saranillio, Dean. *Unsustainable Empire: Alternative Histories of Hawai'i Statehood*. Durham, NC: Duke University Press, 2018.

Saranillio, Dean. "Why Asian Settler Colonialism Matters: A Thought Piece on Critiques, Debates, and Indigenous Difference." *Settler Colonial Studies* 3, nos. 3–4 (2013): 280–294.

Sato, Charlene. "Linguistic Inequality in Hawaii: The Post-Creole Dilemma." In *Language of Inequality*, edited by Nessa Wolfson and Joan Nanes, 256–272. Berlin: Mouton, 1985.

Schleitwiler, Vince. *Strange Fruit of the Black Pacific: Imperialism's Racial Justice and Its Fugitives*. New York: New York University Press, 2017.

Schmitt, Robert C. "Population Estimates and Censuses of Hawaii, 1778–1850." *Hawaii Historical Review* 1, no. 8 (July 1964): 143–154.

Schuessler, Jennifer. "Princeton to Name Two Campus Spaces in Honor of Slaves." *New York Times*, April 17, 2018. https://www.nytimes.com/2018/04/17/arts/princeton-to-name-two-campus-spaces-in-honor-of-slaves.html.

Scruggs, Marc. "Anthony D. Allen: A Prosperous American of African Descent in Early 19th Century Hawai'i." *Hawaiian Journal of History* 26 (1991): 55–93.

Scruggs, Marc. "'There Is One Black Man, Anthony D. Allen.'" In Miles Jackson, "They Followed the Trade Winds," 24–52.

Sexton, Jared. *Amalgamation Schemes: Antiblackness and the Critique of Multiracialism*. Minneapolis: University of Minnesota Press, 2008.

Sexton, Jared. "The Vel of Slavery: Tracking the Figure of the Unsovereign." *Critical Sociology* 42, nos. 4–5 (2014): 583–597.

Shah, Nayan. *Stranger Intimacy: Contesting Race, Sexuality and the Law in the North American West*. Berkeley: University of California Press, 2012.
Sharma, Miriam. "Ethnic Studies and Ethnic Identity: Challenges and Issues, 1970–1998." Ibrahim Aoudé, guest ed. "The Ethnic Studies Story: Politics and Social Movements in Hawai'i." Special issue, *Social Process in Hawai'i* 39 (1999): 19–42.
Sharma, Nandita. Review of *Asian Settler Colonialism*, edited by Candace Fujikane and Johathan Okamura. *Hawaiian Journal of History* 44 (2010): 107–110.
Sharma, Nitasha. *Hip Hop Desis: South Asian Americans, Blackness, and a Global Race Consciousness*. Durham, NC: Duke University Press, 2010.
Sharma, Nitasha. "Over Two Centuries: Black People in Nineteenth-Century Hawai'i." *American Nineteenth Century History* 20, no. 2 (2019): 115–140.
Sharma, Nitasha. "Pacific Revisions of Blackness: Race and Belonging in Hawai'i." *Amerasia Journal* 37, no. 3 (2011): 43–60.
Sharma, Nitasha. "The Racial Imperative: Rereading Hawai'i's History and Black-Hawaiian Relations though the Perspective of Black Residents." In *Beyond Ethnicity: New Politics of Race in Hawai'i*, edited by Camilla Fojas, Rudy Guevarra Jr., and Nitasha Sharma, 114–138. Honolulu: University of Hawai'i Press, 2018.
Sharma, Nitasha. "Rap, Race, Revolution: Post 9/11 Brown and a Hip Hop Critique of Empire." In *Audible Empire: Music, Global Politics, Critique*, edited by Ronald Radano and Tejumola Olaniyan, 292–313. Durham, NC: Duke University Press, 2017.
Shilliam, Robbie. *The Black Pacific: Anti-Colonial Struggle and Oceanic Connections*. London: Bloomsbury Academic, 2015.
Silva, Noenoe. *Aloha Betrayed: Native Hawaiian Resistance to American Colonialism*. Durham, NC: Duke University Press, 2004.
Silva, Noenoe. "The Political Economy of Banning the Hula." *Hawaiian Journal of History* 34 (2000): 29–48.
Silva, Noenoe. *The Power of the Steel-Tipped Pen: Reconstructing Native Hawaiian Intellectual History*. Durham, NC: Duke University Press, 2017.
Simonson, Douglas, Pat Sasaki, and Ken Sakata. *Peppo's Pidgin to da Max*. Honolulu: Bess Press, 1981.
Simpson, Audra. *Mohawk Interruptus: Political Life across the Borders of Settler States*. Durham, NC: Duke University Press, 2014.
Simpson, Leanne. *As We Have Always Done: Indigenous Freedom through Radical Resistance*. 3rd ed. Minneapolis: University of Minnesota Press, 2017.
Smallwood, Stephanie. "Reflections on Settler Colonialism, the Hemispheric Americas, and Chattel Slavery." *William and Mary Quarterly* 76, no. 3 (July 2019): 407–416.
Smallwood, Stephanie. *Saltwater Slavery: A Middle Passage from Africa to American Diaspora*. Cambridge, MA: Harvard University Press, 2008.
Smith, Andrea. "The Colonialism That Is Settled and the Colonialism That Never Happened." *Decolonization: Indigeneity, Education and Society*, June 20, 2014. https://decolonization.wordpress.com/2014/06/20/the-colonialism-that-is-settled-and-the-colonialism-that-never-happened.
Smith, Andrea. "Heteropatriarchy and the Three Pillars of White Supremacy: Rethinking Women of Color Organizing." In *Color of Violence: The INCITE! Anthology*,

edited by INCITE! Women of Color against Violence, 66–73. Durham, NC: Duke University Press, 2016.

Smith, Andrea. "Native Studies Workshop." African American Studies, Northwestern University, May 5, 2015.

Smith, Clay, Jr. *Emancipation: The Making of the Black Lawyer, 1844–1944*. Philadelphia: University of Pennsylvania Press, 1993.

Smyth, Heather. "The Black Atlantic Meets the Black Pacific: Multimodality in Kamau Brathwaite and Wayde Compton." *Callaloo* 37, no. 2 (Spring 2014): 389–403.

Snorton, C. Riley. *Black on Both Sides: A Racial History of Trans Identity*. Minneapolis: University of Minnesota Press, 2017.

Snow, Jade. "Portraits of Gender and Sexual Identities in the Hawaiian Community." *Honolulu*, May 14, 2019. http://www.honolulumagazine.com/Honolulu-Magazine/June-2019/Portraits-of-Gender-and-Sexual-Identities-in-the-Hawaiian-Community.

Solis, Gabriel. "The Black Pacific: Music and Racialization in Papua New Guinea and Australia." *Critical Sociology* 41, no. 2 (2015): 297–312.

Southern Workman and Hampton School Record (Hampton, VA: Hampton Normal and Agricultural Institute) 29, no. 1 (1900): 452–453.

Spady, Sam. "Reflections on Late Identity: In Conversation with Melanie J. Newton, Nirmala Erevelles, Kim TallBear, Rinaldo Walcott, and Dean Itsuji Saranillio." *Critical Ethnic Studies* 3, no. 1 (Spring 2017): 90–115.

Stannard, David. *Before the Horror: The Population of Hawaii on the Eve of Western Contact*. Honolulu: University of Hawaiʻi Press, 1989.

Stannard, David. "The Hawaiians: Health, Justice, and Sovereignty." In *Asian Settler Colonialism: From Local Governance to the Habits of Everyday Life in Hawaiʻi*, edited by Candace Fujikane and Jonathan Okamura, 161–169. Honolulu: University of Hawaiʻi Press, 2008.

Stannard, David. *Honor Killing: Race, Rape, and Clarence Darrow's Spectacular Last Case*. New York: Penguin Books, 2006.

Stark, Heidi. "Criminal Empire: The Making of the Savage in a Lawless Land." *Theory and Event* 19, no. 4 (2016). https://www.muse.jhu.edu/article/633282.

State of Hawaiʻi. "Samoan Population by County, Island and Census Tract in the State of Hawaiʻi: 2010." Department of Business, Economic Development and Tourism Research and Economic Division Data Center, February 2012.

Stinton, Eric. "Black History in Hawaii: From Whaling Ships to Royal Courts." KHON, February 6, 2020. https://www.khon2.com/hidden-history/black-history-month/black-history-in-hawaii-from-whaling-ships-to-royal-courts.

Stinton, Eric. "Black Identity in Hawaii: The Conflicting Experiences of Being Black and Local." KHON, February 29, 2020. https://www.khon2.com/hidden-history/black-history-month/black-identity-in-hawaii-the-conflicting-experiences-of-being-black-and-local.

Stinton, Eric. "Black Music in Hawaii: Hip-Hop's Hawaii Connection." KHON, February 28, 2020. https://www.khon2.com/hidden-history/black-history-month/black-music-in-hawaii-hip-hops-hawaii-connection.

Stockton, Betsey. Journal, Hawaii, November 20, 1822–July 4, 1823. African-American Religion: A Historical Interpretation with Representative Documents. https://aardoc.sites.amherst.edu/Betsey_Stockton_Journal_1.html.

Stone, David Harada. "The Tragic Killing of Kollin Elderts by Christopher Deedy Echoes Trayvon Martin Case." *Daily Banter*, August 5, 2013. https://thedailybanter.com/2013/08/05/the-tragic-killing-of-kollin-elderts-by-christopher-deedy-echoes-trayvon-martin-case.

"Success Story of One Minority Group in U.S." *U.S. News and World Report*, December 26, 1966.

Sumida, Stephen. *And the View from the Shore: Literary Traditions of Hawai'i*. Seattle: University of Washington Press, 1991.

Sundstrom, Ronald. "Being and Being Mixed Race." *Social Theory and Practice* 27, no. 2 (April 2001): 285–307.

Takaki, Ronald. *Pau Hana: Plantation Life and Labor in Hawaii, 1835–1920*. Honolulu: University of Hawai'i Press, 1984.

Takara, Kathryn. "The African Diaspora in Nineteenth-Century Hawai'i." In Miles Jackson, "They Followed the Trade Winds," 1–23.

Takara, Kathryn. *Frank Marshall Davis: The Fire and the Phoenix; A Critical Biography*. Ka'a'awa, HI: Pacific Raven Press, 2012.

Takara, Kathryn. "Frank Marshall Davis in Hawai'i: Outsider Journalist Looking In." *Social Process in Hawai'i* 39 (1999): 126–144.

Takara, Kathryn, comp. *Oral Histories of African Americans*. Center for Oral History, University of Hawai'i, 1990.

Takara, Kathryn. *Pacific Raven: Hawai'i Poems*. Ka'a'awa, HI: Pacific Raven Press, 1979.

Takara, Kathryn [Kay Brundage]. "Who Is the Black Woman in Hawaii?" In *Montage: An Ethnic History of Women in Hawaii*, edited by Nancy Foon Young and Judy Parish. Honolulu: General Assistance Center for the Pacific, College of Education, Educational Foundations and State Commission on the Status of Women, 1977.

Taketani, Etsuko. *The Black Pacific Narrative: Geographic Imaginings of Race and Empire between the World Wars*. Lebanon, NH: Dartmouth College Press, 2014.

Tamura, Eileen. "The English-Only Effort, the Anti-Japanese Campaign, and Language Acquisition in the Education of Japanese Americans in Hawaii, 1915–1940." *History of Education Quarterly* 33, no. 1 (1993): 37–58.

Taylor, Keeanga-Yamahtta. *From #BlackLivesMatter to Black Liberation*. Chicago: Haymarket Books, 2016.

Taylor, Keeanga-Yamahtta. *Race for Profit: How Banks and the Real Estate Industry Undermined Black Homeownership*. Chapel Hill: University of North Carolina Press, 2019.

Teaiwa, Teresia. "The Ancestors We Get to Choose: White Influences I Won't Deny." In *Theorizing Native Studies*, edited by Audra Simpson and Andrea Smith, 43–55. Durham, NC: Duke University Press, 2014.

Teaiwa, Teresia. "bikinis and other s/pacific n/oceans." *Contemporary Pacific* 6, no. 1 (Spring 1994): 87–109.

Teaiwa, Teresia. "Black and Blue in the Pacific: Afro-Diasporic Women Artists on History and Blackness." *Amerasia Journal* 43, no. 1 (2017): 145–146.

Teaiwa, Teresia. "Black in the Blue Pacific (for Mohit and Riyad)." *Social and Economic Studies* 56, nos. 1–2 (March–June 2007): 13.

Teaiwa, Teresia. "Militarism, Tourism, and the Native: Articulations in Oceania." PhD diss., History of Consciousness, University of California, Santa Cruz, 2001.

Teaiwa, Teresia. "Postscript: Reflections on Militourism, US Imperialism, and American Studies." *American Quarterly* 68, no. 3 (September 2016): 847–853.

Teaiwa, Teresia, and Dale Husband. "You Can't Paint the Pacific with Just One Brush Stroke." *E-Tangata*, October 25, 2015. https://e-tangata.co.nz/news/you-cant-paint-the-pacific-with-just-one-brush-stroke.

Teale, Laulani. "Why I Am Boycotting the MLK Parade 2018 in Honolulu and Ask That You Do So, Too." *Iolani* 6, no. 686 (January 14, 2018). http://iolani-theroyalhawk.blogspot.com/2018/01/vol-vi-no-686-part-2.html.

Tengan, Ty. "Embattled Stories of Occupied Hawai'i." In *At Home in the Field: Ethnographic Encounters in Asia and the Pacific Islands*, edited by Suzanne Finney, Mary Mostafanezhad, Guido Pigliasco, and Forrest Wade Young, 246–252. Honolulu: University of Hawai'i Press, 2015.

Tengan, Ty. "The Mana of Kū: Indigenous Nationhood, Masculinity and Authority in Hawai'i." In *New Mana: Transformations of a Classic Concept in Pacific Languages and Cultures*, edited by Matt Tomlinson and Ty Tengan, 55–76. Acton, ACT: Australian University Press, 2016.

Tengan, Ty. *Native Men Remade: Gender and Nation in Contemporary Hawai'i*. Durham, NC: Duke University Press, 2008.

Tengan, Ty. "Re-membering Panalā'au: Masculinities, Nation, and Empire in Hawai'i and the Pacific." *Contemporary Pacific* 20, no. 1 (2008): 27–53.

Tengan, Ty, and Jessie Markham. "Performing Polynesian Masculinities in American Football: From 'Rainbows to Warriors.'" *International Journal of the History of Sport* 26, no. 16 (2009): 2412–2431.

Terrell, Jessica. "OffShore: Hawaii's Not Always Paradise." *Honolulu Civil Beat Podcast*, October 13, 2016. https://itunes.apple.com/us/id1161597030?mt=2.

Teves, Stephanie Nohelani. "'Bloodline Is All I Need': Defiant Indigeneity and Hawaiian Hip-Hop." *American Indian Culture and Research Journal* 35, no. 4 (2011): 73–101.

Teves, Stephanie Nohelani. *Defiant Indigeneity: The Politics of Hawaiian Performance*. Chapel Hill: University of North Carolina Press, 2018.

Thomas, Ashleigh-Rae. "Who Is a Settler, According to Indigenous and Black Scholars." *Vice*, February 15, 2019. https://www.vice.com/en_us/article/gyajj4/who-is-a-settler-according-to-indigenous-and-black-scholars.

"Thomas McCants Stewart." Reprint from *Negro Times*. *Negro World*, January 27, 1923.

Tinsley, Omise'eke Natasha. "Extract from 'Water, Shoulders, into the Black Pacific.'" *GLQ: A Journal of Lesbian and Gay Studies* 18, nos. 2–3 (2012): 263–276.

Trask, Haunani-Kay. "The Birth of the Modern Hawaiian Movement: Kalama Valley, O'ahu." *Hawaiian Journal of History* 21 (1987): 126–153.

Trask, Haunani-Kay. "Feminist and Indigenous Hawaiian Nationalism." *Signs: Journal of Women in Culture and Society* 21, no. 4 (1996): 906–916.

Trask, Haunani-Kay. *From a Native Daughter: Colonialism and Sovereignty in Hawaiʻi*. Honolulu: University of Hawaiʻi Press, 1999.

Trask, Haunani-Kay. "Settlers of Color and 'Immigrant' Hegemony: Locals in Hawaiʻi." *Amerasia* 26, no. 2 (2000): 1–26.

Trenka, Jane Jeong, Julia Chinyere Oparah, and Sun Yung Shin, eds. *Outsiders Within: Writings on Transracial Adoption*. Cambridge, MA: South End Press, 2006.

Tsai, Michael. "All We Want Is to Be Recognized as Human Beings." *Honolulu Star Advertiser*, June 1, 2020. https://www.staradvertiser.com/2020/06/01/hawaii-news/all-we-want-is-to-be-recognized-as-human-beings/?HSA=f5706431d514d0d9da2e9b7808f1a20d502eded5.

Tuck, Eve, Allison Guess, and Hannah Sultan. "Not Nowhere: Collaborating on the Selfsame Land." *Decolonization: Indigeneity, Education and Society*, June 26, 2014. https://decolonization.wordpress.com/2014/06/26/not-nowhere-collaborating-on-selfsame-land.

Tuck, Eve, and K. Wayne Yang. "Decolonization Is Not a Metaphor." *Decolonization: Indigeneity, Education and Society* 1, no. 1 (2012): 1–40.

"2011 State of Hawaii Data Book." Department of Business, Economic Development and Tourism. https://dbedt.hawaii.gov/economic/databook/db2011.

Uperesa, Faʻanofo Lisaclaire. "Fabled Futures and Gridiron Dreams: Migration and Mobility for Samoans in American Football." *Contemporary Pacific* 26, no. 2 (2014): 281–301.

Velasquez-Manoff, Moises. Photographs by Damon Winter. "Want to Be Less Racist? Move to Hawaii." Opinion. *New York Times*, June 28, 2019. https://www.nytimes.com/2019/06/28/opinion/sunday/racism-hawaii.html.

Vinacke, W. Edgar. "Stereotyping among National-Racial Groups in Hawaii: A Study of Ethnocentrism." *Journal of Social Psychology* 30, no. 2 (1949): 265–291.

Vizenor, Gerald, ed. *Survivance: Narratives of Native Presence*. Lincoln: University of Nebraska Press, 2008.

Walcott, Rinaldo. "Reflections on Late Identity: In Conversation with Melanie J. Newton, Nirmala Erevelles, Kim TallBear, Rinaldo Walcott, and Dean Itsuji Saranillio." Edited by Sam Spady. *Critical Ethnic Studies* 3, no. 1 (Spring 2017): 90–115.

Walker, Isaiah Helekunihi. "Hui Nalu, Beachboys, and the Surfing Boarder-Lands of Hawaiʻi." *Contemporary Pacific* 20, no. 1 (2008): 89–113.

Wallace, Don. "Hawaiʻi Football Is Hot Right Now—Here's Why It's Headed for Trouble." *Honolulu*, February 2, 2018. http://www.honolulumagazine.com/Honolulu-Magazine/February-2018/Hawaii-Football-is-Hot-Right-Now-Heres-Why-Its-Headed-for-Trouble.

Walsh, Kenneth. "Obama's Hawaiian Roots Help Shape His Political Beliefs." *US News and World Report*, May 30, 2008. https://www.usnews.com/news/campaign-2008/articles/2008/05/30/obamas-hawaiian-roots-help-shape-his-political-beliefs.

Wang, Oliver. *Legions of Boom: Filipino American Mobile DJ Crews in the San Francisco Bay Area*. Durham, NC: Duke University Press, 2015.

Warren, Joyce Pualani. "Theorizing Pō: Embodied Cosmogony and Polynesian National Narratives." PhD diss., English, University of California, Los Angeles, 2017.

Webb-Binder, Bernida. "Affinities and Affiliations: Black Pacific Art in Aotearoa/New Zealand, 1948–2008." PhD diss., History of Art and Archaeology, Cornell University, 2016.
Weheliye, Alexander. *Phonographies: Grooves in Sonic Afro-Modernity*. Durham, NC: Duke University Press, 2015.
Wilderson, Frank, III. *Afropessimism*. New York: Liveright, 2020.
Wilderson, Frank, III. *Afro-pessimism: An Introduction*. With Saidiya Hartman, Steve Martinot, Jared Sexton, and Hortense Spillers. Minneapolis: Racked and Dispatched, 2017.
Wilderson, Frank, III. Interview with C. S. Soon in "Blacks and the Master/Slave Relation 2015." In *Afro-pessimism: An Introduction*, 15–30. Minneapolis: Racked and Dispatched, 2017.
Wilderson, Frank, III. *Red, White and Black: Cinema and the Structure of U.S. Antagonisms*. Durham, NC: Duke University Press, 2010.
Williams-Leon, Teresa, and Cynthia Nakashima. *The Sum of Our Parts: Mixed-Heritage Asian Americans*. Philadelphia: Temple University Press, 2001.
Wolfe, Patrick. "Recuperating Binarism: A Heretical Introduction." *Settler Colonial Studies* 3, nos. 3–4 (2013): 257–279.
Wolfe, Patrick. "Settler Colonialism and the Elimination of the Native." *Journal of Genocide Research* 8, no. 4 (2006): 387–409.
Wooten, Andre. "Slavery Still Haunts Us at Kalaheo." View Point. *Honolulu Star-Bulletin*, July 19, 1997. http://archives.starbulletin.com/97/07/21/editorial/viewpoints.html.
Wright, Michelle. *The Physics of Blackness: Beyond the Middle Passage Epistemology*. Minneapolis: University of Minnesota Press, 2015.
Wynes, Charles E. "T. McCants Stewart: Peripatetic Black South Carolinian." *South Carolina Historical Magazine* 80, no. 4 (October 1979): 311–317.
Yamamoto, Eric. "The Significance of Local." *Social Process in Hawaii* 27 (1979): 101–115.
Yin, Alice. "Mothers Against Senseless Killings Reclaims Corner Where 2 Women Were Shot Dead." *Chicago Tribune*, July 29, 2019. https://www.chicagotribune.com/news/breaking/ct-breaking-activist-mothers-grieve-2-killed-shooting-mask-20190729-g5djgygdiffevgmvn3hh3vuwry-story.html.
Young, Harvey. *Embodying Black Experience: Stillness, Critical Memory, and the Black Body*. Ann Arbor: University of Michigan Press, 2012.
Young, Nancy Foon, and Judy Parish, eds. *Montage: An Ethnic History of Women in Hawaii*. Honolulu: General Assistance Center for the Pacific, College of Education, Educational Foundations and State Commission on the Status of Women, 1977.
Young, Peter. "Anthony D. Allen." December 2012. http://totakeresponsibility.blogspot.com/2012/12/anthony-d-allen.html.
Young, Peter. "Carlotta." *Images of Old Hawaii*, December 9, 2015. http://imagesofoldhawaii.com/carlotta.
Yuen, Stacy. "Which Ethnic Group Makes the Most Money?" *Hawai'i Business*, October 2013. http://www.hawaiibusiness.com/which-ethnic-group-makes-the-most-money.
Zack, Naomi. *Race and Mixed Race*. Philadelphia: Temple University Press, 1994.

INDEX

Abe, Shirley: on wanting to live in Hawai'i to escape mainland racism, 152
Abercrombie, Neil, 293n40; and racial distinction in politics, 144
access (and lack of): to beaches, 63, 225, 228; to Black community/family/Metropolis, 3, 33, 72, 75, 95-96, 101, 106-17, 124, 134-35, 144, 153-62, 164-65, 170, 188, 261, 265-66; to care, 211, 281n55; to civil rights, 49; to cultural resources, 91, 164, 171; to land/material resources, 21, 17, 73, 82, 144, 173, 175, 199, 230, 236-37, 240, 244, 266-67, 281n55, 283n9, 288n136, 297n88; to nature, 141; to power, 127, 165; to Whiteness, 78, 82. *See also* Hawaiian Homes Commission Act
Adams, John Quincy: on the blackness of diplomat Timoteo Ha'alilio, 48
Adams, Romanzo: on historical identification of Black people in Hawai'i, 42; and the sociological study of Hawai'i, 12, 20, 59-60
adoption, transracial, 77-78, 90, 95-96, 99, 103, 155, 188, 242, 293n40; assumption of, 102
AF3IRM Hawai'i, 215, 254-55
African American Lawyers Association (AALA), 157, 192-93, 202. *See also* Barbee-Wooten, Daphne; Wooten, Andre
Afropessimism, 80, 128, 271; and Black abjection, 126, 231-32, 253, 264; and Black-only spaces, 263; and the erasure of Native peoples, 221
agency: Black, 16, 25-26, 64, 69, 123, 125-27, 224-27, 231-32, 264; of mothers, 91-92; Native Hawaiian, 22, 283n3; of Barack Obama, 127, 252
Aikau, Hōkūlani: on Kanaka experiences abroad, 48; on kuleana, 27. *See also* kuleana (rights/responsibilities)
Akaka Bill, 47, 236, 285n58
Alexander, Michelle: on contemporary incarceration (and the legacy of slavery), 227; on systemic racism against the African American community, 200
Allen, Anthony, 59, 152; and King Kamehameha, 45, 69, 250-51
Allen, Chadwick: on a "trans-Indigenous" method for a "global Native literacy," 258
Amos, Wally: on Hawai'i, 67
Andrews, Courtney-Savali, 15

annexation of Hawai'i, 12, 38, 40-41, 44-46, 51, 59-61, 117, 230-31, 283n14. *See also* Hawai'i; Kingdom of Hawai'i
Anthony, Daniel: on the revitalization of Hawaiian land-based practices, 160, 245.
Aotearoa/New Zealand, 29, 61, 127; and the Polynesian Panthers, 5, 269; and Rastafarianism, 18
apology: to Native Hawaiians (by the US) for the overthrow of the Kingdom of Hawai'i, 236, 283n14; for quotation of racial slurs, 178-79; refusal of an, 198-99; as suggested in lieu of legal action, 192
appropriation: of Black culture, 3-6, 67, 284n30; of Hawaiian culture, 67, 99, 166, 224; of Maori culture, 131, 293n28
Arbery, Ahmaud: murder of, 33
Arista, Noelani: on racial classification in Hawai'i, 46
Armstrong, Clarissa: on the use of the term "nika," 43. *See also* racial slurs
Armstrong, General Samuel, 285n49, 296n73
Arvin, Maile: on the imposition of blood quantum laws, 97; on kapu aloha, 200; on support for an independent Hawai'i, 235. *See also* blood quantum; kapu aloha
Asian settler colonialism, 6, 22-25, 35, 38, 52-54, 59, 77, 123-27, 154, 164, 199, 233, 247, 254, 265; Asian settler allies, 238-39. *See also* settler colonialism
assimilation/integration: of Black people in Hawai'i, 52, 68-69, 154, 246-48; of Cape Verdean sailors, 44; and the "logic of elimination," 221; into patriotic Americans, 173, 186, 190-91, 269. *See also* marriage, interracial
Austin, Lloyd, 224. *See also* military
Australians, Indigenous: and identification with Blackness, 18-19, 61, 256-57, 269

Baldoz, Rick: on early sociological study of Hawai'i, 12
Baldwin, Dwight: on the "blackness" of native Hawaiians, 50
Balibar, Étienne: on "neoracism," 186-87
Ball, Alice, 68; Ball Method treatment of Hansen's disease, 56
Ballard, Susan, 207, 209. *See also* police

Barbee-Wooten, Daphne, 68, 157, 202; on the legal work of T. McCants Stewart, 55. *See also* African American Lawyers Association (AALA)

Bayonet Constitution, 40–41, 49

belonging, 233–60; and exploitation, 23–24; and food, 91, 102; and genealogy, 34–35, 82, 118; and hair, 38, 98, 164, 187, 160, 116, 232–33; and knowledge, 21, 103, 155, 157; to the land, 242–46. *See also* epistemologies: Kanaka; genealogy; self-identification; we-ness

Big Teeze, 68

Bikini Atoll, 227

Black: abjection, 126, 231–32, 253, 264; agency, 16, 25–26, 64, 69, 123, 125–27, 224–27, 231–32, 264; "authenticity," 21, 104, 109, 112–13, 116, 118–19, 144, 153, 262; community/family/Metropolis, 3, 33, 72, 75, 95–96, 101, 106–17, 124, 134–35, 144, 153–62, 164–65, 170, 188, 261, 265–66; culture, 3–6, 16–17, 19–20, 23, 68, 105–17; deviance, 178; dislocation, 25; erasure, 1–11, 18, 36, 54, 59, 61, 171, 173–74, 202, 211–13; as expansive category, 71–119, 211, 218, 256–57, 261, 264; "foreign black," 42–43; invisibility, 1–11, 14, 20–21, 23, 26, 34–35, 37, 41–42, 66, 69, 72, 86–104, 118, 122, 124, 151, 154–56, 162, 171–72, 191, 214, 230, 263, 265–66, 293n43; luminosity/hypervisibility, 151, 171–72, 293n43; missionaries, 45; politics, 5, 17, 19–20, 111, 162, 263, 268–74; *as* politics, 273; settlers, 35, 126, 164, 173–77, 223, 238, 242, 264; stereotypes, 5, 8, 19, 52, 64, 180, 210, 226, 229–30, 296n48; as term, 42–43. *See also* Black Lives Matter movement; Black and Native relations; Black/White binary; Black Pacific; Black Panthers; Blackness; Movement for Black Lives

Black Atlantic, 10, 18, 37–38, 41, 44–46, 80, 130, 213, 263, 284n37. *See also* Black Pacific; Middle Passage

Black Lives Matter movement, 3–6, 33, 36, 159, 168–70, 188, 205–7, 212, 217–18, 254–60, 262, 268, 271, 279n13. *See also* Black; Blackness; Movement for Black Lives

Black and Native relations, 6–9, 23–27, 61–62, 95, 126–27, 173–77, 187, 223, 217–61

Black Pacific, 17–20, 41, 46, 49. *See also* Black Atlantic; racial division of the Pacific

Black Panthers, 5, 269–70, 272–73. *See also* Polynesian Panthers

Black/White binary, 16–22, 38, 52, 58, 70–71, 75–77, 103, 116–17, 120–21, 124, 135, 138, 142, 148–49, 163–64, 170, 197–98, 220, 225–26, 249, 261, 263, 265, 268

Blackness: for Black locals, 105–19; as cultural, 104–17, 242; denial of ("You're not Black"), 104, 116, 144, 222; "earning," 116, 118; escape from, 1, 3, 80, 146, 151–53, 291n55; as ethnicity, 104; expansive, 71–119, 211, 218, 256–57, 261, 264; media depictions of, 110–18, 178, 229; as "not-from-hereness," 87; performed, 113, 116–17, 141–42, 153, 162; and royalty, 50, 73. *See also* Black; Black Lives Matter movement; Black Pacific; Black Panthers; Movement for Black Lives

Bland, Sandra: death of (and resulting #SayHerName movement), 206

Blanding, Don: poetry of, 56–58; "Tutu," 58

blood quantum, 39, 44, 48, 81, 96–100, 104, 173; and access to resources, 21, 73, 173, 219, 244, 266–67, 283n9, 288n136. *See also* Hawaiian Homes Commission Act; hypodescent ("one-drop rule"); racial science

Bright, Reverend Andrew Iaukea: genealogical identification of, 49

Bright, Sol, 49

Brockman, Aozora, 149

Broussard, Albert: on the relative racial tolerance of Hawai'i, 152

Brown, Michael: police murder of (and resultant activism), 206

Brown, Simone: on the surveillance of Blackness, 171–72

Bub, Heidi: *Daughter from Danang*, 188. *See also* adoption, transracial

Bunche, Ralph, 56–58, 287n120

Byrd, Jodi: on Black "arrivants," 127; on bell hooks's framing of White and Black paradigms, 176; on the insistence on difference by some Hawaiians, 251

Caldwell, Ethan, 202, 301n63; on "the colonized-colonizer paradox," 69, 231

Carpio, Myla: on the carceral state, 174; on colonization and relationality, 37; on immigrant complicity in Native dispossession, 24

census, 32, 39, 45, 49, 51–52, 54, 60–61, 65–66, 69, 70–71, 86, 280n27, 280n29, 284nn38–39; and multiracialism, 3, 34, 60, 66, 71, 75, 76, 80, 88, 290n11. *See also* demographics

Chang, David: on marriages between Hawaiians and Native Americans, 48. *See also* marriage, interracial

Chang, Sharon: on multiracial children and anti-Black racism, 178. *See also* multiracialism

"chip on the shoulder" of Black people (according to some locals), 36, 111, 116, 149, 192–93, 198, 211, 240, 277. *See also* localness

Choy, Mary: on the roots of her activism, 269; on supporting an independent Hawaiian nation, 239

citizenship: vs. ancestry, 49, 61–62; in the Kingdom of Hawai'i, 35, 39, 43–44, 49, 60–62, 173, 219, 265, 286n73

Clark, Kenneth: on Black household wealth in Hawaiʻi, 13
class: and Black locals, 88, 119; and Black military men, 69; and Black transplants, 121–22, 196; and police protection, 209; and racism, 196; and self-determination, 36, 139, 238–39, 241, 264
Cleveland, Grover, 48; on the 1893 coup in Hawaiʻi, 12, 40
Clifford, James, 273
Coates, Ta-Nehisi: and learning about Blackness in Pacific sites, 256; on Obama's "blackness quotient," 76
Cocoa Collective, 158, 160
colorism, 179, 187–88. *See also* racism
complicity: in antiBlack racism, 215, 222; in imperialism, 227; in Native dispossession, 22–25, 69, 123, 125, 223–26, 264; in Native erasure, 174; in slavery, 174, 222; in White supremacy, 178. *See also* kuleana (rights/responsibilities)
Cook, James, 44, 274
Cooke, Amos Starr, 45
Cox, Carroll: on institutional racism in Hawaiʻi, 196–97
Crockett, William F. (the elder): and the representation of Black plantation workers, 287n114
Crockett, William F. (the younger), 287n114, 297n90. *See also* Lingle, Linda
Cullors, Patrisse. *See* Khan-Cullors, Patrisse

dance: hula, 28–30, 58, 68, 136, 150, 187, 218, 242, 245, 269; and masculinity, 131–32, 293n28; and the tourism industry, 228
Davis, Angela, 269, 273; on community-building and revolutionary transformation, 34, 261–62; on identity and politics, 128, 261–62; on prisons, 227–28; on Haunani-Kay Trask and solidarity, 273–74
Davis, Frank Marshall: on the Black diaspora and Hawaiʻi's colonization, 249–52. *See also* Obama, Barack
De Lima, Frank, 180. *See also* humor, ethnic/local
Deedy, Christopher: and the murder of Kollin Elderts, 225–26. *See also* Elderts, Kollin
demographics: of Black tourists, 228; and the draw of Hawaiʻi, 137–38, 141, 151; of high school graduation rates, 280n40; of homeownership/rentals, 23, 298n119; of the Honolulu Police Department, 209; of incarceration, 175; of interracial/interethnic marriage, 11, 65; military, 63, 66; population, 11–14, 23, 34, 49, 51–54, 59, 66, 71, 86, 100, 129, 138, 141, 154–55, 163, 197–98; of the University of Hawaiʻi at Mānoa, 201, 270, 298n106. *See also* census
Diaz, Natalie: on Native erasure vs. Black visibility, 221

Diaz, Vicente, 273; on "backing into the future," 237
Dineen-Wimberly, Ingrid: on multiracial identity within the context of the Black experience, 222
disease, 39–40, 51; treating of, 56
dismemberment: from cultural and spiritual practices, 39, 51
DJ Jrama, 68
Dole, Sanford: and the 1893 overthrow of Hawaiʻi, 40
Dominguez, Virginia: on the Kingdom of Hawaiʻi and race, 49; on the unsteadying of the hegemony of US racial terms, 47
dress: and localness, 31, 87, 98, 101, 108, 145, 164, 233; malo, 150, 251, 268; and political affiliation, 272; tapa, 29, 50, 58
Du Bois, W. E. B.: on the color line that "belts the world," 246, 250, 258; on double consciousness, 249–50; on Hawaiʻi "as a land of opportunity," 41
Dunham, Ann, 66. *See also* Obama, Barack

Elam, Jason, 131. *See also* football
Elderts, Kollin: murder of, 206, 211, 225–26. *See also* Deedy, Christopher
Enomoto, Joy, 6, 15; on embracing Blackness in all forms, 257; on the need for solidarity (to achieve sovereignty), 271; on Haunani-Kay Trask's aligning of Hawaiian sovereignty with Black Liberation, 272
epistemologies: of Blackness, 79–80, 264; Kanaka, 26, 33, 47, 49, 51, 72, 80, 86, 173, 257–58, 261, 265–67; Middle Passage 15–16. *See also* belonging; genealogy
erasure: of Alice Ball's work, 56; Black, 1–11, 18, 36, 54, 59, 61, 171, 173–74, 202, 211–13; Indigenous, 22, 25, 174, 220–22; Latino, 54
ethnic studies, 80, 131–32, 202, 254, 268–71, 278, 301n63, 302n104, 303n14
ethnicity, 20, 27, 31, 85, 122, 149, 163, 268, 276; Blackness as, 104; as insufficient, 176–77; and power, 176; vs. race, 20, 24–25, 54, 69, 168, 171, 176–77, 180–82, 185–86, 191, 220; and self-identification, 99–100; and tourism, 5
excess: stereotypes of Black, 180, 210, 296n48; stereotypes of Polynesian, 180, 296nn47–48

Fanon, Frantz, 271–72
Feagin, Joe: on racism (and education) at home, 185. *See also* racism: in the home/family
Fernandez, Ryan Kamakakēhau, 242–44, 246; on ethnicity over race, 96, 99, 104, 182, 186, 193, 242; on learning about Blackness, 103–4; on being "Hawaiian at heart," 96, 99, 104; on history, 251; on the term "pōpolo," 182

first: Black lawyer in the Islands, 55; Black military men who came to Hawai'i, 62; Black president, 107, 122; Black principal in Honolulu, 55; Black secretary of defense, 224; Black woman to live in the Islands, 45, 69; census in Hawai'i, 284; director of ethnic studies at UH, 303n14; Hawaiian-language newspaper, 284n28; international student from Africa at UH, 66; Jewish and woman (Republican) governor in Hawai'i, 297n90; people of the Pacific, 257; rap CD printed in Hawai'i, 112; Royal Hawaiian, 73; tenured Black teacher at Kaimuki High School, 199; tenured Hawaiian professor, 270; woman, 43; woman chief of police (HPD), 209; woman to graduate with a master's of science, 56; woman mayor across the Islands, 58

Floyd, George: police murder of (and resultant activism), 3–5, 33, 188, 203, 205–6

food: and belonging, 91, 102; and Blackness, 104; and colonization, 286n99; and genealogy, 94, 149; as gifts, 256; and localness, 87, 124, 164; and racism, 192; slave, 192; sovereignty, 236; sustainability, 34

football, 130–32; and Sāmoans, 111–12, 130–31, 296n48

Fujikane, Candace: "Asian settler allies," 238; "Asian settler colonialism," 125; on Black people as settler allies, 127. *See also* Asian settler colonialism

future: "Black Futures Ball," 159, 243; vision for the, 26–27, 218, 235–37, 257–60, 264, 269, 278. *See also* self-determination; sovereignty

Gaither, Sarah: on Obama's biracial identity, 83. *See also* multiracialism; Obama, Barack

Garner, Eric: police murder of (and resultant activism), 206

Garvey, Marcus: on T. McCants Stewart's reasons for coming to Hawai'i, 55. *See also* Stewart, T. McCants

Garza, Alicia: and the Black Lives Matter movement 206. *See also* Black Lives Matter movement

Gates, Cedric Solosolo Asuega, 254; defaced campaign banners of, 166–68

Geertz, Clifford, 84

gender imbalance: and Blackness in Hawai'i, 194–95; and entry into Hawai'i, 38–39, 42, 65–68, 92, 131; and family stories of local Black hapas, 88–93, 106, 109, 114–15; and hip hop, 112; and language, 93, 186; and outmarriage, 65, 287n115; and the sovereignty movement, 271; and sports, 131, 143; and racial visibility, 293n43

genealogy: and belonging, 34–35, 82, 118; and humor, 94, 149; Kanaka ideas of, 21, 39, 44, 47–48, 80, 86, 98–99, 118, 135, 242–44, 266–67; and localness, 85; and social status, 39. *See also* belonging; blood quantum; self-identification

Gilmore, Ruth Wilson: on racism, 197

Gilroy, Paul: on Americocentrism, 292n59; on the Black Atlantic, 18, 46

Ginai, 68

Glenn, Dr. Akiemi, 7, 68, 158–59, 207, 213, 256; on antiBlackness in Hawai'i, 3–6, 277, 284n5; on the grief of Hawai'i's Black residents, 10. *See also* Pōpolo Project, The

Glenn, Evelyn Nakano: on dispossession and private property, 27; on Native erasure and White racial identity, 220; on the settler colonial framework and the erasure of Indigenous people in comparative race studies, 22–23

Goeman, Mishuana: on colonialism and private property, 235; on settler "logics of containment," 96. *See also* blood quantum

Gonzalez, Vernadette: on "militourism," 224. *See also* militourism

Goodyear-Ka'ōpua, Noelani, 207, 280n25; on "Asian settler allies," 238; on the complexities of rebuilding Indigenous structures, 128, 234; on "EAducators," 245; on kuleana, 223, 234, 239, 258; on the (historical) neutrality of Hawai'i, 10; on the ongoing conditions of military occupation, 232

Grant, Chantell: murder of, 205

Great Māhele, 274. *See also* land

Guess, Allison: on Black dislocation within the settler state, 25–26

Guevarra, Rudy, Jr.: on racism and dispossession, 185

hair, 133, 190; and aging, 58; and belonging, 38, 98, 164, 187, 160, 116, 232–33; and hula, 187; as liability, 194, 204, 208; and the military, 98, 143, 145, 232; and protest, 212

Hale, Helen, 287n120; political career of, 56–58

Hall, Lisa Kahaleole: on Hawai'i vs. America, 106–7; on Kanaka experiences abroad, 48

Hannah-Jones, Nikole: on the military, 222, 299n23; on responses to the 1619 Project, 221–22

Hannemann, Mufi, 293n40; and racial distinction in politics, 144

Harris, Ellen, 1–3, 31, 155, 198–99. *See also* lawsuits; workplace racism/discrimination

Hawai'i: annexation of, 12, 38, 40–41, 44–46, 51, 59–61, 117, 230–31, 283n14; as expensive, 130, 133, 155; as haven/paradise/sanctuary, 1, 5, 10–15, 17, 20, 34, 37–44, 55, 58–60, 62–63, 68–69, 120–65, 171, 177, 206, 213, 219, 223, 226–27, 241, 262, 265; as isolated, 11, 18, 46, 91, 106–7, 130; as isolating, 155; as not isolating, 139, 190; as racial

laboratory, 12, 15; statehood, 10, 12, 40, 42, 117; as strategic outpost for military, 236; vs. the United States, 106–7, 139, 155. *See also* Kingdom of Hawai'i
Hawai'i Innocence Project, 67
Hawai'i Unity & Liberation Institute, 237; as standing in solidarity with Black struggle, 9. *See also* kia'i (protectors); Pu'uhonua o Pu'uhuluhulu; Thirty Meter Telescope
Hawaiian Home Lands, 68, 73, 96, 99–100, 108, 186, 173, 240, 251, 267, 297n88, 297n88, 297n95. *See also* Hawaiian Homes Commission Act; land
Hawaiian Homes Commission Act, 73, 97, 219, 266–67, 283n9, 288n136. *See also* blood quantum; Hawaiian Home Lands; land
Hawaiian Sugar Planters Association, The: and the importing of Black southern labor, 52. *See also* Asian settler colonialism; plantation economy
Higa, Marion: and the Rex Johnson scandal, 197
Hines, Javonna, 160
hip hop, 6, 110–12, 114–15, 118, 178, 284n30; and gender, 195
Hisatake, Kara: on pidgin, 186
Hobart, Dr. Hi'ilei, 32, 245
Hofschneider, Anita: on response to Black vs. Hawaiian activism, 8
Holland, Sharon: on Black and Native interaction, 23. *See also* Black and Native relations
hooks, bell: on the strategic deployment of antiBlack sentiment, 176
Horne, Gerald: on Hawai'i as a sanctuary for those of African descent, 41; on integration into nonBlack communities, 48
Hoverson, Martha: on the soldiers of the Twenty-Fifth Infantry Regiment, 62
humor, ethnic/local, 36, 173, 180–85, 191–93; as cover for racist comments, 24, 182, 188, 196–202, 211, 213–15; and genealogy, 94, 149. *See also* localness
hyperdescent, 21, 48, 72. *See also* hypodescent ("one-drop rule")
hypersexuality: stereotypes of Black, 19, 64, 226, 229–30
hypervisibility, Black, 151, 171–72, 293n43
hypodescent ("one-drop rule"), 17, 21–22, 44, 48, 59, 72, 74–77, 99, 101, 104, 115–17, 135, 147, 219. *See also* blood quantum; hyperdescent

Idowu, Bankole: on the Rex Johnson scandal, 197. *See also* Johnson, Rex
Imada, Adria: on Kanaka experiences abroad, 48
incarceration, 166, 227–28; Black, 112, 137, 174–75, 203, 212, 239; of children, 248; corporate development of, 137; Hawaiian, 67, 112, 175, 203; and the legacy of slavery, 227; of the Queen, 40; unequal rates of, 199, 203, 212
Ing, Kaniela, 254
Ingram, Reuben A.: on Andre Wooten's $20 million schoolplace discrimination lawsuit, 192
invisibility: Black, 1–11, 14, 20–21, 23, 26, 34–35, 37, 41–42, 66, 69, 72, 86–104, 118, 122, 124, 151, 154–56, 162, 171–72, 191, 214, 230, 263, 265–66, 293n43; and gender, 293n43; racial, 171–72, 230

Jackson, Dr. Miles, 67, 202; on Black locals' community identification, 156; on military reception in Hawai'i, 134
Jackson, Shona: on the real and figurative displacement of Indigenous peoples, 176
James, Chuck, 68
Jarmon, Jamila, 159–60. *See also* Pōpolo Project, The
Jim Crow, 36, 56, 59, 61, 63, 156, 204, 214–15, 250, 254; "New Jim Crow," 174
Johnson, Dwayne "The Rock," 11; on the difficulty he had growing up in Hawai'i, 67
Johnson, Rex: scandal of, 196–97
Johnson, Sylvester: on Black settler colonies, 64

Ka'ahumanu, 50
Ka'eo, Kaleikoa: on the history of the Black Pacific, 257
Kabutaulaka, Tarcisius: on Melanesians (as "the black people of the Pacific"), 19
Kahahawai, Joseph: murder of, 225–26, 275. *See also* Massie Affair
Kahekili II: and reverence for blackness/darkness, 50; and the search for plantation laborers, 53
Kajihiro, Dr. Kyle: and "decolonial tours," 63; on kuleana, 223; on militarized Hawai'i, 224. *See also* kuleana (rights/responsibilities)
Kalākaua, King, 274, 287n103; "Negro-ification" of, 50
Kalaniana'ole, Jonah Kūhiō, 266
Kamehameha I, King, 11, 45, 47, 274; "Negro-ification"/Blackness of, 50, 73, 97
Kamehameha III, King: and Black musicians, 45; "Negro-ification" of, 50
Kamehameha IV, King: on experiencing racism abroad (as Prince Alexander Liholiho), 48
Kamehameha V, King: on experiencing racism abroad (as Prince Lot Kapuāiwa), 48
Kanuha, Kaho'okahi: on the "Kapu Aloha March," 237. *See also* kapu aloha
Kapi'olani, Queen: visits to the continental US, 48
Kapuāiwa, Prince Lot. *See* Kamehameha V, King
kapu aloha, 1, 8–9, 121, 168, 170, 200, 219, 237, 242, 259; appropriation of, 166, 224; Kapu Aloha March, 237

Karuka, Manu: on Black and Indigenous self-determination, 235
Kauai, Willy: on Hawai'i's explicit antislavery stance, 49
Kauanui, J. Kēhaulani: on considering "Hawaiian" a race, 220-21; on the insistence on difference by some Hawaiians, 251; on Kanaka Maoli genealogical practices and kinship, 44, 48; on the racialization of Asian groups, 24; on statist desires for Hawaiian independence, 235
Keel, Terence: on race, 79
Keko'olani, Terrilee ("Auntie Terri"): and "decolonial tours," 63, 270; on ethnic studies and Kānaka activism, 269-70
Kelley, Robin D. G.: on Africans as indigenous to Africa, 244
Kennedy, Randall: on the use of the n-word, 184. *See also* racial slurs
Kent, Noel: on Hawai'i's transformation to a tourist economy, 166. *See also* tourism
Khan-Cullors, Patrisse, 277; on Black freedom as universal freedom, 279n13; and the Black Lives Matter movement, 206, 254-56, 279n13; on Blackness and Hawai'i, 6, 218, 254-55; on support for the protectors of Maunakea, 217-18, 253, 256. *See also* Black Lives Matter movement; kia'i (protectors); Thirty Meter Telescope
kia'i (protectors), 8-9, 217-19, 237, 248, 259. *See also* Pu'uhonua o Pu'uhuluhulu; Thirty Meter Telescope
Kiel, Doug: on assessing Native personhood
Kim, Harry: and Native dispossession, 24; racist comments ("local humor") of, 24, 196, 198-99, 213, 215. *See also* racial slurs; Thirty Meter Telescope
Kimura, Larry: on astronomy and Hawaiian culture, 219. *See also* Pō (darkness)
King, Martin Luther, Jr., 97, 248; antiwar stance of, 270; Martin Luther King Jr. Day Parade, 156-57, 294n51; on the "racial harmony" of Hawai'i, 11
King, Tiffany Lethabo: on Haunani-Kay Trask's work, 126, 271
Kingdom of Hawai'i, 10-12, 26, 35, 39-51, 68-69, 135, 173, 216, 219, 230, 235, 256; and citizenship, 35, 39, 43-44, 49, 60-62, 173, 219, 265, 286n73; overthrow of, 12, 40, 230-31, 235-36, 280n25, 283n14, 287n103; as slavery-free, 39, 49, 68-72, 173, 263, 265. *See also* Hawai'i; sovereignty
Klemm, Adrian, 131. *See also* football
Klopotek, Brian: on the erasure of indigeneity in people with African ancestry, 222
knowledge, 261-78; about the African diaspora, 21, 105, 117-18, 153, 156, 163, 170-71, 173, 212, 215, 274-78; about one's own ancestry, 179, 243; and belonging, 21, 103, 155, 157; about Black culture/politics, 97, 103-18, 135, 171, 212, 215, 263, 268-78; about Hawai'i, 10, 234, 256, 258; racialized (and White possession), 221; of shared oppression, 249
Knowlton, Edgar, Jr.: on migration stories of Cabo Verdeans of African descent, 44
kuleana (rights/responsibilities), 8-9, 26-27, 30, 36, 128-29, 173, 188-89, 215-66, 277-78

Labrador, Roderick: on ethnic/local humor, 185, 191
Lai, Carlotta Stewart: and the Hawaiian educational system, 55-57. *See also* Punahou School
Lake, John Keola, 28-31, 242. *See also* dance: hula
land: abuse of, 237-38; access to, 21, 40, 73, 173, 219, 244, 266-67, 283n9, 288n136; belonging to the, 124, 233, 242-46; land-based practices, 160; redistribution of, 274; restoration of (aloha 'āina), 96, 128, 234, 236, 242, 258; and sovereignty, 233-60, 272. *See also* Hawaiian Homes Commission Act; Hawaiian Home Lands; sovereignty; private property
Langlas, Dr. Charles, 32, 281n53
Lathrop, Dr. George Albert: racism and poor medicine-handling of, 50-51
Lawrence, Charles, 67, 301n63; on Black community in Hawai'i, 158-59, 162; on the Maunakea protectors, 248; on racism and the law, 199-200, 209-12
Lawson, Kenneth, 67. *See also* Hawai'i Innocence Project
lawsuits, 36, 297n95; discrimination, 1-2, 33, 55, 173, 191-95, 198-200, 214; reverse discrimination, 96, 144
Ledward, Brandon: on Kānaka receptivity of "White Hawaiians," 185; on not being recognized by one's own group, 102; on racialization in Hawai'i, 21-22
Lee, Shelley: on early sociological study of Hawai'i, 12
legislation: Akaka Bill, 47, 236, 285n58; Hawaiian Homes Commission Act, 73, 97, 219, 266-67, 283n9, 288n136; Newlands Resolution, 40, 283n14; Organic Act, 40; US Civil Rights Act of 1964, 248
Leong, Karen: on the carceral state, 174; on colonization and relationality, 37; on immigrant complicity in Native dispossession, 24
Leroy, Justin: on Black and Indigenous studies, 174; on settlement and slavery as entangled, 175; on settler-society ideology, 51
Liholiho, Prince Alexander. *See* Kamehameha IV, King
Lili'uokalani, Queen, 58, 274; on the conditions of Native Americans, 47; forced abdication of,

40; "Negro-ification" of, 50; on the overthrow of Hawaiʻi, 287n103; and the use of racial ideology to spur pride, 51; visits to the continental US (as Princess), 48
Lind, Andrew: and the sociological study of Hawaiʻi, 12, 20
Lingle, Linda, 297n90; and the Rex Johnson scandal, 197
localness: and Blackness, 5, 24–26, 35, 71–119, 124–25, 142–46, 152, 164–65, 189–90; deployed strategically, 24, 83, 85, 164; and dress, 31, 87, 98, 101, 108, 145, 164, 233; as expansive, 291n50; and food, 87, 124, 164; and language, 74, 84, 87, 98, 108, 124, 144–45; and temporality, 84, 98, 208. *See also* humor, ethnic/local
logic: of containment, 235; of elimination, 221; of wiping people out, 197
Lonoaea-Alexander, Shayna: on the existence of racism in Hawaiʻi, 3; on the lack of reciprocity between Hawaiian and Black activists, 8–9
Love, Irie, 68
Lyons, Paul: on the sublation of Islander priorities in scholarship around the Black Pacific, 18

Mahtani, Minelle: on the alienation of multiracialism, 172–73. *See also* multiracialism
Makalani, Minkah: on multiracialism as anti-Black, 80. *See also* multiracialism
Malcolm X, 271–73
Marin, Don Francisco: and the use of "Indians" to describe Hawaiians, 47
Mariota, Marcus, 131. *See also* football
Markle, Meghan: on identifying as "mixed-race," 83. *See also* multiracialism
marriage, interracial, 11–12, 41, 44, 48, 55, 65, 69, 81, 100, 108–9, 129, 154, 175, 185, 251, 285n62, 287n115; and the census, 290n11
Mars, Bruno, 289n170
Martin, Trayvon: murder of (and resultant activism), 206, 210, 226
masculinity: and chants, 293n28; and dance, 131–32, 293n28; and language, 186. *See also* gender imbalance
Massie Affair: as bringing locals together (against haole), 125, 225–26; as taught in schools, 275–76
Matsuda, Mari: on the Maunakea protectors, 248
McDade, Tony: police murder of, 33
McGhee, Fred: on the cultural geography of the Black Pacific, 46
McKinley, William: and the annexation of Hawaiʻi, 40. *See also* annexation of Hawaiʻi
media: and depictions of Blackness, 110–18, 178, 229; and depictions of Hawaiʻi, 136, 163. *See also* tourism

Melanesians: and Blackness, 6, 19, 38, 49–50, 61, 273; and colonial division of the Pacific, 16, 18–19, 38, 46, 49–50, 273. *See also* racial division of the Pacific
Micronesians: and disenfranchisement, 13, 54, 211, 227, 229, 241; and integration, 247; racism against, 6, 19, 50, 177, 210–11, 247–48, 275–76; and the racial division of the Pacific, 46, 50, 60. *See also* racial division of the Pacific
Middle Passage, 10, 38, 44–45, 60, 259, 284n37; epistemologies, 15–16. *See also* Black Atlantic
Miles, Tiya: on Black and Native relations, 23, 174–75. *See also* Black and Native relations
military: appreciation of, 222, 227–28, 299n22; assumption of Black people as tied to, 5, 13–14, 17, 26, 34–35, 40, 42, 62–69, 72, 87, 98–99, 123, 140, 142–45, 163, 173, 181, 188, 195, 223–33; Black people as actually tied to, 37–41, 44, 48, 57, 61–69, 85, 87–90, 102, 108–11, 129–30, 133–35, 153–54, 156, 163, 165, 170–71, 187, 190, 222–23, 240, 243, 256, 264; Buffalo Soldiers, 62, 229; and the gender imbalance in Hawaiʻi, 38–39, 42, 65–66; and kuleana, 244; vs. local, 124; occupation of Hawaiʻi, 6, 12, 25–26, 37, 64, 128, 134, 139, 154, 213, 223–33, 252, 264; presence in Hawaiʻi, 3–6, 13–15, 26–27, 121, 128, 130, 139, 213, 223–33, 243, 252, 270; and PTSD, 230–31; Schofield Barracks, 62–63, 181, 232. *See also* militourism
militourism, 121–23, 224–28, 233, 273, 224–30, 292n3. *See also* military; tourism
missionaries, 39–40, 44, 50–51, 191, 224, 283n11; and abolitionism, 52; Black, 45; and ideas of Black inferiority, 16, 46–47, 50, 265
Mock, Janet, 11; on growing up in Hawaiʻi, 67
model minority myth: Asians and the, 122–23, 125
Moreton-Robinson, Aileen: on Native American dispossession and White national identity, 220–21
Morgensen, Scott: on cross-sectional work on Indigenous lands, 257
Mount, Guy Emerson: on postemancipation colonization projects, 289n154
Movement for Black Lives, 3–9, 156, 167, 177, 188, 202–12, 214, 217, 226, 253, 257, 263, 277. *See also* Black Lives Matter movement
Mullen, Bill: on Afro-Orientalism, 133
multiracialism, 185, 247, 291n40; and alienation, 172–73; as "antiBlack," 21, 35, 77, 79–82, 86, 100, 106, 117, 164, 222, 264; and antiBlack racism, 178, 185; in Hawaiʻi, 2–3, 11–17, 20–22, 32–34, 60, 71–120, 127, 154–55, 163, 188, 190, 265–68; in the United States, 20; and sovereignty, 238, 247. *See also* marriage, interracial; self-identification: as multiracial/"Black and ____"

Nathan, Roderick, 4
Native Americans: and Africans, 148, 299n23; elimination/erasure of, 48, 185, 220; and Hawaiians, 47-48, 236, 251-52, 272; and sovereignty, 139; studies, 23, 213, 237; and White national identity, 220
Nelson, Camille, 67, 301n63
Newlands Resolution, 40, 283n14. *See also* annexation of Hawai'i
Ng, Konrad: and the Shangri La Museum of Islamic Art, Culture & Design, 160
Ngoroge, Ngoroge, 301n63
Niheu, Kihei "Soli": on the lessons of past activist movements, 270-72
Nordyke, Eleanor: on the term "haole 'ele'ele" ("foreign black"), 42
Nunn, Willie: as the subject of Mayor Kim's racist remark, 196, 198-99. *See also* Kim, Harry

Obama, Barack, 10-11, 55, 78-79, 82-83, 107, 122, 160, 197, 226, 231, 288n121; agency of, 127, 252; on the beauty of Hawai'i, 137; and Blackness/multiraciality, 2-3, 59, 64-67, 72, 75-76, 96-97, 100, 106-7, 109, 116, 252; and Frank Marshall Davis, 249; and Hawaiian history curriculum, 275; and the influence of Hawai'i, 67, 82; and the (continued) militarization of the Pacific, 252; "the Obama Effect," 65-66; and optimism, 10, 262; on racism in Hawai'i, 166-68, 213
Obama, Barack, Sr. 66
Obama, Michelle, 252; on Barack Obama's relationship to Hawai'i, 2. *See also* Obama, Barack
Okamura, Jonathan: "Asian settler colonialism," 125; on ethnic relations in Hawai'i, 23-24; on ethnicity, 176; on localness, 124; on public schooling in Hawai'i, 280n40. *See also* Asian settler colonialism
Okihiro, Gary: on the travel routes of Hawaiians, 48
oli (chants), 29; and Pō (darkness), 43, 219; and masculinity, 293n28; and one's station in life, 39; as welcome, 248
one-drop rule. *See* hypodescent ("one-drop rule")
Ongelungel, Sha: on anti-Micronesian racism, 211
oppression: contests of, 26, 174-75, 218, 221; linked/shared, 246-60, 266
optimism: of African-descended people, provided by Hawai'i, 10, 78, 186, 262
Organic Act, 40
Ortega, Nadine: on the term "colored," 215
Osorio, Jonathan: on citizenship in nineteenth-century Hawai'i, 286n73; on the effect of nineteenth-century arrivals, 39
ostracism, 95-96, 111, 178, 214, 222; and multiracialism, 173

Osumare, Halifu: on the stylistic origins of Hawaiian protest, 272
Ozoa, Mykie: on the term "colored," 215

Park, Robert: and the sociological study of Hawai'i, 12, 20
Peterson, Luanna, 159-60
pidgin: and gender, 93; as liability, 186; and localness, 74, 84, 87, 98, 108, 124, 144-45
Pierre, Jemima: on Black immigrants vs. African Americans, 149
plantation economy, 13, 15, 23, 26, 37, 52-54, 59, 68, 80, 123-24, 186, 224, 287n114
Pō (darkness), 16, 18, 43-44, 50, 69, 219, 265; "Physics of Pō," 219. *See also* pōpolo; Pōpolo Project, The
police: as community/family, 9, 177, 203-4, 208-9, 227; defunding of, 216; and the Movement for Black Lives, 202-12; violence, 3-4, 8-9, 33, 36, 137, 159, 188, 203-13, 226, 254, 260, 263. *See also* Movement for Black Lives
Polynesian Panthers, 5, 269. *See also* Black Panthers
Polynesians, 18-19, 38, 46, 49-50, 60, 273; and physical excess, 296nn47-48. *See also* racial division of the Pacific; Polynesian Panthers
Pop, Nina: murder of, 33, 206
pōpolo, 273; as a reclaimed term of self-description, 43, 49, 178, 182-84. *See also* Pō (darkness); Pōpolo Project, The
Pōpolo Project, The, 5, 7, 68, 158-62, 182, 207, 209, 212-13, 243, 245, 256, 277, 279n13, 288n127. *See also* Glenn, Dr. Akiemi; pōpolo
private property: and colonialism, 235; and dispossession, 27, 127, 235; vs. land, 242-44, 259; and race, 73; and the sovereignty movement, 127, 238, 241. *See also* Hawaiian Homes Commission Act; land
protest, 3-10, 33, 188, 205-7, 211-12, 215, 237; Black vs. Hawaiian, 8-9, 248, 272; dismissed as rude/not aloha, 168-70, 206, 277; and hair, 212. *See also* Black Lives Matter movement; Thirty Meter Telescope
Punahou School, 55, 88, 106, 189, 285n49. *See also* Lai, Carlotta Stewart; school
Pu'uhonua o Pu'uhuhulu, 9, 218. *See also* kia'i (protectors); Thirty Meter Telescope

racial division of the Pacific, 16, 18-19, 38, 46, 49-54, 60-61, 178, 273. *See also* Melanesians; Micronesians; Polynesians
racial science, 46, 49, 99-100. *See also* blood quantum
racial slurs, 19, 43, 46-47, 50, 95, 121, 166-68, 177-85, 198-201, 211, 213-15, 295n46, 296n47; reclaimed, 43, 49, 178-80, 182-85, 281n53

racism: Asian antiBlack, 24, 189, 198, 200; closet, 152; confronting, 212-16; in Hawai'i, 165-216; in the home/family, 101, 171, 177-82, 214, 259; intangible, 198; without race, 187; in schools, 171, 177, 179, 182, 189-95; in the workplace, 170-71, 173, 177, 185, 195-202. *See also* colorism; racial slurs; reverse racism
Rahsaan, Umar: as the victim of institutional racism, 199. *See also* lawsuits: discrimination
Rastafarianism, 5, 18
reggae, 68; and assumptions about Black locals, 13; as embraced by Pacific Islanders, 5-6, 17; and visible Blackness, 66, 163
reverse racism, 96, 137, 139, 142-44, 146, 247. *See also* racism
Rice, Tadia, 159
Rifkin, Mark, 126
Rock, The. *See* Johnson, Dwayne "The Rock"
Rohrer, Judy: on Black "arrivants," 127; on haole, 143-44, 170
Rokolekutu, Ponipate: on Melanesians as "the black people of the Pacific," 19
Rosa, John P.: on localness, 98, 124, 225. *See also* localness; Massie Affair

Sāmoans, 26, 84; and Blackness, 102-3; and the diaspora of African American soldiers, 15; as disenfranchised, 13, 54, 227; and football, 111-12, 130-31, 296n48; and hip hop, 112; visibility of (in Hawai'i), 3. *See also* Johnson, Dwayne "The Rock"
Sapolu, Jesse, 131. *See also* football
Saranillio, Dean: on settler colonialism in Hawai'i, 85, 125, 238; on sovereignty, 238. *See also* Asian settler colonialism
school: curricula, 274-78; racism in, 171, 177, 179, 182, 189-95. *See also* Punahou School; University of Hawai'i at Mānoa
Scottsboro Boys, 225
self-determination: and class, 36, 139, 238-39, 241, 264; Kānaka, 8-10, 12, 26-27, 211-19, 234-60, 270. *See also* kia'i (protectors); sovereignty
self-identification: as Black only, 21, 34, 65-66, 76, 78, 80-82, 83, 86, 103, 106, 117-19, 135, 146-47, 151, 160, 265, 290n11; as multiracial/"Black and ___," 20-22, 24, 34, 47, 65-66, 71-119, 135, 146-52, 173, 186, 222, 265, 290n11; as Hawaiian (by Black people), 39, 44, 61-62, 66; and (reclaimed) racial slurs, 43, 49, 178-80, 182-85, 281n53. *See also* census; epistemologies: Kanaka; multiracialism
settler colonialism, 6-10, 18-20, 22-27, 35, 83-85, 128, 187, 220, 247; and antiBlackness, 127, 164, 172-77, 199, 213, 217, 244, 265; Asian, 6, 22-25, 35, 38, 52-54, 59, 77, 123-27, 154, 164, 199, 233, 247, 254, 265; "settlers of color," 23, 25, 124-29, 265

sex workers, 163, 195
Sexton, Jared: on colonialism and slavery, 175; on multiracialism as antiBlack, 80-81
Shangri La Museum of Islamic Art, Culture & Design, 160-61
shared/common enemy, 248-49, 252, 254, 258, 269. *See also* oppression: linked/shared; Massie Affair
Sharma, Dr. Miriam, 303n14
Shaw, Nate (b. Nate Cobb), 225
Shilliam, Robbie, 18
Silva, Noenoe: on the racialization and denigration of Hawaiians by American cartoonists, 50
Simms, Sandra, 68; and the African American Lawyers Association, 157. *See also* African American Lawyers Association (AALA)
Simons, Doug: on astronomy and Hawaiian culture, 219. *See also* Pō (darkness)
Simpson, Leanne: on indigenous relationship to land, 127
1619 Project, 221-22
slurs. *See* racial slurs
Smallwood, Stephanie: on historical accounts of slavery that commodify (rather than humanize), 44; on settler colonialism and slavery, 238
Smith, Andrea: on the notion of land *belonging* to someone, 244
Smith, Nolle, 56
Solis, Gabriel, 18
sovereignty, 36; food, 236; movement, 40, 127, 139, 164, 228, 232-63, 269-72; and shared struggle, 257, 271; usurpation of, 40. *See also* Kingdom of Hawai'i; self-determination; Thirty Meter Telescope
spirits: ancestral, 81; of Hawai'i, 1, 136, 141; spirituality, 39, 242, 262
Stannard, David, 272, 275
statehood: of Hawai'i, 10, 12, 40, 42, 117
"staying in one's lane": as advisable, 239; as a limited perspective, 221-22
Stewart Lai, Carlotta. *See* Lai, Carlotta Stewart
Stewart, T. McCants: as first practicing Black lawyer in the Islands, 55
Stockton, Betsey, 55, 68, 152, 285n49; and early Black residents of Hawai'i, 45, 50; and the Hampton Institute, 45, 191; sitting with the queen, 47, 69
Stone, David Harada: on the murders of young, unarmed men of color, 226
Stoudemire, Andrea: murder of, 205
Sub Zero, 68
Sultan, Hannah: on Black dislocation within the settler state, 25-26

Sundstrom, Ronald: on multiracial identity, 74, 79, 82
surveillance: of Blackness, 137, 155, 163, 171–72, 204

Takara, Dr. Kathryn Waddell, 62, 67–68, 120, 134, 136, 159, 202, 275, 301n63; on the anxiety of claiming "Negro origins," 60; on Frank Marshall Davis, 250; on the dynamics of being Black in the Islands, 194–95, 250; Pacific Raven Press, 67, 134, 157; on the shift toward antiBlack ideas in Hawaiʻi, 61; and the Winter Institutes on Black Studies, 276. *See also* Waddell, Dr. William
Tanuvasa, Maʻa, 131. *See also* football
tattooing, 50, 160, 236
Taylor, Breonna: police murder of, 33, 205
Teaiwa, Teresia, 15, 269, 271–73; on "militourism," 224, 273; on the "saltwater people" of Hawaiʻi, 160. *See also* militourism
Teale, Laulani: on reaction to military involvement in the Martin Luther King Jr. Day Parade, 294n51
temporality: and localness, 84, 98, 208; and race, 281n55
Tengan, Ty: on illegal US intervention in Hawaiʻi, 11–12; on pidgin and masculinity, 186; on the sublation of Islander priorities in scholarship around the Black Pacific, 18
Teves, Stephanie: on antiBlackness in defiant indigeneity, 188
Thirty Meter Telescope: activism against, 8–9, 24, 58, 64, 188, 198–99, 217–19, 237, 248, 253, 256, 259. *See also* kiaʻi (protectors); Puʻuhonua o Puʻuhuluhulu
Tometi, Opal: and the Black Lives Matter movement, 206. *See also* Black Lives Matter movement
tourism, 5, 11–12, 166; and Black people, 26, 66, 101, 123, 130, 136, 143, 163, 169–70, 213, 224, 228–30; calls to end, 228; Hawaii Tourism Authority, 166, 196; and kuleana, 244; and White supremacy, 34. *See also* militourism
Trask, Haunani-Kay: on the importance of genealogy in Pacific Island cultures, 81–82; on letting Hawaiians direct their own path toward sovereignty, 239; and the lessons of Black social movements, 269–74; on "local," 125; on "settlers of color," 23, 25, 125–26
Trask, Mililani: and the insistence on difference, 251

Tuck, Eve: on Black dislocation within the settler state, 25–26

universalism: as apparent solution to racism, 182, 192–93
University of Hawaiʻi at Mānoa, 12, 56, 66–67, 130–34, 143, 200–202, 268–70, 301n63; ethnic studies, 254, 268, 301n63, 302n104; Faculty of African Descent (FAD) group, 276–77, 304n40; and the Rex Johnson scandal, 197; and the Thirty Meter Telescope, 64
Uperesa, Dr. Faʻanofo Lisaclaire: on Black vs. Hawaiian political action, 268

violence: police, 3–4, 8–9, 33, 36, 137, 159, 188, 203–13, 226, 254, 260, 263; stereotypes of Black, 5, 8, 19, 52

Waddell, Dr. William, 62. *See also* Takara, Dr. Kathryn Waddell
Walcott, Rinaldo: on "the wonderful thing about blackness," 20
Warren, Joyce Pualani: on the concept of "Pō," 43. *See also* Pō (darkness)
we-ness, 27, 61, 84, 124, 164, 263. *See also* belonging
Webb-Binder, Bernida, 18
whaling industry: and Black arrivals to Hawaiʻi, 38–39, 44, 54, 59, 69
"What (are) you?," 21, 72, 82, 93, 98, 99–102, 146, 148, 151–52, 265. *See also* genealogy; multiracialism; self-identification
White, Elisa Joy, 301n63; and the Winter Institutes on Black Studies, 276
Wilderson III, Frank: on being a slave, 292n16; on Haunani-Kay Trask, 271
Wolfe, Patrick, 126; on the "logic of elimination," 221; on settler colonialism, 247
Wooten, Andre, 157, 202; on schoolplace racism and potential remedies, 192–94, 199. *See also* African American Lawyers Association (AALA)
workplace racism/discrimination, 170–71, 173, 177, 185, 195–202
World War II: and the importing of racist paradigms, 197, 229–30; and the resulting diaspora of African American soldiers, 15, 42, 48, 63, 171, 173, 178. *See also* military
Wright, Michelle: on "Middle Passage epistemologies," 15–16. *See also* Middle Passage